WINNING THE PEACE

About the Post-Conflict Reconstruction Project

In the fall of 2000, the Center for Strategic and International Studies (CSIS) and the Association of the United States Army (AUSA) embarked on a joint venture to address the U.S. government's ineffective response to the challenges of post-conflict reconstruction. The project analyzed U.S. capabilities and sponsored a distinguished bipartisan commission that made a number of policy recommendations. This volume is a direct outgrowth of that collaboration.

Today, the Post-Conflict Reconstruction Project is a global center for innovation and information on rebuilding after war. Its pursuit of reforms now extends beyond the U.S. government to include international capacity. For more information, visit www.csis.org/isp/pcr/.

About CSIS

For four decades, the Center for Strategic and International Studies (CSIS) has been dedicated to providing world leaders with strategic insights on—and policy solutions to—current and emerging global issues. Headquartered in Washington, D.C., CSIS is a private, bipartisan, tax-exempt organization with 190 researchers and support staff.

About AUSA

The Association of the United States Army (AUSA) is a private, nonprofit, professional educational organization dedicated to supporting the needs and interests of the U.S. Army, promoting a strong defense industrial base, and upholding and strengthening the ethical base, knowledge, skills, and standards of the American profession of arms.

■   ■   ■

The views expressed in this volume should be understood to be those of the authors and not necessarily the views of their organizations, or of CSIS, or of AUSA.

Significant Issues Series
Managing editor: Roberta L. Howard
Timely books presenting current CSIS research and analysis of interest to the academic, business, government, and policy communities.

The CSIS Press
Center for Strategic and International Studies
1800 K Street, N.W., Washington, D.C. 20006
Telephone: (202) 887-0200 Fax: (202) 775-3199
E-mail: books@csis.org Web: www.csis.org

WINNING THE PEACE

An American Strategy
for Post-Conflict Reconstruction

Edited by Robert C. Orr

Foreword by John J. Hamre
and Gordon R. Sullivan

A publication of the Joint CSIS/AUSA Project
on Post-Conflict Reconstruction

THE CSIS PRESS

Center for Strategic
and International Studies
Washington, D.C.

The publisher gratefully acknowledges permission to include revised versions of articles originally appearing in the *Washington Quarterly*:

Scott Feil, "Building Better Foundations: Security in Postconflict Reconstruction," *Washington Quarterly* 25, no. 4 (Autumn 2002). © 2002 by the Center for Strategic and International Studies and the Massachusetts Institute of Technology.

Michèle Flournoy and Michael Pan, "Dealing with Demons: Justice and Reconciliation," *Washington Quarterly* 25, no. 4 (Autumn 2002). © 2002 by the Center for Strategic and International Studies and the Massachusetts Institute of Technology.

Johanna Mendelson Forman, "Achieving Socioeconomic Well-Being in Postconflict Settings," *Washington Quarterly* 25, no. 4 (Autumn 2002). © 2002 by the Center for Strategic and International Studies and the Massachusetts Institute of Technology.

Robert Orr, "Governing When Chaos Rules: Enhancing Governance and Participation," *Washington Quarterly* 25, no. 4 (Autumn 2002). © 2002 by the Center for Strategic and International Studies and the Massachusetts Institute of Technology.

Significant Issues Series, Volume 26, Number 7
Printed on recycled paper in the United States of America
Cover design by Robert L. Wiser, Silver Spring, Md.
Cover photograph: © AP/ Wide World Photos/ Jerome Delay. U.S. Marine in a gun turret atop a truck deliverying food to a CARE warehouse in Somalia, December 1992.

08 07 06 05 04   5 4 3 2 1

ISSN 0736-7136
ISBN 0-89206-444-7

Library of Congress Cataloging-in-Publication Data
Winning the peace : an American strategy for post-conflict reconstruction / edited by Robert C. Orr / foreword by John J. Hamre and Gordon R. Sullivan
    p. cm. — (Significant issues series ; v. 26, no. 7)
    "A publication of the Joint CSIS/AUSA Project on Post-Conflict Reconstruction."
    Includes bibliographical references and index.
    ISBN 0-89206-444-7 (pb : alk. paper)
    1. United States—Foreign relations—2001 – 2. National security—United States. 3. Postwar reconstruction—Afghanistan. 4. Postwar reconstruction—Iraq. 5. Postwar reconstruction—Bosnia and Hercegovina.   I. Orr, Robert C. (Robert Cameron), 1964– II. Center for Strategic and International Studies (Washington, D.C.) III. Title. IV. Series.
    E895.W56 2004
    355.02'8'0973—dc22
                              2004011959

CONTENTS

FOREWORD

John J. Hamre and Gordon R. Sullivan

Failed states matter. One of the principal lessons of the events of September 11, 2001, and since is that we ignore failed states like Afghanistan at great peril. Such states pose not only huge humanitarian challenges but national security challenges as well. If left to their own devices, they can become sanctuaries for terrorist networks with a global reach, not to mention havens for international organized crime and drug traffickers who exploit the dysfunctional environments. Likewise, a post-war environment like Iraq, if not managed properly, can spawn new threats. Indeed, defeated as well as failed states can pose a direct threat to the national interests of the United States and to the stability of entire regions.

From Afghanistan to Iraq to various parts of Africa, Asia, and Latin America, we have already seen evidence of how terrorist groups have exploited the vacuum of state authority. As much as some in the United States would like to avoid involvement in nation building, failed states are a reality that cannot be wished away. Indeed, some of the possible candidates for failure in coming years are those countries in which the United States already has a defined national security interest—from a struggling post-war Iraq and the Occupied Territories in the Middle East to North Korea and Cuba.

If regional stability is to be maintained, economic development advanced, lives saved, and transnational threats faced, the United States and the international community will have to develop a strategy to enhance capacity for pursuing post-conflict reconstruction. Significant international

John J. Hamre is president and CEO of the Center for Strategic and International Studies. Gordon R. Sullivan is president of the Association of the United States Army.

interventions to help rebuild countries are certainly not the answer for every failed or failing state; nevertheless, international involvement will be essential in many cases. Even when other options are pursued—such as quarantining failed states, carving them up, absorbing them into larger entities, establishing a transitional authority, or backing a party in the hopes it can win a war and re-establish order—these will most often succeed when reconstruction capabilities exist and can be used to supplement whatever other measures are undertaken.

If the United States has learned one thing during the last decade of crisis, it is that it cannot wait for the next crisis to begin before it prepares. Even in Afghanistan, where it has clear national security interests at stake and high-level governmental commitment, the United States has used ad hoc mechanisms to try to address pressing needs. The United States has therefore not maximized its leverage with both external and internal actors, and its response has at times lacked coherence and been slower, less effective, and more costly than necessary.

To succeed in the future, the United States must act now. Especially in the post–September 11 environment, the United States cannot wait until the next crisis to try to build its post-conflict reconstruction capabilities. Indeed, U.S. leadership will only be credible if the United States gets its own house in order. In some instances, this effort may require new or reformed institutions, while in others it may require new legislative and executive authorities. In any case, there has long been a need to identify the most important issues, the comparative advantages of the United States and other actors, and the gaps in current capabilities.

In 2000, concerned that the United States was not sufficiently focused on the problems posed by failed and weak states, the Association of the United States Army (AUSA) and the Center for Strategic and International Studies (CSIS) embarked on a joint venture to address the challenges of "post-conflict reconstruction." We recruited an extraordinary staff with deep experience at a wide range of U.S. government agencies— from the Departments of State and Defense, to the U.S. Army, the National Security Council, USAID, and the Peace Corps. In particular we would like to recognize the codirectors of this ambitious project, who provided the leadership and intellectual guidance necessary to bring it to fruition: Michèle Flournoy and Robert Orr at CSIS and Scott Feil and Johanna Mendelson Forman at AUSA.

These individuals led the team that produced an extensive set of white papers on the problems of failed and weak states and what the

United States needs to do to address those challenges. These in turn were reviewed by a distinguished bipartisan commission on post-conflict reconstruction that consisted of members of Congress, military leaders, and senior policy experts who have served in the U.S. government, international organizations, and the not-for-profit sector. (See appendix 2 for a full list of commissioners and project staff.) Many of the chapters in this volume benefited along the way from the input and advice of working groups and the commission. They also benefited from the incisive comments provided by Vinca LaFleur. The conclusions in the chapters, of course, are those of the authors themselves.

We would like to thank the United Nations Foundation and the William and Flora Hewlett Foundation for their support of this project. Long before the challenges of Afghanistan and Iraq brought "nation building" back in vogue, these two foundations recognized the need for work in this area. Their respective leaders, Tim Wirth and Paul Brest, are both visionaries who are interested in seeing practical changes made that will improve people's lives around the globe. Their continuing support has made both the bipartisan commission and this book possible. We would also like to thank Rick Barton and Sheba Crocker, both of CSIS, for leading ongoing efforts to mobilize domestic and international interest in this vital subject.

We think that the analysis and recommendations in this volume offer a realistic, achievable vision of a more coherent and effective U.S. post-conflict reconstruction capacity. We hope that the reader will think so too.

Luckily, the United States will not have to build its post-conflict reconstruction capacity from scratch. It already has some key institutions and a wealth of human, organizational, and material resources on which to draw. With a concerted, coherent, bipartisan push, the United States can position itself for the brave new world that confronts it. Enabling the United States to catalyze indigenous and international reconstruction efforts will help to protect U.S. interests. Doing so will also help others to pursue that which U.S. citizens hold most dear—life, liberty, and the pursuit of happiness.

PREFACE

Robert C. Orr

The United States is in the nation-building business. As this book goes to press in the summer of 2004, the United States is more involved in nation building around the globe than at any time in its history, save the period immediately following World War II. After occupying and running Iraq for more than a year, over 135,000 American troops remain the principal authority on the ground throughout the country. In Afghanistan, U.S. civilian government employees and nongovernmental organization workers put their lives on the line to build the new government as thousands of American forces provide security by keeping Taliban and Al Qaeda fighters on the run. Back on the other side of the world, U.S. Marines patrol the streets of Haiti and render assistance to a struggling new government, a story repeated many times in that troubled land. After a decade, U.S. and allied forces continue to anchor peace in the Balkans, despite periodic rumblings about downsizing. In these and many other places around the world, Americans are on the frontlines of rebuilding societies after war.

The demands on the United States to rebuild countries—for their good and our own—show no sign of abating. Indeed, we might expect post-conflict reconstruction to be a fixture of international life in the twenty-first century. Since the end of the Cold War, the United States has engaged in a new post-conflict rebuilding operation every 18 months on average. With global terrorism a reality, the United States does not have the luxury of ignoring troubled countries no matter how small, how poor, or how distant. The forces that prey on lawlessness and instability have proved they can effectively use the least powerful countries in the world to strike the most powerful.

The question facing American policymakers and citizens, therefore, is not whether to get involved in reconstructing weak and failed states, but rather when and how to do so. This book examines the reconstruction challenge, what the United States has done in the past, what capability it has now to reconstruct countries, and what it would need to do to improve the chances of success in the future.

The first section of the book introduces the contours of the reconstruction challenge in post-conflict environments. In chapter 1, Robert Orr presents the four pillars of reconstruction: security; governance and participation; economic and social well-being; and justice and reconciliation. By laying out the universe of options, both this chapter and the Post-Conflict Reconstruction Task Framework in appendix 1 seek to provide a starting point for identifying and prioritizing what needs to be done. In chapter 2, Robert Orr explores the problem of designing a coherent international response despite often-chaotic environments where a whole host of outside actors is involved, including other governments, international organizations, private-sector actors, and various types of nongovernmental organizations (NGOs). This chapter proposes a set of principles, the implementation of which would create a more cohesive and strategic international response.

The second section of the book focuses on how the United States must enhance its post-conflict reconstruction capabilities in four core areas in order to be able to rebuild countries more effectively. In chapter 3, Scott Feil addresses the challenges in the area of security in terms of providing public safety as well as developing legitimate security institutions. In chapter 4, Robert Orr examines the twin challenges of helping to create structures for channeling popular will and enhancing the capability of the local institutions to deliver security, social and economic, and political goods to the population. In chapter 5, Johanna Mendelson Forman explores improving capacity to address a range of needs in social and economic well-being—the most diverse of the four pillars of post-conflict reconstruction. In chapter 6, Michèle Flournoy and Michael Pan address justice and reconciliation, two distinct sets of activities that share the common goal of establishing processes for war-torn societies to address grievances and wrongdoing.

The third section of the book explores how the United States will have to enhance four "critical enablers"—those crosscutting capabilities that would improve performance in all functional pillar areas. In chapter 7, Michèle Flournoy explores the needs in the area of strategic planning and management of post-conflict operations. In chapter 8, Johanna Mendelson Forman and Michael Pan describe the need for, and the contours of, a civilian rapid response capability within the U.S. government. In chapter 9, Michele Flournoy focuses on training and education needs, both for people in the countries trying to rebuild themselves and among the many individuals who would come from outside to help in such situations. In chapter 10, Robert Orr and Johanna Mendelson Forman explore the final, and perhaps most crucial, "enabler"—funding—in terms of both the volume and the flexibility and effectiveness of current U.S. government funding mechanisms.

The fourth section of the book provides a series of historical case studies to explore the complexity of very different operations as well as demonstrate the evolution of the U.S. approach to post-conflict reconstruction.

In chapter 11, Robert Orr examines the central case of "first-generation" post-conflict reconstruction efforts—the United States' occupation of Japan after World War II. The second generation of post-conflict reconstruction efforts is that of the so-called "humanitarian interventions" of the post–Cold War world. In chapter 12, Bathsheba Crocker evaluates the relatively successful intervention of the United States and its European allies in Kosovo. In chapter 13, Robert Orr reviews another relatively successful case, that of East Timor, and what it implies about the United States' role as a junior partner in some cases. In chapter 14, Milan Vaishnav and Bathsheba Crocker evaluate Sierra Leone, an extraordinarily challenging case in Africa where the United States played a subordinate role to the United Kingdom and the United Nations.

The third generation of post-conflict reconstruction efforts, those spawned by concerns about terrorism and weapons of mass destruction in the wake of the September 11, 2001 attacks on the United States, raises some similar and some different sets of issues. In chapter 15, Milan Vaishnav lays out the foundations of the "light footprint" model in Afghanistan and evaluates the potential weaknesses of this model. In chapter 16, Bathsheba Crocker analyzes recent post-conflict operations in Iraq, one of the United States' most ambitious, yet problematic, post-conflict reconstruction efforts to date.

The concluding chapter by Robert Orr applies the insights from the case studies to the question of when and how to apply the U.S. post-conflict reconstruction capacity described earlier in the book. Every country is different, and each country's needs after war will be different. A "one-size-fits-all" approach is not appropriate for the broad array of cases that the United States will face in the coming decades.

By the end of this book, it is hoped that the reader will have a better understanding of what it takes to do post-conflict reconstruction, and what it will take to do it more successfully. Neither the United States nor the world can afford failure.

ACKNOWLEDGMENTS

We would like to thank the United Nations Foundation and the Better World Fund and the William and Flora Hewlett Foundation for their ongoing commitment to the Post-Conflict Reconstruction Project.

PART ONE

THE POST-CONFLICT CHALLENGE

CHAPTER ONE

THE UNITED STATES AS NATION BUILDER

FACING THE CHALLENGE OF POST-CONFLICT RECONSTRUCTION

Robert C. Orr

This book seeks to answer three fundamental questions: What is needed to rebuild countries after war? How can the United States improve its capacity to succeed at post-conflict reconstruction? And, when and how should the United States use this capacity?

The answers to these questions are extremely important to the United States today because war-ravaged countries are no longer just a threat to their own citizens and their neighbors, but to the United States and the whole world.

Indeed, although weak, failed, and defeated states have long been a part of the international landscape, the threat they pose today to the United States and the civilized world is greater than ever. Terrorist and criminal networks can and do use these weak links of the international state system to wreak damage and commit crimes anywhere around the globe.[1] Lawless and unstable post-conflict environments that are lacking institutional means to address their internal problems provide almost perfect laboratory conditions for those who would hatch terror plots and recruit and train terrorists, as well as finance and manage global terror operations from a safe distance.

While weak states are clearly an international problem and an international responsibility, the United States has a special interest in addressing these issues. As the world's richest and most powerful country with a truly global presence, the United States is a prime target for those who would use weak states as a base of operations. In a world of increasingly globalized threats from terrorist networks and from weapons of mass destruction (WMD), the United States has a disproportionate interest in ensuring a functional international system. As President George W. Bush himself acknowledged in his *National Security Strategy*: "America is now threatened less by conquering states than we are by failing ones."[2]

In this era of heightened threats, however, the United States has done little to enhance its ability to address these challenges. Perhaps due to President Bush's early antipathy to "nation building" and competing priorities since 9/11, the U.S. government has been very slow in responding to the challenge and has been either unwilling or unable to make the kind of internal changes that would improve U.S. capacity to do post-conflict reconstruction right.

The United States has not always tied its own hands in this regard. To figure out how to address current gaps, therefore, a good place to start is to examine what the United States has done previously.

The United States has a long history of nation building. In addition to building its own nation, the United States has actively sought to help build and rebuild numerous other countries over the course of the last century. The United States got an early start by trying its hand at colonialism in the Philippines and through "gunboat diplomacy" in the early twentieth century when it sought to establish stable and sympathetic regimes in the Caribbean and Central America. From these early efforts to the rebuilding of Europe and Japan after World War II, and from Vietnam War–related efforts in Southeast Asia during the 1960s and 1970s to the post–Cold War humanitarian interventions of the 1990s, the United States has historically cut a broad swath as the modern world's most active nation builder.

GENERATIONS OF U.S. NATION BUILDING AND POST-CONFLICT RECONSTRUCTION EFFORTS

The United States has undertaken nation-building efforts outside its borders for over a century. In general historical terms, there have been five eras of nation-building efforts: the era of quasi-imperialism in the Philippines and throughout the Caribbean and Central America at the end of the nineteenth and the early part of the twentieth centuries; the post–World War II occupations of Japan, Germany, Italy, and Austria, as well as the virtual protectorates in the Republic of Korea and the Republic of China on Taiwan; Cold War counterinsurgency, as epitomized by U.S. efforts in Vietnam; post–Cold War "humanitarian intervention" in the 1990s; and, finally, post–9/11 interventions under a shadow of global terrorism and weapons of mass destruction, as epitomized by U.S. efforts in Afghanistan and Iraq.

Understanding how the various generations of nation-building efforts are similar and different requires examining many factors. What is the impetus behind the effort? Is the effort during conflict or after? Is the United States party to the conflict or a relatively "neutral" third party? Who are the principal external actors involved—are they primarily civilian or military, U.S. or multinational?

Using these criteria, the quasi-imperial and Cold War containment eras stand out as different. In contrast to the other eras, these two consisted principally of counterinsurgency pacification efforts. Nation-building efforts, to the extent they were pursued, were a subordinate outgrowth of a war-fighting strategy. Not surprisingly, the U.S. military was by far the dominant actor, affecting the intervention's fundamental character. Finally, the quasi-imperial era and the Cold War era differed from the others in that they had as their fundamental motivation the desire to gain and hold territory—either directly or through surrogate regimes that would back the United States against an outside threat (European colonialism in the case of the quasi-colonial era, and Soviet communism in the case of the Cold War). This book will examine only those generations of nation-building efforts that are nonterritorial in nature and that take place wholly or largely after war, thereby falling under the "post-conflict reconstruction" rubric: post-World War II; post-Cold War; and post–9/11.[3]

First-Generation Post-Conflict Reconstruction: Post–World War II Occupations

The heart of the "first generation" of post-conflict reconstruction was an attempt to put vanquished powers back on their feet after World War II. Leaders in the United States knew that the destruction of World War II and the ensuing destitution could spur a return of fascism or accelerate the growth of communism. As such, U.S. leaders undertook massive rebuilding efforts to establish security and prosperity in the defeated countries. There were strong differences between the two most important cases—Japan and Germany—and the United States used a wide variety of political, economic, and military instruments in each to undertake wide-ranging programs of reform and institutional rebuilding, from writing new constitutions and establishing courts to reshaping labor management relations and creating a free press. Although the U.S. military was central to implementation in both cases, it played a relatively larger role in Japan. In Germany, the role of multilateral institutions and countries other than the United States was much more significant than in Japan.

In the cases of Italy and Austria, a less ambitious, more political strategy was used toward similar ends. By "picking winners" and supporting their parties, the United States achieved the goal of ensuring that neither Austria nor Italy would revert to fascism or fall to a resurgent communism. The Republic of Korea and the Republic of China on Taiwan, while not formally occupied by the United States, hosted large numbers of U.S. troops for decades, and had their political, economic and social policies strongly affected by the wishes of their American protectors.

Second-Generation Post-Conflict Reconstruction: Post-Cold War "Humanitarian Interventions"

With the end of the Cold War, the demand for peace operations and accompanying rebuilding efforts dramatically expanded throughout the course of the 1990s. From Somalia, to Haiti, Bosnia, and Kosovo, the United States was sufficiently motivated by the need for stability as well as by humanitarian concerns to put significant numbers of U.S. troops on the ground.

In a whole range of other cases—from Cambodia and El Salvador, to Mozambique, Guatemala, East Timor, Ethiopia and Eritrea, and Sierra Leone—the United States made financial and political contributions, but let other countries and the United Nations take the lead.

In all these cases, international actors were deeply involved, and the United States intentionally set its operations within a multilateral context. In virtually all these cases, the United States and the international community were not initial protagonists in the war, though in some cases they were dragged in by circumstances on the ground. A broad range of political and military strategies were used during the 1990s, but there was an obvious "learning curve" as the United States sought to apply lessons learned from previous cases. The United States sought to build coalitions wherever possible and drew on both civilian and military resources as appropriate to the situation. While by no means problem-free, the U.S.-led and supported interventions at the end of the decade were in the main much more successful than those in the first half of the decade.

Third-Generation Post–Conflict Reconstruction: Post–9/11 Interventions in an Era of Global Terrorism and WMD

Following September 11, 2001, rapidly growing concern about terrorism and weapons of mass destruction (WMD) led the Bush administration to intervene first in Afghanistan, then in Iraq.[4] Although both cases involved major military interventions, the approach to post-conflict reconstruction could not have been more different.

In Afghanistan the Bush administration pursued a war against Al Qaeda and the Taliban, but when it came to reconstruction it tried to hand the vast majority of the tasks to international actors. Because a broader coalition with clear objectives had not been built before launching the war, however, many potential international partners doled out limited assistance. Peacekeepers were limited to Kabul, insecurity continued to block widespread reconstruction efforts in most parts of the country, and the U.S. military remained the key set of actors on the ground.

Iraq is the case that could define the newest generation of nation building. The situation on the ground and how the Bush administration responds to it will determine whether this effort becomes a real post-conflict reconstruction effort or else becomes a counterinsurgency strategy that uses post-conflict reconstruction tools. It is the largest initiative, arguably with the most at stake for the United States, since the occupations of Japan and Germany.[5]

Despite the Bush administration's initial promises of a clean victory and a relatively rapid withdrawal of American forces, the U.S. military has been the primary protagonist in the ongoing effort. Because resistance continued long after President Bush declared the end of major combat operations on May 1, 2003, and general insecurity reigned, U.S. troops remained the central actors long after it was hoped they would have gone home. The United States fought and won the war as the far-and-away dominant member of the military coalition. In the reconstruction phase, the United States remained the dominant player—due both to its larger stake in the outcome and to the fact that other major players could not be recruited on Washington's terms following the war.

The reconstruction effort itself has been quite ambitious—seeking to develop an unprecedented democratic political structure, create a new security infrastructure, revive and reform a shattered economy, and bring many of the former regime leaders to justice. The scope of the vision, combined with huge challenges on the ground resulting from ongoing resistance and 30 years of degradation and neglect of the country's people, institutions, and infrastructure, make for a "grand experiment" that will establish a new point of reference for all future efforts.

THE CHALLENGES OF WEAK, FAILED, AND DEFEATED STATES IN THE TWENTY-FIRST CENTURY

President Bush asserted that the United States faces a major threat from "failing states" following 9/11.[6] In fact, a wide spectrum of states could be considered weak, failing, or failed. State failure is a matter of degree. Many states in Africa, for example, are weak, having never developed a state apparatus capable of meeting even the most basic needs of the vast majority of their population. In the process, these weak states run the risk of losing the loyalty and control of the population. Other countries, such as the former Yugoslavia in the 1990s or Somalia today, might be considered "failed states" in that they did not or do not have a functioning central government at all. Others, such as Afghanistan, Pakistan, Colombia, and the Democratic Republic of the Congo today fall somewhere in between on the continuum, as they have central governments but ones that are unable to control major parts of their territory.

Although there have been relatively few cases of completely failed states in recent years, the number of weak or failing states that face the potential of widespread conflict and state failure is much greater. In this category one might identify approximately 30 cases, or more than 15 percent of the world's countries.[7] State weakness or failure in these countries affects, or has the potential to affect, a significant portion of the world's population, economic potential, and regional stability.

Beyond the question of degree of state weakness, there are various reasons why states fail. Three distinct paths to state failure account for the vast majority of cases. The first path to state failure, and perhaps the most common, is that of civil war. Violent internal conflicts often lead to a sudden collapse of state institutions, sometimes accompanied by dissolution of a stable political consensus. A second path to state collapse or failure is military defeat by an outside power. In some cases the institutions and people necessary to the functioning of the state are destroyed in the war. In others, the defeat by an outside power leads to a crisis of legitimacy of the government, sometimes leading to the collapse of the state. The third path to state failure—intrinsic weakness due to underdevelopment—is often less dramatic, playing out over time, but is no less serious in its consequences.

Of course, any given country can suffer from one or all of these maladies. But it is useful to distinguish between them, as each situation poses different challenges to any outside actor that would aspire to rebuild the country.

The most striking common denominator of the three major paths to state failure is war. In the first case, civil war directly triggers the conversion of a functioning, capable state into one that can no longer maintain order or provide basic services to its population. Military defeat at the hands of an outside power likewise often leads to a collapse of institutions and political legitimacy of those people or parties that might hold a nation together. Defeated countries are particularly vulnerable to virulent nationalism, violent power struggles, and general chaos if the power vacuum left by a defeated regime is not filled expeditiously. The third path, intrinsic weakness due to underdevelopment, can also be linked to war. In many developing countries, spending to prepare for the possibility of war, whether internal or external, can contribute substantially to economic, social, and political underdevelopment that erodes a state over time.

In part because these distinct paths to state weakness and failure often share the common denominator of war, they also share some commonalities in the types of solutions required to put states back on their feet.

NATION BUILDING AND POST-CONFLICT RECONSTRUCTION

In the age of global terrorism, transnational crime networks, and border-hopping disease, state weakness and failure are a real threat to Americans and their way of life. Weak states in the international system can enable or facilitate the ability of those threats to reach across the globe and affect Americans where they live. Defenses against these threats therefore require not only strong military and law enforcement tools, but also the tools of nation building. Until the weak links in the international system are firmed up, they will continue to be exploited by any number of opportunistic threats.

The United States must re-energize its focus on weak, underdeveloped countries generally. Significant improvements to paltry, ineffective foreign assistance programs and improved trade regimes are required if the United States is to help address the needs of the vast majority of the world's people, gain their support for the fight against terrorism, and provide them with the means to do something about it in their own countries. Likewise, the tools of nation building are needed when the United States goes to war. Dominance on the battlefield will be squandered if the United States does not have the tools to win hearts and minds and secure lasting peace out of its military engagements.[8]

This book, however, will not focus on nation building as a general phenomenon. Although the United States may need to improve its long-term development tools and those that will complement its war-fighting ability, the true center of the problem the United States faces is in "post-conflict" environments. This is where both the real dangers and the biggest opportunities are. After war, physical and institutional infrastructure is usually badly damaged. Human capital is depleted due to the death toll and war-induced brain drain. The population remaining is often vulnerable and capable of choosing many different paths. All political, economic, and social processes are accelerated. The potential to dramatically improve the situation is heightened, as is the potential for it to unravel further.

Not only are the stakes higher and the range of motion of the local population greater in post-conflict environments; the external factors are different as well. The post-conflict window is the time at which the international community is most focused on the country in question and therefore most able to help shape the situation positively.

The focus on post-conflict environments in this volume does not mean that nation-building tools are not sometimes important during war as an element of a war-fighting strategy, or in the absence of war as part of a long-term development strategy. Rather, the volume focuses on post-conflict countries largely because this is where the biggest "bang for the buck" is to be had in policy terms.[9] Policy is all about prioritizing. The post-conflict arena is a valuable target intrinsically, but it is doubly so because the United States and the international community have seriously underperformed in this area. Investment of time, attention, and money in this field is likely to pay greater dividends to American security than just about any other investment that could be made. Thus, for policy reasons the focus of this book is not "nation building" but rather "post-conflict reconstruction."

THE FOUR PILLARS OF POST-CONFLICT RECONSTRUCTION

Post-conflict reconstruction is not a new concept. The World Bank has used the term since 1995 to describe the need for "the rebuilding of the socioeconomic framework of society" and the "reconstruction of the enabling conditions for a functioning peacetime society [to include] the framework of governance and rule of law."[10] In this book, however, "post-conflict reconstruction" is understood more broadly to denote efforts by the United States and other outside actors to help local actors build up a minimally capable state in four key areas: security; governance and participation; social and economic well-being; and justice and reconciliation. Each of these distinct yet interrelated sets of tasks constitutes a pillar of efforts to rebuild countries after conflict.[11]

The *security pillar* addresses all aspects of public safety, in particular establishment of a safe and secure environment and development of legitimate and stable security institutions. Security encompasses the provision of collective and individual security and is the precondition for achieving successful outcomes in the other pillars. In the most pressing sense, it concerns securing the lives of civilians from immediate and large-scale violence and the restoration of territorial integrity.

The *governance and participation pillar* addresses the need for legitimate, effective political and administrative institutions and participatory processes. These are most often guaranteed through a representative constitutional structure. Governance involves setting rules and procedures for political decisionmaking, and strengthening public-sector management and administration to deliver public services in an efficient and transparent manner. Participation encompasses the process for ensuring active and open participation of the citizenry in the formulation of government and its policies, including through advocacy groups, civic associations, and media that help ensure the generation and exchange of ideas.

The *social and economic well-being pillar* addresses fundamental social and economic needs of the population, in particular the provision of emergency relief, restoration of essential services, laying the foundation for a viable economy, and initiation of an inclusive, sustainable development program. Often accompanying the establishment of security, well-being entails protecting the population from starvation, disease, and the elements. As the situation stabilizes, attention shifts from humanitarian relief to long-term social and economic development.

The *justice and reconciliation pillar* addresses the need for an impartial and accountable legal system and for ways to deal with past abuses; in particular, creation of effective law enforcement, an open judicial system, fair laws, humane corrections systems, and formal and informal mechanisms for resolving grievances arising from conflict. These tasks encompass the provision of mechanisms to redress grievances, exact appropriate penalties for previous acts, and build capacity to promulgate and enforce the rule of law. Incorporating the concept of restorative justice, they include extraordinary and traditional efforts to reconcile ex-combatants, victims, and perpetrators.

A minimally capable state is an appropriate goal in the short to medium run because outside actors must be realistic, even humble, about what they can achieve in the context of a failed state or a devastated postwar environment. The long-term goals of addressing the root causes of conflict in the country and building a durable nation are beyond the scope of what external actors can realistically aspire to. The people of the country in question and their leaders must be the ones who achieve these long-term goals, albeit, one would hope, with support from outside actors characterized by "normal" economic (trade and aid), military (liaison), and political (diplomatic) relations between sovereign countries.

THE ROLE OF THE UNITED STATES

The question for the United States at the beginning of the twenty-first century is not *whether* to engage in post-conflict reconstruction but, rather, *how* to do so most effectively. U.S. interests in combating breeding grounds for terrorism will require action on this front, and American ideals will often support those American leaders who would seek to use American power and capability toward humanitarian ends in these and other cases.

The United States is by no means the only actor involved in post-conflict reconstruction efforts. As the sole superpower, however, the United States has a dominant interest in maintaining a coherent and stable international order. Therefore, although the exact nature of the U.S. role will vary case by case, depending on the U.S. interests at stake, it is safe to assume that the United States will be involved in some way in most major reconstruction efforts. When vital interests are at stake, the United States will most often choose to assume a direct leadership role. When such interests are less clear, however, the United States will often encourage other international actors to take a lead while it makes a limited contribution. In some cases the United States may try to avoid involvement altogether.

Decades of experience suggest, however, that U.S. participation and leadership are often a crucial determinant of an operation's success or failure. This should come as no surprise given the significant military, political, and economic resources that the United States can bring to bear. In Bosnia and Kosovo, for example, direct application of U.S. diplomatic and military resources reversed the pre-existing trends toward ethnic cleansing and borders drawn by force and laid the foundation for success. The United States cannot and should not take a lead role in every post-conflict operation. But its global reach may often mean that the United States is capable of making a difference even in some of the most remote and least integrated countries, as was the case of Mozambique in the early 1990s where diplomatic support and targeted foreign assistance led to a peaceful and increasingly prosperous outcome. Even when the United States is not a central player, targeted U.S. support can help an intervention led by other nations to succeed, as in the cases of U.S. support for Australia in East Timor and the United Kingdom in Sierra Leone. The United States can also have a great impact when it provides serious political and financial support for interventions run by the United Nations, as in the cases of El Salvador, Cambodia, and Guatemala.

When the United States does not have overriding national interests and chooses not to take a leadership role, it should not underestimate its ability to catalyze action by other international actors. When the United States makes a meaningful contribution to a rebuilding process, this action improves confidence in the mission and raises prospects for success by making others more willing to assume leadership roles and raise their own contributions. In short, the United States has unique political and financial leverage that should not be underestimated.

Because it cannot afford to meet every post-conflict reconstruction need, the United States can and should promote an international division of labor. To be effective this division of labor in turn requires identifying areas where the United States and other international actors hold a comparative advantage—those capabilities or assets that a given country can bring to the table. U.S. military power, for example, gives U.S. negotiators particular leverage in some cases, even as that same power may make the United States a less appropriate leader in other cases. Another area where the United States has a consistent comparative advantage is its economic market, which can be used to enhance trade opportunities for post-conflict countries. Yet another comparative advantage that the United States enjoys is a multicultural population with refugees and immigrants from just about any country where an intervention might take place. Finally, the United States' global presence and unique logistical and technical capacity give it a comparative advantage in identifying needs in a timely manner and mustering a quick response.

U.S. contributions will vary from operation to operation. Still, U.S. leaders need to make judgments about what assistance options they want to have available for potential engagements. The notion of comparative advantage should be central in helping the U.S. government determine the portfolio of long-term capabilities and mechanisms that should be cultivated.

In recent years, some in the United States have argued that enhancing U.S. capacity to work in post-conflict environments is a recipe for automatically dragging the United States into "other people's messes." In fact, nothing could be further from the truth. Enhancing U.S. capacities to work on a broader spectrum of post-conflict reconstruction issues will give the United States more, not less, flexibility. The United States would have the ability, one it does not currently enjoy, to choose different tools and varying levels of commitment depending on the situation. Indeed, it will also provide the United States with more leverage to determine what role to play and what roles to ask other international and indigenous actors to play. Far from limiting U.S. options, building post-conflict reconstruction capacity is a recipe for more judicious and more effective interventions.

ADDRESSING AMERICA'S CAPACITY GAPS

Despite a long and deep history of involvement in post-conflict reconstruction efforts and growing demand over the last decade, the United States has failed to undertake a significant reform of its approach to and capabilities for post-conflict reconstruction. For all its ability to wage war, the U.S. military is unprepared to mount major stability operations and secure a lasting peace. Of even greater concern, U.S. civilian agencies lack the tools to take the job over from the military. Likewise, the U.S. government's capacity to plan for and oversee both civilian and military post-conflict operations is wanting. In short, the United States is unprepared for the real challenges of the twenty-first century.

Although the Bush administration came to office concerned about the overuse of the military, it has rapidly accelerated the tendency to use the military as the primary instrument for post-conflict reconstruction. During the 2000 campaign, candidate Bush cautioned: "I would be very careful about using our troops as nation builders. I believe the role of the military is to fight and win war... I believe we're overextended in too many places." [12] In his first year in office, he and his top officials followed that same line. Even after the terrorist attacks on the United States on September 11, 2001, official attitudes in the Bush administration toward nation building changed only slowly. [13] President Bush himself continued to demonstrate his unease with the concept and the term. [14]

And yet, by mid-2003, President Bush had deployed significant numbers of forces to Iraq (150,000 coalition, including 130,000 U.S.) and Afghanistan (6,000 NATO and 9,000 U.S.) where they became deeply enmeshed in fundamental nation-building efforts, remaining in both places in similar quantities for more than a year despite plans to scale back dramatically.[15] In addition, the Bush administration maintained significant force levels in two ongoing nation-building projects: Bosnia (13,000 NATO, including 3,000 U.S.) and Kosovo (20,000 NATO, including 1,500 U.S.).

This military, however, has not been prepared to do the job of post-conflict reconstruction. It had not been trained for the types of duties it is now undertaking, it does not have the doctrine necessary, nor has it received a mandate to do the job. One artillery officer in Iraq, for example, when asked if he had any training or doctrine on how to set up and run a local governing council, a task for which he was currently responsible, replied, "No sir. I guess it's good I paid attention in my civics class… back in 8th grade." [16] In fact, many of the soldiers on the ground insist that they are not supposed to be doing nation building even as they practice it.[17] The simple fact is that American troops have succeeded to the extent they have because of the dedication, hard work, and entrepreneurial spirit of individual soldiers on the ground, not because of the way they were prepared to do their job. Appropriate doctrine, organization, and training could dramatically improve the outcome.

Although the military can and should play an important role in some cases, civilian actors have a comparative advantage in addressing many of the wide range of needs in post-conflict reconstruction. Nongovernmental organizations, the private sector, international organizations, multilateral development banks, and civilian agencies of multiple donor governments all have a crucial role to play in addressing post-conflict needs.

Unfortunately, civilian capacity to do post-conflict reconstruction has lagged behind. Insufficient attention has been paid to building up civilian capacities in a systematic way so that these actors' natural comparative advantages can be marshaled in the struggle to rebuild countries. Indeed, it is a question not just of creating new capabilities, but rather, in many cases, of rehabilitating civilian capacities that once existed in the U.S. government but that have been allowed to decay.

In addition, it is time to re-examine all the instruments of government that have been designed for "normal" countries and "normal" relations.

If an external intervention is required, there is a good chance that the countries in question are anything but normal. Providing development assistance, enhancing trade, and promoting democracy in weak, failed, and defeated states is a very different challenge, one for which the United States must adjust its tools.

Ultimately, what is required is (1) a standing set of instruments capable of addressing a wide range of needs in a wide range of countries, and (2) a conceptual and institutional framework capable of deploying them appropriately. Only if the United States improves its capacity and develops a more coherent strategy for addressing failed, weak, and defeated states will it be prepared to defend its national security and uphold its historic values in the twenty-first century. It is to this end that this book has been written.

Notes

[1] The modern international system is premised on sovereign nation states. In reality, however, not all states created in the modern era have had the ability to exercise actual sovereignty over their territory. As globalization has accelerated, the problems of theoretical but not actually realized sovereignty have become global problems as opposed to simply local or regional ones.

[2] The White House, *The National Security Strategy of the United States of America*, September 2002, p. 1.

[3] Though the initial phase of the U.S. efforts in Afghanistan and Iraq has been undertaken largely by military actors in hostile environments, these cases are included in this volume both because of the nonterritorial aims of the interventions and the open-ended possibility of what these operations may become.

[4] Although in retrospect the Bush administration's case concerning an imminent threat from Iraqi weapons of mass destruction appears weak, it was the heart of the administration's case to Congress, the American public, and potential coalition partners that allowed the intervention to proceed.

[5] Although the approach in Iraq was very different from the approach in Japan and Europe after World War II, the sums of money allocated for Iraq approach the same levels as those for the reconstruction of Japan as well as Europe under the Marshall Plan. By November 2003 the United States had already appropriated well over $20 billion (in both regular budget and supplemental spending) for the first year of reconstructing Iraq, an amount exceeding the $19 billion (in inflation-adjusted 2003 dollars) spent during the seven-year occupation of Japan. The White House's estimate of a $50-$75 billion requirement for rebuilding Iraq put it roughly at the level of resources

needed to rebuild Britain, France, and Germany after World War II. The cost of the Marshall Plan to rebuild all of Europe between 1948 and 1952 was $13 billion, or approximately $100 billion in inflation-adjusted 2003 dollars. See Richard W. Stevenson, "78% of Bush's Postwar Spending Plan Is for Military," *New York Times*, September 9, 2003, p. A12.

[6] The only official U.S. government definition of "failed states" is that used by USAID: "Failed states are those in which the central government does not exert effective control over, and is unable or unwilling to assure provision of vital services to, significant parts of its own territory." See Bureau for Policy and Program Coordination, *U.S. Foreign Aid: Meeting the Challenges of the Twenty-first Century* (Washington, D.C.: USAID, January 2004), p. 19.

[7] See Robert Rotberg, "The New Nature of Nation-State Failure," Washington Quarterly 25, no. 3 (summer 2001): 85–96 (identifying eight completely failed states). See also National Intelligence Council, "Global Humanitarian Emergencies: Trends and Projections, 2001–2002" (identifying 17 failed countries in 2001 and another 6 countries in immediate danger for failure in 2002), at www.cia.gov/nic/special_globalhuman2001.html (August 2001). See also the report of the State Failure Task Force (SFTP), which identifies 137 state-failure events between 1955 and 2000; for a list of the cases and methodology used to determine them, see *State Failure Task Force Report: Phase III Findings* (September 2000), and *State Failure Problem Set: Internal Wars and Failures of Governance, 1955-2000*, at www.cidcm.umd.edu/inscr/stfail/.

[8] The distinction here is between using nation-building tools to win hearts and minds as part of a war-fighting strategy and using nation-building tools in a "post-conflict" environment where there is a government or at least leaders that are inclined to head in the same direction with the United States, whether through natural sympathies, corresponding interests, or the outcome of a war—whether by capitulation to the United States or a negotiated settlement among parties that the United States can support.

[9] Many of the rebuilding activities can, and in fact usually do, occur while conflict is still taking place in some parts of a country. "Post-conflict" does not mean that conflict is concluded in all parts of a given country's territory at the same time. The term simply recognizes that most reconstruction tasks cannot be addressed until at least major parts of the country's territory, especially major population centers, have moved beyond conflict. Therefore, the term "post-conflict" applies to those areas where conflict has indeed subsided, but not necessarily to all parts of a nation's territory at the same time.

[10] See World Bank, *Post-Conflict Reconstruction: The Role of the World Bank* (Washington, D.C.: World Bank, 1998); Robert Muscat, "The World Bank's Role in Conflict Prevention and Post-Conflict Reconstruction" (prepared for the Task Force on Failed States, World Bank, Washington, D.C., November 27, 1995).

[11] See appendix 1 for a breakout of the pillars into 39 distinct sets of tasks within a single framework, as elaborated under the auspices of the Post-Conflict Reconstruction Project jointly sponsored by the Center for Strategic and International Studies and the Association of the United States Army.

[12] George W. Bush, remarks during presidential debate, October 3, 2000. This was by no means a one-off comment. As early as January 2000, future National Security Advisor Condoleezza Rice was arguing that the military was meant to be a lethal instrument, "not a civilian police force. It is not a political referee. And it is most certainly not designed to build a civilian society." *Foreign Affairs* 79, no. 1 (January-February 2000): 53.

[13] National security adviser Condoleezza Rice, for example, six weeks after the attacks stated, "There's nothing wrong with nation building, but not when it's done by the American military." Condoleezza Rice, "Foundation for a Nation," *Washington Post*, October 29, 2001, p. A17. Defense Secretary Donald Rumsfeld, writing more than two years after 9/11 while over 130,000 U.S. troops were involved in the largest nation-building exercise since World War II's aftermath, continued to show his unease with the concept, "Beyond Nationbuilding," *Washington Post*, September 25, 2003.

[14] George W. Bush, at a White House press briefing on October 12, 2001, noted, "It would be a useful function for the United Nations to take over the so-called 'nation-building'—I would call it the stabilization of a future government—after our military mission is complete." CNBC News transcripts.

[15] The U.S. Department of Defense, Directorate of Information Operations and Reports, listed 270,000 troops for Operation Iraqi Freedom in September 2003, but approximately half were stationed in Kuwait. The Bush administration also increased the number of U.S. troops and retired U.S. military contractors in Colombia, but because they were involved most directly on counternarcotic and counterinsurgency missions, their involvement will not be considered "post-conflict reconstruction" in this analysis, despite significant U.S. support for the Colombian government, which has been involved in a major nation-building effort.

[16] Numerous interviews conducted by the author with U.S. Army soldiers and Marines in Baghdad, Mosul, Kirkuk, Erbil, Sulamaniya, al Hillah, Karbala, and Najaf from June 27 to July 7, 2003.

[17] One soldier in Afghanistan actively participating in a range of reconstruction activities, for example, noted to a journalist that anything that smacks of "nation building" earns a "non-concur." See Susan B. Glasser, "Soldiers in Civilian Clothing," *Washington Post*, March 28, 2002, p. A20.

CHAPTER TWO

CONSTRUCTING A COHESIVE STRATEGIC INTERNATIONAL RESPONSE

Robert C. Orr

In many post-conflict environments, the chaos on the ground is paralleled only by the chaos of the international response. Various governmental agencies, international organizations, international financial institutions, and nongovernmental organizations come from all parts of the globe to help. They bring much-needed resources, expertise, and energy, but they also bring very different assumptions, working styles, and goals. Sometimes, making the international response cohere seems almost as challenging as rebuilding the country itself. And yet, if the international community is to maximize the likelihood of successful assistance and minimize the chance of exacerbating problems on the ground, it must take on that challenge.

Cooperation among international actors, while important, is not sufficient. Rather, a strategic approach that ensures unity of effort is essential to success. Although creating a perfectly cohesive effort in any post-conflict country is not possible, there are a number of straightforward actions that can be taken to maximize the unity of international effort. Below are ten essential principles for unifying efforts and operational guidelines that should be followed to help realize them.

One. The people of the country in question must own the reconstruction process and be its prime movers.

Following conflict, indigenous governance structures are often very weak or nonexistent. At the same time, the local human resource base is greatly diminished through war-induced deaths, brain drain, displacement, and forgone investment in people (due to destroyed or underfunded education and health systems as well as closed private enterprise). This bleak starting point often forces outside actors to play, at least initially, a disproportionately large role in the rebuilding process. While this reality cannot be denied, all efforts must be taken to ensure that the external presence dedicates itself to building indigenous capacity and governance structures as quickly as possible. A number of steps can and should be taken to ensure that the affected population does not come to depend on external actors for their basic goods and services, and makes good use of the presence of outside experts by receiving training and coaching. In the end, mobilizing the country's population is the only way that key goods and services will be delivered over time.

Host-country control and ownership are also central to building momentum for internal cohesion, forcing external collaboration (the more unified and autonomous the government, the more unified the external actors need to be), and creating a long-term sustainable political and economic balance.

In keeping with this principle, the international community should follow two key operational guidelines. First, leadership roles in the reconstruction effort must be given to host country nationals at the earliest possible stage of the process. Even if capacity is limited, host country representatives should chair or cochair pledging conferences, priority-setting meetings, joint assessments of needs, and all other relevant processes. In ideal circumstances the representatives should be elected or otherwise legitimate representatives. In other situations, peace accords may designate which civil society actors beyond the parties to conflict should participate in specified aspects of the rebuilding process. Where these initial avenues do not exist, the international community must help create mechanisms for legitimate host country leaders to be elected or appointed. The Afghanistan process outlined in Bonn is just one example of this type of immediate leader identification with phased participatory, legitimizing processes.[1]

The second operational guideline is that international actors should seek out host country counterparts from day one. If host country counterparts do not exist, international actors should help to create them and impart the knowledge and skills necessary to succeed in the job. For all tasks that will eventually need to be performed by the host country population, international organizations should pair their functionaries with locals (through either election, appointment, or competitive hiring mechanisms). Creating or developing effective host country counterparts should be one of the criteria on which the various external organizations and individuals are judged, including in their performance reports.

Two. A coherent international strategy based on internal and external parties' interests is crucial.

Virtually all major international donors have called for strategic coordination in post-conflict settings.[2] In parallel, the United Nations has attempted to create and implement "strategic frameworks" for coordinating the UN system. Despite the need and compelling rationale for these frameworks, bureaucratic resistance and difficulties on the ground doomed the effort as the first two attempts in Afghanistan and Sierra Leone fizzled.[3] The simple fact is that no general processes or models for strategy development and coordination exist among major international actors.

For any strategy development exercise in these difficult environments to succeed, it must be based on at least three key assumptions. The first assumption is that all involved must recognize that post-conflict reconstruction is not a technical or "normal" developmental process, but rather a fundamentally political one.[4] Although the United Nations has accurately acknowledged that "the overriding criterion for the selection and establishment of [aid] priorities is political," in fact neither the UN nor other international organizations have conducted their assistance programs in a manner that conforms to the primacy of politics in these settings.

A second key assumption is that any outside intervention must be designed with the interests of all the involved key actors, both within the country and outside. Just as the fundamental interests of the parties to conflict must be evaluated and influenced to create a stable peace, so too must the interests of other key actors in the society, as well as those of neighbors, regional actors, and international powers. If a realistic interest calculation is not done with and for the indigenous players, then any intervention may unwittingly empower spoilers or disempower legitimate, peace-seeking actors. At the same time, the interest calculations of key international actors must be taken into account to maximize their ability to help the peace process and minimize their ability to undermine it.

Finally, although a coordinated strategic plan may exist on paper, a third key assumption is that only a small team of key external actors working in-country will be able to effectively leverage international resources and influence the interest calculations of key actors. Major international support, if delivered ad hoc through myriad agencies, may meet some immediate needs within the country, but will be unlikely to constructively address the needs of those who could re-ignite the conflict. Thus senior-level international actors, whether envoys or special representatives, must be resourced to make the in-country financial, security, and operational decisions that make or break the reconstruction process.

Accordingly, the international community should adopt three key operational guidelines. First, in order to ensure strategic coherence throughout the process, international organizations and countries should designate top international and national leadership—experienced, operationally minded, and culturally savvy—and deploy them to the field as soon as possible. Where the United Nations is heavily involved, Special Representatives of the Secretary General (SRSGs) should be given additional authority to coordinate UN actors and shape the strategic direction of the overall international response. In addition, major donors like the United States should field senior, operationally oriented "directors of reconstruction" to ensure a coherent national response.

Second, representatives of the international community in partnership with host country representatives should conduct joint assessments of needs so that all players have a common frame of reference. The host country should be a leader in the process of assessing local and regional actors and estimating the capacity of factions to advance or undermine the peace process. Local leaders will best be able to identify security risks, assess priority infrastructure needs, point out quick-impact opportunities for international actors who need to gain credibility, and identify local resources that could be channeled toward reconstruction.

Third, based on this joint assessment, international and indigenous representatives on the ground should develop a strategy for addressing priority needs and objectives and provide strategy suggestions to help shape any pledging conference. Whether they are an indigenous or intervening actor, those working in the field will be the most able to realistically evaluate and prioritize needs.

Three. The international community must address the problem of post-conflict reconstruction holistically, building and deploying capacity to address a broad range of interrelated tasks.

Military leaders are often among the first to realize that the tools their forces possess are not sufficient to the complex task of post-conflict reconstruction. General John Abizaid, the regional commander of U.S. forces spearheading U.S. reconstruction efforts in Iraq, identified the problem succinctly: "There is no strictly military solution to the problems we face.... It requires that we move together on the political front, on the economic front, on the reconstruction front in a manner that is synchronized and coordinated. If we don't do that, I do not believe that we can be successful. So you can pay the military to stay there, but you are only paying us to stay forever."[5]

And yet it is not enough that the international community "move together" on the range of issues. It requires a single, coherent strategy. As United Nations Secretary General Kofi Annan has noted, "All [the] tasks—humanitarian, military, political, social, and economic—are interconnected, and the people engaged in them need to work closely together. We cannot expect lasting success in any of them unless we pursue all of them at once as part of a single coherent strategy. If the resources are lacking for any one of them, all the others may turn out to have been pursued in vain."[6]

The range of tasks that should be considered in any given post-conflict reconstruction operation are easily identified and fall into four main areas: security; justice and reconciliation; economic and social well-being; and governance and participation.[7]

Operationally this means that a broad survey, or "capacity map," of capabilities currently held by national governments, international organizations, international development banks, and nongovernmental organizations should be undertaken. Gaps in capacity to conduct the requisite activities should be identified and filled. This would require hardheaded analysis of comparative advantages of the different actors and a level of cooperation among them that does not currently exist.

Four: Security is the sine qua non of post-conflict reconstruction.

Though every case is different, there is one constant—if security needs are not met, both the peace in a given country and the intervention intended to promote it are doomed to fail. Unless security needs are addressed up front, spoilers will have undue leverage to affect the political outcomes, vitiating the peace. In an insecure environment, elevated risk will impede the mobilization of pro-peace constituencies. In addition, if the international community gets significantly involved without sufficient security and the blood of those providing assistance is spilled, there will be a risk of an abrupt pullout—leaving the country, and those involved in the operation, significantly worse off than before.

While security is essential, it will never be one hundred percent guaranteed. Crucial initial efforts in justice and reconciliation, social and economic well-being, and governance and participation must not be sacrificed for vain attempts to establish a completely stable and secure environment. The perfect must not become the enemy of the good.

There are two important guidelines that the international community needs to follow in this area. First, "coalitions of the willing" and UN peacekeeping operations need coherent military leadership and core troops that provide the backbone of the operation. This is most easily ensured when both are provided by a "lead nation" (or the equivalent), as the United States and then Canada did in Haiti, NATO did in Bosnia and Kosovo, and Australia did in East Timor. However, no single, failure-proof model exists. Various other configurations have worked in other instances such as Sierra Leone (where the British have provided core capabilities and South Asian and African troops have provided leadership and the bulk of the forces).

Second, because personal security and internal order are essential and often in scarce supply in a post-conflict environment, policing is a major need.[8] The international community must enhance its ability to deploy civilian police to address temporary needs, and it must build additional training and organizing capacity to help develop indigenous police forces in a timely manner.

Five: Success is made on the ground.

Although the distant headquarters of various international actors can facilitate or impede success, the key to effective international involvement in post-conflict reconstruction efforts is empowering and organizing representatives in the field. Strategy in a post-conflict environment must be closely tailored to the particular characteristics of the country and, as such, should be heavily informed by those closest to the situation. To operate strategically and effectively, the key international actors must be close to key host country actors, both because they must know what their interest calculations are and how to influence them, and because they must be able to respond flexibly to difficult situations on short notice.

Because actors with various—sometimes even contradictory—mandates are in the field at any given time, they must be left to devise an appropriate division of labor at the country level. Adhering too closely to the interests of distant capitals, headquarters, and mandates is a recipe for failure. Redundancy, overlap, and unhealthy competition are the likely results. Those who are looking at the same situation every day are much more likely to find areas of agreement on how to proceed than those who follow guidance based on abstract authorities and bureaucratic politics generated in distant places.

Therefore, first, donors and international organizations need to begin to structure their post-conflict authorities to devolve maximum power, money, and authority to their representatives in the field. This will require strong leadership at the political level to overcome the natural bureaucratic instinct to hold power and authority at the respective headquarters. Only through intentional decisions to devolve power and responsibility can a truly effective system be created.

Second, "country teams" should be created that include representatives not only from the UN system and/or the lead nation, but also the major donors, multilateral development banks, and key NGOs. They should jointly conduct assessments, provide input to strategic planning, and coordinate all activities throughout their stay in country.

Third, Civil-Military Operations Centers (CMOCs) or Civil-Military Cooperation Centers (CIMICs) should be a standard part of the package where military or peacekeeping operations operate alongside other reconstruction efforts. To succeed, civilian and military strategies must be coordinated: they must come together to form a common culture and site for information sharing and operational coordination. Both military and humanitarian groups must dedicate staff and time to the communication of their activities, assets, and limitations in order to build credibility, manage expectations, and build trusting dependable relationships across organizational lines. CIMICS must be readily available to the humanitarian community—that is, they should be located "outside the wire" of a military compound. Yet they must also have immediate access to the force commander, military logistics, and operations. Since Operation Provide Comfort (Northern Iraq 1991) and Operation Provide Relief (Somalia/Kenya 1992-1993), the coordinating mechanism of the Civil-Military Operations Center has been incorporated into U.S. military doctrine. Meanwhile, humanitarian organizations have begun to build internal frameworks for collaboration, such as the Humanitarian Community Information Center (HCIC) in Kosovo or the UN's Office of the Coordinator of Humanitarian Affairs' (OCHA) Structured Humanitarian Assistance Reporting (SHARE). [9]

Fourth, "friends groups," which formally bring together governments with means and interests in supporting the peace and reconstruction process, should be cultivated and formed at early stages of the process. According to one major study that reviewed 16 different cases, friends groups were a part of virtually all cases of successful strategic coordination.[10]

Six: Needs must be rigorously prioritized and activities sequenced accordingly.

Dire post-conflict environments rife with needs often lead locals and international interveners to determine that "everything is a priority." Yet if everything is a priority, then nothing is. As difficult as such discipline is in the face of extreme want, a strategic approach demands that host country leaders and outside actors agree on top priorities. Although every case is different, certain issues—security, for one—need urgent attention in virtually all cases. Safety is often followed closely by meeting food security needs—not just immediate humanitarian assistance, but also the revival of agriculture and functional market and distribution mechanisms. Another top priority is putting people back to work. Although new economic activity that spurs employment is preferable, temporary work programs are often required to get people off the streets and spur economic activity and hope.

To maximize impact, the international community not only must prioritize needs; it must also pay serious attention to the sequencing of the various aspects of its intervention. If top priorities are addressed in the wrong order, there can be perverse side affects. In Bosnia, for example, the position of spoilers was unintentionally strengthened when economic privatization programs were pursued before rule of law and anticorruption mechanisms were in place.[11]

Operationally, this means that country teams composed of all the major international actors, together with the host government, should establish priorities and a notional sequence for implementing them. The UN Special Representative of the Secretary General or other senior official coordinating the international response with the host government should have the authority and responsibility to accelerate or slow certain agencies' programs based on prioritization and sequencing requirements.

Because not all tasks can be a priority, and sequencing cannot happen as it would in a laboratory, risks and trade-offs must be communicated to citizens of the host country who may be affected. In many cases, for example, hundreds of thousands of refugees may want to repatriate before public health needs such as providing sufficient sanitation, repairing damaged infrastructure, or clearing mine fields can be sufficiently met. Afghanistan in 2002 is one such dramatic case.[12]

Seven: International interventions are extraordinary and should take all necessary measures to avoid undermining local leaders, institutions, and processes.

A significant international presence is often needed in a post-conflict situation in order to provide security, reassure the indigenous population of international financial and moral support, deliver needed services, and build lasting internal capacity. Although a large international presence may be both necessary and appropriate in initial phases, a dominating presence can be damaging over the long term. A large international presence, if not managed properly, can have such negative consequences as (1) encouraging dependency, both physical and psychological; (2) distorting the local economy, including markets for goods, labor, real estate, and currency; (3) distorting local norms, values, and practices, especially those relating to age and gender; and (4) damaging the health and well-being of the population due to increased sexual contact and the transmission of HIV/AIDS and other sexually transmitted diseases.

The first operational guideline that the international community should follow is hiring locals to do as much of the reconstruction as possible. If a job can be done by someone local, it should be. Provide incentives, such as good publicity and additional resources, to international and nongovernmental organizations that do this well. Employing locals helps boost long-term economic and social well-being and morale, and at the same time reduces the size of the international presence with its negative economic side effects such as inflation, parallel economies, and housing shortages. Increasing local employment can also provide incentives for locals to support peace—people with jobs are more likely to support a stable political order. On a cautionary note, employing locals must be done in such a way that jobs are distributed in a manner that is perceived to be "fair" by most people (e.g., by ethnicity, geography or political persuasion)—otherwise a delicate political balance can be disrupted.

Second, the international actors must establish salary structures for local hires that are competitive, but not exorbitant. Donor agencies must compete for the highest-skilled workers without drawing them all away from government and indigenous private-sector opportunities. Where necessary, donors may even provide temporary supplements to the fledgling host government in order to make key government and private-sector positions more attractive.

Third, international actors must balance their desire for a "light footprint" with the need to have sufficient presence on the ground to help shift the balance of power toward key groups and individuals. Reformers within the host country can often author the strategy and organize broad support, but certain groups may require particularly visible outside support. For example, in the post-Taliban reconstruction of Afghanistan, UN Special Representative Lakhdar Brahimi selected as his gender adviser Fatiha Serour, an Afghan woman without international experience, in order to build reform that fit within Afghan mores. The UN Security Council expressed support for human rights reform, declaring that "it was 'essential' for the future government to respect the human rights of all Afghan people, regardless of gender, ethnicity and religion, and welcomed the Interim Authority's 'bold steps' to promote the rights of women—including appointing female Cabinet Ministers."[13]

Eight: Mechanisms are needed to rapidly mobilize and coordinate needed resources and sustain them for appropriate periods of time.

Given the great diversity of actors, agendas, funding sources, authorities, and methods of disbursement involved, it is little wonder that funding post-conflict operations is complex and that current methodologies have proved quite resistant to change.[14]

Bilateral donors, UN agencies, and international financial institutions are generally more eager to script their own role in post-conflict reconstruction than to coordinate with other international or local actors. The World Bank was established with a mandate of post-conflict reconstruction, and over the course of the last decade has again become by far the largest funder of activities in post-conflict situations. Between 1989 and 1998, for example, the Bank disbursed over $6.2 billion in loans to 18 countries experiencing or emerging from conflict. By 1999 a full one-quarter of its concessional lending went to countries other than China and India.[15] Individual OECD donor countries have also provided large amounts of funding, as have regional development banks. Ultimately, the 22 members of the OECD's Development Assistance Committee are responsible for approximately 99 percent of global overseas development assistance.[16] And the UN, while its monies are much smaller, sometimes plays an important role in managing the politics of a post-conflict reconstruction process, thereby becoming involved in the coordination of resources.

To date, virtually all these major actors have examined current funding mechanisms and found them wanting. Yet attempts to mobilize funding for these types of operations more rapidly have failed. Not only did the UN Strategic Framework model fail in Afghanistan; it was never fully developed in Sierra Leone despite a commitment in 1999 to do so. In an attempt to mobilize funds more effectively, the UN Consolidated Inter-Agency Appeal (CAP) was modified into an Expanded Consolidated Inter-Agency Appeal (ECAP), both of which have marginally improved coordination to meet priority needs. Likewise, the OECD's Development Assistance Committee developed *Guidelines on Conflict, Peace, and Development Cooperation*, but these have had little impact. The World Bank continues to appeal for a trust fund that would house post-conflict funds committed by all reconstruction participants. Programmatically, the World Bank developed a Post-Conflict Reconstruction program (now the Conflict Prevention and Reconstruction Unit) and is seeking to build upon a limited Post-Conflict Fund. The United States has developed the modestly resourced Office of Transition Initiatives within the United States Agency for International Development (USAID), and Canada has developed a similarly limited Peacebuilding Fund within the Canadian International Development Agency (CIDA).

To bridge the gap, some have proposed innovative solutions.[17] Donors, however, have jealously guarded their sovereign or institutional prerogatives to dole out money on a case-by-case basis. In the United States, for instance, the role of the U.S. Congress is central and must be factored into any solutions in this area.

Based on various funders' acknowledgments that efforts to help post-conflict countries have been severely hindered by current funding mechanisms, these funders should agree to craft a new resource-mobilizing infrastructure for post-conflict situations. A joint effort should be undertaken by the World Bank, the UN, the regional development banks, and the OECD bilateral donors to create a new funding mechanism to address the needs of countries in crisis or emerging from it.[18] Individual contributing governments will also need to improve their ability to commit to flexible reconstruction assistance and move money quickly. [19]

Pledging conferences, in which donor nations tend to extend promises far beyond what they will truly deliver, require mechanisms for monitoring and accountability. Afghanistan is yet another example of the damage done by slow-disbursing aid.[20] Indeed, even the United States, which proved to be far and away the most generous donor to Afghanistan's reconstruction through the early stages of the rebuilding there, designated close to half its money over the first half year of Afghanistan's reconstruction to rebuilding its own national facilities, while the United Nations received the lion's share of the other money, leaving the host government without any means to improve its capacity.[21]

A third operational guideline for providing funding to post-conflict operations is that governments and organizations need to provide disbursement authorities to operation-level strategists, such as Special Representatives of the Secretary General or Directors of Reconstruction, rather than retaining those authorities at UN headquarters or foreign capitals. As a result of working from the field, these senior representatives on the ground will have better knowledge of genuine priorities, credible mechanisms for resource transfer, and suspected or known spoilers than they possibly could from their home cities.

Nine: Accountability is essential for both host country and international actors.

Holding both host country and international actors accountable in post-conflict settings is as important as it is difficult. Chaos exists after a conflict because no legal or institutional framework has the authority to hold people accountable in economic, political, and personal affairs. Too often, force or the threat of force mediates justice, while actors seeking to build the legitimacy of civic recourses lack the clout and structure to deter dishonorable conduct. At the same time, the influx of foreign resources into a resource-scarce environment raises the potential for corruption and tests the accountability of both local and international actors.

Conditionality can and should be used to ensure accountability, but it must be carefully designed, focused on specific high-value issues (corruption, key parts of the peace accords, etc.), and rigorously coordinated so as not to pull the incipient government apart.

Before being dispatched to a post-conflict site, international staff members should be required by their sponsoring organization to receive appropriate training and indoctrination on codes of conduct and accountability systems. The UN Department of Peacekeeping Operations (DPKO) and the Office of the High Commissioner for Human Rights (OHCHR) already require basic courses in human rights for peacekeepers and police commanders, but recent evidence of sexual exploitation by UN staff suggests that current curricula and enforcement measures are tragically insufficient. The so-called Brahimi Report on reforming UN peacekeeping notes "...the importance of training military, police and other civilian personnel on human rights issues and on the relevant provisions of international humanitarian law" (No. 41) and commends the Secretary-General's bulletin of August 6, 1999 entitled "Observance by United Nations forces of international humanitarian law." [22]

In addition to imparting basic human rights covenants and principles, training should teach (1) internal legal aspects of a mission such as standing operating procedures, codes of conduct, and clearly delineated disciplinary procedures, as well as (2) external legal requirements such as the laws and norms of the host country, the requirements of the international actors' home country, and the policies of the sponsoring organization. If indigenous or generic procedures and penal codes have been set up, staff must be trained in these legal frameworks and the legal implications of abridging those laws.[23]

International actors also need to design and rigidly enforce codes of conduct for themselves. Although a host country may not yet have acculturated to robust norms and may lack mechanisms for enforcement and punishment, intervening organizations retain the authority over their staff to require adherence to a strict code of conduct. In addition to observing all local laws (and being imprisoned or immediately expelled if they do not), international staff should be penalized in job evaluations and public information campaigns if they behave inappropriately. Civil and military professionals remain accountable to the sovereign law of their home countries.

Ten: The timing of an operation must be driven by circumstances on the ground, not by artificial deadlines or by externally driven bureaucratic imperatives.

Timing of international actions can be a crucial determinant of success or failure. Unfortunately, the international community is neither nimble nor prompt when getting into the field or when transitioning from one phase of an operation to another. Likewise, international actors are often indecisive about the indicators for handing off authority and departing at the appropriate time.

Fielding appropriate resources quickly enables international actors to maximize their leverage when the peace is both most fragile and most malleable. Timing is no less a concern, however, once actors are in the field. Phasing actors in and out (peacekeepers, police, etc.) and designing hand-offs to host country actors from the beginning is crucial to addressing needs appropriately, maintaining momentum and, ultimately, making an intervention sustainable.

Getting in: The effectiveness of post-conflict reconstruction is often a race against time to act while the opportunity for establishing rule of law is greatest. Thus, to achieve maximum leverage of finite resources, the United States must improve the pace at which civilian capacity responds to international complex contingencies. Its ability to react rapidly—and with appropriate breadth of engagement—will require significant structural and cultural reform in the areas of anticipatory planning, rate of deployment, and funding mechanisms.[24]

Transitioning: To sustain political support and enable smoother transitions from one phase of an operation to the next, requires establishing measures of success at the beginning of a mission and evaluating progress constantly. For example, the World Bank established nine-month objectives in Afghanistan to assess its progress and hold itself accountable to its shareholders. Its objectives encompassed the areas of governance and civil service, fund management, employment and education, infrastructure, agriculture, and business development, as well as the organization of donors led by Afghan authorities and enhanced knowledge by the bank and international community of Afghanistan's needs for longer-term development. [25] Establishing measures of success and notional transition points is a key to managing the expectations of both the local population and the international community.

Getting out: A realistic time horizon is essential to achieving a mission's goals and calibrating expectations accordingly. Different actors may be central in different time periods, but the major actors must make an overall commitment to stay engaged over time. Any artificial deadlines for withdrawal, like those set by the United States in Bosnia, simply enable spoilers to wait the international community out. Achieving success is the only true exit strategy. Anything less risks forcing return involvement at a later date.

CONCLUSION: WORKING TOGETHER

Given the immense social, financial, military, and political expense of assisting a nation in its recovery from conflict, and the grim consensus that so-called failed states will continue to demand international attention, lead nations and organizations in reconstruction have every incentive to build disciplined, effective methods for getting the job done well and quickly. With the lessons of 1990s, we now have sufficient knowledge of the pitfalls and opportunities of post-conflict reconstruction to become more sophisticated and systematic in our approach. The numerous donor agencies, international organizations, and NGOs must not be allowed to pursue their mandates in a way that compromises long-term local sustainability. Countries emerging from conflict succeed to the extent that they achieve a united vision, accountability, and well-organized capacity—and international actors must remain committed to these goals for themselves as well as for the country they assist.

Notes

[1] See James Dobbins et al., *America's Role in Nation-Building: From Germany to Iraq* (Santa Monica: RAND, 2003), pp. 129–148. See also Barnett Rubin, Abby Stoddard, Mumayun Hamidzada, and Adib Farhadi, "Building a New Afghanistan: The Value of Success, The Cost of Failure" (New York: Center for International Cooperation, New York University, March 2004), www.cic.nyu.edu/pdf/Building.pdf.

[2] See, for example, the formulation agreed to by all the world's major aid donors in Organization for Economic Cooperation and Development/ Development Assistance Committee (OECD/DAC), *Conflict, Peace, and Development Cooperation* (March 1997), pp. 33,48, www.jha.ac/Ref/r017.pdf, and April 2001 supplement.

[3] See "Strategic Framework for Afghanistan Towards a Principled Approach to Peace and Reconstruction" (September 1998), www.pcpafg.org/Programme/strategic_framework. In 1999, the UN planned to develop a strategic framework for Sierra Leone, which never materialized; see United Nations System Chief Executives Board (CEB), "Generic Guidelines for a Strategic Framework Approach for Response to and Recovery from Crisis" (April 1999), http://ceb.unsystem.org/hlcp/documents/manual/D11-2.pdf.

[4] For a good volume that makes this case clearly based on multiple case studies, see Elizabeth M. Cousens and Chetan Kumar, eds., with Karin Wermester, *Peacebuilding as Politics: Cultivating Peace in Fragile Societies* (Boulder, Colo.: Lynne Rienner, 2001).

[5] General John Abizaid, testimony before the House Appropriations Committee, Subcommittee on Foreign Operations, Export Financing and Related Programs, September 24, 2003.

[6] Kofi Annan, speech to the UN General Assembly, New York, February 2002.

[7] See the Post-Conflict Reconstruction Task Framework in appendix 1.

[8] On the training and use of international civilian police (CIVPOL) in peace operations, see William Lewis, Edward Marks, and Robert Perito, "Enhancing International Civilian Police in Peace Operations," United States Institute of Peace (April 22, 2002), www.usip.org/pubs/specialreports/sr85.pdf. See also conclusions of the so-called Brahimi report (*Report of the Panel on United Nations Peace Operations*, Lakhdar Brahimi, chairman of the panel), for example, nos. 87 and 118 under part 3 of the report, "United Nations capacities to deploy operations rapidly and effectively." A/55/305–S/2000/809 (August 21, 2000), www.un.org/peace/reports/peace_operations/. See, in this volume, chapter 6: "Dealing with Demons: Enhancing Justice and Reconciliation," by Flournoy and Pan.

[9] United States Institute of Peace, "Good Practices: Information Sharing in Complex Emergencies," Report from Roundtable on Humanitarian-Military Sharing." 2001 Worldwide Civil Affairs Conference, 2001, www.usip.org/vdi/vdr/11.html. For more information on OCHA's mechanism SHARE, see www.proventionconsortium.org/files/disastersdb_020501/recaldekingdavis.pdf.

[10] See Bruce D. Jones, "The Challenges of Strategic Coordination: Containing Opposition and Sustaining Implementation of Peace Agreements in Civil Wars," IPA Policy Paper Series on Peace Implementation (New York: International Peace Academy, June 2001).

[11] Chris Hedges, "Leaders in Bosnia Are Said to Steal Up to $1 Billion," *New York Times,* August 17, 1999, p. 1; and "Better Luck Next Time," *The Economist,* April 29, 1999).

[12] ReliefWeb, "Let Afghans Themselves Decide If They Are Ready to Go Home, Says UNHCR," June 26, 2002, www.reliefweb.int.

[13] United Nations Chronicle, online edition, "Afghanistan: On the Road to Recovery," by Horst Rutsch, 2002 issues, issue 1, *Today, in Afghanistan,* www.un.org/Pubs/chronicle/2002/issue1/0102p7.html.

[14] The best work on international funding coordination has been done by Shepard Forman and Stewart Patrick. The analysis here draws on their work, although some of the conclusions presented here may differ. Shepard Forman and Stewart Patrick, eds., *Good Intentions: Pledges of Aid for Postconflict Recovery* (Boulder, Colo.: Lynn Rienner, 2000).

[15] Ibid., p. 45. "Concessional lending" refers to loans made with favorable terms, generally at better than market rates.

[16] Forman and Patrick note that global mechanisms for reporting aid flows do not provide a means to verify aid delivery. They note that the best sources available for obtaining aid flow statistics are through the *Creditor Reporting System on Aid Activities. Gazette—Creditor Reporting System: Quarterly Report on Individual Aid Commitments.* Development Assistance Committee (DAC). ww.oecd.org/department/0,2688,en_2649_33721_1_1_1_1_1,00.html.

[17] One proposal has been the Global Post-Conflict Reconstruction Fund (GRF), whose key multilateral stakeholders would include the World Bank, the leading international finance organizations, the United Nations Development Program (UNDP), and the United Nations High Commissioner for Refugees (UNHCR). However, Forman and Patrick anticipate that resistance to such a fund would be greatest from DAC members "determined to avoid regular budgetary assessments and to maintain sovereign control of their assistance in politically charged environments." In January 1999, donors rejected the GRF proposal as unrealistic. UNHCR and World Bank "Roundtable on the Gap," cited in Forman and Patrick, *Good Intentions*, p. 24.

[18] Working from a model similar to GRF, the World Bank has long discussed developing a post-conflict trust fund. This financial mechanism would similarly be a single monetary account designed to fill the gap in funding for various types of activities between the phases of emergency relief and normal long-term financing mechanisms. Rather than fund specific reconstruction programs and activities, the trust would have specific eligibility criteria for expenditures, unified disbursement procedures, and oversight by an accountable, broad-based governing body. Currently, the Bank is piloting a post-conflict fund (PCF) housed within the Conflict Prevention and Reconstruction Unit that "supports planning, piloting and analysis of reconstruction activities by funding governments and partner organizations in the forefront of this work. The emphasis is on speed and flexibility without sacrificing quality."

[19] Report on UN Consolidated Inter-Agency Appeal (CAP) and the Expanded Consolidated Inter-Agency Appeal (ECAP), cited in Forman and Patrick, *Good Intentions*, p. 39. For one proposal to improve United States government capacity along these lines, see, in this volume, chapter 10 by Orr and Mendelson Forman, "Funding Post-Conflict Reconstruction."

[20] On August 15, 2002, Secretary Rumsfeld noted his frustration in a Pentagon briefing: "Money has not been coming in as fast as it needs to come in. I'm told that less than a third of the aid pledged for this year, at the Tokyo conference has arrived thus far, and it's September almost. In many cases the promised contributions are spread out over several years, and in still other instances, they are in kind as opposed to in cash, and that means that managing it is more difficult than it would be with cash, although all of it's helpful and all of it's needed and all of it's appreciated. Others of the donations are saddled with

various prohibitions…. It all helps, but it does need to be increased." For the impact of slow funding on prospects of success, see also Susan B. Glasser "Reconstruction of Afghan Roads Stalls, Despite Promises; New Government Sees Donors Leave," *Washington Post*, August 11, 2002; Ahmed Rashid, "Foreign-Aid Shortage Hinders Karzai's Efforts against Warlords," *Wall Street Journal*, July 18, 2002; and Peter Baker and Susan B. Glasser, "Miles to Go before Kabul Can Be Left Behind," *Washington Post*, June 9, 2002. According to the Associated Press, "During a Tokyo reconstruction conference in January, international donors pledged $4.5 billion. Only a fraction of that—an estimated $100 million—has been given. That will continue to be the case as long as Afghanistan is seen as an unstable nation." Tini Tran, "Groups Seek Afghan Peace Expansion," Associated Press, June 22, 2002.

[21] According to Michael Ignatieff, over half a year into the project, "at the Afghan Assistance Coordination Authority, the Afghan and other international officials trying to coordinate reconstruction believe that as much as $700 million of the money pledged at Tokyo has so far gone to U.N. agencies, while only $100 million or so has gone to the Afghan administration itself." In "Nation-Building Lite," *New York Times Magazine*, July 28, 2002.

[22] United Nations document ST/SGB/1999/13, www.un.org/peace/st_sgb_1999_13.pdf

[23] These topics for training were among those proposed for a fall 2001 UN "Seminar on Management Training for Civilian Police for Peacekeeping Missions."

[24] For recommendations to meet this challenge of rapid reaction, see, in this volume, chapter 8, "Filling the Gap: Civilian Rapid Response Capacity for Post-Conflict Reconstruction" by Mendelson Forman and Pan. See also the Brahimi Report (note 7, above), which states, "The first 6 to 12 weeks following a cease-fire or peace accord is often the most critical period for establishing both a stable peace and the credibility of the peacekeepers. Credibility and political momentum lost during this period can often be difficult to regain. Deployment timelines should thus be tailored accordingly." (No. 87).

[25] World Bank Group, "Afghanistan Transitional Support Strategy," March 12 2002. Report No. 23822. www-wds.worldbank.org/servlet/WDSContentServer/WDSP/IB/2002/03/29/000094946_02032004020914/Rendered/PDF/multi0page.pdf.

PART TWO

ENHANCING U.S. RESPONSE CAPABILITIES
IN CORE AREAS

CHAPTER THREE

LAYING THE FOUNDATION

ENHANCING SECURITY CAPABILITIES

Scott Feil

During the 1990s, peace operations became a growth industry. The absence of human security in certain countries and parts of the world emerging from conflict has become a significant issue confronting the United States and the international community. The trend observed during the last decade of the twentieth century has, if anything, become an even more salient issue pervading international relations in the twenty-first.

As of this writing, and for the foreseeable future, tens of thousands of U.S. and international military personnel are engaged in operations that mean the difference between life and death for hundreds of thousands of people. Where U.S. military personnel have been involved in these operations, significant initial progress has almost always been made. People stop killing, and many more stop dying. And although the U.S. military's history is mixed, the record shows that successes outweigh failures, from the significant successes at the end of World War II and the Korean conflict in the 1950s to more modest gains made in Latin America, the Balkans, Haiti, and East Timor.[1]

Clearly, the ongoing situations in Afghanistan and Iraq illustrate the pressing need to establish the security component of the post-conflict equation quickly and permanently. The inability of the international community to create a capable Afghanistan in the aftermath of the Soviet withdrawal has had direct and tragic consequences for international and U.S. security. The security and political vacuum left in Afghanistan after Soviet withdrawal in 1989 allowed the penetration of the ruling Taliban by the Al Qaeda network and indeed was characterized not as a case of state-supported terrorism but as a terrorist-supported state. In

Iraq, the inability to maintain momentum in building a secure environment for post-conflict reconstruction in the wake of a brilliant military campaign in the spring of 2003 has threatened to unravel the results of that campaign. At a minimum, it set less than optimal conditions for the emergence of a responsible representative government and liberal market democracy.

WHAT IS "SECURITY"?

Post-conflict situations, by definition, have at their core a significant security vacuum that is often the proximate cause for external intervention. Indigenous security institutions are either unable to provide security or are operating outside generally accepted norms (e.g., corruption, as in the case of Panama; abuse of power, as in the Balkans; or threats to regional security based on internal instability, as in Africa's Great Lakes region, Afghanistan, and Iraq). This absence of physical human security differentiates post-conflict interventions from interventions conducted solely for humanitarian reasons (e.g., natural disasters), although post-conflict situations almost always have a large humanitarian component.

Undeniably, the four pillars of post-conflict reconstruction—security, governance and participation, social and economic well-being, and justice and reconciliation—are inextricably linked, and a positive outcome in each area depends on successful integration and interaction across them. Yet, security is the necessary foundation on which progress in the other issue areas rests. To be lasting, security must ultimately be provided by indigenous actors on behalf of the country itself, but in the interim it is often provided by outside agencies.

In the most pressing sense, security means protecting the lives of citizens from immediate and large-scale violence and restoring the state's ability to maintain territorial integrity.[2] Conceptually, security means a condition of acceptable public safety, particularly the establishment of an environment wherein citizens can conduct daily business relatively free from violence or coercion directed at them by the government, organized crime, political organizations, and ethnic groups. Schools operate, business is conducted free of corruption or protection rackets, markets provide goods and services without evading laws and regulations, and those laws and regulations are enforced objectively, with avenues of citizen recourse. The government can prevent undue influence by other state and nonstate actors. Reciprocally, the government collects revenue and delivers services through legitimate, transparent, and fair mechanisms. While providing this capacity in the interim, the assisting forces must lay the foundation and begin the process of developing legitimate and stable security institutions. Additionally, during the post-conflict reconstruction process, a secure environment must be provided in order to facilitate the operations of other assisting organizations from the international community.

The role of the external security provider depends on specific circumstances. Indigenous institutions may be able to execute selected groups of tasks, so that the international assisting agencies can focus on tasks that are beyond the ability of fledgling national and local administrations. In many cases, however, a country's domestic security apparatus may be completely unable to perform, forcing outside entities to assume more responsibilities. The goal of the assisting agencies—whether other nations, a coalition, or a mixed government/private partnership—is therefore to execute immediate security tasks that the host nation cannot, while reconstructing or strengthening the self-sufficiency of indigenous institutions.

ORDER VS. SECURITY

Just as the absence of conflict is not peace, the imposition of order is not the provision of security. Research indicates that only half of the attempts to stabilize a post-conflict situation and prevent a return to large-scale violence have been successful.[3]

The potential for a return to violence is so strong that, once international military forces have intervened to improve or stabilize a security situation, they are extremely difficult to extract. Transition to conditions conducive to long-term developmental assistance conducted by government, international agencies, nongovernmental organizations, and private enterprise often stalls, leading to a two-dimensional problem from both a U.S. and an international standpoint. On one dimension, international military forces find themselves executing tasks for which their comparative advantage is eroding; yet they are unable to transfer responsibility to either more appropriate international agencies or local actors. Military resources are applied with less and less effect and increasing cost. On the second, related dimension, this continuing and less effective engagement is manifest in extended commitments, tying down military forces and making them less available for future contingencies. In a spiral of avoidance, these extended commitments with reduced return strengthen the political and military resistance to conduct these operations, thereby delaying intervention in many cases to the point where sustaining the operations becomes more onerous.

Although military forces are well suited to coercion, deterrence, and the imposition of order, building a stable security environment in post-conflict reconstruction situations has proved difficult, with a less than satisfactory return on investment when using the military to apply resources of people, organization, and money. Much of that difficulty can be traced to an inability to develop, access, organize, and focus U.S. and international capabilities that could contribute to security under the dynamic conditions that characterize these operations.

The basic security question is two-dimensional: who and what must be protected, and from whom?[4] Among the elements to be protected are the general populace (especially the most vulnerable groups, such as women and children); selected key individuals; infrastructure; institutions; humanitarian aid workers; and the intervening security force itself.

A defensive focus on protection must complement an equally persistent offensive effort to remove the capacity for groups and individuals to engage in illegitimate violence. To control belligerents, cease-fires must be enforced (either in the context of a larger political agreement or as a measure that leads to such an agreement). Comprehensive efforts must be made to disarm, demobilize, and reintegrate combatants either into their hometown communities or into reconstituted or rebuilt military and nonmilitary security forces and organizations. Territory must be secured through a combination of border/boundary, movement, and point-of-entry controls. Finally, this entire effort must be pursued in the context of regional security initiatives to gain cooperation and prevent unhelpful interference from regional actors.

Clearly, this universe of security tasks encompasses much more than just defeating an adaptive enemy organized in identifiable groupings and organizations. The post-conflict security situation requires personnel and organizations that can employ a seamless, agile blend of capabilities that provide the security as "public goods" (those benefits for which any individual is not suited by interest or capacity in providing, and therefore become the purview of a collective entity) in an ambiguous and dangerous environment.

   Provision of security is dependent on both military and policing forces. The interplay between these forces is important in any post-conflict operation. In most capable states, the military focus is on the external, extraordinary event or threat. In contrast, police focus on the internal, recurring, steady-state provision of public safety. History indicates that when police operate as part of a justice system that integrates policing with the judicial, legal counsel, and correctional components of the system, police are more responsive, restrained, and capable. In many post-conflict and developmental cases, however, police institutions that are closely associated with, or an outgrowth of, military security institutions are not integrated into a system of civil restraints and oversight. Therefore, if the goal is to provide a capable and integrated justice function, then policing ought to be addressed in concept, plan, and execution as part of that system. For this reason, policing issues will be addressed in a later chapter of this volume relating to justice and reconciliation.[5]

   A second reason why policing is handled in this volume principally as it relates to justice rather than to security is because research shows that the development of the rule of law often suffers because policing—the most visible aspect of the entire justice system—is addressed through military channels and capabilities. The reconstruction of a capable judiciary, legal profession, humane correctional institutions, regulatory and oversight framework, and civil and property codes often languishes while the police operate as an extension of a military security force. Considering the development of police capacity within the justice pillar can serve to highlight the need for integrated development of these other components of the justice pillar and can serve a forcing function to draw resources, planning and execution capacity to crucial justice issues.

ADDRESSING KEY U.S. GAPS AND SHORTFALLS

In any post-conflict environment, the populace must feel secure as a necessary precursor to "normal" activities. Refugees and internally displaced persons will wait until they feel safe before they go home; former combatants will wait until they feel safe before they lay down their arms and reintegrate into civilian life or a legitimate, restructured military organization; farmers and merchants will wait until they feel that fields, roads, and markets are safe before engaging in food production and business activity; and parents will wait until they feel safe to send their children to school, tend to their families, and seek economic opportunities.

How the intervening force provides this security is of secondary significance, if any, to the affected population.[6] It is essential that this force retains control of the security situation, however, and that it limits the influence of opponents of the peace process. Change will continue to happen in the post-conflict environment as the nation/society knits itself together. Security must be the single constant in an environment where other conditions of life are "to be determined." The question for U.S. policymakers should not be, "Do we need robust policemen or constrained military forces?" but rather, "How can security be best achieved?"

Two general analytical perspectives have characterized past post-conflict interventions. In situations perceived as only slightly more unstable than normal, operations emphasize efficiency. They strive to maximize benefits while minimizing risks and costs (including to the security forces themselves) and will consist of a small deployment of minimally armed and constrained forces—so as not to inflame the situation and to present as little affront as possible to the sovereignty of the host nation. In order to meet minimum expected requirements, the intervening forces will need only to "dial up," or add, capabilities to an observer/monitor force. Rwanda in the aftermath of the Arusha accords in 1993–1994,[7] the Balkans in 1994–1995, and Kosovo in 1998–1999 exemplify this approach.

In dynamic situations only slightly less violent than war, intervening forces use a different approach. In the Balkans in 1995 and 1996, in Sierra Leone in 1999, in the later stages of operations in Kosovo, and initially in Afghanistan and Iraq, ground forces were deployed with the clear capacity to make war and intimidate violent groups. These security forces had the ability both to respond and to preempt. Yet, even these extraordinary military efforts, largely successful at the outset, were oriented around belligerent forces and organizations, neglecting the potential for long-term security problems. In the Balkans, central actors in the conflict were not held immediately accountable, and members of belligerent organizations reverted to crime as well as corrupt economic and political activities to the detriment of final comprehensive settlements.

In Afghanistan, problems arose when the Integrated Security Assistance Force was not expanded to provide security to the entire nation. Relationships with regional power brokers (made for necessary and expedient reasons to pursue a successful military campaign), coupled with the inability of the central government to expand its writ to the countryside, led to a situation of limited central government in competition with regional warlords. In the conflict with Iraq, intense discussions about the nature and extent of U.S. and international involvement in the post-invasion security of the country began well prior to the campaign, continued through traditional military operations between March and May 2003, and colored the discussions between the United States and the Iraqi Governing Council and the international community.

To improve, develop, access, organize, and focus U.S. capability in providing post-conflict security, five key areas demand attention: unity of effort; integration of security forces; disarmament, demobilization, and reintegration (DDR); regional security and reconstruction of security institutions; and information and intelligence.

Unity of Security Effort

Dozens of U.S. agencies play a vital role in providing security in post-conflict situations. At the national level, the National Security Council (NSC), the Departments of State and Defense, and the Central Intelligence Agency are often the lead actors. The U.S. Agency for International Development, the Departments of Justice and the Treasury, and other government agencies are also involved. Although the U.S. ambassador, as a representative of the president, retains overall responsibility for U.S. activity within a given country, the Defense Department has the most robust structure for global planning and execution. Other agencies in the region may have quite specific responsibilities, rather than broad authorities.

These layers of hierarchy, "stovepipes," lack of infrastructure, and widely disparate capabilities to plan, communicate, and operate in austere environments are not conducive to clear direction and effective, efficient action. Reforms are needed to redress the fragmentation in guidance, planning, and execution of security efforts at the national and regional levels and to provide necessary staffing to the responsible leadership on the ground.

Beginning with small steps in response to demands of conflict in Afghanistan and Iraq, some improvements are being made in concept and on the ground. In 2002, staff members from nongovernmental organizations were stationed with the military Central Command to provide liaison between military and NGO efforts in Afghanistan. The U.S. Joint Forces Command is crafting operational concepts for new organizations—a Joint Interagency Coordinating Group (JIACG) located at the regional combatant command headquarters, improving on the model established in the domestic counterdrug Joint Interagency Task Force and implemented in the regional combatant commands with a narrow focus on counterterrorist operations. This coordinating group has the potential to significantly improve coordination between government agencies and should provide additional opportunities to engage and communicate clearly with staffs from international organizations (IOs), intergovernmental organizations (IGOs), and nongovernmental organizations (NGOs) that are operating within a region. There has been an ambitious program of outreach and inclusion of agencies and organizations with the recognition that integration of key capabilities not resident in the military is key to improving the security conditions in a country, releasing the military to focus on its core competencies.

In January 2003, President Bush directed that national planning efforts focus on post-conflict Iraq.[8] At the direction of the president, the secretary of defense established an Office of Reconstruction and Humanitarian Assistance with the express purpose of integrating U.S. government agency efforts in the field, as the campaign in Iraq was to transition from a military to a reconstruction focus. Organized along lines that substantially parallel the post-conflict issue areas, the office comprised an interagency staff of civilian and military experts, with substantive operational subunits headed by civilians with relevant experience and authority seconded from U.S. government agencies. Administration of the post-conflict effort was further focused through a system of regional administrators. The largest USAID Disaster Assistance Response Team (DART) ever assembled deployed to the Iraqi theater in March 2003.

Establishing an experienced, practiced, and integrated civil/military staff that conducts assessments, develops operational plans, and provides supervision and centralized guidance to on-the-ground operational organizations is a major step forward and must be institutionalized with the authority to anticipate and move resources as needed. Subsequent initiatives by the Coalition Provisional Authority (CPA) included co-location of the CPA civil headquarters with the military headquarters and continuing initiatives to provide staff analysis and communication tools to facilitate integrated decisionmaking and policy development.

However, even in the face of progress in the region, significant national organizational obstacles exist. Unity of effort suffers from a lack of consistency in regional responsibilities. For example, while the State and Defense Departments have regional deputy assistant secretaries responsible for African policy, the military commander responsible for all but the Horn of Africa (USEUCOM) is also responsible for Europe, parts of Central Asia, and Russia. The military commander (CENTCOM) for the Middle East is also responsible for the Horn of Africa. Agencies must therefore plan, operate, and coordinate not only among their own different levels of staff, but also with multiple leaders at each level of other agencies. In fact, none of the regional authorities set up by the Departments of State, Defense (in security cooperation or the Unified Command Plan), USAID, or other government agencies correspond to one another.[9]

To remedy key U.S. gaps and shortfalls in this area, the United States should provide each regional combatant command's new permanent JIACG with staff to integrate other government agencies, coalition partners, international organizations, and international governmental organizations into its planning and operational functions, and provide the opportunities for NGOs to harmonize operations. The Defense Department should accommodate expanded interagency and international staffing at the combatant commander level, and should continue to expand military unit training and mission rehearsals and offer participation opportunities to government agencies, international partners, and NGOs involved in post-conflict reconstruction.

In addition, USAID's humanitarian assessment teams and disaster-assistance response teams should be expanded to include the broader interagency and NGO communities. These assessment and assistance response teams should provide comprehensive assessments of the in-country situation to the NSC, combatant commanders, and the JIACG.

Finally, the government should align the areas of responsibility within the Defense and State Departments, USAID, the Central Intelligence Agency, the Joint Staff, and the regional combatant commands.

Integrated Security Forces

As conditions change, the overall security situation no longer warrants the large presence of military forces prepared to engage in high-intensity combat. This achievement, however, often occurs well before legitimate indigenous security institutions are organized, trained, and equipped to assume security responsibilities. The strains within the intervening military forces as they adapt their roles and force levels to the changing security situation, coupled with the inability of the indigenous security forces to assume increased responsibility, creates a security gap.[10]

To address this gap effectively, security organizations must conduct a combination of integrated defensive and offensive measures oriented at the local level, while retaining the appropriate interactions with international organizations and fledgling state entities. The security situation calls for diverse capabilities—including border patrol; customs support; weapons collection; large-scale (belligerent groups) and targeted (indicted persons) apprehension conducted in coordination with police; and DDR— that do not fall directly within the purview of a military force focused on high-intensity conventional combat.[11]

According to conventional wisdom, "Soldiers can make peace, but peacekeepers can't fight wars."[12] From this perspective, extended peace-support missions degrade a military's combat capability. With combat skills as the core competency of military forces, many have viewed peacekeeping and peace enforcement operations as "lesser-included cases." It is thought that the military can conduct these missions with limited pre-deployment training, and that dedicated units specifically equipped, organized, and trained for post-conflict security operations are unnecessary; one need only "dial down" the rules of employment and engagement for traditional military forces. However, the combination of unparalleled Western military power and the seemingly intractable current security challenges are forcing a reevaluation. Some have called for reestablishing not only medium-weight forces that can more rapidly respond while carrying significant combat capability, but also forces to bridge the capabilities gap between lightly armed forces that cannot achieve escalation dominance and modernized forces that are tailored for high-intensity combat.[13] They find tank patrols ill suited for post-conflict operations.

Two major Western traditions, based on national culture, have been used to produce forces for executing security tasks in post-conflict settings. One is an Anglo-American perspective that eschews national paramilitary police forces internally and is not comfortable generating such a force. For the Americans and the British, it has been more palatable to take traditional military forces organized, equipped, and trained for combat, and to give them specialized training prior to a post-conflict mission. The British, based on their experiences in Northern Ireland, have established a training center, doctrine, and a program for forces to receive specialized training and equipment exchange prior to deployment. For U.S. forces, the National Training Center in California, the Joint Readiness Training Center in Louisiana, and the Combat Maneuver Training Center in Germany have, for several years, included missions that exercise peacekeeping and peace-enforcement abilities, and forces bound for post-conflict missions conduct rigorous, specific scenario-driven rehearsals at these sites. Higher headquarters staffs have undergone mission rehearsals before deploying to lead operations in the Balkans and Kosovo.

The second major Western tradition may be called "continental" and is exemplified by countries with a tradition of national police organizations that possess paramilitary skills (notably Germany, France, Spain, and Italy). These forces offer capacity that spans the gap between normal policing and military forces. They are specially equipped and trained for either large-formation operations as an adjunct to the military or for more dispersed and localized police functions. They are employed within their own countries for law enforcement purposes, however, and may not be as available as military forces. A security force with the requisite staffing, organization, and equipment to execute the broad range of integrated security tasks necessary to fill the security gap described above could conduct preemptive measures; support DDR; conduct border surveillance and patrol; engage in crowd control; pursue and engage belligerent groups; and support police apprehensions.[14] Such a force could more effectively accomplish the transition tasks that so often plague post-conflict reconstruction efforts, while relieving international military units of many of the operational deployments that allegedly drain combat effectiveness.[15]

Some countries, instead of trying to advance combat capability, have sought to carve out niche functions with a comparative advantage in peacekeeping and peace-enforcement capabilities. Canada has moved most aggressively to shift the central rationale and training focus of their conventional ground forces to preparing for and executing peacekeeping and peace-support operations. Germany, France, Spain, and Italy offer manpower and training capacity. European countries have had some success organizing multinational forces under broad mission statements that encompass post-conflict peacekeeping and peace enforcement (the Baltic Battalion, the Nordic Brigade, and the Multinational Peace Force Southeastern Europe, or MPFSEE).

Despite the domestic challenges and potential friction within coalitions assembled to address post-conflict situations, without a real commitment of resources and organizational energy from the United States, other nations will not integrate their efforts prior to deployment. This

will lead to artificial and inhibiting divisions of labor and ineffective security efforts on the ground. To redress this critical security gap, the
United States should take the lead in creating and supporting a multinational Integrated Security Support Force, providing units specially
organized, equipped, trained, and manned to execute post-conflict security tasks, integrated in the revised NATO Rapid Reaction Corps.

Disarmament, Demobilization, and Reintegration (DDR)

Dealing with combatants, whether they are organized in formal national security forces, paramilitary units, or private militias, is the most
pressing and recurring challenge of any post-conflict situation. Failure
to respond to this problem adequately and to promote combatants' in-
corporation into a legitimate security organization, or more frequently
a return to civilian life, leads to long-term difficulties across all areas of
reconstruction. Where organized subgroups and individuals have access to funds and the means of violence, spoilers emerge.[16] The experience in the Balkans illustrates this principle, where factional organizations
transformed into political parties and factional leaders turned to criminal
enterprises. These criminal enterprises, including human and drug trafficking, extortion, and protection rackets, generated funds that were
used to further their organizations. Coupled with the easy availability of
weapons, these criminal enterprises have carved out significant niches
and emerged as alternative sources of power to fledgling governments.

Further, releasing demobilized combatants into a disrupted economy
both exacerbates the unemployment situation and denies the central
government access to an organized labor pool, that, properly paid,
trained, and employed, could significantly add to the indigenous capacity of the country to recover with public works projects.

Although DDR is not a clean three-step process, a viable and seamless strategy must dismantle command and control structures; relocate
soldiers to communities; limit the circulation and individual possession
of weapons and small arms; and provide employment, educational opportunities, and community reintegration programs. U.S. responsibility
and capacity for DDR currently stretches across various government
agencies.[17] To coordinate strategy and promote a more holistic response,
the United States should create an office to handle matters concerning
DDR. Located within USAID, this unit would possess lead responsibility
for developing a coherent strategy for DDR, coordinating it, and managing it financially. The office would include staff from relevant agencies in

the State and Defense Departments in order to strengthen planning capacity and the ability to respond to urgent DDR needs.

Regional Security and Reconstruction of Security Institutions

The regional context in which reconstruction efforts are undertaken offers both opportunities and obstacles. Interested regional parties often wield considerable local influence, possess substantial infrastructure, offer proximity, and can act as a source of intelligence, information, and access. However, they also may have an interest in promoting factionalism that could skew reconstruction efforts. Often in these regions, the mechanisms to channel interests into productive and supportive relationships are limited. The existence of regional security arrangements can help curtail the detrimental influence of those who wish to continue violence or to bend the reconstruction efforts to their own advantage, while providing a conduit for positive influence and "peer pressure" to conform to improving norms.

Two benefits accrue from enhancing regional security. First, this capacity will provide additional leadership potential as post-conflict situations arise. Put simply, more nations will have the ability to adopt the lead role and intervene to stop or alleviate the conflict at an early stage. Regional interaction gives the United States more confidence in and access to military and government leaders and national facilities. Finally, professional security forces that are inculcated with the rule of law and higher standards of conduct are less likely to contribute to continued or resurgent conflict.

Beyond bilateral programs, regional organizations can disseminate ethics and skills and build cross-national confidence in tense regions. Successful examples of bilateral and multilateral organizations and training for peacekeeping and peace enforcement include those conducted under NATO's Partnership for Peace initiative, the Multinational Peace Force Southeastern Europe, and the African Contingency Operations Training Assistance Program (ACOTA, formerly the African Crisis Response Initiative).

In a related area, established professional norms and related training institutions ensure that progress within countries and regions is sustainable, thereby reducing the need for continued extraordinary external assistance and oversight. Current programs and procedures for the reconstitution or reform of indigenous security forces are fragmented and unfocused, however. Education and training programs for indigenous military and security forces tend to be organizationally, rather than functionally, conceived, and lack integrated goals, instructional materials, and methodology. Training, education, and information exchange programs for indigenous security forces are spread between various departments and are separated by statutory and regulatory restrictions that inhibit comprehensive, integrated, and responsive engagement.[18]

Recent trends in using private military companies (PMCs) to provide training and expertise have further complicated the issue.[19] There are concerns about role modeling, cost, accountability, and transparency. In addition, there is some long-standing fear that training and advising will lead to operational employment of PMCs in combat roles. Countering the notably poor experiences in the 1960s and 1970s in Africa, recent operations in Sierra Leone have shown that under some conditions, PMCs are capable of providing security in a post-conflict situation.

Finally, formal education and reconstitution programs focus on the uniformed military rather than on conducting a comprehensive reconstitution and reform of all government agencies that possess coercive capability. The result is a patchwork effort on the ground and an ineffective method of transferring expertise and a system of professional ethics to the country's security institutions.

The United States can take a number of measures to encourage regional security and the reconstruction of indigenous security institutions. First, it should support and strengthen regional efforts to provide forces that can respond to post-conflict requirements, such as ACOTA and MPF-SEE, and seek other venues within established regional organizations to support the development of similar regional security capabilities.

Second, all aspects of training transfer should be revised and rationalized to improve the ability to provide progressive and sustainable institutional training to host-nation security forces, both military forces and police. The State, Defense, and Justice Departments should form an interagency task force to this end. International military exchanges must be focused, with individual training and assignments complementing unit training and combined exercises. Assessment methods should be devised to determine, in conjunction with the host country, the needs and the plans for institutionalizing the training of indigenous security forces.

Finally, the United States should review the use of PMCs to provide training and education where appropriate and successful, thus allowing government organizations to focus on the direct provision of security.

Information and Intelligence

A relative lack of information and intelligence has also hampered security forces engaged in post-conflict reconstruction, with considerable negative impact at both the strategic and operational levels. In the Great Lakes Region of Africa, for example, one U.S. defense attaché oversaw multiple countries in the 1990s. The situation was similar in the Balkans in the 1990s when the U.S. attaché in Austria was accredited to multiple countries in the region, several emerging from the Warsaw Pact and the splintered Yugoslavia. One staff member in one embassy clearly cannot respond to demands from six other embassies, nor can that staff member be expected to maintain currency and contacts within a region covering thousands of square miles and millions of people.

Fragmented information- and intelligence-sharing systems compound the problem. IGOs, IOs, and NGOs frequently possess valuable information but are reluctant to share intelligence with security forces for fear of reducing their rapport with the population they serve and increasing their own risk by appearing partial. For their part, security organizations loathe sharing information with NGOs because sharing information risks compromising operations and sources. The various proprietary interests and variations in mechanisms for information exchange reduce the ability to see and operate on a common operational understanding.

Additionally, the U.S. government specifically denies itself access to information sources that could be useful. Currently, returning Peace Corps volunteers are prohibited from work as linguists or analysts with any U.S. agency that gathers intelligence. The practice of separating Peace Corps members from intelligence gathering activities while they are on assignment in a country has an historic, legitimate rationale, but safeguards could be established to allow returning volunteers with knowledge of a country to impart their analytical and language skills to agencies here in the United States. Several other agencies also currently honor the Memorandum of Agreement between the CIA and the Peace Corps, which prohibits returning volunteers from working for the agency.

Current initiatives to remedy these information and intelligence gaps are promising, but they are not yet adequate to the task. Military commanders already form humanitarian-assistance survey teams, for example, that can provide initial, up-to-date information on military operations, threat assessments, mapping support, and contact lists, thus sharpening military support for humanitarian assistance. These teams, however, fall short of providing a comprehensive liaison with IOs, IGOs, and NGOs. Civil-Military Operations Centers (CMOCs) that bring civilian agencies and organizations into appropriate military planning, coordination, and execution activities have been successfully used at the operational and tactical level to exchange information. NGO participation is voluntary, however, and threats to cut military support have at times been used to coerce attendance.

To improve the development and distribution of information and intelligence, the United States should increase staffing for defense attaché positions and foreign-area officers. In addition, relevant agencies should review their prohibition on employing returned Peace Corps volunteers as analysts and linguists, and look for a way to simultaneously access the skills possessed by returning volunteers and protect the status of in-country volunteers and the impartiality and objective nature of the Peace Corps itself.

Finally, the director of Central Intelligence should be given the lead in creating a system for sharing information in post-conflict reconstruction operations at the national level and between government agencies and the NGO community.

CONCLUSION

Indigenous populations and agencies remain ultimately responsible for improving and sustaining their situation, and returning the execution of security tasks to the host country must be the paramount objective. But the international community, including the United States, possesses enormous capability to have a positive influence on the security situation in states and regions emerging from conflict.

Calls for U.S. leadership and international participation in post-conflict reconstruction will continue for the foreseeable future. If the United States is to continue to lead the international community and secure its global interests without scattering its military around the globe in long-term deployments in which it does not have comparative advantage, then it must develop and focus military and civilian talent and capabilities to accelerate the transition from external security assistance to sustainable indigenous capacity.

Notes

[1] See David Bentley and Robert Oakley, "Peace Operations: A Comparison of Somalia and Haiti," Strategic Forum, Institute for National Strategic Studies

(INSS), National Defense University, no. 30, May 1995; Steven Metz, "The American Army in the Balkans: Strategic Alternatives and Implications," Strategic Studies Institute, U.S. Army War College, January 2001; "Report of the Panel on United Nations Peace Operations," www.un.org/peace/reports/peace_operations/docs/part3.htm (hereinafter Brahimi Report).

[2] See appendix 1, Post-Conflict Reconstruction Task Framework.

[3] Jean-Paul Azam, Paul Collier, and Anke Hoeffler, "International Policies on Civil Conflict: An Economic Perspective," December 14, 2001, mimeo, p. 2, http://users.ox.ac.uk/ ~ball0144/research.htm.

[4] For a discussion of how security concepts have changed with the dynamics of state and nonstate actors, see James N. Rosenau, "Strategic Links in an Emergent Epoch: From People to Collectivities and Back Again" (paper presented at the Conference on the New Strategic Discourse, sponsored by the Jaffee Center for Strategic Studies and the Cummings Center for Russian and East European Studies, in collaboration with the Doctrine Division, Israel Defense Forces, Tel Aviv University, May 28–June 3, 2000); Lloyd Axworthy, "Human Security: Safety for People in a Changing World," Department of Foreign Affairs and International Trade, Canada, April 1999, www.summit-americas.org/Canada/HumanSecurity-english.htm.

[5] See chapter 6 in this volume, "Dealing with Demons: Enhancing Justice and Reconciliation," by Flournoy and Pan.

[6] World Bank, *Voices of the Poor* (Washington, D.C.: World Bank, 1999), p. 186.

[7] See Scott Feil, "Preventing Genocide: How the Early Use of Force Might Have Succeeded in Rwanda," Carnegie Commission on Preventing Deadly Conflict, Carnegie Endowment for International Peace, 1998.

[8] Testimony of Undersecretary of State Marc Grossman and Undersecretary of Defense Douglas Feith, U.S. Senate Foreign Relations Committee, 108th Congress, 1st Session, February 11, 2003. Interviews with the Office of Secretary of Defense, Office of Reconstruction and Humanitarian Assistance, February–March 2003.

[9] In response to the terrorist attacks of September 11, 2001, the Department of Defense Unified Command Plan (UCP) was recently revised to add the U.S. Northern Command, responsible for military organization, employment, and support to homeland security requirements. The UCP delineates Defense Department and Regional Combatant Commander geographic and policy planning responsibility for the global activities of the uniformed organizations of the department. The U.S. government still has not seized the opportunity for coherent foreign policy implementation through alignment of all structures within the Departments of State and Defense along the same geographic and functional lines.

[10] William Durch, *Security and Peace Support in Afghanistan: Analysis and Short- to Medium-Term Options* (Washington, D.C.: Henry L. Stimson Center, June 2002).

[11] Although the Brahimi Report (see note 1) did not recommend a UN force, it did make recommendations on staffing, integrated planning, and rapid deployment. See also Thomas Ricks, "The Price of Power—Ground Zero: Military Must Change for 21st Century," *Wall Street Journal*, November 12, 1999, p. A1; Elaine Sciolino, "Bush Aide Hints Police Are Better Peacekeepers than Military," *New York Times*, November 17, 2000; U.S. General Accounting Office, *European Security: U.S. and European Contributions to Foster Stability and Security in Europe*, GAO-02-174 (Washington, D.C.: U.S. Government Printing Office, November 2001); Ann Scott Tyson, "Wider Mission Stretches Military," *Christian Science Monitor*, May 2, 2002, p. 1.

[12] T. R. Fehrenbach, *This Kind of War* (New York: Bantam, 1991). See also Charles E. Heller and William A. Stofft, eds., *America's First Battles: 1776–1965* (Lawrence, Kans.: University of Kansas, 1986).

[13] See about Army Transformation at www.army.mil/vision/transformationinfo .htm. See also Douglas MacGregor, *Breaking the Phalanx: A New Design for Landpower in the 21st Century* (Westport, Conn.: Praeger, 1997); Carl Conetta and Charles Knight, *The Logic of Peace Operations: Implications for Force Design*, Project on Defense Alternatives, Commonwealth Institute, Cambridge, Mass., September 1997, www.comw.org/pda/webun.htm.

[14] Based on interviews and working groups of NATO and other defense attachés and Department of Justice personnel at the Association of the United States Army (AUSA), August 2002.

[15] For a discussion on whether PCR security duties degrade combat capability, see Charles Moskos, "Peacekeeping Improves Combat Readiness," *Wall Street Journal*, April 26, 2001, p. A20. This piece is based on a larger study conducted for the Supreme Allied Commander, Europe. Dr. Moskos, a respected military sociologist, has argued that there may be a "market" for volunteers who would not ordinarily consider a military career, but who would be interested in a shorter term of service (18 months vice two or three years) for the opportunity to serve in peace-support units.

[16] David Jablonsky and James S. McCallum, "Peace Implementation and the Concept of Induced Consent in Peace Operations," *Parameters* (Spring 1999): 54–70.

[17] See Office of African Affairs, International Security Affairs, Office of the Secretary of Defense, "Policy Options Paper: Improving United States Support to Demobilization, Demilitarization, and Reintegration in Sub-Saharan Africa," May 2002.

[18] As an example, the International Military Education and Training Program, or IMET, which sends international military officers to yearlong service colleges at the mid- and senior-grade level, is managed by the Department of State. Additionally, a senior government official stated that about 700,000 foreign military and civilians have been educated and trained under the auspices of the U.S. government here in the United States over the last decade, but the government has no comprehensive capability to keep track of its "alumni." The potential to monitor and influence the impact of training efforts is clearly underused. U.S. Army Peacekeeping Institute, Conference on "The Power of Information in Peace Operations," U.S. Army War College, June 12, 2002.

[19] See Tony Vaux et al., "Humanitarian Action and Private Security Companies: Opening the Debate," International Alert, undated report, www.international -alert.org/pdf/ pubsec/humanitarianaction.PDF.

CHAPTER FOUR

GOVERNING WHEN CHAOS RULES
ENHANCING GOVERNANCE AND PARTICIPATION

Robert C. Orr

The extent to which a coherent, legitimate government exists or can be created is arguably the most important factor in determining the success or failure of a post-conflict reconstruction effort. Having such a government is key to providing essential security, justice, economic, and social functions and to channeling the will, energies, and resources of both the indigenous population and the international community.

Yet, as we have seen from places as diverse as Iraq and Afghanistan to Bosnia and Sierra Leone, countries emerging from conflict often have neither a legitimate government in place nor agreement on a process to determine what would constitute a legitimate government. Even if a government is in place and deemed legitimate by many citizens, war and the attendant chaos often incapacitate the government's ability to deliver services to the population. At the same time, many citizens are hesitant to become overly involved in the political rebuilding process, having been conditioned by wartime realities to defer to individuals who exercised authority through the barrel of a gun. In addition, potential spoilers— those with an interest in undermining both a peace accord and the development of a new order—abound.

Given these realities, the international community must find ways to support an indigenous self-governing capability. The effort involves at least three sets of activities:

- helping to support a process for constituting a legitimate government;
- enhancing the government's capacities; and
- helping to ensure broad participation in the government and the reconstruction process.

All these steps help identify and progressively isolate potential spoilers and their independent bases of power.

While seeking to build up local governance and participation capacity, the international community must observe the cardinal rule of governance: ensuring indigenous ownership of the process. Even when local actors are disorganized and disempowered in the wake of conflict, they must be given a leadership role in the rebuilding process. Likewise, even when international actors must assume certain functions temporarily, they must always train and empower indigenous counterparts if they hope to succeed.

Unfortunately, the international community's existing instruments for undertaking activities to enhance governance and citizens' participation are poorly adapted to the special requirements of post-conflict environments.

GOVERNANCE AND PARTICIPATION

Good government requires an interactive two-way process between the government and the governed. The first challenge is to ensure that the government has the ability to deliver the security, economic, social, political, and justice goods that the population demands—the top-down process of "governance."

The definition of governance, as the term is used here, is consistent with definitions used by the U.S. Agency for International Development (USAID) and the United Nations Development Program (UNDP). According to USAID, "Governance issues pertain to the ability of government to develop an efficient and effective public management process ... [that is able] to deliver basic services."[1] According to the UNDP, "Governance is the exercise of economic, political, and administrative authority to manage a country's affairs at all levels and the means by which states promote social cohesion, integration, and ensure the well-being of their populations. It embraces all methods used to distribute power and manage public resources, and the organizations that shape government and the execution of policy."[2]

The UNDP definition contains an additional quality that can be considered the essence of participation: "[Governance] encompasses the mechanisms, processes, and institutions through which citizens and groups articulate their interests, exercise their legal rights, meet their obligations, and resolve their differences."[3] The World Bank's definition of governance—"the manner in which power is exercised in the management of a country's economic and social resources"—is significantly narrower.[4]

In post-conflict situations, building the capacity for governance involves a broad range of tasks.[5] "National constituting processes"—such as a national dialogue, a constitutional convention, or a *loya jirga* as in the case of Afghanistan — can help forge agreement on how the political system should be structured, or even who should have a say in helping to design it. In some cases, a transitional administration will be needed to exercise power before a new legitimate regime can take office. Another set of governance tasks consists of strengthening institutions, either in the executive branch or the legislative branch, that deliver goods to the population at the national or local level. A final major challenge involves ensuring transparency in the delivery of goods and services, as corruption can severely undermine all other efforts.

The second essential component of good government is the ability to enable citizens to make their views heard and to act on those views—the bottom-up process of "participation." Participation encompasses the processes that give the population a voice through formal governmental mechanisms such as elections and political parties and through the development of a vibrant civil society, including the generation and exchange of ideas through advocacy groups, civic associations, and the media.

Even though the top-down process of governance and the bottom-up process of participation can be separated analytically, in practice they are intimately related. Transparent, effective governance is difficult to achieve if participation is insufficient to ensure that government programs respond to the will and needs of the people and remain channeled toward public ends, not private. Likewise, participation produces little if a government is incapable of delivering basic security, economic, social, justice, and political goods to the population. Only through encouraging sufficient participation and ensuring effective governance can a government establish a degree of legitimacy and stability over time.

CURRENT U.S. APPROACH AND CAPABILITIES

During the last decade, attention to governance and participation has expanded dramatically. Bipartisan recognition that democracy promotion is consistent with U.S. values and interests has led Democratic and Republican administrations alike to expand democracy promotion programs, with a budget now approaching $1 billion annually.[6] Even though the United States has led the charge, programs to promote governance and democracy have also emerged among a number of European donors, at the UN, and at some regional organizations such as the Organization of American States. Similarly, the World Bank and other multilateral development banks are increasingly integrating governance concerns into their development programming.

While this activity has vastly improved the capacities of the United States and the international community to engage in governance and participation issues, the international community, including the United States, remains poorly prepared to address them in post-conflict settings. As the targets of U.S. "democracy" money reflect, the democracy promotion paradigm was developed over the years principally in Eastern Europe and Latin America. Not only are the environments in which most of today's post-conflict challenges take place quite different from those formerly communist and authoritarian regimes, but they also lack the institutional capacity and resources upon which those regimes could draw. In addition, current challenges inhibit resolution of a whole range of additional problems arising from the legacy of protracted armed conflict.

All too often, governance efforts in post-conflict settings have boiled down to supporting formal election processes (allowing the international community to leave after a legitimate government has been elected), and funding a wide range of nongovernmental organizations (NGOs) in an inchoate attempt to "build civil society." From Cambodia to Angola to Haiti, this minimalist approach to governance as an exit strategy has led to crucial reversals of peace processes, costing thousands of additional lives and wasting millions of international dollars, major effort, and credibility. Establishing a comprehensive approach to governance and participation, one that addresses the full range of institutions and tasks and that presupposes support lasting well beyond the first election, is necessary.

ADDRESSING KEY CAPABILITY GAPS AND SHORTFALLS

If peace is to be sustainable in more cases, outside assistance for governance and participation activities must be improved in five areas: supporting national "constituting processes"; mobilizing broad peace constituencies and civil society actors to progressively marginalize spoilers; building state capacity, particularly civil administration; addressing corruption; and, crafting a coherent system of conditionalities to support good governance and peace.

Supporting "Constituting Processes"

As violent conflict comes to a close, the establishment of a new order usually requires resolution of a number of fundamental questions: What should the new political structure be? How is power to be shared or administered during the transitional period? Who are the citizens of the country? What are the rights and responsibilities of citizens and of former combatants?

Sometimes, a peace accord at least partially answers these questions; in other cases, peace accords create or call for processes to answer these questions; in still others, existing political structures are expected to work out the uncertainties. Regardless of the form of the peace process in question, some sort of "constituting process" is always needed.

The role of outside actors can be decisive. Choosing which actors to recognize, which ones to work with, and what processes and projects to support can tilt the balance of power either toward or away from a stable peace. Although choosing sides in internal power struggles does not generally produce the desired consequences, establishing clear ground rules and acting accordingly can often have a strong positive effect. Ultimately, for a new government to survive and thrive, its own citizenry and the international community will need to perceive it as legitimate. This outcome involves a careful balancing act, attempting to conform to two different sets of standards—on the one hand, international standards of respect for the peace agreements, the rule of law, and a range of other international norms and practices; and, on the other, local standards based on recent history, traditional political practices, the local balance of power, and acceptability of working with outside players. In essence, any national constituting process must first and foremost achieve internal legitimacy, even as it conforms to standards that provide external legitimacy and maintain corresponding international support—a political tightrope exercise in which everything is in play and everything is at stake.

Despite the fundamental importance of outside actors in many constituting processes, external assistance for these types of activities is paltry, and what exists is currently handled in an uncoordinated, ad hoc manner. Special envoys are often dispatched without clearly articulated mandates, training, or any significant means of supporting the political processes. Coordination among envoys is left to happenstance. Little direct linkage exists between the individuals who negotiate the hard political questions and those who support the long-term political and economic developmental process that will implement the solutions. Expertise in this highly specialized area of nation design is widely dispersed, with few mechanisms for retaining it on call. Additionally, while negotiations to end a conflict tend to be highly centralized, it is rare to find the same level of international coherence to implement agreements among the parties or between the parties and the donors.

The United States should take a number of steps to deal with these realities. First, the U.S. government should create new "director of reconstruction" (DR) posts responsible for directing U.S. efforts in specific countries in which the United States has intervened (e.g., a "U.S. director of reconstruction for Afghanistan"). Unlike traditional special envoys who negotiate or shepherd political agreements, these DRs would be responsible for implementing large, multidisciplinary U.S. government programs after an agreement has been reached and, as such, should be civilians with significant operational experience. Their posts would be lodged in the U.S. Department of State but supported by the logistical and operational authorities and capabilities of USAID and the Department of Defense. Interdepartmental memorandums of understanding and standard operating procedures should be drafted, approved, and in place prior to the appointment of a specific DR.

To support directors of reconstruction and special envoys, the U.S. government should create an integrated mechanism within the State Department and USAID. This action would require a line item in the State Department budget (initially set at approximately $5 million) to fund the operations of various special envoys and DRs and the establishment of a small support unit under the secretary of state's auspices. The support unit would provide functional expertise to these posts and serve as a repository of lessons learned and a link to standing capacity within the system (i.e., the State Department's regional bureaus and Legal Affairs Office; USAID's regional bureaus and Bureau of Democracy, Conflict, and Humanitarian Assistance; and the Defense Department's logistical operations).

To be able to spring into action quickly when needed, the support unit should develop and maintain on-call lists of people with experience in negotiating settlements, designing new political orders, and writing new constitutions. The State Department and USAID also should streamline the disbursement processes for monies required to support the initial establishment of governments constituted by legitimate processes.

A second major way to support constituting processes would be to further strengthen the roles and capabilities of the UN Special Representatives of the Secretary General (SRSGs) and build broad support for them among UN member states. This would involve authorizing a more direct, more central, and better-funded role for SRSGs in post-conflict countries, rather than expecting them simply to pick up UN agency scraps as they try to establish a coordinated international position on sensitive political questions. Such an initiative would give the United States real options when it chooses not to take a lead or when the circumstances require a non-American at the helm.

Mobilizing Disenfranchised Sectors of the Population

Peace and democratic development depend on incorporating marginalized constituencies into a new political order. Armed conflict tends to heighten political exclusion of all but certain political elites and armed combatants. Enabling disenfranchised groups to play a role in determining their country's direction and mobilizing them to defend a new peaceful order facilitates democratic development and helps to progressively squeeze armed combatants, warlords, and other spoilers out of the picture.

Previously marginalized noncombatants stand to gain the most from peace. Mobilizing "peace constituencies" (often including women and politically disenfranchised groups) is difficult, however. Armed combatants, warlords, and political elites frequently strive to protect their privileged positions by keeping political decisionmaking processes highly circumscribed. The disenfranchised groups often hang precariously on the edge of survival; they therefore focus on immediate needs rather than on political participation. In addition, wartime conditions have often so beaten down these constituencies that they are bereft of hope.

Mobilizing the disenfranchised therefore requires providing them with a concrete basis for hope and incentives for participation. Their material needs far outstrip the available resources of the local government or international community; as a result, initial programs need to target top priorities for these constituencies and provide for processes whereby they themselves determine how international monies are spent in their communities.

In recent years, both USAID's Office of Transition Initiatives (OTI) and the World Bank have developed programs and methodologies for getting small amounts of money to villages quickly. By making the money available for any type of development priorities, as long as the village pursues an inclusive participatory process in determining those priorities, OTI and the World Bank (at least in some cases) have been able to show results quickly, broaden participation, and build support for peace. The challenges now are to extend these programs to reach more local communities, to find ways to translate participation at the local level into comparable participation at the national level, and to meld them more effectively with long-term development programs.

To mobilize the disenfranchised sector of the population, the United States should take a number of steps. First, it should enhance support dramatically for quick-disbursing community-based approaches that can immediately reach grassroots constituencies and provide them the means to enhance participation at the local level. The easiest way to accomplish this goal is to increase OTI's budget for this purpose. Simultaneously, OTI should be charged with ensuring linkage of these local processes to a national peace implementation strategy (created by the government, in conjunction with donors). This could be done through funding the participation of local actors in national constituting and peace implementation processes, including paying for their transportation, lodging, and other types of logistical and administrative support.

Second, the United States should request a study of community-based approaches used by the World Bank. Based on the study's conclusions, the U.S. government should be prepared to increase support for participatory models for World Bank and other multilateral development bank programs by working out cooperative agreements at the country level. Given the lack of field presence by the World Bank and multilateral development banks, these programs should be implemented through NGOs. Doing so is not only likely to improve immediate success rates and free the World Bank to focus on its comparative advantages; it would also help to build crucial institutional links between these programs and long-term development programming.

Third, the United States should develop a strategy and capacity within USAID civil-society promotion programs for designing and funding projects that enhance the standing of marginalized groups at the earliest possible stage of the reconstruction process. This effort should involve, but not be limited to, bolstering political parties through NGOs such as the National Endowment for Democracy, the International Republican Institute, and the National Democratic Institute; ensuring free information flow; and targeting the marketing of at least some programs and opportunities to these groups.

Building Sustainable Civil Administration Capacity

Any new government must earn the support of its people by building sufficient state capacity to begin delivering basic security, justice, economic, social, and political goods to the population. The state's legitimacy and effectiveness also depend on its ability to provide a simple set of rules and structures that help to organize basic political, economic, and social life. No institution is more central to providing this structure than civil administration at the district, provincial, and national levels.

U.S. democracy and governance programs have four principal objectives: to strengthen the rule of law and respect for human rights; to develop more genuine and competitive political processes; to foster the development of a politically active civil society; and to promote more transparent and accountable government institutions.[7] Even though these goals are laudable, consideration of the more fundamental question facing post-conflict societies—building basic state capacity to deliver essential public goods—is largely absent. Limited programs intended to strengthen local government exist, but they are not complemented by any similar focus on enhancing the capabilities of the executive branch of central government.

The other major players in this arena—the multilateral development banks—do have programs dealing with civil administration, but these tend to concentrate on reforming public administration, with a focus on cutting bloated bureaucracies to save on government costs. For example, the focus of the World Bank's 169 operations to reform civil service in 80 countries between 1987 and 1998 "has been and remains on addressing fiscal concerns ... [by] reducing wage bills, compressing salaries [and] reducing employment."[8] In post-conflict settings, however, the primary concern is too little government, not too much.

One critical area where the World Bank has made a significant contribution is that of reforming tax systems—one of the key elements of revenue-generating capacity necessary to sustain the ability of a state's public administration to function effectively. In fact, during the 1990s approximately 120 of the World Bank's loan operations in 67 countries had components involving the reform of some aspect of the tax system, at an outlay of about U.S.$13.9 billion.[9] Despite extensive experience, however, a comprehensive study of these programs concluded, "Background work is essential to improve Bank assistance for revenue administration [and] a strategy needs to be articulated for the Bank."[10]

To help build a sustainable civil administration capacity in post-conflict states, the United States should first create a mechanism for fielding

U.S. civil administration experts, including seconding federal government employees, and recruiting and paying state and local officials. The United States should also build a mechanism for assembling interagency, interdisciplinary teams that specialize in building civil administration capacity. Because this activity is primarily developmental with a focus on building indigenous capacity, USAID should establish and the Congress should support a line item for these activities, and USAID should develop a core of specialists to lead the U.S. government's civil administration efforts. The USAID civil administration unit should also work with other donor governments whose civil administration systems and capacities may be different than those of the United States. In some cases, working with another government whose system is more like the one of the country in question may be more productive.

To complement and augment U.S. bilateral capabilities, the United States should urge the Bank to enhance the capacity-building elements of its civil service reform programs and to develop a strategy for reforming tax systems and building them from scratch in post-conflict countries.

Addressing Corruption

Weak institutional structures, patterns of behavior exacerbated by war, a semi-lawless environment, and a shortage of well-paying jobs combine to create a hothouse environment ripe for corruption in virtually all post-conflict societies. The prospect of infusions of new money from the outside world during peacetime only heightens the challenge and the stakes. In addition to threatening economic reconstruction, corruption jeopardizes the country's political stability and its prospects for peace. Corruption siphons money from needed government services, scares off investment, inhibits economic development, empowers spoilers, and leads to a dangerous lack of confidence in the new order.

Since 1994, the international community has begun to talk about corruption much more openly. The UN, the World Bank, the U.S. government, and many other donors have developed programs to combat corruption. New international NGOs aimed at eliminating corruption—Transparency International, for example, with local chapters in more than 90 countries—have come into their own.

No single solution exists to combat corruption. Different institutions have approached this dilemma in various ways, but at a minimum, an anticorruption package should include serious self-policing among donors; building anticorruption institutions (inspector generals, ombudspersons, civil service training); passing legislation; developing rule-of-law programs; establishing strong enforcement mechanisms; monitoring; developing free media and civil-society mobilization; and improving the transparency of the government budgeting processes.

To address the problem of corruption in post-conflict states, the United States should take three steps. First, the United States should develop a set of procedures with international financial institutions and the UN to share information and collectively sanction entities found guilty of corruption. This effort would involve everything from terminating contracts and sources of financial support to freezing assets and enforcing targeted smart sanctions, as well as pursuing legal cases against individuals and entities guilty of corrupt practices.

Second, USAID should be charged with developing a comprehensive set of resources within its anticorruption programming specifically designed for post-conflict countries that have little or no infrastructure. This step will require a significant institution-building component (i.e., establishing ombudspersons and inspector general offices as well as strong civil service programs). Through USAID, the U.S. government should also provide more support for a range of local and international watchdog NGOs that keep an eye on corruption by local and international actors, and should sponsor information-sharing networks that build the anticorruption movement into a permanent fixture of international society.

Third, the United States should support the free flow of quality information by building institutional centers like the Center for Public Integrity, which sponsors the work of investigative journalists; by providing technical assistance for designing and implementing information programs via all means of communication; by ensuring a capacity to tap into U.S. agency expertise on such important decisions as allocating radio spectrum and television licenses; and, in extreme cases, by blocking "hate" media that helped to drive places as dissimilar as Rwanda and the Balkans into conflict.

Crafting an Appropriate System of Conditionalities

The international community has long used conditionality on developmental assistance to promote macroeconomic goals and transparent economic-related governance. Conditionality related to politics or democracy has been much more controversial. Some analysts have pointed out that good political governance is a worthy objective and is also essential to ensuring the effective use of foreign assistance monies; they have therefore argued that political governance is a legitimate target for conditionality. Others have argued that politics is the sole province of the citizens of the country in question and thus should not be subject to conditionalities of any sort.

As debate in the United States intensifies about targeting foreign assistance to "deserving countries" that meet performance indicators—particularly those related to the substantial new funds that the Millennium Challenge Account will make available—bipartisan concurrence by the executive and legislative branches on the role for governance conditionality is important. Even though conditionality is an important tool both to ensure U.S. taxpayers that their money is well spent and to leverage difficult policy decisions, direct "democracy conditionality" is likely to backfire. If the United States and other outside parties demand a particular political process in exchange for U.S. funding, accusations of imperialism and U.S. meddling in internal affairs are likely to undermine the basic goals of the United States.

"Peace conditionality," a mechanism designed to ensure compliance with agreements made by the parties to the conflict themselves, is a viable alternative, however. Another area where conditionality is likely to be useful relates to the issue of corruption. Tailoring "microconditionality" to individuals and organizations to ensure transparency and to punish those who violate anticorruption norms not only improves the odds of getting an honest government but also enhances locals' views of the international community. Where conditionality is less effective is on the priorities of specific donors. Even on such high priorities as ensuring full participation of women and other marginalized groups in the political process, conditionality can be counterproductive. In these areas, carrots are more likely to produce results than sticks: forcing groups into the process against the will of the dominant interests almost guarantees their isolation over the long run.

Finally, to be effective, conditionalities must be tightly coordinated by donors. If donors fail to agree on conditionalities, and if more than a single entity (an SRSG-type figure or a country team) metes them out, leverage is dispersed and donors run the risk of destroying government coherence by pulling in different directions.

To achieve U.S. objectives in post-conflict situations, the United States should propose a clear set of distinct guidelines on the use of conditionality for post-conflict and institutionally weak countries. The

White House, in conjunction with the Treasury Department, USAID, and the State Department, should carefully coordinate this undertaking with the relevant actors on Capitol Hill, such that any enabling legislation for the Millennium Challenge Account (or a new parallel account designed for post-conflict countries) includes an agreement on how the government should use conditionalities in post-conflict situations (acknowledging that performance indicators in these situations will almost always be very different from those used for top economic performers that are not burdened by conflicts).

Finally, U.S. foreign assistance administrators and U.S. representatives to the multilateral development banks and the UN should be instructed to coordinate conditionality tightly through country teams composed of major donors, multilateral development banks, and UN representatives. Leverage is best exercised when those closest to the peace process coordinate their efforts.

THE EARLIER, THE BETTER

Patterns for governance and participation are not open for discussion during a conflict and are most malleable in the period soon after the conflict ends. For the United States and other international actors to have any hope of affecting these fundamental issues, they must be ready to engage before lines harden. This serious undertaking will require adapting existing democracy and governance mechanisms to post-conflict environments and enhancing those mechanisms' flexibility and ability to deploy quickly. While the role for outside actors in governance and participation will always be limited, it is nonetheless crucial. Both the hearts and minds of the local population will determine the ultimate success or failure of any reconstruction effort. With this knowledge, and with keen attention to local sensibilities, the international community must be more bold in this area. Pulling back from governance issues and hoping that locals will naturally fill the vacuum is a recipe for failure. Locals will fill the vacuum, but not those that can deliver a long-term peace. These hard lessons need to be learned from difficult experiences from Bosnia to Afghanistan. Investing early, helping shape the field of play, and being willing to remain involved long enough to see positive governance and participation structures develop are keys to shorter, more successful interventions.

Notes

[1] U. S. Agency for International Development (USAID), "Democracy and Governance: A Conceptual Framework," PN-ACC-395, November 1998, www.undp.org.

[2] Ibid.

[3] Ibid.

[4] World Bank, *Governance and Development* (Washington, D.C.: World Bank, 1992).

[5] For a comprehensive, systematic listing of potential governance and participation tasks in a post-conflict environment, see the Post-Conflict Reconstruction Task Framework in appendix 1.

[6] The Bush administration has budgeted over $1 billion for democracy and governance activities in fiscal year 2004, including $193 million for general USAID democracy and governance programs (in the Development Assistance account); $325 million in Economic Support Funds used for similar activities; $250 million in democracy- and governance-oriented assistance for Eastern Europe and the Balkans; $167 million for similar assistance in the independent states of the former Soviet Union; $30 million for democracy promotion under the Andean Counterdrug Initiative; and $55 million in the Transition Initiatives account. See www.usaid.gov/policy/budget/cbj2004/summary_tables _table2.pdf.

[7] USAID, "Program, Performance and Prospects" (Democracy and Governance section), *Budget Justification FY 2002*, www.usaid.gov/pubs/cbj2002/prog_pref 2002.html.

[8] World Bank, *World Bank Poverty Reduction and Economic Management Notes*, no. 31 (Washington, D.C.: World Bank, October 1999).

[9] Luca Barbone et al., *Reforming Tax Systems: The World Bank Record in the 1990s* (Washington, D.C.: World Bank, 1999), p. 3.

[10] Ibid., p. 31.

CHAPTER FIVE

RESTORING HOPE

ENHANCING SOCIAL AND ECONOMIC WELL-BEING

Johanna Mendelson Forman

It is no coincidence that states emerging from conflict are also among the world's poorest. Fifteen of the world's 20 poorest countries have experienced internal conflicts in the last 15 years.[1] These wars have spilled refugees over borders, often destabilizing neighboring states. Any visitor to these war-torn states recognizes that without economic hope there can never be peace. But reconstruction creates the competing demands of peace-building and economic stabilization.[2] Although poverty is not a direct cause of violence or civil war, it is a symptom of the decline of a state's capacity to protect and provide for its citizens.[3]

For post-conflict reconstruction generally, success is clearly premised on three conditions: establishing security; restoring good governance, which includes the rule of law; and creating economic opportunity. Recent research on the political economy of developing nations suggests that a good policy environment is essential for economic performance.[4] Despite more than a decade of experience in post-conflict reconstruction, however, the U.S. government has yet to form a coherent vision of dealing with these tasks. It lacks a deliberate program for linking immediate post-conflict needs with medium- and long-term development. Even with the funding available through the U.S. Agency for International Development (USAID), the notion of a smooth transition from one phase of reconstruction to another is illusive.

Intractable conflict and its economic roots have yet to become a serious subject matter for congressional deliberation or legislative action. U.S. foreign assistance lacks a focus on conflict prevention.[5] It also has no tools to deal with conflicts driven by resources rather than ideologies. Two major deficiencies that further inhibit U.S. policy to address countries in conflict are (1) slow response times in delivering assistance in war-torn countries, and (2) lack of any form of flexible credit that would permit local actors to engage in any reconstruction effort, reflected by limitations imposed by statutes that govern foreign assistance. Until recently, socioeconomic tasks were considered part of long-term development assistance programs that could only begin once peace was at hand. We now know that development can and should take place even when parts of a nation are at war. Research also shows that at the end of conflict, a small window of opportunity exists to restore economic hope and social well-being. Without U.S. leadership it will be lost. This chapter addresses some of the gaps in U.S. policy and provides some recommendations to consider in dealing with them.

The events of September 11, 2001, were central to rethinking the U.S. government's development assistance in much the same way that security is currently being reassessed.[6] Where once it was not popular to advocate more foreign aid, it is now a central feature of President George W. Bush's response to preventing terrorism.[7] As the president noted in 2002 in his address to the International Conference on Financing for Development in Monterrey, Mexico, "We must accept a higher, more difficult, more promising call. Developed nations have a duty not only to share our wealth, but also to encourage sources that produce wealth: economic freedom, political liberty, the rule of law and human rights."[8] This articulation of U.S. development objectives is mirrored in the work on human security currently under way at the United Nations. It recognizes that poverty alleviation implies not only economic growth, but also personal security as a condition precedent to any other type of socioeconomic progress.[9]

Of the four pillars of post-conflict reconstruction, social and economic well-being is the most varied, and therefore the most comprehensive.[10] A basic assumption is that good governance goes hand in hand with economic growth. The challenge in post-conflict reconstruction is finding the balance between external demands for reform by the United States and the international donor community and capacity inside the affected country to step up to the types of political changes required to ensure progress. Economic performance in the post-conflict period is affected by two conditions: the commitment of the affected state's leadership to support specific types of reform, including respect for basic human rights and the rule of law, and open, transparent economic transactions. Aid conditionality without specific economic reconstruction objectives will not achieve the required reforms. Post-conflict settings are considered to be poor policy environments, and thus not likely to abide by the good governance conditions of donors.[11]

SOCIOECONOMIC NEEDS AND CURRENT U.S. GOVERNMENT CAPABILITIES AND GAPS

After conflict, certain minimum conditions are necessary to enable a country to progress from decay to development. Six priority areas continue to be insufficiently addressed:

- establishing a legal regulatory framework that supports basic macroeconomic needs;
- effectively managing the natural resource components of many conflicts;
- engaging the private sector;
- jumpstarting international trade;
- establishing basic education services; and
- combating HIV/AIDS in post-conflict settings.

Early assistance in each of these areas, by the United States government in coordination with the international community and the international financial institutions, can help lay a solid foundation for social and economic well-being.

Those in leadership positions in affected countries also need to play an important role in advancing local interests. Bringing stakeholders into the process of economic and social reconstruction will create ownership of both policies and processes. Believing that such a partnership between local and international actors will make the achievement of economic development fast or easy would be foolish, however. Fragile political environments, reluctance of the private sector to invest in unstable states, concentration of wealth and resources in the hands of a few powerful figures, thinness of the financial sector and markets, and weak governance capacity will challenge both external actors and stakeholders.

The U.S. government has the capacity to provide humanitarian assistance, recognized as the essential core for saving lives and laying the foundation for social and economic reconstruction. U.S. humanitarian assistance programs, implemented primarily by nonprofit U.S. private voluntary organizations (PVOs) and local nongovernmental organizations (NGOs) are effective for three main reasons. First, they are well organized and funded. Second, they have the skills needed both during crises and during the reconstruction process, including emergency management, vulnerability assessments, and development of early warning systems for disaster preparedness. Third, U.S. government agencies manage short- term relief projects simultaneously with efforts to create medium- and long-term economic growth in a rare example of interagency coordination (involving USAID's Office of Foreign Disaster Assistance (OFDA), the Department of State's Bureau for Population, Refugees and Migration, and the Department of Defense through the Office of the Secretary of Defense and the relevant theater commanders who may be engaged in humanitarian operations). If there is any issue about humanitarian assistance, it relates not to the quality or quantity of American generosity, but to its use as a substitute for diplomatic preventive action and its dissociation from the broader reconstruction needs that follow a humanitarian crisis.

A missing element of U.S. assistance in the humanitarian phase is deliberate planning or linkage of assistance to needs beyond the immediate emergency. This is evident in U.S. emergency agencies' inability to contract for so-called quick impact programs (QUIPS) for longer than nine months, lest they become full-blown development projects. Indeed, given the understanding of conflict and the immediate aftermath, planning on the war-to peace transition will require a longer time line for assistance to effectively transition from international activities to local ownership. Without a medium- to long-range view up front, the emergency assistance provided by the U.S. government to international NGOs in the field will fail to yield either hope or sustainability to those most vulnerable after war.

GETTING THE U.S. HOUSE IN ORDER

To address the six gaps noted above, the U.S. government must get its own house in order. This will require central, coordinated leadership at the highest levels of government. There is a *lack of a coherent, overarching strategy* among U.S. policymakers on how to promote economic and social well-being in post-conflict countries, let alone within a greater framework incorporating security, justice, and governance. Too often the overwhelming demands of rebuilding a war-torn country have far outpaced the capacity of the U.S. government to respond in a holistic manner. There has yet to be a deliberate program that links immediate

post-conflict needs, upon conclusion of emergency programs, with me-
dium-and long-term development. As an early responder to emergencies, the Department of Defense (DOD) has interests in the military's
need to exit and hand off activities not related to security. Many DOD
assets currently available are unknown to many officials in agencies
dealing with economic development and recovery.[12] Even with transition funding available through USAID, the lack of systematic procedures, inadequate information sharing, and resource gaps combine to
work against the notion of a smooth handoff to the private sector or to
U.S. government and other bilateral development programs. Without a
comprehensive, long-term approach to social and economic well-being,
it is doubtful that external assistance can prevent the recurrence of a future conflict.

Since September 11, the U.S. government has recognized the ease of
money transfers intended for nefarious purposes. Diaspora populations have frequently provided resources that have fueled conflict in
war-torn states. These resources have also, in some instances, supported
terrorism. Foreign remittances not only support families in need of assistance, but also provide money to purchase weapons and salaries to
sustain fighters. Recent evidence of this phenomenon was clear in the
case of funds for the Kosovo Liberation Army (KLA) in Kosovo, the
Irish Republican Army (IRA) in Northern Ireland, and the Palestine
Liberation Organization (PLO) in Palestine. In light of recent events in
Afghanistan, much remains to be done to limit diaspora money that
helps support and sustain fighting.

To improve coordination of efforts in the economic and social arena,
the president should create an Office for Economic International Security to help bring together all the relevant tools of the U.S. government
in a timely manner. This body would facilitate coordination—with international financial institutions; the State, Treasury, and Commerce
departments; the U.S. Agency for International Development; the Office of the U.S. Trade Representative (USTR); the Trade Development
Agency; the Export-Import Bank; and the Overseas Private Investment
Corporation (OPIC)—to provide centralized and coherent responses
to the immediate reconstruction needs, including maintaining a roster
of private-sector companies capable of rapid deployment for emergency reconstruction work.[13]

To deal with the threat and the opportunity posed by diaspora communities residing in the United States, the Department of the Treasury

should set up a regulatory mechanism to oversee the international distribution network for remittances. Such an office would provide citizens of foreign countries with a more reliable and secure means of receiving funds from accredited agencies while also preventing money from going into the hands of illegal organizations from the outset.

The Treasury Department, through a Memorandum of Understanding, should also work with the Department of Defense to create an ongoing information-sharing system on potential economic crises. Such a system would keep the U.S. military alert to places of emerging crises, thus giving DOD a more extended time line for planning emergency response initiatives. Where U.S. lives and property are at risk, the U.S. military is often tasked to support humanitarian and emergency extraction operations without warning, or comprehension of the policy issues.

ESTABLISHING A LEGAL REGULATORY FRAMEWORK

Creating governing systems that are predictable and impartial, along with establishing economic rules for development is crucial to any postconflict economic reconstruction. Real equity investments will follow the development process only after the groundwork of a rule of law system and microeconomic systems have been put in place.[14] This means that a judicial system must be able to uphold contracts, protect property rights, and ensure that commercial interests have a process that produces reliable and enforceable results. No country can be part of the international economic community without this. Often the economic aspects of legal reform are treated as secondary to the immediate need to provide justice to victims of war. The two areas, however, are equally important in creating the foundation for economic and social rebuilding.

Any legal system must reflect stakeholder laws and traditions, even if the international community plays an initial role in providing technical assistance and resources. Local approaches to justice should integrate existing practices that will provide immediate relief in commercial disputes rather than creating new systems of adjudication that may not be sustainable once assistance ends. USAID has some capacity to support this area, but in the last decade U.S. government assistance in legal regulatory law has declined and programming is done ad hoc. The U.S. government has delegated this type of assistance to the World Bank. The Department of Commerce supports some programs to help provide assistance on alternate dispute resolution and to provide assistance for export and trade. None of these programs in either agency are geared to dealing with the immediate post-conflict legal needs.

To address these needs, three steps need to be taken. First, as part of their emergency conflict management activities, USAID's democracy programs should establish a separate rule-of-law initiative for post-conflict countries to establish basic legal and regulatory regimes. Second, USAID and the Treasury, Justice, Commerce, and State departments all need to coordinate their various legal regulatory activities among themselves and with the World Bank and the International Monetary Fund (IMF). Third, congressional appropriations should be increased for the Department of the Treasury's Office of Technical Assistance in order to enhance U.S. government capacity to assist countries emerging from conflict to develop the important legal and regulatory architecture for entering the global economic market and for getting their own economies moving.[15]

EFFECTIVELY MANAGING RESOURCE-DRIVEN CONFLICTS

In the last decade research on civil wars has pointed to the central role that natural resources play in fueling violence. "War may be a continuation of economics by other means" is a play on Clausewitz' famous maxim.[16] Civil wars have created great opportunities for profits through underground economies that are often not available during peace. Weakened states, no longer able to manage economic policy and the institutions that govern them, are targets for rent-seeking groups. Criminals engaged in illicit economic transactions pay no taxes, and armed groups that can exact cash or resources through extralegal activities act as spoilers to any peaceful resolution of conflict. Contrary to popular wisdom, greed seems to be a key factor in perpetuating civil wars. This is particularly the case when personal security is transformed from a public to private good. Most citizens lose from war, but a few powerful figures can perpetuate fighting. In countries where a natural resource is a primary export commodity (where export income accounts for more than 25 percent of gross domestic product [GDP]), the chances of these resources becoming a means to fuel instability and conflict are greatly increased.[17]

In spite of this evidence that reducing the profits of war is one way to restore stability, the U.S. government has yet to develop a coherent strategy that addresses this issue. U.S.-based extractive industries (e.g., oil;

gas) must be engaged with the U.S. government to develop both short-term and long-term solutions to this difficult problem.[18] The situation in Angola is but one example of how the United States and the private sector are not working to address the way oil wealth can destabilize a fragile peace. Few if any tools exist that can address this issue except the good will and responsiveness of private corporations to act responsibly. In 2002 in Angola it was the private sector that put the Dos Santos government on the spot when an NGO, Global Witness, exposed the discrepancies between the tax revenue collected from oil and the revenue reported by the Ministry of Finance.[19] Transparency about corporate operations and earnings can be powerful in rallying citizens against corrupt, rent-seeking elites. On the public front, it is ultimately a diversified economy that will reduce dependence on single-commodity economies. Development policies that view economic diversity as a key component of reconstruction may in the long run be the best response to this difficult economic reconstruction hurdle. There are, however, immediate actions that, if taken, could curtail the impact of conflict entrepreneurs.

The U.S. private sector should develop specific industry-designed codes of conduct on war profits in conflict-ridden countries. As part of this self-regulation, U.S. corporations operating in post-conflict environments should promote transparent accountings of their revenues in country so citizens of war-torn states are aware of government revenues from extractive industries.

The U.S. government should work with the World Bank to create a public-private trust fund as part of a natural resources revenue strategy. This trust fund would capture income from international extractive industries operating in post-conflict states so that it could be used to meet recurrent costs for essential services and recurrent costs of the government.

ENGAGING THE PRIVATE SECTOR IN RECONSTRUCTION

In countries emerging from conflict, the role of local business and entrepreneurs in supporting immediate investment needs is essential for rebuilding human and social capital, promoting good economic governance, and building the foundations for international investors. Those who have survived the conflict or who have returned from neighboring states must be provided incentives by the international community to restore local markets and invest profits locally. Accordingly, support must first be given to local investment and indigenous business development as a first step toward economic well-being. During this time, the international community will be called on to support programs that provide microfinance and microcredit as part of a process of restoring long-term capacity to sustain economic development.

Private-sector strategies are not a magic bullet for international investors unless fortified with U.S. government support. Instability, coupled with inadequate security, is a major deterrent to international investment. This means support must be developed for local investment and indigenous business development, while ensuring that social spending needs and recurrent costs are met. The international community may have to support the salaries of the civil service, the armed forces, and the police, and support meeting pension and other obligations of the public sector. Not only will this demonstrate the tangible benefits of peace. It will ensure some stability to those who are essential to the restoration of any economic infrastructure in a post-conflict environment.

In spite of a certain reluctance by the international private sector to invest in high-risk environments, much could be done through U.S. corporate tax incentives to manage investment risks while also providing medium- to long-range incentives for fostering new markets and international partners. New partnerships between the U.S. government and the private sector must foster a better understanding of the needs of countries emerging from conflict, something that the U.S. government has ignored, in spite of the fact that developing countries represent 40 percent of global trade.

Wars also create waves of "brain drain." Often the most educated and capable citizens are forced to flee conflict zones, thus robbing states of important human capital and capacity. A return of talent is essential for a country to recover not only its social capital but also its economic growth. Those who leave a country often do not return because restrictive immigration policies of their new homes provide no incentives for them to help their countries after conflict. This is certainly the case under U.S. immigration law. Reversing this loss of talent would go a long way toward creating a capable, economically viable post-conflict state.

To help reverse brain drain, the immigration service within the Department of Homeland Security should review its immigration rules for U.S. permanent residents who would like to participate in "return of talent" programs to countries undergoing post-conflict reconstruction. A simple regulatory fix could provide incentive to many permanent residents to return home for extended stays by creating a release from their necessary time-in-class requirements for U.S. citizenship. Currently no such waivers exist, thus inhibiting U.S. permanent residents from participating in reconstruction and development.

A second way to get much-needed talent into post-conflict environments would be for USAID to support training for masters of business administration students seeking experience in managing post-conflict reconstruction. A fellowship program, similar to those already established with the American Association for the Advancement of Science, should include internships in key private-sector enterprises and promote an understanding about the demands and potential opportunities of high-risk investment environments.

To help facilitate private-sector investment, a number of actions should be taken. First, the administration and the Congress should agree to expand the mandate of the Trade Development Agency to include specific funding mechanisms to assess the private-sector investment climate in countries emerging from conflict. Second, the Overseas Private Investment Corporation should create a one-stop source of credit for U.S. businesses seeking guarantees to invest in post-conflict countries. A specific fund with less restrictive criteria should be created for emergency high-risk credits to support immediate investments. Third, U.S. embassies in post-conflict countries should be given additional economic officers whose responsibilities would include supporting local investment opportunities and providing intelligence on the potential risks and benefits for the private sector.

Finally, to get the indigenous private sector moving again after conflict, USAID should develop a long-term flexible funding mechanism to provide microcredit at the community level, with a focus on enhancing local capacity. Such a new fund would bridge the gap between the emergency grants of USAID's OFDA and regional bureau programs.

JUMPSTARTING TRADE

Opening domestic markets to foreign exporters should go hand in hand with U.S. efforts to engage foreign businesses in commercial trade ventures. Even though developing countries are the United States' fastest-growing export markets and will soon account for 40 percent of global trade, U.S. programs to support trade are geared only to normal conditions. Little or no capacity exists to support initiatives in the post-conflict rebuilding process.[20]

Breaking down trading barriers with certain regions such as parts of Africa and Asia could provide important incentives to American businesses. Trade initiatives could support significant investment opportunities in such places as the Balkans, East Timor, Angola, or Afghanistan.[21] Today the U.S. government has two ways to grant developing countries increased market access and beneficial trade preferences: the General System of Preferences (GSP) and Preferential Trade Waivers. The latter are more useful in post-conflict environments because they offer unilateral trade preferences on exports entering the United States. The 1983 Caribbean Basin Initiative (CBI), established under President Reagan, and the 2000 African Growth and Opportunity Act (AGOA), enacted under President Clinton, provide models for duty-free and reduced-duty treatment. The CBI and AGOA both seek to expand foreign and domestic investment in nontraditional sectors and to diversify beneficiary country economies and expand their export bases.

To jumpstart trade in these tough environments, the United States needs to take a number of concrete steps. First, Congress should authorize and fund a new version of trade benefits for qualifying post-conflict countries that could be modeled on the CBI and the AGOA. Using such a fund could require presidential authorization, and it could have a limited time frame (10 years). This would not only provide the incentive for importers to work with businesses in these states, but also help U.S. commercial interests to gain access to potential markets. Successful participation in such an initiative could lead to qualification for the GSP programs.

Second, under the auspices of the Office of the U.S. Trade Representative, the Trade Policy Review Group should establish a specific subcommittee on post-conflict states for addressing trade and investment-related issues. This subcommittee should be tasked with developing a policy framework for the U.S. government in states emerging from war.

Third, the Small Business Administration, which currently supports technical assistance to developing nations, should be granted authority to expand its work in post-conflict countries, to train local entrepreneurs in ways to reach U.S. import markets.

Fourth, the Foreign Commercial Service of the Department of Commerce should establish a post-conflict capacity to address investment opportunities for U.S. businesses.

ESTABLISHING BASIC EDUCATIONAL SERVICES

Wars disrupt education, with long-term impact on a state's capacity to grow economically. Even under normal development conditions, the U.S. government has devoted scant resources to improving the education of young men and women. In post-conflict environments, no consistent approach exists for this type of assistance. Some resources go to communities with returned refugees. Others go to on vocational programs for former combatants and demobilized soldiers.[22]

Over the last decade we have decreased our assistance in this area, relegating education to a minor component of our development assistance.[23] The results are evident from the net decline of literacy that accompanies economic downturns and wars. A state's inability to support basic education also leaves room for religious schools that exclude women or indoctrinate young men to elevate violence as a political means. The madrassa schools in Pakistan provided school and feeding to thousands of young men and served as a recruiting ground for the Taliban. Finally, unemployed youths ages 15–25, who are often part of the demobilized population, pose the greatest threat to peace in post-conflict countries.

Restoring education immediately after conflict sends a signal of hope to families whose lives have been turned upside down by conflict. In Haiti, for example, the restoration of schools in almost every district in 1994–1995 sent a powerful sign to Haitians that life had begun to return to normal. Returning children to school also has an important deterrent power. Removing young men from the streets limits opportunities for recruitment into militias. Schools also provide employment for many individuals in a community. Yet the government of Haiti was unable to sustain its support to its education system because international development money did not reach Haiti in the late 1990s.

Accordingly, a special post-conflict education fund, similar to the Wars Victims Fund, should be established inside USAID to address emergency education needs in post-conflict societies. It should be authorized with "not withstanding authority" to avoid any delays in disbursement. Community-based education funding should be the priority for using these resources. This fund could provide seed money for partnerships with NGOs and other international agencies to support the immediate restoration of educational services and the return of teachers from refugee camps, and to provide books and school supplies.

In addition, the Peace Corps should designate certain post-conflict countries to a special high-priority category for placement of volunteers with education backgrounds, to support the training of teachers as well as the management of education in countries moving out of conflict.

COMBATING HIV/AIDS IN POST-CONFLICT SETTINGS

Health care is a recurrent cost of any government, but in post-conflict societies health delivery systems are often inadequate or nonexistent. The most urgent priority in post-conflict environments is the prevention of HIV/AIDs. Not only does HIV/AIDS spread rapidly in post-conflict environments, but it also undermines future generations through the destruction of human capital. This is especially true in African conflicts. More men and women have died of HIV/AIDs in the Democratic Republic of the Congo than from that country's internal war. Prevention programs in refugee camps and dealing with soldiers returning to communities after any demobilization program must make HIV/AIDs education and prevention a serious part of the effort to improve social and economic conditions. No serious social and economic reconstruction program can turn a blind eye to this great threat. Even though more than half the U.S. public supports funding for HIV/AIDS prevention abroad, the proven record of support by the U.S. government is uneven.

Two concrete steps could be taken by the U.S. government to help address this crisis. In addition to the $200 million that the U.S. government has committed to the Joint World Bank/United Nations AIDs Trust Fund, Congress should mandate that all U.S. government reconstruction programs provide for HIV/AIDs assessment, counseling, and prevention support.

Second, the Department of Defense's onetime Africa-oriented HIV/AIDs prevention program, directed at regional militaries, should be made an ongoing program. Members of the armed forces comprise a mobile and high-risk population. Similar training programs should also be added to work in Eastern Europe, Asia, and the Caribbean. Additionally, this training and education should be integrated into the curriculum at institutional educational centers (like the U.S. war colleges) and also into unit-level and individual-level combined training and educational exercises and exchanges.

CONCLUSION

Crisis is part of the development process. Thus, the integration of humanitarian programs and programs that look toward more stable and sustainable development is the best approach to recovery and reconstruction. The donor community has come to recognize that man-made disasters have set back development gains. U.S. leadership is needed to support programs that achieve sound economic governance and address the immediate needs of countries emerging from conflict. Effective measures to start a country's economic engines will ultimately prevent conflicts and help restore social capital. For the United States to ignore the social and economic well-being of a post-conflict state is to do so at our peril. After the events of September 11 this should be apparent. U.S. commitment to poverty reduction and human security that is needed to achieve economic growth is our best strategy for addressing the new security threats that we face in the years to come. We must develop effective tools that address these challenges.

Notes

[1] World Bank, *Post Conflict Reconstruction: The Role of the World Bank* (World Bank: Washington, D.C., 1998), p. 2. There are 78 countries considered to be the poorest in the world, representing about 2.4 billion people. Thus, approximately one-fourth of this group has also been conflict-ridden since the end of the Cold War.

[2] Organization for Economic Cooperation and Development, *Conflict, Peace and Development Cooperation on the Threshold of the 21st Century* (OECD: Paris 1998), p. 76.

[3] Poverty reduction, a long-term goal of development, is a matter of many different factors that will remove the world's poor from the misery of insecurity, the absence of adequate education and health care, or the inability to earn a living wage. Poverty reduction is the obvious end of which foreign assistance is a means, but unlike the World Bank, whose development mission is a world free from poverty, bilateral donor assistance has both short-term objectives, such as political stability, and objectives such as the promotion of democratic governance and other specific objectives that support the U.S. national interest.

[4] Recent research on the political economy of policy reform suggests that the influence of the governance context on economic performance is determinant. See David Dollar and Lant Pritchett, *Assessing Aid: What Works, What Doesn't, and Why,* World Bank Policy Research Report, no. 18295, November 30,1998, available at www-wds.worldbank.org; Stephen Haggard, *The Political Economy of the Asian Financial Crisis* (Washington, D.C.: Institute for International Economics, 2000); and Carlos Santiso, "Governance Conditionality and the Reform of Multilateral Development Finance: The Role of the Group of Eight." G8 Governance, Number 7, March 2002, available at www.g8.utoronto.ca/governance.

[5] A five-year effort by the Carnegie Commission on Preventing Deadly Conflict to explore all aspects of conflict prevention has articulated many options for the U.S. policy community and international actors in its series of reports. See Carnegie Commission on Preventing Deadly Conflict, www.wilsoncenter .org/subsites/ccpdc/index.htm

[6] Sebastian Mallaby, "Does Poverty Fuel Terror?" *Washington Post,* May 20, 2002, p. A21.

[7] At the end of the World War II, development assistance accounted for $4 for every $1 of private investment. Today the situation is reversed. The vast majority of financing for development comes not from aid, but from trade, domestic capital, and foreign investment. Developing countries received approximately $70 billion in aid in 2002, in comparison to foreign investment of almost $200 billion in annual earnings from exports of $2.4 trillion (World Bank, "2004 World Development Indicators," April 23, 2004, p. 336). Private investment in developing economies is by far the largest form of support. If free markets and greater trade are central to foreign assistance objectives, the United States must work to create the means by which investors can partake of the potentially rich investment environments that exist in countries emerging from conflict.

[8] Remarks by George W. Bush, March 22, 2002. In dollar terms the United States spends more on aid ($13.5 billion) than any other country except Japan. As part of President Bush's commitment to development assistance, the administration is proposing a special performance-based Millennium Development Account. As currently conceived, its purpose would not address countries undergoing post-conflict reconstruction. Thus, a separate account is also needed to reward countries emerging from conflict through different performance measures that use humanitarian indicators rather than solely measures of good governance. This program would supplement already designated reconstruction funds. For additional discussion of this account, see chapter 4, by Orr, "Governing When Chaos Rules: Enhancing Governance and Participation."

[9] The Commission on Human Security, a joint undertaking of the UN and chaired by Sadako Ogata, former UN High Commissioner for Refugees, and

Amartya Sen, Nobel Laureate economist, is defining these relations in the work currently under way. See also *Voices of the Poor*, the 1999 World Bank study on global poverty, which identified personal security as the main obstacle to moving out of poverty, available at www.worldbank.org/poverty/voices/reports.htm#lands.

[10] See appendix 1, Post-Conflict Reconstruction Task Framework.

[11] In recent years the international community has advocated smart sanctions to produce economic pressure as a means of more effectively convincing elites to changes objectionable policies that inhibit international support. Recent examples of this tactic are evident in Serbia, where continued U.S. government assistance toward reconstruction was directly linked to the elected leadership delivering indicted war criminals to the International Criminal Tribunal in The Hague.

[12] In 1996–1997, the Department of Defense contracted with the Institute for Defense Analysis to create an economic reconstruction game, SENSE, which was developed out of the military's frustration about its inability to exit Bosnia because of the lack of economic planning by civilian development institutions for post-war Bosnia. To exit Bosnia, the military felt that civilian development agencies needed to jumpstart economic life, yet they did not see progress in this area.

[13] See David Rothkopf's monograph *The Price of Peace: Emergency Economic Intervention and U.S. Foreign Policy,* (Washington, D.C.: Carnegie Endowment for International Peace, 1998), which discusses this need.

[14] The author thanks J. Brian Atwood, a national commissioner on the Joint CSIS/AUSA Post-Conflict Reconstruction Project, for providing important insights and comments on this aspect of this chapter.

[15] Currently staffed by fewer than 40 persons, and with a budget of just under $10 million, the office could expand its reach in developing budgets, banking authorities, and financial governance and in providing technical assistance to post-conflict states.

[16] David Keen, "Incentives and Disincentives to Violence," in *Greed and Grievance: Economic Agendas After Civil Wars,* ed. Mats Berdal and David Malone, (Boulder, Colo.: Lynne Rienner, 2002), p. 27.

[17] Paul Collier, "Doing Well Out of War," in *Greed and Grievance* (note 16), p. 97.

[18] Ibid., pp. 101–103.

[19] Rachel L. Swarns, "Angola Urged to Trace Its Revenue from Oil," *New York Times,* May 14, 2002, p. A9.

[20] Several U.S. government programs to provide emergency credit to exporters exist through the Department of Agriculture (e.g., Public Law 480 Food for Peace program and the Foreign Agriculture Export Credits).

[21] President Bush did restore normal trade relations treatment to Afghanistan on May 3, 2002. This action, however, only starts the process of providing that state with the minimum threshold for trading relations with the U.S. government; see Public Law 990190, {118.

[22] Demobilization programs include educational components as part of the reintegration efforts. For additional information on demobilization programs, see, in this volume, chapter 3 by Feil, "Laying the Foundation: Enhancing Security."

[23] In USAID's most recent reorganization, education is subsumed as a minor component of the new Economic Growth and Agricultural Development Bureau.

CHAPTER SIX

DEALING WITH DEMONS
ENHANCING JUSTICE AND RECONCILIATION

Michèle Flournoy and Michael Pan

The failure to establish, quickly and decisively, the rule of law in Bosnia-Herzegovina, repeated in Kosovo, is something for which we have paid a high price. That is why the looting in Baghdad and Basra, even though expected, has to be treated seriously.... Unless law and order is consolidated quickly and comprehensively, peace will not take hold and the benefits of the coalition victory will be swiftly lost as criminals and corruption swarm into the vacuum.... As in Bosnia, so in Iraq, everything depends on the early establishment of the rule of law: a functioning economy, a free and fair political system, the development of civil society, public confidence in the police and the courts. The process is sequential.... In Bosnia and Kosovo we paid a bitter price for not establishing the rule of law early. It is not a mistake we should repeat in Baghdad.

Paddy Ashdown, High Representative for Bosnia and Herzegovina, April 22, 2003

Mechanisms and institutions for upholding the rule of law and dealing with past abuses are crucial to rebuilding societies emerging from conflict. More often than not, however, such countries lack these very tools. Justice and reconciliation must therefore be a central pillar of post-conflict reconstruction assistance—one that should receive priority attention early and throughout the life of an operation.

While justice and reconciliation activities are very different in nature, they share the common goal of establishing processes for war-torn societies to address grievances and wrongdoings, past and present, in hopes of forging a more peaceful future. The past decade of international experience in post-conflict assistance—from Somalia and Haiti to Bosnia and Kosovo to East Timor and Sierra Leone—suggests that there are substantial gaps in the ability of the United States and the international community both to rapidly assist in these areas and to develop an integrated justice/reconciliation strategy. Indeed, this has been a primary area of poor performance, if not outright failure, in many interventions. The explosion of lawlessness, corruption, and crime that often accompanies post-conflict vacuums can undermine all gains made by international assistance. Therefore, justice assistance must be timely in order to be effective.

To date, international assistance in the justice arena has focused too narrowly on the question of re-establishing a functioning police force to maintain public safety. While this is indeed a critical task, a much more comprehensive approach to justice and reconciliation must be taken if we are to be successful. Specifically, this pillar of post-conflict reconstruction should include six key elements:

- law enforcement instruments that are effective, responsive to civilian authorities, and respectful of human rights;
- an impartial, open and accountable judicial system;
- a fair constitution and body of law;
- mechanisms for monitoring and upholding human rights;
- a humane corrections system; and
- formal and informal reconciliation mechanisms for dealing with past abuses and resolving grievances arising from conflict.[1]

Every effort should be made to build upon acceptable indigenous practices, laws, and institutions that were in place before the conflict. Indeed, the guiding principle for international assistance in the justice and reconciliation arena should always be to seek to empower local actors and promote the building of sustainable indigenous capacity while reinforcing respect for human rights and international norms. In practice, this means an early assessment of indigenous justice and reconciliation systems must be made to determine what can be salvaged and built upon and what must be discarded and replaced. Local actors must be given an active role in the design and implementation of programs to help ensure sustainability once the period of extraordinary international intervention ends. Given the poor track record of the United States and the international community on these issues, there is an urgent need to reform existing capacities to better promote the twin goals of justice and reconciliation.

DEFINING JUSTICE AND RECONCILIATION

The justice and reconciliation pillar of post-conflict reconstruction includes several distinct but interrelated tasks that may be undertaken over the life of an operation. Here, it is useful to think in terms of four key categories: emergency justice measures by international actors to "fill the gap" until indigenous processes and institutions can take over; longer-term efforts to rebuild indigenous judicial systems; the establishment of international and national reconciliation mechanisms for addressing grievances and past atrocities; and, finally, critical pre-deployment enablers—things that should be in place in advance to facilitate a rapid and effective international response.

Emergency justice measures are designed to establish as quickly as possible the bare essentials of an interim justice system to deal with the most urgent law and order issues. This may involve deploying international police either to monitor and mentor indigenous police forces or, in rare cases like East Timor, to exercise executive police functions. It may also include the simultaneous deployment of legal experts to help establish an interim legal code as well as international judges, prosecutors, defense attorneys, and court administrators to help indigenous actors set up interim courts to deal with immediate issues like the status and fate of individuals detained by security forces. With every experience from Bosnia to Iraq, improvements in this area have been made, but reform remains piecemeal and disjointed. In this critical early period, it is important to ensure that vital justice and reconciliation issues are properly addressed. Failure to do so can lead to the loss of gains in other areas, like security, governance, and well-being. For example, in Kosovo, the inability of coalition forces to establish the rule of law led to an explosion of corruption and organized crime. Whenever there is a justice vacuum, criminal elements will find a way to fill it.

At the same time, the international community should be launching its assistance to help develop more permanent, indigenous justice processes and institutions. Although such assistance usually extends over many years, it is imperative that it be part of the initial response in a post-conflict operation given the very long lead times involved in institution building. Activities to promote a culture of justice and reconciliation should be transparent and accessible to the broad population in order to support public security and counter any claims of international bias. Typically, international and regional efforts to support the development of a viable rule-of-law infrastructure could include development and training of indigenous law enforcement personnel; organization and stand-up of an independent judicial system; training for indigenous legal professionals; construction of key judicial infrastructure, including prisons and courts; revision of the constitution and legal codes; and training of indigenous human rights monitors. These should also be accompanied by a parallel effort to develop and support vital civil society and nongovernmental institutions that promote reconciliation and healing. The importance of local feedback and ownership should be reflected in the establishment of appropriate liaison mechanisms and ombudspersons for the citizenry. Due to the advocacy of the United Nations High Commissioner for Human Rights in Geneva, this worked well with UN experiences in both East Timor and Kosovo.

Immediate attention should also be given to establishing mechanisms for addressing abuses that occurred during the conflict, such as war crimes or gross violations of human rights. Based on an assessment of the needs of the society in question, it may be appropriate for the international community to establish and administer international courts or tribunals to deal with alleged war crimes, help establish truth commissions to deal with past abuses, and help create programs to support the rebuilding of communities and the healing and empowerment of individuals. If such efforts are indeed undertaken, they should begin as soon as possible, but they should not be expected to produce instant results. While not as high-profile or formal, support to civil society groups and nongovernmental entities involved in alternative dispute resolution and other nonjudicial remedies should also be provided.[2] In this regard, many international organizations are better placed than the U.S. government to provide alternative models to meet indigenous needs.

Finally, the United States and the international community should consider the "critical enablers" that should be in place before an actual operation begins in order to facilitate a rapid and effective international response to justice and reconciliation needs. These could include arrangements such as rosters of trained personnel available for rapid deployment, advance training in various justice and reconciliation tasks, standard operating procedures and contingency plans in key functional areas, standing capacities for material and private-sector support, and memorandums of understanding and contract vehicles among key international actors.

ADDRESSING KEY CAPABILITY GAPS AND SHORTFALLS

There are substantial gaps in the capabilities of the United States and the international community to provide the justice and reconciliation assistance that may be necessary.[3] Taking a holistic approach to justice and reconciliation in post-conflict reconstruction operations is a Herculean task. But failure to coordinate the delicate and complex relationship between justice and reconciliation carries great risks, as the absence of a viable justice system or adequate reconciliation mechanisms can undermine the security and stability essential to sustainable reconstruction efforts. For example, in Sierra Leone, the international community sponsored the simultaneous work of an international war crimes tribunal and a truth and reconciliation commission (TRC). The war crimes tribunal's resources and mandate were limited to prosecuting only a handful of top rebel and militia leaders, resulting in an unrealistic workload for the TRC in the absence of any national judicial mechanism. As every situation will be different, the international community should have the widest possible range of tools available to meet specific needs in an appropriate fashion.

While it will not always play a lead role, the United States should be prepared to provide limited, but critical, assistance in areas where it has strong comparative advantage, such as training, communications, and logistical support. In many cases, actions taken by the United States will in fact help provide incentives and demonstrate political support for other international partners to join the effort.

Policy and Strategy

One of the most fundamental gaps in U.S. capacity to assist in the justice and reconciliation arena is the absence of clear policy guidance from the president on these issues. Previous attempts to organize and implement needed changes within the U.S. government in the area of international assistance for judicial development fell short of their lofty objectives.[4] Currently, there is no policy basis for determining what sort of justice and reconciliation assistance the United States should be prepared to provide, which agencies should have lead responsibility for which tasks, how interagency programs should be coordinated, and where additional investment should be made to improve U.S. capacity in this critical area. Perhaps more troubling, currently no single office or individual within the U.S. government is responsible for this set of issues, leading to glaring gaps and ad hoc responses often dominated by short-term political goals. This is highly problematic at a time when the proliferation of ad hoc international and national institutions to address long-term justice and reconciliation issues has made coordination even more critical to ensure that scarce financial and political resources are not squandered.

In light of this situation, the United States government needs to develop and implement a National Security Presidential Directive (NSPD) on post-conflict reconstruction that, among other things, addresses U.S. strategy, capabilities, and interagency responsibilities and coordination in the area of post-conflict justice and reconciliation assistance. In addition to addressing constabulary force and international civilian police (CIVPOL) issues, this NSPD should define an integrated approach to providing judicial, corrections, and legal code development assistance. The directive should also address existing legislative and statutory restrictions that impair the efficiency and effectiveness of U.S. government assistance in this area.

A second improvement would be to establish a policy coordination committee (PCC) for post-conflict reconstruction, including strategy development for and coordination of U.S. government justice and reconciliation activities. Lead responsibility for the PCC should be assigned to a senior director at the National Security Council. This person would be responsible for leading the interagency process to draft and implement the new NSPD and empowered to interface directly with Congress. The PCC should also include the offices of U.S. representatives to international institutions, such as the World Bank and specialized agencies of the UN.

Rapidly Deployable Capabilities

As we have seen in Kosovo, Afghanistan, and Iraq, another critical gap in U.S. and international capacity is the lack of rapidly deployable capabilities to temporarily fill immediate "emergency justice" needs. The response time is chronically slow—often ranging from six months to one year. In Kosovo, for example, it took close to one year for the UN to deploy 4,000 international police.

Within this area, there are several specific shortfalls. The first is inadequate mechanisms for calling up and deploying appropriately trained international constabulary forces to safeguard public security until indigenous police forces are able to do so.[5]

The second shortfall is a shortage of qualified CIVPOL who are available for short-notice deployments as monitors and mentors of indigenous police forces or, in rare cases, to exercise executive policing authority. Due to the post–9/11 demands placed on our federal, state, and local law enforcement agencies, the United States may not be able to sustain its past role as a major provider of CIVPOL without major reforms. However, the United States can make a meaningful contribution in this area by seeking to improve access to and availability of specific kinds of American law enforcement expertise, such as planning, training, organization, and finance.

A third shortfall is the absence of rapidly deployable legal experts who can assist indigenous actors in establishing an interim legal code and interim courts to deal with pressing judicial issues. Even if the international community manages to rapidly deploy adequate numbers of well-trained constabulary and CIVPOL forces in the future, such forces cannot operate effectively without appropriate laws and courts to hear cases regarding detainment and alleged violations.

A fourth shortfall is inadequate materiel and equipment, such as generators and transport, to support judicial initiatives. One of the most critical gaps in material support is the lack of deployable public information assets such as shortwave radio transmitters, photocopiers, and translators.

Given this situation, there are four actions the U.S. government can take to speed up deployment of critical justice-related assets. First, the United States should launch a diplomatic initiative to increase the availability of national constabulary forces and international CIVPOL as interim guarantors of public security. Specifically, this would include endorsement of the European Union's plans to develop a rapid reaction police force, as well as active U.S. government support for the implementation of the UN's Brahimi Report recommendations regarding interim justice capabilities.[6] CIVPOL training courses could be provided by U.S. agencies to countries requesting assistance.

Second, the U.S. federal government, working with state and local law enforcement institutions, should design and organize a civilian reserve police system to support both national homeland security needs and post-conflict reconstruction. Units from such a volunteer force could be mobilized and deployed abroad on order of the president to serve U.S. national interests in post-conflict reconstruction operations. These individuals would have rights and protections similar to military reserve forces. Specifically, the president should establish a task force of federal, state, and local police representatives to design a police reserve system.

Congress should then authorize the creation of such a reserve based on the task force's recommendations.

Third, the U.S. government should reform its CIVPOL program to take advantage of specific U.S. comparative advantages. Agreements should be negotiated with sponsoring international organizations to ensure that U.S. experts in planning, training, organization, and finance are matched with specific jobs utilizing their particular skills and experience. Reform should include taking steps to assure better quality control and accountability, as well as extending tours to reduce the harmful effects of high turnover. Furthermore, the administration and Congress should work together to close the jurisdictional loophole for prosecuting American CIVPOL who commit crimes abroad.

Fourth, the U.S. Agency for International Development (USAID) should enhance its contracting capacities for rapidly deployable public information equipment, programs, and experts. Drawing on expertise and experience from nongovernmental organizations (NGOs), such as Internews, USAID should have the ability to help promote justice and reconciliation activities and disseminate legal information through rapidly called-upon radio, print, and other communication resources.

Capacity Building

Similarly critical gaps exist in both international and U.S. capacity to assist nations in the longer-term tasks of rebuilding or developing new judicial processes and institutions—in particular, the absence of an agreed-on, integrated approach to such assistance and the lack of trained, available personnel who could deploy to provide such assistance in a timely manner. The international community also lacks standard operating procedures for assessing justice and reconciliation needs in post-conflict societies as well as mechanisms for gaining access to a wide pool of experts to assist indigenous actors with the rewriting of legal codes, organization and operation of courts, vetting and training of police forces, compensation of indigenous judicial officials, strengthening of the legal education system, establishment of corrections systems, and the range of nonjudicial reconciliation mechanisms.

While the United States may not have a particular comparative advantage in reconstituting judicial systems, especially in countries with civil (vice common) law traditions, it does have significant capacity to assist with the development of bar associations, administrative systems, and antiterrorism and anti-organized crime units, and to provide material support. For each operation, an interagency assessment, drawing on existing U.S. government field personnel, ongoing UN and World Bank programs, and input from local actors, should be conducted at the outset to develop a feasible plan and integrated approach to building capacity throughout the judicial, police, security, and NGO sectors.

Specifically, the U.S. government should build its capacity in four ways. First, the U.S. government must expand its legal authority and capacity to train indigenous police forces. Specifically, Congress should replace Section 660 of the Foreign Assistance Act of 1961, as amended, with new legislation outlining available authorities. Until then, U.S. agency lawyers should better utilize the often ignored 1996 "post-conflict waiver" in Section 660 to allow U.S. assistance to be used for training indigenous police. The replacement act should maintain appropriate conditions on funding to protect human rights objectives and ensure accountability, while rationalizing and consolidating the numerous amendments and simplifying the mechanisms for applying resources to legitimate requirements.

Second, the president should move the International Criminal Investigative Training Assistance Program (ICITAP) from the Department of Justice (DOJ) to the Department of State's Bureau for International Narcotics and Law Enforcement Affairs (INL) to enable more effective integration of U.S. support for training indigenous police forces and support for community policing. Community policing programs should be developed in close coordination with USAID, and the Department of Justice should remain involved in helping to identify and recruit U.S. national experts in justice administration and policing. The president should request, and Congress should fund, a robust increase in funding for police training in post-conflict settings.

Third, the White House should assign lead responsibility for coordinating private-sector and material support for justice assistance to the State Department's Bureau for Democracy, Human Rights, and Labor (DRL). Functions would include facilitating "sister city" bar association partnerships and law school exchange programs, as well as coordination and disbursement of donated or U.S. government "excess property" equipment, texts, and furniture. U.S. government "space available" programs should be expanded to include support for courts, offices, and correctional facilities. Working with the Justice Department's Office of Litigation Support, DRL should also design "material justice support" packages for procurement on short notice.

Fourth, the secretary of state should dedicate a portion of the State Department's human rights budget to discretionary purposes. With appropriate congressional oversight, emerging PCR needs rather than year-old programming would drive this funding. Setting aside $20 million in an already-existing DRL account would dramatically improve the surge capacity of justice and reconciliation assistance throughout the entire U.S. government. Funding should be transferred to USAID's Bureau of Democracy, Conflict, and Humanitarian Assistance as necessary to ensure that legal development programs are balanced with civil society-based justice initiatives. Funding should also be used to provide language experts to support justice and reconciliation efforts in need of translators and interpreters.[7]

International Courts and Commissions

Another set of capability shortfalls lies in the area of U.S. support for both international and national truth commissions and war crimes tribunals.[8] Despite almost a decade of experience with the ad hoc criminal tribunals for the former Yugoslavia and Rwanda, the U.S. government still has difficulty finding appropriate mechanisms to support UN-sponsored initiatives for justice and reconciliation. The vast needs of these initiatives, ranging from evidence collection and legal assistance to funding and qualified personnel, are daunting. It is important to note that in many of these areas, international and local NGOs possess a significant comparative advantage; they are far better suited to lead such efforts than the U.S. government. That said, the United States can often provide invaluable support in the form of funding, logistics, equipment, and experienced personnel.

There are four specific ways in which the United States can help to fill this capability shortfall. First, Congress should amend relevant legislation to extend U.S. government drawdown authority to justice and reconciliation institutions based upon certification by the president. Current law restricts this assistance to the narrow category of UN-sanctioned ad hoc criminal tribunals. As truth commissions, hybrid tribunals, and specialized UN courts are becoming increasingly common in post-conflict societies, extending this assistance would have a large impact at a relatively modest cost.

Second, the U.S. government should create a mechanism at the U.S. Institute for Peace or the National Endowment for Democracy to allow tax-deductible, private contributions to UN trust funds to support international tribunals and commissions. Direct contributions to the United Nations are not tax-deductible; however, contributions to non-profit organizations and foundations are.

Third, the White House should facilitate the creation of interagency agreements between the Departments of State, Justice, and Defense to enable DOJ and DOD resources, such as the Armed Forces Institute of Pathology, to provide teams of forensics and evidence-collection experts in support of international atrocity documentation efforts.[9]

Fourth, the U.S. government must improve its process for rapidly declassifying records on human rights violations in other countries in response to requests from international judicial institutions and com-missions—assuming release of these records does not threaten U.S. na-tional security. The Freedom of Information Act (FOIA), which allows the release of classified documents after 25 years, is inadequate to assist countries investigating past criminal abuses. Previous attempts, such as the Human Rights Information Act, have failed to gain the necessary leg-islative momentum.

Critical Enablers

The last set of significant shortfalls lies in the area of "critical en-ablers"—those actions that can be taken in advance to improve the speed and quality of the international or U.S. response. Several such shortfalls are particularly important. Currently, the international com-munity lacks any agreed-on legal code for use as part of an interim jus-tice package in post-conflict operations. Consequently, this wheel is reinvented in every new operation, at considerable effort, expense, and loss of valuable time. In addition, there are no common principles or standard operating procedures governing the use of international CIVPOL and no standard training or certification procedures. The UN and other international organizations also lack adequate mechanisms, such as rosters and databases, to gain timely access to trained and avail-able experts across the range of judicial and reconciliation functions. They further lack the staffs and tools for planning and executing an inte-grated assistance program in this area.

The first thing the U.S. government could do to enhance the U.S. and international response would be to support recommendations in the UN's Brahimi Report of 2000 regarding the development of interim le-gal codes for ongoing peace operations. Until the report's recommenda-tions are implemented, a commission of international legal experts, including government lawyers and representatives from the NGO community, should be convened by a nonpartisan institution to develop an international consensus about basic interim laws.[10] Furthermore, the U.S. government could assist UN efforts to establish common principles, standard operating procedures, and training for international CIVPOL, including offering U.S. experts to participate in the effort. When appropriate, U.S. government training programs should be made available to selected international CIVPOL candidates.

Second, the United States should develop ready rosters of U.S. judicial specialists, police, penal officers, planners, and human rights monitors. These lists would specifically include those available for rapid deployment to help establish and develop interim courts. Responsibility for vetting, background checks, and call-up should be assigned to a stand-alone staff working for the State Department's undersecretary for global affairs.[11] A separate roster of mental health and psychological service professionals should be developed to assist U.S. government interagency teams conducting assessments of reconciliation needs in post-conflict societies. These rosters should be made available to the UN Department of Peacekeeping Operations and the Office of the UN High Commissioner for Human Rights.

Third, the secretary of state should be empowered to temporarily waive or modify personnel, medical, and other bureaucratic restrictions regarding the immediate secondment and deployment of U.S. government experts to assist critical justice and reconciliation initiatives. The inability of policymakers to meet the various federal and state employment requirements often causes unacceptable delays in the internal transfer of U.S. government employees.

Fourth, the United States should establish pre-deployment training to familiarize U.S. experts with international humanitarian law, other applicable international laws, local laws, the requirements of the specific mission, the operating environment to which they are deploying, and existing U.S. government programs and plans already in theater. A similar training module should be established and included in courses for new ambassadors and USAID mission directors at the State Department's National Foreign Affairs Training Center.

CONCLUSION

The damage wrought by mass atrocities and lawlessness in post-conflict societies usually takes years, if not decades, to begin to repair. But failure to address justice and reconciliation needs on a priority basis is a recipe for failure in reconstruction operations. Despite more than a decade of experience, the international community still lacks a coherent approach and adequate capacity to assess and address justice and reconciliation needs in war-torn societies. While the United States does not possess comparative advantages across the entire spectrum of needed justice and reconciliation assistance, it can play a unique and important role in enhancing international capabilities in the key areas of strategy, deployable resources, capacity building, support for international courts and commissions, and critical enablers to foster credible processes that promote sustainable peace. Given the importance of this pillar to success, the United States should take steps today to enhance its capacity to assist in this critical aspect of future post-conflict operations.

Notes

[1] The "rule of law" focus of this chapter is primarily in the criminal sector. Critical legal foundations in the areas of economic and social well-being are dealt with in chapter 5 by Mendelson Forman, "Restoring Hope: Enhancing Social and Economic Well-Being."

[2] Reconciliation initiatives include programs in areas such as public education, mass media, interfaith workshops, commemoration, and cultural exchange. See "Nature of Reconciliation" by Daniel Bar-Tal, prepared for the Stockholm International Forum on Truth, Justice, and Reconciliation (April 22-23, 2002). As reconciliation models are best derived from within society, this chapter deals more with justice initiatives, which more often require significant outside assistance. Nevertheless, the authors believe that reconciliation initiatives are as important as justice activities.

[3] The following recommendations focus primarily on gaps in U.S. policy and capacity for assisting post-conflict justice and reconciliation, although some attention is also paid to how the United States might encourage the enhancement of international capacities in key areas where the United States lacks a comparative advantage.

[4] The Clinton administration's Presidential Decision Directive 71, "Strengthening Criminal Justice Systems in Support of Peace Operations," has been neither adopted nor replaced by the Bush administration, and its implementation in the final year of the Clinton administration was limited by several factors, including the lack of appropriate resources and National Security Council-level leadership.

[5] This is addressed at greater length in chapter 3 in this volume, "Laying the Foundation: Enhancing Security Capabilities," by Feil. Although the United

States does not have any national constabulary forces, a number of other countries—including many of our closest European allies—do. And yet the international community has not been able to access these forces rapidly for post-conflict reconstruction operations.

[6] See UN Document A/55/305-S/2000/809, "Report of the Panel on United Nations Peace Operations" (Brahimi Report), August 2000, http://daccess-ods.un.org/TMP/4215316.html.

[7] Resources at the National Foreign Affairs Training Center, the Foreign Broadcasting Information Center, and the Peace Corps should be tapped to support these initiatives.

[8] In light of U.S. legislative restrictions on the International Criminal Court, U.S. engagement in this area will likely be with ad hoc international tribunals and commissions.

[9] Past initiatives have included investigations on behalf of the International Criminal Tribunal for Yugoslavia (ICTY) and the International Commission for Missing Persons, and portable morgues for use in Kosovo to perform on-site autopsies.

[10] An initial effort along these lines has already been undertaken by the United States Institute for Peace's Project on Peacekeeping and the Administration of Justice. More work would have to be done to refine the formulation and gain adoption.

[11] Placing the function within the purview of the undersecretary for global affairs would cut across the Democracy, Human Rights, and Labor (DRL) and International Narcotics and Law (INL) worlds of expertise without creating new administrative burdens for either bureau.

PART THREE

ENHANCING U.S. CAPACITY ENABLERS

CHAPTER SEVEN

INTERAGENCY STRATEGY AND PLANNING FOR POST-CONFLICT RECONSTRUCTION

Michèle Flournoy

The idea that "no plan survives contact with the enemy"[1] has made many in Washington skeptical of the value of interagency planning for complex contingency operations, including those aimed at assisting post-conflict reconstruction. But for those who have actually participated in such operations, another premise holds even truer: no operation succeeds without a strategy and a plan. One of the most powerful lessons learned during the 1993 operation in Somalia was that the absence of rigorous and sustained interagency planning and coordination can hamper effectiveness, jeopardize success, and even court disaster. The difficulties encountered by the United States in post-conflict Iraq a decade later further underscore this lesson.

Given the sheer complexity of post-conflict reconstruction efforts, developing a clear strategic plan of action at the outset is critical to success. Such a plan should articulate the U.S. interests at stake and define as clearly as possible U.S. objectives for the intervention. Developing a common set of objectives across the U.S. government is of paramount importance to creating unity of effort among disparate agencies and actors. The plan should also lay out the strategy for achieving those policy objectives, and a clear division of labor delineating who is responsible for what aspects of the plan's implementation. Obviously, any U.S. strategic plan must be developed in the context of and in coordination with the broader international effort of which U.S. operations are a part.

Perhaps even more important than the plan itself is the strategy development and planning *process*. While strategy obviously informs planning, in practice planning also helps refine strategy by framing and assessing alternative approaches, identifying trade-offs, and highlighting policy "disconnects" for decisionmakers. The process produces more than just a set of documents: it allows key players to build working relationships, subject assumptions to more rigorous scrutiny, hammer out differences, identify potential inconsistencies and gaps, synchronize their actions, and better understand their roles and responsibilities. Smoothing out such wrinkles is much less costly in terms of blood and treasure before an operation begins than during its execution. Interagency planning also provides an antidote to some of the more disruptive effects of the high turnover in military and foreign service personnel.

RECENT INTERAGENCY PLANNING EFFORTS: FROM HAITI TO IRAQ

As planning began in mid-1994 for operations in Haiti, lessons from Somalia were in the forefront of many participants' minds. The Deputies Committee of the National Security Council (NSC) established an Executive Committee (ExCom) at the assistant secretary level to be chaired by the NSC's senior director for global and multilateral affairs, with a mandate to develop policy options and plans for a possible U.S.-led intervention in Haiti. The Haiti ExCom developed the first-ever interagency political-military plan, which articulated the overall objectives of the mission, an interagency strategy for meeting them, and a division of labor delineating which agencies had responsibility for which tasks. This plan was rehearsed before the Deputies Committee prior to the launch of the U.S.-led multinational force.

The strides made in planning for Haiti led several participants to seek a way to institutionalize lessons learned and best practices from the experience. This resulted in Presidential Decision Directive 56 on Managing Complex Contingency Operations (PDD-56), which was signed by President Bill Clinton in May 1997.[2] PDD-56 called for the Deputies Committee to establish an interagency Executive Committee to assist in policy development, planning, and execution of complex contingency operations; the development of a political-military implementation plan as an integrated planning tool for coordinating U.S. government actions; an interagency rehearsal or review of the plan's main elements prior to execution; an after-action review of each operation; and interagency training to support this process.

Although PDD-56 was never fully implemented, the Clinton administration's use of some aspects of the PDD in the major complex contingency operations that followed did generate many useful planning processes and tools. As political-military plans were prepared for the Deputies Committee for crises in Kosovo, East Timor, and elsewhere, several innovations were adopted to strengthen the U.S. government's limited planning capacity. Some of those innovations, which continue today in some form, include the development of an advance planning process; establishment of the interagency contingency planning working group; creation of standing interagency working groups for humanitarian response, information operations, and public security; inclusion of civilian agency requirements in the Pentagon's deliberate planning process—the so-called Annex V of various military plans; and the inclusion of coalition-building efforts as a major component of the interagency planning effort. While these innovations made substantial progress in building institutional capacity in the Clinton administration, there remained some pockets of resistance to interagency political-military planning for crises, reflecting both an anti-planning bias on the part of some senior regional officials (at the State and Defense Departments and the NSC) and an overestimation of the time and resources needed to undertake a full-fledged planning effort.

After coming into office, the Bush administration decided to develop National Security Policy Directive (NSPD) "XX,"[3] which builds on PDD-56 but is broader in scope, in that it provides guidance on providing warning, advanced planning, prevention, and response options for complex contingency operations. With regard to interagency strategy and planning, the NSPD calls for the establishment of an NSC-chaired Contingency Planning Policy Coordination Committee (CP-PCC) at the assistant secretary level to lead the development of interagency contingency plans for emerging crises with a focus on U.S. objectives, a desired endstate, policy options, interagency responsibilities, resource issues, and strategies for various aspects of the operation.

When it came time, however, to prepare for operations in Afghanistan in response to the terrorist attacks of September 11, 2001, the Bush administration did not follow the guidance laid out in its own (still unsigned) NSPD. Specifically, there was no person or entity below the Deputies Committee designated to be in charge of interagency planning and coordination and no clear process for integrating the military, diplomatic, humanitarian, and other elements of the U.S. planning for the intervention.

Similarly, when the administration began to prepare for war and post-conflict operations in Iraq in the winter of 2003, the guidance laid out in NSPD-XX was once again largely ignored. Initial NSC-led planning efforts were ultimately overtaken by the appointment of a former U.S. Army general to lead U.S. preparation for post-conflict operations in Iraq. Thenceforth, the locus of interagency planning for Iraq moved to the Pentagon, greatly limiting the participation of other agencies.

Unfortunately, interagency planning frequently falls short of achieving its full potential, largely due to recurring bureaucratic factors and inexperience at senior levels. Past shortcomings underscore the need for capable NSC leadership from the outset; improved methods to overcome bureaucratic inertia, personal rivalries, and internal communication disconnects during the planning process; and better ways to monitor implementation of agency plans as an operation unfolds.

KEY ELEMENTS OF SUCCESS

Accountability

Perhaps the most significant determinant of success in interagency planning is the degree to which participants are held accountable for meeting U.S. objectives and for the roles they play in the process. Accountability begins with putting someone clearly in charge of strategy development and planning. Ideally, the president's "point person" for this should be a senior director on the National Security Council staff positioned to act as an honest broker and empowered with the authority to task other agencies to assist in the planning process. Past attempts to put senior officials from the State Department or the Defense Department in charge have proved unsuccessful, either because the officials in charge lacked the authority to hold their counterparts in other agencies accountable for their elements of a plan or because they failed to adequately integrate the perspectives and capabilities of other agencies.

The second aspect of accountability is ensuring that the head of each department or agency is held responsible for delivering on his or her organization's part(s) of the plan. For example, the secretary of state might be held responsible for developing the political, diplomatic, and humanitarian assistance aspects of the plan, while the secretary of defense might be held accountable for the military aspects of the security mission. Accountability also requires ensuring that agency representatives have the resources they need to deliver on the commitments they make. Furthermore, all agencies responsible for some aspect of policy implementation must be represented at the strategy and planning table, including those traditionally outside the NSC process, such as USAID, Treasury, Justice, Commerce, and parts of the State Department like the Bureau for Population, Refugees, and Migration (PRM) and the Bureau for International Narcotics and Law Enforcement Affairs (INL). These agencies and offices must also be given appropriate incentives to play— particularly the opportunity to influence the development of the strategy and how their resources will be used. Bringing additional parties to the table will require aggressively avoiding overclassification of plans as well as prudent handling of genuine operational security issues that may exist.

A third aspect of accountability is adequate consultation with Congress during the planning process. Key members of Congress should be consulted early and often as an administration develops its strategy and plans for a given post-conflict reconstruction operation. As the ultimate allocator of resources for such operations, Congress should be briefed not only on the objectives and basic strategy for an operation but also on anticipated funding requirements, measures of success for various aspects of the plan, and key handoff or transition points in the operation.

Leadership

Too often in the past, lessons learned and best practices have been ignored because the national security adviser and the NSC staff allowed anti-planning biases to trump the president's planning guidance. More often than not, when an ExCom is created for a particular complex contingency operation, a functional NSC director is put in charge but ignored by regional NSC directors and regional assistant secretaries. Given concerns about putting too much of evolving U.S. policy down on paper for fear of the diplomatic ramifications of leaks, and a desire to avoid having functional experts meddling in their work, senior regional experts often come to the table disinclined to develop formal interagency plans for an operation. The national security adviser needs to ensure that an effective interagency strategy and planning process that reflects the president's priorities is developed early on, if not in advance of a crisis, and that the necessary players participate in the process.

Responsiveness

To be effective, the strategy and planning process must be responsive to the requirements of the anticipated post-conflict reconstruction operation and start early enough to allow participants adequate time to prepare. In the past, planners have been given anything from months, as in Haiti, to hours or days, as in Rwanda. Ensuring that planning gets started early enough to make a difference argues for establishing a trigger mechanism for the planning process. Commendably, NSPD-XX calls for a quarterly review by the Deputies Committee of crises that could result in complex contingency operations and a determination as to whether the initiation of planning is warranted. Such a determination should trigger not only the launch of an interagency planning process but also the suspension of certain staffing constraints to allow the NSC to augment its planning staff with detailees from other agencies. In addition, having a known, exercised process in place would allow for planning to get started more rapidly.

In addition to time, senior agency representatives also need the authority and flexibility during the planning process to rapidly commit the resources that their agencies can bring to bear in an operation. Too often in the past, planning has been delayed by interagency debates about funding authorities, resources, and arrangements. Several aspects of this issue will need to be addressed, including possible revision of agency authorities, increased resources and capacities in specific task areas, and empowerment of senior participants in the process to make commitments on behalf of the agencies they represent.[4]

Shared Frame of Reference

In the past, several mechanisms have been used to help get participants working off the same sheet of paper, including a comprehensive interagency assessment of the crisis situation. Frequently, this process begins well before a crisis takes shape in the minds of policymakers. Such an assessment can help focus the strategy and planning effort from the outset by aiding the development of a common appraisal of what needs to be done on the ground to achieve policy objectives. It can also help to establish ways of sharing information over the course of the planning process. While any such assessment should be revised over time, it provides an invaluable foundation for developing a common view of policy aims, strategy, and plans. It is essential that this assessment process include the "reality check" of perspectives from personnel in the field. In the wake of Somalia, such assessments became a critical part of the Clinton administration's planning for complex contingency operations throughout the 1990s; however, they did not play a central role in the Bush administration's initial planning for Afghanistan and Iraq.

The strategy development and planning process may also be greatly assisted by the establishment of a common template or generic plan. Equally important is codifying a set of standing interagency arrangements for U.S. government post-conflict reconstruction efforts (similar to arrangements agreed to in the Federal Response Plan used by the Federal Emergency Management Agency (FEMA) for domestic disasters). Such a template could conceivably be tailored on a case-by-case basis, depending on factors such as the complexity of the operation and the level of U.S. involvement. It focuses analysis and debate on the key issues that must be resolved at the strategic level. It also provides a shared foundation on which individual agencies can build their own operational responses. In any case, planning done at the Washington interagency level should avoid preempting more detailed planning that is more appropriately done at the operational level.

A third key aspect of establishing a shared frame of reference is putting into place mechanisms to help ensure coordination along three axes: between civilian and military agencies of the U.S. government; between Washington (the planners) and the field (the implementers); and between the U.S. government and other elements of the international community such as coalition partners, international organizations, and NGOs playing key roles in post-conflict operations. Effective interagency planning is necessarily a multilayered process; planning and coordination must occur at and between both the strategic and operational levels. Again, it is invaluable, if not critical, for each party to know what the others are planning on doing and to identify any issues that need to be resolved before execution.

Adequate Capacity

A successful strategy development and planning process requires a degree of capacity—particularly trained and available personnel—on the NSC staff and in participating agencies. In the past, such efforts have been hampered by the fact that each agency representative in the process was effectively a one-person show, and most had additional responsibilities completely unrelated to planning. For example, the assistant secretary of state responsible for the diplomatic and coalition-building aspects of a particular pol-mil plan is also likely to be responsible for overseeing U.S. diplomatic strategy for a number of other countries in the region. Planning requires devoting quality NSC personnel to the process on a full-time basis. In addition, as noted above, during the planning process the NSC should be allowed to temporarily augment its staff with personnel on loan from other agencies. In agencies where planning is not a routine or valued endeavor, and other priority areas may already be understaffed, building the internal capacity necessary for success will require substantial leadership and a culture change initiated at the highest levels.

Rehearsals and Training

A critical but often neglected part of effective interagency planning is the rehearsal—that is, a seminar-style walk-through of the plan as if it were being implemented. Rehearsals are an invaluable and low-cost way of discovering gaps and problems in a plan before an operation actually begins—and without placing U.S. lives, credibility, and resources on the line. They can also be critical to ensuring smooth handoffs of responsibility from one agency or actor to another. Ideally, rehearsals should be conducted not only prior to an operation's initiation, but also before any major transition. Lessons learned from rehearsals can provide invaluable "fixes" to interagency plans and can anticipate discontinuities for which planners may want to develop additional contingency plans. The challenge here is to ensure that insights gained at senior-level rehearsals actually "trickle down" to implementers in the field.

Over the longer term, interagency training is a key element of success for post-conflict reconstruction operations. Both PDD-56 and NSPD-XX called for interagency training programs to develop a cadre of professionals capable of planning for complex contingency operations. There are valuable planning skills that can be honed in advance and one should have opportunities to make mistakes and learn lessons in a training environment, without the pressures and high stakes of a real-time operation. Training also provides an opportunity for building familiarity with and buy-in to the shared frame of reference described above. Ensuring that interagency training actually occurs, however, will require increased emphasis on and funding for training.[5] Personnel selected for training should be assigned to positions where their training will have the most beneficial impact on the planning process.

AN ACTIONABLE AGENDA FOR THE U.S. GOVERNMENT

There are several concrete steps that the U.S. government can take to meaningfully enhance its capacity plan and prepare for future complex contingency operations, including post-conflict reconstruction efforts.

Creating a Standing Interagency Process

The current ad hoc strategy and planning process for addressing post-conflict reconstruction situations should be replaced with a standing comprehensive interagency process. Specifically, the president should sign and fully implement a National Security Presidential Directive on complex contingencies similar to NSPD-XX and develop a companion NSPD specifically designed to organize U.S. government participation in post-conflict reconstruction efforts. The national security adviser should give priority to ensuring that this guidance is actually followed in practice. In addition, the national security adviser should designate and appropriately staff and fund a directorate at the NSC to be in charge of interagency strategy development and planning for post-conflict reconstruction operations. This office should have the capacity to lead the development of more than one interagency plan at a time.

Incorporating Field Knowledge

All agencies with implementation responsibility should be included in the strategy development and planning process and a mechanism should be established for including key field representatives on a regular basis. It is particularly important to involve relevant ambassadors, the military combatant commanders, the USAID Disaster Assistance Response Team (DART) leader, and the USAID mission director, among others, to give interagency planning in Washington periodic "reality checks." This might be accomplished by consulting them periodically during the planning process, in person or by secure video teleconference, as well as requiring them to participate in rehearsals. Regular consultations over the life of an operation are essential to both synchronization of U.S. government efforts and smooth handoffs of responsibility from one agency to another.

Maintaining a Planning Template and Rehearsal Process

Building on an NSPD-XX-like foundation, the NSC staff should develop a generic interagency planning template for use in interagency planning for complex contingencies. Having in place such a template as well as an agreed division of labor among the relevant agencies not only would avoid the problem of having to reinvent one's planning approach for each new operation, but also would provide the interagency training program with an authoritative and solid foundation.

Integrating Planners into the Regional Staffs

Developing planning expertise and capacity in key offices likely to play important roles in designing post-conflict reconstruction operations, particularly the State Department's regional bureaus, is critical to improving U.S. government performance. Currently, there is little strategic planning expertise outside the U.S. military, and little training done on the civilian side.[6] To enhance planning capacity in the State Department, each regional assistant secretary of state should be given at least two staff people trained as political-military planners.[7] This will require additional billets and resources. In times of calm, these personnel could be used to support deliberate planning and interagency coordination and training efforts. Over time, integrating planners into regional staffs could go a long way toward changing the anti-planning culture that pervades several civilian agencies, such as the State, Treasury, and Justice Departments.

A Secure Intranet

Within the U.S. government there is a strong need for a secure intranet for interagency planners, including relevant intelligence and information, collaborative planning tools, and decision support tools. A shared virtual space that enables interagency participants to communicate, share information, and coordinate with one another on a real-time basis could meaningfully improve both the quality and speed of the interagency planning process. It could also enable finished products to better reach individuals in the field responsible for operational implementation of the strategic plan. The technologies and tools exist, and a modest investment could substantially increase efficiency.

International Liaison

To anticipate the complex needs and resources of all the international players in an intervention, the U.S. government should establish mechanisms for early and regular consultation with other key international players, including international organizations like the United Nations, regional organizations, NGOs, and coalition partners. The U.S. government needs mechanisms for determining what other key players in a post-conflict reconstruction effort plan on doing, as their actions may directly affect the United States' ability to achieve its objectives in an operation—and vice versa. It may also be in the U.S. government's interests to provide support, direct or indirect, to the efforts of various international actors. In addition to meeting regularly with key partners and organizations early in the planning process, the NSC should consider inviting key non-U.S. government and international participants to a rehearsal of the U.S. plan. The United States should also consider including its closest allies as partners in the U.S. planning process. While there may be legitimate operational security concerns, these could be managed, as they are in the U.S. interagency process.

CONCLUSION

Interagency strategy development and planning at the strategic level is critical to success in post-conflict reconstruction operations. The past decade of experience offers a number of invaluable lessons to be learned and some clear guidelines for improving the United States government's performance in this area. The key elements of success are known and largely accepted. By taking the steps recommended above, the president and his national security adviser could, with a minimum expenditure of political capital, meaningfully improve the U.S. government's ability to develop an integrated approach to post-conflict reconstruction operations and to increase the chances of success on the ground.

Notes

[1] Attributed to nineteenth-century Prussian field marshal Helmuth von Moltke.

[2] See PDD-56 White Paper, at http://clinton2.nara.gov/WH/EOP/NSC/html/documents/NSCDoc2.html.

[3] The NSPD is designated "XX" as it is still awaiting the president's signature.

[4] On the question of revising agency funding authorities to make them more flexible and responsive, see chapter 10 by Orr and Mendelson Forman, "Funding Post-Conflict Reconstruction." On the question of increasing resources and capacity in some areas, see chapter 8 by Mendelson Forman and Pan, "Filling the Gap: Civilian Rapid Response Capacity for Post-Conflict Reconstruction."

[5] For greater detail, see chapter 9, "Training and Education for Post-Conflict Reconstruction," by Flournoy.

[6] There is, however, substantial planning expertise in pockets of the U.S. government like USAID, but this agency often gets left out of interagency strategy and planning processes.

[7] For a more detailed analysis of the need for an interagency training program to develop such a cadre of professionals, see chapter 9 by Flournoy.

CHAPTER EIGHT

FILLING THE GAP

CIVILIAN RAPID RESPONSE CAPACITY FOR POST-CONFLICT RECONSTRUCTION

Johanna Mendelson Forman and Michael Pan

The post–Cold War world and the global war on terror have underscored a significant capacity gap between U.S. military operations and the civilian operations to which they hand off. It has now become commonplace for the U.S. military to remain in theater performing nonmilitary missions precisely because no civilian agencies are ready or able to deploy. As General Anthony Zinni, former commander of Central Command, has noted, the U.S. military have become the "stuckees," the force that gets stuck with all of the cleanup because no other alternative exists to fill the emergency gaps. Similarly, Condoleezza Rice, the president's national security adviser, has warned that "none of us should be forever using military forces to do what civilian institutions should be doing."[1] Until the U.S. government develops sufficient rapid civilian reaction capacity, the military will continue to be called on to accomplish "civilian" tasks, greatly limiting the strategic choices of the U.S. government at home and abroad.[2]

RAPID RESPONSE AND POST-CONFLICT RECONSTRUCTION

Rapid response is not a stopgap measure. It lays the foundation for long-term development strategies and permits the military to complete its war-fighting missions. It should become part of a well-defined approach to post-conflict events, which also include humanitarian aid and security protection as part of the triad of requirements.

The two most urgent tasks in post-conflict reconstruction are enhancing citizen security and initiating democratic processes. Citizen security requires the presence of international civilian police and the transition to indigenous policing capacity. It also requires an emergency justice package that would meet basic needs of resolving conflict with internationally accepted legal norms. Democratic processes include the steps needed to create a legitimate governing authority. Beyond elections, creating local decisionmaking over specific emergency needs is as important to building a foundation for economic investment as is the development of national ministries.

Civilian rapid response capacity, as defined here, is not humanitarian assistance, but rather the ability to deploy critical political, social, and economic development assistance needed in the immediate post-combat phase of an external intervention, when a window for civilian skills can make a difference in securing the peace. The relief-to-development continuum is not a viable concept in light of more than a decade of U.S. government experience in responding to complex emergencies. Anyone who has worked in manmade disasters, such as Bosnia, Rwanda, East Timor, Iraq, and Afghanistan, understands that humanitarian aid exists side by side with initial political development tasks.

What distinguishes civilian rapid response from humanitarian aid is that it begins at the cessation of hostilities. What has become more difficult to define has been where it ends. The reasons for this are manifold. For example, elections of officials in a post-conflict setting do not immediately ensure the presence of capable institutions of governance. Communities that have suffered during a conflict will require immediate assistance to jumpstart and rebuild both the social capital and physical infrastructure that will provide the basis for longer-term development assistance.

After violent conflict, a special environment is needed for political development. Civilian rapid response involves short-term interventions that can lay the foundation for what can be accomplished after the immediate crisis has been resolved. Civilian rapid response requires taking risks and focusing attention at the local or community level, and it must be done immediately to establish positive and tangible results that all people can see.

Across the spectrum of post-conflict reconstruction tasks, several operational gaps require immediate attention. The U.S. military provides a rapid response to security threats and humanitarian emergencies and possesses the greatest capacity to respond to these types of emergencies. For our purposes here, however, civilian rapid response refers to the U.S. government's capacity to provide immediate post-conflict assistance in justice and reconciliation, governance and participation, and socioeconomic well-being. It assumes that security—which must be maintained and supported for these other areas to flourish—is a joint effort of both civilian and military forces.

U.S. GOVERNMENT CAPACITY AND GAPS IN RESPONSE CAPABILITY

The existing civilian capacities for post-conflict rapid response were created in an ad hoc fashion, leaving gaps in either institutional capacity or resources to perform specific tasks. The Office of Foreign Disaster Assistance (OFDA), consolidated in 1992 under the U.S. Agency for International Development (USAID), brought together interagency personnel, a grants program, and coordination with U.S. military assets to ensure delivery of humanitarian aid and short-term relief.

In 1994, USAID's Office of Transition Initiatives (OTI) was founded to provide immediate programming in the area of political development in countries emerging from war or conflict. Complementing OFDA, in the short run OTI was able to do many of the most important activities aimed at redressing the most basic causes of the conflict. But this effort has generally been a small-scale response to an ever-growing global need to provide immediate resources to places where hope is the only survivor of war. In Iraq in 2003, OTI was the only effective civilian response mechanism on the ground, although even that mission was compromised by deteriorating security conditions and the competing civil affairs role of the U.S. military.

The Department of Justice currently houses two programs for international police (International Criminal Investigative Training Assistance Program, or ICITAP) and prosecutorial training (Office of Overseas Prosecutorial Development, Assistance, and Training, or OPDAT). The Department of State has expanded its work in policing through the Bureau for International Narcotics and Law Enforcement Affairs (INL). Both agencies do security-related work without the capacity to respond to the increasing emergency demands that arise from new threats in the post–Cold War environment. The State Department's Bureau of Democracy, Human Rights, and Labor (DRL) has resources for governance and justice activities. However, these funds are not immediately available for the period of transition from a military to a civilian environment in a post-conflict setting; nor does the bureau have any presence in the field to disburse the resources. The Department of Commerce's International Trade Administration (ITA) promotes long-term economic development but fails to provide immediate advice to jump-start foreign investment. Similarly, the Treasury Department's office that oversees funding for the international lending institutions has little immediate impact to support economic demands that accompany a crisis environment. Many other U.S. government agencies also possess a mandate in support of long-term development, but they too are not equipped to respond to the transitional needs of war-torn societies. In many of the post-conflict reconstruction efforts during the 1990s and in Afghanistan in 2001, the United Nations and regional multilateral development partners executed the majority of the rapid response mission.

AN ACTIONABLE AGENDA FOR THE U.S. GOVERNMENT

In the wake of 9/11 it is time to revisit the question of rapid civilian response so that all U.S. government assets, civilian and military, can be brought to bear on the challenges of post-conflict reconstruction. After more than a decade of active involvement by the United States in multinational peace operations and complex emergencies, it is apparent that the civilian capacity to respond rapidly is uneven, lacks specific legislative authorities, and is resource-starved. What capabilities are needed to round out the U.S. government's capacity to respond?

No single "silver bullet" exists to fix these problems. The current U.S. approach to post-conflict challenges strongly adheres to specific agency missions, thus reinforcing a civilian/military mission dichotomy that does not exist in reality. There is no unambiguous line between securing the peace and "handing off the mission" when the fighting stops. U.S. military doctrine is still evolving in this area so that field commanders fully understand and appreciate what different civilian groups can do. Significant transformation is needed in the form of a set of interlocking innovative reforms, implemented across agencies, to create a more effective architecture for civilian rapid response. While individual agencies will need to tackle institution-specific challenges, recommendations should be seen as a broad "package" for reform.

The Department of Defense applies the concept of "DOTML-P"—Doctrine, Organization, Training, Materiel, Leadership, and People—as a requirements checklist based on a specific strategy. The components of DOTML-P are critical considerations when developing the necessary tools for achieving success. Strong capabilities in each of these areas allow the U.S. military to achieve dominance in the security theater. There is no counterpart to this type of strategy analysis in civilian agencies when it comes to responding to post-conflict challenges. One approach to solving the gaps in timing, capacity, and resources is to implement a similar concept that would give military and civilian planners a common vocabulary for specific emergency requirements. A comprehensive framework for post-humanitarian intervention would also facilitate planning for the medium- and long-term development programs.

A civilian counterpart of DOTMIL-P would require additional capacity in five areas: strategy and planning; organization; coordination; trained and deployable people; and available funding.

Strategy and Planning

Where everything is a priority in the emergency phase of a reconstruction process, this framework would provide clear policy guidance and direction for the broad range of agencies involved in both the immediate response and the long run. Any strategy or planning for civilian rapid response must take into account the importance of addressing the root causes of conflict prior to full-scale intervention.[3] To fill this critical gap, the U.S. government should strengthen the mandate and capacity of the interagency process to develop strategy and planning, and should create joint military-civilian planning headquarters in the field to support directors of reconstruction as they seek to implement those plans.[4]

Organization

With over a dozen offices spread out across the U.S. government's interagency bureaucracy, redundancy and gaps are inevitable. The principal civilian agencies, USAID and the Department of State, are complemented by a host of other agencies such as the Departments of Justice and Commerce, the Overseas Private Investment Corporation (OPIC), and the Office of the U.S. Trade Representative (USTR). No roadmap exists that would help a military planner develop a hand-off plan that would embrace all the tools available on the civilian side. The problem is exacerbated by separate funding streams, time lines, operational speeds, and legislative requirements. Most, if not all, of these actors bring distinct comparative advantages to reconstruction at different times, including interface with international institutions and other bilateral donors. Like any concert orchestra, a strong conductor is needed to pull together the divergent players into a seamless strategy.

Solving organizational challenges in this very complex field of endeavor requires understanding what the current organizational structure of the U.S. government is with respect to these issues. To this end, the national security adviser should task each civilian agency to provide the National Security Council (NSC) with a list of its capacities for field implementation, both in budgetary and human capacity terms. Using this information, the NSC should develop a "capacity map" that would help identify current weaknesses. It should be matched by a parallel process that helps to identify international capacity for rebuilding.

Second, the national security adviser should establish an interagency task force to examine ways to improve liaison and coordination across all relevant participants in reconstruction. Proposals for improving international liaison components of domestic agencies, such as Treasury, Commerce, and Justice, should be given special attention. The task force should also study human resource and personnel changes needed in order to better integrate organizational structures, particularly between the State Department and USAID.

Coordination

The National Security Council, currently charged with coordination, has no budget authority to implement plans. In times of crisis this often results in the NSC becoming a prisoner of agency intransigence when it comes to mounting civilian rapid response. Those agencies with budgets and people to address the needs identified by the interagency process essentially decide how, and at what speed, they will use their resources. This amounts to a de facto veto power for agencies.

To maintain a close linkage between policy setting and implementation, the NSC should retain responsibility for policy coordination of rapid response capacities inclusive of all agencies, civilian and military. In addition, the NSC should work with the Office of Management and Budget to provide active monitoring of funds in these types of operations.

In addition, a civilian rapid response plan for humanitarian response, modeled on the Federal Response Plan of the Federal Emergency Management Agency (FEMA), should be created. Such a plan would codify interagency protocol on coordination and standing arrangements and memorandums of understanding for emergency conflict response. It would also provide a framework of tasks, phased in by needs in different stages, to allow adequate strategic planning between civilian and military agencies to go forward.

People

A pool of trained and readily deployable civilian experts to complement the military components of a post-conflict intervention is sorely needed. Experience from each intervention over the past decade shows that the deep disparity between civilian and military human resources hampers the effectiveness of the overall endeavor. In times of greatest need, the right people with the right skills are nowhere to be found. As highlighted in recent reports by the General Accounting Office and the U.S. State Department Advisory Commission on Public Diplomacy, the U.S. government is suffering from a critical shortage of human talent.[5]

The first step to having a pool of readily deployable civilian reconstruction experts would be to create a cadre of "on-call" civilians. These individuals would be experts in critical early response areas who could be immediately seconded to an interagency task force responsible for coordinating the U.S. government's reconstruction effort. Unlike a Disaster Assistance Response Team (DART), these individuals would work to ensure that both resources and capacities of their respective agencies are brought to bear immediately on the diverse needs of the crisis. The "on-call" list should also include former ambassadors and senior diplomats willing to be act as high-level civilian advisers to the military, international organizations, and host governments.

A second initiative that would help to mobilize the range of experts needed would be to expand DART-team membership to include more interagency partners. Specialists from the Commerce, Defense, Justice, and State departments should receive DART training and join USAID to actively assess interagency division of labor and cooperation. These individuals would also focus on scope, timing, and exit strategy for U.S. government military and civilian assets.

A third initiative is a long-overdue Peace Corps-based database of thousands of former and current volunteers with the appropriate language and cultural skills willing to be deployed on short notice. The database would also include information about the technical skills held by these individuals. While some progress has been made in bringing the Peace Corps community into the U.S. national security arena, current efforts have failed to truly integrate this valuable resource into either the planning process or on-the-ground operations.[6]

Funding

Funding complex operations on short notice is a major challenge. Currently, multiple funding accounts with overlapping authorities and requirements create obstacles for rapid disbursement.[7] A number of actions can and should be taken to speed an effective civilian response.

One option would be to create a mechanism so that during a crisis programmed funds in a regional account's foreign aid budget could be amended to allow for "notwithstanding" authority, thus freeing programmed assets into more fungible categories. Triggered by the declaration of a crisis by the president, this would provide the USAID administrator with greater flexibility for mobilizing resources. The U.S. Congress should work with the administration to ensure that adequate checks, such as a "waiver cap," are in place to prevent abuse.

A second option would be to allow easier transfer of non-International Disaster Assistance (IDA) funds into IDA program budgets. After a crisis declaration by the president, the secretary of state should have the authority to immediately transfer State/Economic Support Funds (ESF) and Defense/Overseas Humanitarian, Disaster and Civic Aid funds into emergency response programs to avoid drawing down scarce IDA resources.

Another concrete measure that could be taken to increase response times would be to raise the ambassador's Disaster Assistance Authority (DAA) to $100,000. The 1961 Foreign Assistance Act currently allows $25,000 to be made immediately available following a disaster declaration by the chief of mission or the regional assistant secretary of state. Although it is a relatively small amount, the DAA moves extremely quickly and signals to other donors and the local population the immediate engagement of the U.S. government.

A fourth measure to help speed response times would be to develop an inventory of Department of Defense support arrangements for civilian agencies that could be called on in times of crisis, including in the areas of training and planning. Where possible, memorandums of understanding should be pre-negotiated by the relevant agencies. Where not, procedure should be agreed on for shaping a decision for the president on short notice.

CONCLUSION

Effective civilian rapid response is at least partly a function of civil-military coordination. With the exception of USAID's Office of Foreign Disaster Assistance and, to a lesser extent, the Office of Transition Initiatives, there is little in the way of ensuring that the skills needed from civilians are readily available after conflict. Indeed, the high demand within the U.S. armed forces for experienced civil affairs officers attests to this gap in civilian response. As post-conflict reconstruction remains a central part of the U.S. military mission, it is essential that new doctrine be developed that embraces the importance of civilian capacity so that field commanders are able to plan for their own transitions from warfighting to peace building.

Current civilian response capacity also requires better collaboration with the United Nations in the field. In the absence of using the UN and other multilateral civilian support capacity, however, such as seen in Iraq, the U.S. government must evaluate its response capacities when such a gap exists.

Finally, if the United States pursues a doctrine of preemptive action, there must also be a concomitant set of skills and resources available to back up military success so that the short- and medium-term political development needs that exist after conflict receive the highest level of attention and resources.

Notes

[1] Condoleezza Rice, as cited in "The People's Justice in the Balkans," *Washington Times*, August 6, 2001.

[2] Civilian response depends on two factors: the state of security after conflict, and the resources available to civilian agencies.

[3] Reports by the International Commission on Intervention and State Sovereignty (*The Responsibility to Protect,* International Development Research Centre, Ottawa, December 2001), the Carnegie Commission on Preventing Deadly Conflict (*Preventing Deadly Conflict,* Carnegie Corporation, New York, December 1997), and the UN Secretary General (*Report of the Secretary General to the Security Council on the Protection of Civilians in Armed Conflict,* United Nations, S/2002/1300, November 26, 2002) all highlight this point.

[4] On specific proposals for interagency reforms, see, in this volume, chapter 7 by Flournoy on strategy and planning. On specific proposals for directors of reconstruction and creating coherent implementation capacity in the field, see chapter 4 by Orr on governance and participation.

[5] Our most recent experience in Iraq underscores the inadequate response in the U.S. government when it comes to identifying trained civilians for post-conflict positions on short notice.

[6] During the crisis in Rwanda in 1994 an effort by USAID to create a database for the returned Peace Corps volunteers never saw the light of day. Clearly, this need was identified almost a decade ago, but never acted on for various interagency bureaucratic reasons.

[7] For a complete analysis of current funding amounts and funding mechanisms for post-conflict reconstruction, see, in this volume, chapter 10 by Orr and Mendelson Forman on funding.

CHAPTER NINE

TRAINING AND EDUCATION FOR POST-CONFLICT RECONSTRUCTION

Michèle Flournoy

Training and education are critical to the success of post-conflict reconstruction operations in two very different ways. First, they can significantly enhance the performance of the outsiders providing assistance; and second, they can help develop indigenous human resources and capacity in areas central to enabling the society's transition to durable peace and stability.

TRAINING U.S. PERSONNEL FOR POST-CONFLICT RECONSTRUCTION

The training of U.S. government personnel to assist in post-conflict operations has been uneven at best. Some organizations—like the U.S. Agency for International Development's Office of Foreign Disaster Assistance (OFDA) and elements of the U.S. military—have developed excellent training programs for the personnel they send into the field. Others, however, routinely deploy people to reconstruction operations with little or no specialized training for the post-conflict environment. Even when U.S. personnel receive solid training in their particular task or skill area, they rarely have an opportunity to train with the representatives of the other U.S. agencies, nongovernmental organizations (NGOs), and international actors with whom they will have to work in the field. The same is true at the strategic or headquarters level.

This is true for several reasons. First, many U.S. agencies do not have a "training culture"—that is, training is not generally valued as a means of either improving performance or gaining advancement. Indeed, few agencies outside the Departments of Defense and State offer any routine opportunities for training and education beyond initial, entry-level indoctrination and job-specific skills training. The training culture that exists in the U.S. military is truly an exception; most civilian U.S. government agencies expect their personnel to acquire the skills they need on the job rather than giving priority to training them for anticipated requirements. This raises the question of how to create the necessary incentives and accountability to ensure that the right people get the training they need to be successful in their assigned responsibilities in managing or executing post-conflict reconstruction operations.

A second reason is a lack of consensus on what the substance of training for post-conflict reconstruction operations should be. For example, whereas the Clinton administration's Presidential Decision Directive (PDD)-56 on Managing Complex Contingency Operations defined an interagency process that could be used as the basis for an interagency training program aimed at policymakers and their staffs in Washington, the Bush administration's reluctance to sign and issue National Security Policy Directive (NSPD) XX and a follow-on NSPD on post-conflict reconstruction left existing interagency training programs without a clear conceptual foundation upon which to build a curriculum, even as Operation Iraqi Freedom got under way.

Finally, there is little agreement on the question of who should receive training when. One approach is to train as many people as possible as part of routine professional development. For example, the State Department could include a course on post-conflict reconstruction issues and lessons learned in the curriculum for foreign service officers at the National Foreign Affairs Training Center, and the Defense Department could incorporate post-conflict reconstruction issues into its professional military education programs. Integrating post-conflict reconstruction into the professional development courses of all the relevant agencies is certainly necessary to build an appreciation for its complexities. Still, this foundation is unlikely to be sufficient to ensure that the right people get trained in the right skills at the right time.

Another approach is to provide targeted, in-depth training for smaller cadres of key personnel at both headquarters and field levels. Indeed, this concept animated the PDD-56 effort to train a cadre of interagency political-military planners who could be drawn on in the earliest stages of preparing for a complex contingency in which the United States might intervene. It has also been used by, among others, OFDA to develop a pool of qualified people prepared to serve as Disaster Assistance

Response Team (DART) leaders, by the U.S. military to develop Joint Task Force (JTF) staffs, and by the Federal Emergency Management Agency (FEMA) to develop a cadre of crisis managers prepared to serve as interagency coordinators for response to domestic disasters. Such an approach could conceivably be used to develop a cadre of professionals qualified to serve as "directors of reconstruction" and on their staffs, as previously recommended.[1]

In addition, a third axis is required to complement general "professional development courses" and more in-depth training for those who are likely leaders and participants in post-conflict reconstruction efforts. Pre-deployment training for those who are tapped to take part in a specific operation is an absolute necessity. Competent execution on the ground will maximize the effects of good planning and strategy (and may even be able to salvage a poor plan). Incompetent execution can cause even the best plans and international programs to fail. While practitioners have sometimes argued that once a crisis arises, the people involved in orchestrating and executing the response simply do not have time for training, the U.S. military and USAID have routinely provided intensive, scenario-specific training to their personnel prior to deploying them to an actual operation, with substantial positive impact on their performance. In truth, some combination of all three of these approaches is warranted.

Priority Shortfalls to be Addressed

Given the complexity of post-conflict operations—and the fact that the United States should focus on its areas of comparative advantage—efforts to improve training for U.S. personnel participating in these operations should be targeted at areas that are most critical to the success of an operation; those in which U.S. personnel are likely to play lead or important roles; and those in which current training programs are inadequate or nonexistent. Based on these criteria, efforts to improve training and education for U.S. personnel involved in post-conflict reconstruction should focus on the following areas.

Interagency assessment of post-conflict reconstruction needs for a given operation. Understanding the situation on the ground, the history of the conflict, the indigenous and international actors on the ground and their respective objectives and capacities, the particular challenges likely to be encountered, and numerous other factors is critical to developing effective strategies for reconstruction. Yet, too often, the personnel conducting the assessments on which key policy decisions and operational plans will be made have not been given the training they need to even ask the right questions in a post-conflict environment, let alone answer them. Training personnel for this critical task should be given a high priority.

Interagency strategy development and planning at the headquarters level. As the last decade of experience has demonstrated, an interagency process for developing an integrated strategy and plan for U.S. assistance in a post-conflict operation is critical to unity of effort and, ultimately, achieving successful outcomes. Yet there is no guarantee that such a process will take place unless it is led by the National Security Council staff and there is a common approach (such as that identified in PDD-56 or NSPD XX) that the key participants are prepared to undertake.[2]

Interagency coordination in the field. Nearly every "lessons learned" report from nearly every post-conflict operation of the last decade has flagged interagency coordination in the field as at best an area in need of some improvement, and at worst a profound problem. And, too often, the interagency coordination wheel has been reinvented with each new operation. Building on best practices from past operations, training in this area could substantially enhance unity of effort and overall performance on the ground.

Integrated approaches to justice and reconciliation. To be successful, meeting emergency justice needs and helping to rebuild indigenous justice and reconciliation mechanisms in countries emerging from conflict requires a comprehensive approach that integrates legal, judicial, police, corrections, human rights, and reconciliation elements. At present, no training exists to help U.S. personnel involved in these aspects of post-conflict reconstruction to design or implement such an approach.[3]

Anticorruption measures. In operation after operation, U.S. and international efforts to help jump-start economic activity, rebuild indigenous institutions and capacity, and reestablish the rule of law have been undermined by the corruption that is often rampant in post-conflict societies. This was certainly the case in operations ranging from Haiti to Bosnia and more recently proved true in the Afghan countryside. Training U.S. personnel in the design, implementation, and monitoring of anticorruption measures could have a meaningful impact on the degree of success in future operations and the time required to achieve it.

TRAINING INDIGENOUS PERSONNEL TO BUILD LOCAL CAPACITY

Training and education programs for indigenous organizations and individuals can be a vital form of assistance in helping a post-conflict society transition to sustainable peace. The primary objectives of such programs are to develop the human resources and build the institutional capacities of the host country. Such efforts are essential in all four pillars of post-conflict reconstruction: security; governance and participation; social and economic well-being; and justice and reconciliation. While the United States and the international community have developed significant programs in areas such as training indigenous military and police forces, there are a number of critical areas in which effective training and education programs are sorely lacking.

In developing and implementing such training and education programs, the United States and the international community face several challenges. The first is determining the content of the training—what should be taught. In many post-conflict reconstruction task areas there is little consensus on what is necessary to support the successful development of a society. The second challenge is ensuring that any knowledge imported from the outside is adequately adapted or tailored to specific, local conditions. The substance of the training needs to be rooted in local norms and culture if it is to be sustainable over time. For example, the use of the *loya jirga* in Afghanistan is a compelling example of drawing on a society's traditions in support of a post-conflict objective, like establishing an enduring democracy.

Another challenge is ensuring that programs have the scope and duration necessary to have lasting impact. Programs must reach not only the right people (vetted, in key positions, etc.), but also adequate numbers in a given area if they are to create the critical mass of capacity necessary to create lasting change. In this regard, "training the trainers" and establishing indigenous training institutions (such as police, military, and civil service academies) can be very effective "force multipliers" for the international community. Doing so can significantly magnify the impact of the initial training program and create a capacity for continuing the development of the society's human capital long after the period of extraordinary international intervention ends. Programs must also consider the longer-term needs of those who receive training, and how to remain engaged with them over time.[4]

Finally, there is the perennial challenge of translating theory into practice—of helping new ways of doing business to take root and grow in often-inhospitable environments. This challenge highlights the importance of treating training and education as a process, not a one-time experience, and of supplementing such programs with ongoing opportunities for mentoring and "on–the-job" training to sustain progress.

Priority Shortfalls to be Addressed

The list of areas in which the United States could conceivably provide training and education assistance to post-conflict societies is virtually endless—and prohibitively costly. Priorities for U.S. training and education assistance should be identified based on three criteria: (1) the relative importance of a given task area to the success of the society's transition from conflict to sustainable peace; (2) the existing capability of existing programs offered by the United States or others in the international community; and (3) the comparative advantage of the United States vis-à-vis other international actors in terms of expertise, access, resources, or training programs in the task area.

Based on these criteria, several post-conflict reconstruction areas stand out as possible areas of focus for the United States.

Development of indigenous militaries and civilian mechanisms of democratic control. Establishing civilian control of the military is one of the key metrics of success in the development of a post-conflict society. As demonstrated in several recent post-conflict reconstruction operations (and a number of developing countries), the U.S. military has substantial expertise in assisting with the development of indigenous military forces under civilian control. Equally important, but less well established, are civilian-run programs to develop a cadre of host-country civilians capable of providing appropriate oversight of and direction to military forces. Given its history, expertise, resources, and cadre of experienced civilian defense officials, the United States is uniquely positioned to address this shortfall.

Development of indigenous police forces and civilian mechanisms of democratic control. Similarly, establishing competent police forces that are responsive to civilian authorities and respectful of human rights is another key measure of successful reconstruction. And here again, the United States has well-established expertise: for example, ICITAP—the International Criminal Investigative Training Assistance Program under the Department of Justice—is currently managing programs in 18 countries as well as a regional program in the Newly Independent States (NIS). Yet these programs have been both consistently underfunded by both administrations and Congress and somewhat constrained by the nature of the mechanisms used to fund them.

Training of legal, judicial, corrections, and human rights personnel. Too often in the past, international assistance efforts have focused on training indigenous police forces without adequate regard for developing the broader justice system in which they must operate. Establishing (or reestablishing) a fair, impartial, and transparent system of justice is one of the most critical tasks of reconstruction. This requires a comprehensive approach that touches all aspects of the justice system, from lawyers to judges to corrections officials to human rights monitors. As yet, however, no integrated approach to training indigenous personnel for this broad range of tasks has been developed.

Training and mentoring of local entrepreneurs. Creating economic vitality and growth in post-conflict economies is one of the greatest and most important reconstruction challenges. And, in most cases, local entrepreneurs are the real engines of economic change. While many governments and NGOs have launched successful programs in this area, few have the capacity to create lasting change on a national scale. Given the size, experience, and diversity of the U.S. entrepreneurial base, the United States has a great deal to offer in providing technical assistance to local businesses.

Training of civil servants and administrators. Creating the capacity for good governance in a post-conflict society requires developing a cadre of people with the skills, experience, and incentives to administer a broad array of government programs—from education to health programs to public works—with integrity, effectiveness, and efficiency. Yet progress in many cases has foundered on precisely this issue. In Afghanistan, for example, everyone has recognized the importance of building a central government, but the entire project is stalled—not only by political wrangling between the central government and the warlords, but even more importantly by the fact that there is no capacity whatsoever to train competent civil servants and administrators. Even in more successful cases like East Timor and Kosovo, the inability to train and field competent administrators has slowed progress significantly. The international community could do much more to strengthen its assistance in this area, and the United States is well positioned to contribute.

Design and implementation of anticorruption programs. Corruption often runs rampant in post-conflict societies, and rooting it out must be a top priority of any reconstruction effort. To date, however, international assistance efforts in this arena have been ad hoc in nature, and often too little too late. As a country with a strong anticorruption culture and well-established anticorruption measures in every sector of society and at every level of government, the United States is uniquely positioned to help design and implement anticorruption programs as part of its post-conflict assistance efforts.

AN ACTIONABLE AGENDA FOR THE U.S. GOVERNMENT

Providing better training and education to the U.S. personnel who participate in the planning and execution of post-conflict operations—both at the headquarters level and in the field—is critical to improving performance in future operations. Based on the analysis above, the United States should implement a package of recommendations.

First, the president, working with Congress, should establish a U.S. Training Center for Post-Conflict Reconstruction Operations. The U.S. Training Center would have five key missions:

- training key interagency personnel in assessment, strategy development, planning, and coordination for post-conflict reconstruction;
- developing and certifying a cadre of post-conflict reconstruction experts who could be called to participate in future operations at both the headquarters and field levels;
- providing pre-deployment training to interagency personnel tapped for specific operations;
- developing a cadre of rapidly deployable training packages for use in the field; and
- conducting "after action" reviews of real-world operations to capture lessons learned, best practices, and tools and designing mechanisms to feed them back into training and education programs.

This center would need to provide training for both civilian and military personnel, and would need to work closely with existing training entities in the Department of Defense and other U.S. government agencies to promote maximum "jointness."

Second, the U.S. government should make interagency training for strategy development and planning a de facto requirement for all key participants in the process. The national security adviser, working with his or her counterparts in the cabinet, should emphasize the importance of such training by articulating an expectation that everyone involved in U.S. post-conflict reconstruction operations, from the deputies on down, will receive the appropriate training, and should then work with his or her counterparts in the cabinet to ensure that such training actually takes place. Specifically, the National Defense University should be tasked with creating, under the sponsorship of the National Security Council, a short exercise for deputies, a slightly longer exercise for assistant secretaries and others serving on relevant Policy Coordination Committees, and a more in-depth exercise for the deputy assistant secretaries, office directors, and staff who support them. Whenever possible, such training should also include key U.S. representatives from the field (such as the relevant combatant or JTF commander, ambassador, deputy chief of mission, head of USAID mission). This training should be offered frequently enough to accommodate personnel changes and to keep the participants current.

Third, the U.S. government should develop new simulation tools for use in interagency training programs. The more realistic a training experience, the more powerful it tends to be. Simulations offer a way of replicating real-world conditions and experiences outside an operational environment. They can also enable policymakers to explore the impacts of alternative courses of action before making real-world decisions. Yet the U.S. government currently lacks simulation tools that accurately portray the full range of post-conflict reconstruction challenges with which U.S. decisionmakers must grapple.[5] Developing such tools should be explored on a priority basis. These simulation tools should be capable of serving not only as generic training devices, but also as mission rehearsal tools that can be rapidly tailored to reflect specific situations.

Fourth, the U.S. government must better integrate post-conflict reconstruction issues into regularly scheduled U.S. government training and education courses. This should include, but not be limited to, courses offered at the National Defense University, the service war colleges, the Naval Post-Graduate School, and other institutions offering professional military education, as well as the National Foreign Affairs Training Center and other relevant U.S. training and education centers. The U.S. government should also seek ways of promoting teaching on post-conflict reconstruction in graduate programs in American universities.

Fifth, all new and existing U.S. training programs should expand the participation of NGO, international organization, and other international personnel in U.S. training programs for post-conflict reconstruction at all levels. U.S. efforts to assist post-conflict reconstruction always take place in an environment that requires working with a wide range of non-U.S. government actors. U.S. personnel are greatly disadvantaged if they do not understand how organizations such as the United Nations, NGOs, regional organizations, and others operate. Including representatives of these organizations in training programs is essential. The U.S. government should also look for opportunities to send its personnel to UN and other international training programs that include the full range of actors likely to be involved in post-conflict operations.

Sixth, the U.S. government should make interagency training in post-conflict reconstruction a de facto requirement for U.S. personnel assigned to key field positions. Given the importance of interagency unity of effort in achieving success in post-conflict reconstruction operations, advanced training in interagency operations should be treated as a required qualification for any U.S. official assigned to a key operational position, such as U.S. special envoy or "director of reconstruction," U.S. ambassador, Joint Task Force commander, or head of a USAID mission. Making appropriate interagency training a de facto requirement for such positions would almost certainly provide a very real incentive for more mid-level and senior officials to get such training over the course of their careers.

Seventh, the U.S. government must invest in training a cadre of personnel who are qualified to serve as directors of reconstruction as well as members of their staff. Building on the demonstrated successes of the OFDA and FEMA models, this would involve developing a roster of senior and mid-level civilians who would be qualified and trained to serve in such positions in future operations as well as a clear career path in post-conflict reconstruction.

Eighth, the U.S. government must enhance specialized training programs in the key areas of justice and reconciliation and anticorruption measures. The Department of Justice, with support from the Defense and State Departments, should be tasked with establishing a program for training U.S. personnel in integrated approaches to justice and reconciliation in post-conflict environments. Similarly, the Department of Treasury, with support from the State Department, should be tasked to develop and implement a training program on anticorruption measures.

In addition, the United States should enhance its ability to provide training for indigenous personnel in post-conflict societies in critical areas. To do so, the U.S. government should take a number of actions. First, it should design and develop rapidly deployable training assistance programs for post-conflict societies in each of the following key areas: civilian control of the military; training of legal, judicial, corrections, and human rights personnel; training of local entrepreneurs; training of civil servants and administrators; and anticorruption measures.

Second, the U.S. government could identify and train cadres of on-call U.S. experts in each of the above areas. This would involve developing databases of U.S. experts who are qualified and potentially available to deploy within weeks to post-conflict operations.

Third, the U.S. government should enhance indigenous capacity through increasing the funding available for training of police forces in post-conflict societies. Specifically, ICITAP funding for this purpose could and should be increased.

Fourth and finally, the U.S. government should examine the need for increasing funding available for longer-term educational assistance in post-conflict societies. This is imperative for sustainable development and the transition to sustainable peace.

CONCLUSION

Imagine a future in which U.S. involvement in post-conflict reconstruction operations was planned by personnel highly trained in assessment, strategy development, planning, and coordination of such operations and deeply knowledgeable about lessons learned from experience. Imagine that the execution of an interagency plan was then led by a team of people whose skills had been honed by years of training for and gaining experience in the conduct of post-conflict operations. And imagine the United States had, at the ready, rapidly deployable teams of trainers ready to help a post-conflict society rebuild in critical areas like the rule of law and civil administration. In such a future, the United States' ability to achieve its objectives in post-conflict operations in less time and at less cost would be radically increased. As the above recommendations suggest, such a future is within our grasp. All that is needed is the political will to implement them.

Notes

[1] See, in this volume, chapter 4 by Orr, "Governing When Chaos Rules: Enhancing Governance and Participation."

[2] The recommendation that such a common approach and template be established is made in chapter 7, "Interagency Strategy and Planning for Post-Conflict Reconstruction," by Flournoy.

[3] For more on the requirements of an integrated approach to justice and reconciliation in post-conflict operations, see, in this volume, chapter 6 by Flournoy and Pan, "Dealing with Demons: Enhancing Justice and Reconciliation."

[4] It is estimated that the U.S. government has trained more than 700,000 foreign personnel in government programs over the last 10–12 years, but the government has no comprehensive system for tracking "alumni," ensuring that their skills are put to good use, and developing their potential through further training. (Info Operations in Peacekeeping, CJCS [Chairman, Joint Chiefs of Staff] Conference at the U.S. Army War College, May 2002.)

[5] Perhaps the most well-developed simulation tool to date is SENSE (Synthetic Environments for National Security Estimates), an interactive computer-based program that provides a virtual decisionmaking environment for some aspects of post-conflict reconstruction training. At this point in its development, however, SENSE is primarily an economics-based program, teaching responsible financial management and basic free-market economics as means to rebuilding a collapsed economy. The current version of SENSE does not adequately treat the crucial security, justice, and governance aspects of post-conflict reconstruction. To be made more effective for post-conflict reconstruction training, the simulated environment would need to be refined to introduce realistic variables such as re-emerging conflict, security threats, public health issues, arrests and trials, elections, civic unrest, infrastructure and institutional capacity weakness, warlords, donor fatigue, and other unpredictable forces that complicate reconstruction. If these indicators could be linked to one another—e.g., a rise in unemployment causes civic unrest and requires increased security—then participants would better appreciate the need for interagency and cross-sector collaboration.

CHAPTER TEN

FUNDING POST-CONFLICT RECONSTRUCTION

Robert C. Orr and Johanna Mendelson Forman

In the wake of the attacks on the United States on September 11, 2001, the Bush administration, and indeed the American people, has recognized the need to adequately support a broad range of international programs to address the threatening new environment Americans face. As the president himself has said,

> We have a great opportunity to extend a just peace, by replacing poverty, repression, and resentment around the world with hope of a better day....In our development aid, in our diplomatic efforts, in our international broadcasting, and in our educational assistance, the United States will promote moderation and tolerance and human rights. And we will defend the peace that makes all progress possible.[1]

Delivering on this inclusive vision costs money. And as Secretary of State Colin Powell has noted, "We cannot do any of this—we cannot conduct an effective foreign policy or fight terrorism—without the necessary resources."[2]

And yet even though the public constituency in support of increasing foreign aid is high,[3] the challenge is not only, or even principally, a question of increasing resources to foreign affairs budgets. It is also about *how* we fund foreign affairs. This question of "how" was recognized to be a problem well before 9/11.[4] Foreign assistance monies are authorized in the Foreign Assistance Act of 1961 (FAA), a law that has been amended multiple times and is encumbered by its origination as tool of foreign policy within the Cold War paradigm. Since the Cold War has passed, sitting administrations have failed to provide the bureaucracy with a coherent, rationalized, and actionable strategy for use of foreign aid.

Funding post-conflict reconstruction is particularly problematic, from both military and civilian perspectives, because it involves security, development, political, and humanitarian activities, all of which are normally funded out of different accounts.

Both the previous Bush and Clinton administrations, to varying degrees, attempted to substantially rework foreign assistance legislation, but they met with little success.[5] This is hardly surprising considering the lack of trust between the executive branch and Congress on foreign aid matters. [6] President George W. Bush has also begun the process of reevaluating and retooling the foreign affairs funding machinery, this time by proposing an important initiative with respect to development funding. In March 2002, the president proposed the creation of a Millennium Challenge Account that would increase U.S. core development assistance by 50 percent over three years, resulting in a $5 billion annual increase over 2002 levels.[7] In announcing this fund, President Bush noted that "persistent poverty and oppression can lead to hopelessness and despair. And when governments fail to meet the most basic needs of their people, these failed states can become havens for terror." [8]

While the proposal for a Millennium Challenge Account is a promising development—one that could help introduce an important element of competition into development assistance if it is passed by Congress[9]—it is unlikely to affect the countries that are most likely to spawn or provide safe haven for terrorism. Indeed, the failed states cited by the president, and weak states emerging from conflict, do represent an opportunity for terrorists who thrive in the cracks of the international system. The problem is that these same weak and failed states emerging from war have myriad problems and little or no institutional capacity that might enable them to meet the prerequisite benchmark criteria for receiving funding.[10] These countries, the ones that have the most potential to threaten U.S. interests by creating vacuums that will be exploited by terrorists, suffer from a range of conditions and face an array of needs that will make competing for Millennium Challenge Account funds almost impossible.

Because the Millennium Challenge Account is unlikely to have a significant impact on U.S. capacity to effectively support countries emerging from conflict, we should therefore examine other funds and funding mechanisms currently at our disposal for addressing post-conflict reconstruction needs.

THE CURRENT CHALLENGES OF FUNDING POST-CONFLICT RECONSTRUCTION

Five major challenges stand out to be addressed if the U.S. government is to improve its ability to successfully fund post-conflict operations: coherence; speed; relative volume of resources; flexibility; and contracting and procurement mechanisms.

Coherence

To have even the beginnings of coherence of effort in any undertaking, one needs a vision of an end goal or product, an understanding of the tools available and necessary to reach that goal, and unity of effort (i.e., coordination) to move toward that goal. These steps are especially difficult to accomplish in the area of post-conflict reconstruction due to the wide range and complexity of tasks involved even under the best of circumstances.[11] U.S. efforts are disabled from the start because of an incoherent mass of funding mechanisms, resulting from a lack of trust between Congress and the executive branch and from the lack of a modern, articulated vision of foreign assistance that directs the relevant departments. The incoherence is seen in the implementation of the budgeting and appropriations process as well as in the budget structure itself.

Foreign affairs are principally financed through four different congressional bills, each of which has to undergo a lengthy and complex budgeting and appropriations process.[12] The essential problem of the process, however, is not its bureaucratic complexity, but instead that it is not favorable to long-term planning. A comprehensive approach to post-conflict reconstruction, aimed to produce sustainable results, must have a multiyear program commitment. Yet annual funding appropriations limit use of monies in most accounts to a single year with few guarantees for future funding. There is neither a secure time horizon in which to plan and operate nor freedom to expend funds in a situation-appropriate time frame. There is a crucial need for longer-term funding mechanisms that allow for dynamic field operations.

A further result of the limits of annual appropriations is that funds may run out by the end of the fiscal year and not be compensated for in supplemental appropriations. For example, crises occurring within the first quarter of the fiscal year are the least well-timed for action funded under the Overseas Humanitarian, Disaster, and Civic Aid fund, the Department of Defense's primary post-conflict noncombat account, because funds from the previous fiscal year will have expired and new funds may not yet be appropriated or disbursed. In contrast, most Department of Defense funds are used for increasing military readiness, an activity well suited to a long planning lead time fitting with the budget cycle. Reliance by the Defense and State departments and USAID on supplemental appropriations for unexpected operations actually exaggerates the budget cycle problem because supplementals generally focus on one-off, short-term needs yet have relatively slow disbursement. For example, in the case of Iraq, the $18.4 billion supplemental of 2003 had disbursed only $2.3 billion by April 2004.[13] Moreover, supplemental appropriations are not easy to attain for smaller-scale contingencies that have not been provided for in the regular budget.

The principal problem of the U.S. budget structure is the division of monies among so many accounts. This is true between military and civilian agencies, both of which are usually needed in post-conflict countries, as well as within agencies. The division often creates gaps in the capacity to respond and in the quality of programming that can be offered to societies in desperate need. A lack of retooling foreign aid mechanisms and anemic funding levels in several accounts translate into lack of coordination, resulting in less cohesive and effective efforts.

Civilian post-conflict reconstruction operations, for example, are funded out of a wide range of authorities, including many within the patchwork of the FAA as amended many times over the years. This patchwork has led to fiefdoms within agencies and within Congress, which impede coherent funding for complex operations. The wide range of authorities also means that funding decisions and oversight are managed by a wide range of congressional committees and subcommittees, not all of whom agree on the specifics of a given mission.

Further, interagency strategy and planning for post-conflict reconstruction operations is done in an ad hoc manner, making it hard for Congress and the various agencies involved in the funding process to anticipate what might be called for generally or in a given operation.[14] This, and the large number of executive branch agencies involved, leads to bureaucratic politics that impede a rational funding process. In lieu of rationalized, coherent direction from the top, the various parts of each agency are left to pursue their own funding objectives and processes. The problem extends to the armed services, which experience intense infighting over operations that are funded by more than one service.

Finally, within agencies, the State Department and USAID budgets have not adapted as effectively or quickly for complex contingencies as that of the Defense Department. By the early 1990s, for example, DOD had included resources for a variety of operations in all theatres of engagement that it called "military operations other than war," whereas major changes to State and USAID were either limited geographically to the former communist and newly independent states or were very small-scale, as with the Office of Transition Initiatives at USAID. At each level of decisionmaking, therefore, U.S. efforts are fragmented by the very legal and regulatory structures that are supposed to facilitate a concerted government response in the national interest. This initially incoherent foundation for action, in both the budgeting process and structure, produces a wave of fragmentation within the entire U.S. system of funding post-conflict reconstruction.

Speed

Whereas the U.S. military may draw upon pre-deployed resources while waiting for additional emergency funding, U.S. civilian agencies generally have little ability to fund foreign crisis operations in a timely manner. The slow speed with which the U.S. government can act in the critical window of opportunity after the end of conflict is one of the greatest challenges facing post-conflict reconstruction today, second only to lack of coherence. In part, this is because foreign assistance was not setup to respond to contingencies, with narrowly tailored rapid response mechanisms only evolving in certain areas over time.[15] As a result, the U.S. government is able to use some accounts on short notice, but relies on a usually slow supplemental appropriations process to make possible actions under the authority of the other accounts. The net result is that the United States is not able to bring its full range of capabilities to bear at the same time in any given situation.

The FAA presents problems for speed of response just as it does for coherence. As it has evolved over 41 years, the FAA is a sprawling web of authorities with many competing priorities and restrictions. A general lack of trust between the executive and legislative branches has led to the imposition of a wide range of cumbersome constraints and notification requirements. Every expenditure from the Economic Support Fund, for example, must be approved at the deputy secretary of state level or above.[16] These constraints can be addressed, but only with a lot of time and energy. The reliance on supplemental appropriations also slows the response time, especially when the appropriations are loaded with notification requirements and an expiration date.[17]

Finally, bureaucratic problems also slow the movement of funds. Tussles between and within departments over who should fund what often makes timely funding impossible. Even for less contentious projects, the State Department funding process has become so snarled that every expenditure of funds from three key accounts—Economic Support Fund (ESF), Foreign Military Financing (FMF), and Peacekeeping Operations (PKO)—is given a separate congressional notification, resulting in a slow and inconsistent process of project approval. Moreover, once legal and bureaucratic agreement has been established within Washington, speed of disbursal to the field and use of the monies in the field are often slow as well.[18]

Funding Balance

While the overall volume of funding for foreign affairs in general is a significant issue,[19] perhaps one of the most difficult problems is not the absolute shortage of funds, but rather the *relative* shortage of funds in certain agencies and parts of agencies. Post-conflict reconstruction operations include both military and civilian activities; however, funding for the military side of reconstruction does not have parallel funding from the foreign assistance accounts.

The disparity between budgets is particularly acute in post-conflict operations because there is significant overlap between tasks and a blurred distinction between relief and development as operations progress over time. Indeed, because the State Department and USAID have such small pots of money to address the issues for which their funds are authorized, often far less than immediate needs require, they often seek to involve the Defense Department in operations so that its significantly larger budget might be brought into play.[20] Unfortunately, this often leads to using, and overusing, certain funding options, such as equipment drawdowns and compelling the military to undertake operations best suited to civilian agencies. Rising tensions resulting from the asymmetry in budgets makes for neither effective, unified reconstruction efforts in the field nor a positive environment for cooperation in Washington.

Funding balance within agencies is problematic as well. Politically popular accounts receive much more money than less popular accounts. There is ample support for humanitarian assistance, but much smaller amounts available for transition and development programs. For example, USAID's Office of Transition Initiatives, which is charged to bring countries from war to sustainable peace, received only $50 million in fiscal year 2002, compared to the International Disaster Assistance fund's $236 million. Development assistance to support governance, rule of law, and anticorruption efforts pale in comparison with some of the special programs that different constituencies want funded through the foreign assistance appropriation. For example, Congress has basically turned much of USAID into a health agency through the child survival funds.[21] Even with the increased demand to work on post-conflict matters, without supplemental funding there is little room for diverting resources to different parts of the agency in the event of a major reconstruction effort.

Flexibility

A chief complaint of many implementers of foreign assistance is the lack of flexibility in funding mechanisms. A general and continuing breakdown of trust between Congress and the executive branch, largely a result of U.S. involvement in Vietnam and Central America, has led to an inflexible, uncoordinated raft of legal restrictions, earmarks, and directives.[22] What were legitimate concerns decades ago are now serious impediments to broadly accepted needs. Section 660 of the FAA, for example, prohibits FAA funds from being used to train, advise, and financially support foreign law enforcement forces even though there is a clear need to do so to secure most post-conflict settings.[23] At the same time, however, the Defense Department has been able support the training and deployment of civilian police. The decline in the amount of earmarks imposed on the State Department and USAID since Colin Powell became secretary of state has been more than offset by a rise in restrictions formally written into appropriations laws and by directives informally mandated (or "suggested") in official and unofficial reporting by Congress. In fiscal year 2001–2002 alone, USAID operated with 274 restrictions, directives, and earmarks reported out of the appropriations process, resulting in a staggering lack of flexibility that left a small fraction—some estimate well below 7 percent—of the roughly $7 billion managed by that agency annually available for discretionary use.

The Defense Department is known to have the most flexibility of any U.S. government agency, but even it suffers from major constraints. The main inflexibility is that most DOD monies are intended for increasing military readiness, not for foreign aid. Supplemental appropriations offer greater flexibility than regular appropriations because they are usually so large, but they are not provided for small-scale contingencies, such as East Timor, and take too long in reaching military theaters. The Defense Emergency Response Fund has been pared down from a contingency fund that allowed for proactive and immediate response in post-conflict settings into residual mission money that is used reactively to offset costs of named operations. This change has damaged the "go-to" edge of the U.S. military by reducing its flexibility in action.

Finally, a certain level of inflexibility is due to self-imposed limitations coming from an overly cautious bureaucratic culture. Strict statutory interpretations within each agency, particularly USAID, both protect pots of money and help avoid congressional scrutiny of more "risky" programs. For example, the International Disaster account statute allows for "relief, rehabilitation, and reconstruction," but activities have tended to stay closer to the more politically accepted meeting of basic humanitarian needs rather than forming a basis for a transition to sustainable development in post-conflict societies. [24] A recent example concerns Nigeria, where use of International Disaster account funds to support the promotion of democratic policing after the fall of the authoritarian regime was denied because Nigeria was not considered "post-conflict," but rather in a state of transition. This problem is not limited to USAID, however. Like so many of the funding problems discussed in this chapter, these self-imposed limitations are somewhat understandable, but ultimately just add one more layer to an already inflexible system. Lost opportunity can lay the foundation for potential trouble in not addressing a critical need in a country's democratic development trajectory.

Substantial political will on the part of the executive branch and Congress can overcome the inflexibility of today's funding authority machinery, but the will is usually lacking for post-conflict states. The primary and easiest way to get needed flexibility for foreign assistance monies, therefore, is through "notwithstanding authority," or other special authorities, which authorize the use of foreign assistance monies for activities otherwise prohibited by law.[25] Understandably, this authority is generally granted only to narrowly defined accounts with finite needs (e.g. Emergency Refugee and Migration Assistance) or to politically popular accounts (e.g., Support for East European Democracy). Even where it is available, practical use of notwithstanding authorities within specific accounts can be limited by reluctance to use this authority for certain geographic areas or in activities or programs that are known to be politically unpopular. The president also has extraordinary notwithstanding authority under section 614 of the FAA, although it is not broadly effective due to its dependence on political will, the often slow pace of the attendant bureaucratic processes, and the annual limit on overall funds that can be provided in any given fiscal year pursuant to section 614.[26]

Contracting and Procurement

If speed and flexibility are essential elements for delivering resources to societies in transition, a major roadblock remains in the contracting and procurement problems that plague the U.S. government. Although the Department of State has some issues in moving money quickly, the amount of money moving out the door is much smaller than that of USAID or DOD and the number of transactions are far fewer. Most of the State Department's contracting and procurement problems actually arise in reconciling its statute interpretation with that of the other agencies. For example, the State Department may transfer money to DOD for procurement of equipment under the Foreign Military Financing program. DOD often adds the equipment onto existing contracts, the fulfillment of which is first allocated to DOD, or undergoes its normal, lengthy competitive bidding process, which the State Department asserts is unnecessary under the terms of the FAA. Interpretive reconciliation between the agencies is needed. Although the it has some bottlenecks in its own contracting system, the Defense Department also has quick deployment mechanisms for fielding contracting officers that temper its problems. USAID, on the other hand, suffers from severe difficulties.

USAID's role in foreign assistance is essentially that of a bank from which most foreign assistance resources flow into the private sector and then into the field. Over the last decade, each new USAID administrator vows to overhaul the system and, unfortunately, each leaves frustrated in his failure to accomplish this basic reform. The urgency of remedying the contracting bottleneck is apparent, as there are thousands of transactions per year, often moving only small amounts of money. In total, however, in 2002 USAID contracted $1.9 billion out of Washington and an equal amount in the field. This is significant, given that the total USAID budget is just over $5 billion.

Three central problems plague USAID's contracting system. First, it has only 126 bonded contract officers to process on average over 2,000 transactions per year. This is in part because of the lack of career incentives for contracting officers, which creates a continuous personnel turnover, and it is complicated by USAID's use of individuals from other federal agencies who are not knowledgeable about the needs of a development or emergency environment. The principal factor, however, is an overly restrictive procurement program that keeps small contracts bound in Washington. This can slow the contract process by days if not months.

Second, outdated information technology plagues efficient contracting within USAID. Today USAID relies on two separate software systems, the NMS (New Management System) and Phoenix. Lack of integration between the two deprives the field missions and Congress of a full picture of spending. Moreover, the accounting system and the procurement system are separate entities, creating impossible situations for tracking money. "[USAID's] accounting systems do not produce reliable and timely information," notes a 2002 report of the House Appropriations Committee, which further states, "The Committee finds it distressing that the agency does not possess a system that allows agency managers to track procurement activity worldwide to monitor the efficiency, fairness or competitiveness, and consistency with objectives across countries and regions."[27] The situation is so dismal that the Office of Foreign Disaster Assistance uses a private contractor to help it move its emergency money through the system.

Third, use of larger contracting vehicles, known as Indefinite Quantity Contracts, may make moving large sums of money easier, but it also tends to limit the choices that field missions have to obtain technical assistance. A few companies have a hold on providing technical support to the field, so that choosing the best possible types of services is often compromised by the need for speed. For many years, different offices at USAID have developed several ad hoc mechanisms to move resources from their bank accounts to the neediest populations, finding ways around the plodding Office of Procurement machinery. But such a system, without any standardization, does not solve the larger problem of a broken procurement system. What is truly needed is an overhaul of the procurement system, the essence of which should allow mission directors to authorize small contracts, leaving Washington to handle major contracts.

Finally, and perhaps most important, while the contracting and procurement systems are inherently technical, their regulation must tie into a larger vision of foreign aid. A key missing element of U.S. assistance is the ability to deliberately plan and link the emergency humanitarian phase of aid with longer-term assistance. This is evident in U.S.

emergency agencies' inability to contract for quick impact programs (QUIPS) for longer than nine months, lest they become full-blown development projects. The planning for war-to-peace transition requires a longer time line. Without a medium- to long-range view up front, the emergency assistance provided by the United States to the international NGOs in the field will be incapable of giving hope to or sustaining the needs of the most vulnerable after war.

THE WAY AHEAD

After 9/11, President Bush, with great support from Congress and the American public, repeatedly made a strong case for increasing foreign assistance as a tool for securing a safe world. Yet this call was not matched by adequate funding authority recommendations. The problems facing the funding of post-conflict reconstruction are complex. The solutions, however, are quite straightforward. We recommend an approach that would expand and integrate post-conflict funding vehicles and also address the mechanics of the funding process that require immediate remediation. For these recommendations to be successful, however, the administration and Congress must articulate a clearly defined vision of post-conflict reconstruction. This vision for rebuilding countries must include a comprehensive approach that integrates security with political and economic development, with an eye to preventing further conflict.

Establishing an Account for Post-Conflict Reconstruction

First and foremost, when the president decides that a mission is in the interests of the United States, he must have the ability to bring the full force of wide-ranging U.S. capabilities to bear on the situation in a timely manner, while at the same time enabling U.S. programs to respond to needs as they evolve on the ground.

Creating an account specifically to deal with unique post-conflict realities that complements current accounts in this area is the key to improving coherence, speed, and flexibility.[28] This new account, which could be named the Marshall Security Development Account (MSDA) in honor of the greatest reconstruction effort in modern history, would be structured along the lines of the highly successful Emergency Refugee and Migration Assistance (ERMA) account,[29] but would be mandated to address an integrated package of top reconstruction needs in four priority areas, namely, the "four pillars" of post-conflict reconstruction: security; governance and participation; urgent social and economic needs; and justice and reconciliation.. The MSDA would help the current foreign assistance account structure meet the challenges of reconstruction not by meeting all needs itself, but by rounding out the existing account structure in three ways: addressing immediate post-conflict needs that are not authorized for in existing emergency accounts (surge capacity); supplying bridge money between current emergency funds and long-term development funds (both U.S. and international); and providing for necessary activities that are not presently covered in existing accounts.

Many of the activities funded by the MSDA would be ones that currently are inadequately covered, if they are funded at all. In the security realm, for example, funds could be used to support early and voluntary disarmament, demobilization, and reintegration efforts (DDR) as well as provide short-term support for non-American troops or police who might be deployed in lieu of American troops or police (as with Turkey's deployment in Afghanistan). In the area of justice and reconciliation, where little money is available for emergencies, funds could be used to field an emergency justice package, deploy human rights monitors, or support reconciliation efforts at the national or local level. In the economic and social arena, MSDA funds could be used to jumpstart economies, provide temporary employment, reverse brain drain, or address critical social needs. In the area of governance and participation, MSDA funds could be used during the short-term window amenable to reform to support national "constituting processes" (such as the *loya jirga* in Afghanistan), anticorruption efforts, civil administration needs (including funding recurrent costs during the transition period), and civil society strengthening efforts.

The administration and Congress should work together to craft legislation that would create a new MSDA account with the following characteristics:

■ Funds would be used solely for activities designed to secure peace in the wake of conflict and to prevent a re-occurrence of conflict. They could be used only in extraordinary circumstances—in conjunction with a U.S. military intervention or in lieu of one—and would not be used for normal development activities.

■ Use of funds would require a presidential determination that a given country or region in crisis qualified for such funds.

- Requests for such a determination would be made by a director of reconstruction appointed by the president. [30] The director would be responsible for assessing needs, drafting requests, deciding how allocated funds would be used, and full accounting of all funds disbursed through regular reports to the chairmen of the Senate Foreign Relations Committee and House International Relations Committee as well as the Appropriations Committees.

- To prepare a budget request, an interagency assessment team with representatives from the State, Defense, Justice, and Treasury departments, USAID, and other relevant agencies—under the direction of the director of reconstruction—would be fielded in order to evaluate the needs for reconstruction, provide realistic funding estimates, and identify potential funding sources.

- The director of reconstruction's requests would be considered by a standing subcommittee of the Deputies' Committee, co-chaired by the deputy national security adviser and the deputy director of the Office of Management and Budget. This committee would be responsible for adjudicating amounts of money from which accounts would be used and to determine the necessity of a supplemental budget request. Their conclusions would recommend to the president the ultimate amount of money to be authorized for a given contingency (under such terms and conditions as the president may determine).

- The Marshall Security Development Account would have authority for immediate "emergency" activities as well as longer-term projects that would help to fill the transition gap until "normal" U.S. or other international programs could resume.

- Monies will be available to be implemented through U.S. agencies as well as through international and nongovernmental organizations.

- No operational time limit would be placed on the mission (as was the case with the Transition Initiatives account, to the great detriment for U.S. effectiveness).

- Rather than the traditional "use it or lose it" arrangement, authorities would be flexible and would represent money that could be spent over several years, allowing funds to be quickly disbursed to U.S. or other governments' agencies, international organizations, or nongovernmental organizations.

- The monies in the account would be available until expended ("no year") and "notwithstanding any other provision of law."
- As the monies in the account are depleted in any given year, they should be replenished up to a set level though the normal budget process.
- Supplemental requests or annual appropriations would be expected to pick up ongoing activities over time. Specific arrangements for designing smooth handoffs to existing accounts – such as that between ERMA and the Migration and Refugee Assistance account (MRA) – should be designed as part of the creation of this account.

To operationalize this proposal, the Office of Management and Budget, along with the National Security Council, should cochair an interagency process to review all existing accounts that provide funding in areas related to post-conflict reconstruction. This process should identify the functions and the monies that should be taken from existing accounts to provide a base funding level. In addition, this process should cost out the likely needs for activities not funded by current existing accounts, such as in the area of building civil administration capacity. Based on the outcome of that study, the administration should submit a proposal to Congress for the new account, the required funding level, and recommendations on the sources of financing it. Notionally, this account will probably need to have between $350 and $450 million available annually.[31] For large post-conflict operations, such as currently in Iraq and Afghanistan, this money could fill in for immediate operations until supplemental appropriations are legislated and disbursed to the field.

Establishing Funding Symmetry

Currently the Defense Department's annual appropriation for its "050" account is more than 15 times as large as the State Department's "150" account.[32] This imbalance is serious, and it is growing with every passing budget cycle. The State Department and USAID budgets will never be as large as that of the Department of Defense, but a serious look at the imbalance and the problems it causes is long overdue. The need to balance funds is not a blanket call to raise foreign assistance, nor is it an assumption that simply adding money to the current pots will increase post-conflict reconstruction effectiveness. Balancing funds as described here is a call to put money where one wants the policy authority and oversight to lie. A first step toward remedying these programmatic asymmetries would be to appropriate more money for specific accounts on the State and USAID side that would enable them to address the tasks in post-conflict reconstruction for which they are authorized without having to "raid" DOD monies.

The proposed new post-conflict account will cover the gaps in U.S. capacity. At the same time, there are standing authorities in certain areas of reconstruction that should be bolstered so that they can be effectively used in conjunction with the new MSDA. These standing accounts should not be so strapped for funds that their implementers must "raid" DOD's or other accounts, via drawdowns or political wrangling, to meet their operational needs. Nor should the legitimate programs that these accounts are, and should be, funding be cut to meet an inappropriately small budget. Existing authorized accounts must be funded at a level to allow their use for appropriate and authorized purposes as have already been legislatively agreed upon.

Seven key accounts require attention. The first is the Transition Initiatives (TI) account. The TI account, operationalized by the Office of Transition Initiatives (OTI) at USAID, is charged to bolster "democratic institutions and processes, revitalize basic infrastructure, and foster peaceful resolution of conflict."[33] The success of OTI's programming is vital to state recovery after conflict. It is also an expression of how much Americans value democracy and peace. The current $55 million budget[34] should be doubled to allow for comprehensive, well-planned and coordinated, and targeted programs.[35]

The second account, the International Disaster account, authorizes assistance for the "relief, rehabilitation, and reconstruction" of "people and countries" affected by natural and man-made disasters.[36] With the authority to go beyond traditional humanitarian assistance, the account has been—and can be more so with a broader interpretation of the statute—an important tool for bridging the gap between humanitarian intervention and development assistance. The need for the substantial $40 million supplemental request in March 2002 to pay for USAID work in Afghanistan and the $144 million emergency wartime supplemental request for Iraq in January 2003 demonstrated that the current levels of International Disaster funding do not provide enough contingency reaction flexibility.[37] As already discussed, supplemental appropriations are too slow to meet the needs of the critical window of opportunity directly after conflict.

The International Disaster account needs approximately an additional $90 million annually. However, it will be important to thoroughly review programming to ensure that the line between International Disaster and Development Assistance monies is properly drawn. Further, the International Disaster account should be raised by an additional $5 million to cover an increase in the Ambassador's Disaster Assistance authority, which is drawn from the International Disaster account after a declaration of emergency, from $25,000 to $100,000 annually. These monies are increasingly important for signaling the United States' commitment to its allies for obtaining their early participation in relief support.

The third account, Peacekeeping Operations (PKO), authorizes assistance for non-United Nations assessed peacekeeping operations and other programs in furtherance of the U.S. national security interests. The value in this account is the great flexibility it gives the president to act with allies without overtaxing the U.S. military. For example, it funds programs, such as the African Crisis Response Initiative in Africa, designed to build foreign capacity in peacekeeping operations, which ultimately relieves future burdens on the United States. Further, having substantial funds readily available also enables the United States to leverage its allies to provide proportionate funding to peace operations.

The PKO request for fiscal year 2004 is just $95 million, reduced from slightly over $108 million in fiscal year 2003.[38] Especially considering the need to increase African peacekeeping capacity, the account should be appropriated an additional $60 million annually.

The fourth account is that for Emergency Refugee and Migration Assistance or ERMA. The ERMA fund is narrowly defined to meet, with presidential declaration, "unexpected and urgent refugee and migration" needs.[39] This fund is crucial in meeting the urgent humanitarian needs of both refugees and internally displaced persons because it can be dispersed rapidly. The cap on this account is $100 million—far above what is generally spent annually. However, as outflows have been greater than appropriations in recent years, the account is in danger of being maintained at too low of a level, making it ineffective for all but a few emergencies annually. Congress should ensure that funding for ERMA stays at $100 million annually, which on average will increase appropriations for this account approximately $35 million per year.

The fifth account that needs attention is the Nonproliferation, Antiterrorism, Demining, and Related Programs (NADR) account. The "demining" portion of the NADR budget is particularly important to post-conflict reconstruction as the presence of mines, most recently seen in Angola and Afghanistan, impedes the return of refugees and

IDPs, humanitarian assistance, infrastructure reconstruction, agricultural sustainability, and a variety of other essential tasks.[40] The NADR account currently contributes $40 million annually to the U.S. Humanitarian Demining Program. Given recent experience with the paralyzed efforts at rapid demining, an additional $35 million should be appropriated for demining activities, as well as an additional $15 million to build regional demining capacity in Africa and South and East Asia.

Sixth, the Trade Development Agency (TDA) is an independent, commercially oriented foreign assistance agency that promotes economic development and facilitating trade with U.S. companies. It has its own line item of $45 million in the FY03 request.[41] While it is unlikely that U.S. companies will invest in the immediate post-conflict environment, with an additional $15 million the TDA could fund feasibility studies, provide consultancy, give training to local entrepreneurs, and advise project planning efforts to establish a baseline for instituting markets and for quick U.S. private investment—guaranteed through the Overseas Private Investment Corporation (OPIC) and the Export-Import Bank—to revitalize the local economy.

Seventh, attention should be paid to Treasury International Affairs Technical Assistance (TIATA). Realizing the extreme importance of the private sector in the stabilization and growth of developing economies, the United States should give more resources to the creation of a suitable climate for private investment. The Department of the Treasury's International Affairs, Office of Technical Assistance offers expertise in areas ranging from budgeting to anticorruption and should be given an additional $5 million to expand its efforts in promoting the private sector.

Needed support for these seven existing authorities totals only $320 million dollars a year. Although a good portion of this will need to be new money, the remaining could be drawn from other, less productive sources following a review of their programs and mandates by the Office of Management and Budget. In any case, $320 million at a minimum is an extremely cost-effective investment to avoid risking failure, as we have in Afghanistan and Iraq.

Fixing the Broken Machinery

Creation of the MSDA and balancing of funds should be a top priority. However, there are also immediate remedies available to address the problems in process and procedure. If the U.S. government is serious about transforming its foreign assistance objectives in today's world, then it is urgent that executive agencies, working together with Congress, be given the resources to fix what is clearly broken in a timely fashion. The following five recommendations are meant to bridge the gap until structural reform is possible.

First, the U.S. government should extend the time horizon of emergency and intermediate funding authorities. Concretely, this would entail extending deadlines for dedicating monies in the Overseas Humanitarian, Disaster, and Civic Aid (OHDACA) account, within the Department of Defense, until the funds are expended. With responsible management, this will give program managers more flexibility to respond to unexpected needs without regard to where an emergency falls in the budget cycle. OHDACA funds should be appropriated to maintain a constant level, as is done with the ERMA account. This would also involve authorizing monies provided in emergency supplemental appropriations for post-conflict aid to be dedicated in multiyear time frames. This would allow for more efficient use of monies and implementation of more sustainable projects. Finally, this would involve eliminating the new proposal requirement for renewal of quick impact projects (QUIPs). Instead, the QUIPs initial contract duration should be extended from 9 months to 12 to 24 months, depending on local need and economic assessment.

Second, the U.S. government should enhance use of contracting authority for reconstruction. The president should further amend Executive Order 10789 to include the Department of State and USAID as agencies authorized to utilize contracting authority in 50 U.S.C. 1431.[42] This contracting authority allows certain departments and agencies to enter into contracts for which Congress has not yet appropriated funds when the president has declared that doing so will facilitate national defense. The president should also clarify his interpretation of "national defense" in this context in light of his views of foreign aid as part of the war on terrorism and protecting the homeland. Agencies should then make better use of the contracting authority as bridge money to fill the gap in funds created from the budget process and the transition period between relief and development. Congress should amend 50 U.S.C. 1431 to exclude, with the president's authorization, contracts entered or amended under the contracting authority from regular contracting statutes.

Third, the administration, working with Congress, should reformulate USAID's procurement system by allowing contracts under $1 million to be authorized by mission directors. A reduced procurement staff in Washington would be in charge of contracts in amounts more than $1 million. Such a system would need to ensure appropriate training of personnel for foreign aid and development work and have internal security arrangements. A second component of reforming USAID's contracting system would involve upgrading the information technology required to track U.S. government resources for foreign assistance by incorporating both accounting and procurement systems for USAID into one, easily accessible system.

Fourth, the U.S. government should reconcile procurement processes between departments. General counsels of the State and Defense departments and USAID should meet to come to an understanding of the legal interpretation of the various procurement statutes and regulations that apply to transferred monies. They should then report to the principals committee (cabinet secretaries) for administrative implementation.

Fifth, the State Department should streamline its funding processes. First, department leadership should provide explicit guidance on the principles of how monies should be spent. This could produce a filter within the department to weed out extraneous proposals and produce increased consistency across the department, making high-level approval, such as at the deputy level, unnecessary. In addition, in consultation with Congress, the State Department should adapt the annual congressional budget justification to take the place of separate congressional notifications for every program under the Economic Support Fund, Foreign Military Financing, and Peacekeeping accounts. This may be modeled on USAID's congressional budget justification.

CONCLUSION

U.S. efforts in Iraq marked a sharp departure from the way that the United States had handled post-conflict reconstruction over the decade of the 1990s. Among other things, the dramatic shift away from interagency responsibility for post-conflict operations to almost sole responsibility held by the Department of Defense showed the weakness of the existing funding model. Responsibility was shifted to the one part of the U.S. government that had the financial and manpower resources to do the work, instead of broadening resourcing and capability throughout the civilian agencies that could make their own unique contribution.

Why did this happen after more than a decade of experience in post-conflict rebuilding? The Bush administration abandoned any inter-agency planning process that could have provided an immediate outline of what resources were in hand and what could be anticipated from the international community. In addition, no mechanism was es-tablished early enough to work with other donors. For the future, the United States needs to undertake a thorough mapping of all its funding authorities, and it should work cooperatively with other countries to initiate a larger review of resourcing for international post-conflict re-construction. The United States must mesh its resourcing capacity with that of other countries. Unlike after World War II, the United States can-not bear the entire burden for rebuilding. Funding of post-conflict ac-tivities also requires an important outreach component that would provide American citizens with a sound and positive rationale for the use of U.S. monies to secure U.S shores.

In the absence of any interagency planning process that takes on the mission of medium- and longer-term post conflict contingencies, it will be important for Congress to assert leadership again on how U.S. tax dol-lars are allocated to protect our citizens, support our military, and create new symmetry between civilian and military resources for post-conflict reconstruction. To this end, Congress should establish a Select Commit-tee on Post-Conflict Requirements that includes representatives with committee responsibilities for defense, foreign assistance, and law en-forcement. Such a select committee could properly focus its time and energies on finding the appropriate balance that the United States must create for civilian and military agencies to be prepared for future con-tingencies.

Even as the United States rethinks its long-term foreign aid strategy in light of 9/11, measures can be taken in the short term that will address the problems made apparent by the lack of effective post-conflict re-construction assistance. The cost of the proposed new MSDA, combined with a replenishing of the other current post-conflict related accounts, will most likely total less than $500 million annually. This is a small but important investment. Given ongoing needs in Afghanistan, Iraq, the Balkans, and Africa, as well as numerous potential challenges around the corner, the United States requires new funding capacity to meet the ex-pected and unexpected challenges ahead. It can hope to succeed only if it equips itself with the proper tools and its agencies are able to collabo-rate without competing over resources.

Notes

[1] Remarks by President George W. Bush at the 2002 graduation exercise of the United States Military Academy. West Point, New York, June 1, 2002. The need for a multifaceted, comprehensive foreign aid program as a means of securing peace and freedom as well as achieving U.S. security interests is well known in recent U.S. history. See Secretary of State George C. Marshall's declaration of the Marshall Plan for the reconstruction of Europe after World War II (commencement address at Harvard University, Cambridge, Massachusetts, June 5, 1947) and President John F. Kennedy's announcement of the Alliance for Progress for the democratic development of Latin America in the 1960s (address at a White House Reception for Latin American Diplomats and Members of Congress, March 13, 1961).

[2] Testimony of Secretary of State Colin L. Powell before the U.S. Senate Appropriations Subcommittee on Foreign Operations, Washington, DC. April 24, 2002.

[3] According to a survey in April 2002 by the Pew Research Center for the People and the Press, in conjunction with the Council on Foreign Relations and the *International Herald Tribune*, 53 percent of Americans approve of an increase in the U.S. foreign aid budget. See "Bush Ratings Improve But He's Still Seen as Unilateralist: Americans and Europeans Differ Widely on Foreign Policy Issues," Pew Research Center for the People and the Press, Council on Foreign Relations, and *International Herald Tribune*, April 17, 2002. See question 2e at http://people-press.org/reports/print.php3?ReportID=153.

[4] See Richard N. Gardner, "The One Percent Solution: Shirking the Cost of World Leadership," *Foreign Affairs* (July/August 2000): 2–11.

[5] In 1991, the Bush administration attempted to rewrite the FAA, and in 1994 the Clinton administration wanted to repeal the FAA and replace it with a new account structure. These attempts, although failing in their ultimate goals, had limited successes—the establishment of special accounts for the former communist countries of central and eastern Europe and the newly independent states of the former Soviet Union, as well as the establishment of funding for the Office of Transition Initiatives (OTI) at USAID. For an overview of the history of U.S. foreign assistance, see "A History of Foreign Assistance" and "Brief Chronology and Highlights of the History of U.S. Foreign Assistance Activities," available at www.usaid.gov.

[6] Cold War history is wrought with dubious "foreign aid" operations undertaken in a highly polarized world. Especially following the Vietnam conflict, lack of trust between Congress and the executive branch led to a highly restricted foreign aid budget. Various administrations since then have not earned back the lost trust.

[7] Office of the Press Secretary, White House, "Fact Sheet: A New Compact for Development," March 22, 2002.

[8] Remarks by President George W. Bush on Global Development at the Inter-American Development Bank, March 14, 2002.

[9] The House Committee on Appropriations noted in its report on the Foreign Operations bill that "to date, the Administration has made no legislative proposal or budget request for a pilot program [for the Millennium Challenge Account]. It is the Committee's understanding that the interagency process has reached no common approach regarding management or implementation of the proposal. For these reasons, the Committee does not recommend funding for a pilot to test and perfect the Millennium Challenge Account concept. The Committee expects to be consulted as development of the Millennium Challenge Account proceeds within the Executive branch. While the Committee welcomes new approaches to foreign aid, it remains determined to protect Congress's constitutional power of the purse." From "Report together with Additional Views [To accompany H.R. 5410]," U.S. House of Representatives, *House Report 107-663-Foreign Operations, Export Financing and Related Programs Appropriations Bill, 2003*, September 19, 2002, p. 5.

[10] In his speech in Monterrey, the president laid out three major criteria for evaluating countries' requests for Millennium Challenge Account funding: "ruling justly, investing in their people, and encouraging economic freedom." Measurement benchmarks are currently being designed to evaluate requests, and many officials close to the process acknowledge that conflict-stricken, impoverished countries will have a difficult time meeting them.

[11] While every situation is unique, a general matrix of tasks to be addressed in post-conflict reconstruction can be found in the Post-Conflict Reconstruction Task Framework (appendix 1).

[12] As pertains to foreign affairs, the Departments of Commerce, Justice, and State, the Judiciary, and Related Agencies (CJS) bill funds the operations of the State Department, U.S. diplomacy, and assessed contributions to international organizations and United Nations peacekeeping. The Foreign Operations, Export Financing, and Related Programs (Foreign Ops) bill funds most foreign aid programs, such as development and humanitarian assistance except food aid, bilateral military assistance, and contributions to voluntary UN programs and multilateral development banks. The Agriculture Appropriations bill funds food aid programs. Finally, the Department of Defense Appropriations bill includes funding for U.S. military involvement overseas, including civil and humanitarian programs.

[13] Richard Simon, "$25 Billion More for Iraq, Afghanistan," *Los Angeles Times*, May 6, 2004.

[14] On the need for a new interagency strategy and planning process, see chapter 7 by Flournoy, "Interagency Strategy and Planning for Post-Conflict Reconstruction."

[15] The Office of Transition Initiatives was one example that demonstrated the recognition of this timing problem. But with a mere $20 million at its creation and only $55 million budgeted in FY 2004, it can hardly begin to touch the myriad of reconstruction tasks that post-conflict countries face.

[16] This restriction was legislated in the Consolidated Appropriations Resolution, 2003 (Public Law No. 108-7). It is currently included in both the House and Senate versions of the Foreign Operations, Export Financing, and Related Programs Appropriations Act, 2004 (HR2800, June 21, 2003).

[17] A recent Government Accounting Office (GAO) report of the U.S. government response to non-post-conflict reconstruction after Hurricanes Mitch and Georges devastated parts of the Caribbean and Latin America illustrates the timeliness problem with supplemental appropriations. Reconstruction was funded by a supplemental appropriation approved in March 1999, yet it took seven months for the monies to reach the field because of legislative and administrative restrictions. Use of these monies was also constrained by their December 31, 2001, expiration date. As the GAO reported: "USAID and the other agencies almost unanimously agreed that the December 31, 2001, deadline was a major factor in how they planned, designed, and implemented disaster recovery activities, and it also affected the extent to which sustainability could be built into the program." See "Foreign Assistance: Disaster Recovery Program Addressed Intended Purposes, but USAID Needs Greater Flexibility to Improve Its Response Capability," GAO Report to Congressional Committees, GAO-02-787, July 24, 2002.

[18] Some of the obstacles to speedy disbursal of funding are discussed in the "Contracting and Procurement" section of this chapter. On impediments to speed related to interagency coordination and U.S. government civilian capacities, see, in this volume, chapter 7 by Flournoy, "Interagency Strategy and Planning for Post-Conflict Reconstruction," and chapter 8 by Mendelson Forman and Pan, "Filling the Gap: Civilian Rapid Response Capability for Post-Conflict Reconstruction."

[19] Following the passage of the Foreign Assistance Act of 1961, U.S. foreign aid levels in 1962 were 0.58 percent of GDP. In fiscal year 2002, foreign aid was just 0.11 percent of GDP. Even if a $5 billion annual increase under the Millennium Challenge Account, or MCA, is added to a constant level of current monies, foreign aid has been estimated to be just 0.135 percent of GDP in 2006 (the year in which the MCA will reach full levels). See Isaac Shapiro and David Weiner, "The Administration's Proposed Millennium Fund—While Significant—Would Lift Foreign Aid to Just 0.13 Percent of GDP" (Washington, D.C.:

Center for Global Development and Center on Budget and Policy Priorities, March 2002).

[20] Anne C. Richard discusses funding problems confronting the State Department and other international affairs agencies in "Superpower on the Cheap? The Difficulty of Funding U.S. Foreign Relations," Institut Francais des Relations Internationales (IFRI), 2002.

[21] In fiscal year 2003, approximately $1.47 billion went to the Child Survival and Disease/Health Programs fund at USAID, compared to $1.36 billion into the Development Assistance fund. According to the president's fiscal year 2004 request, $1.49 billion will be allocated for the Child Survival and Disease/Health Programs fund, while $1.34 will go to the Development Assistance fund.

[22] There is an argument to be made that a certain degree of inflexibility is inherent in a budget system with so many accounts, each with its own statutory mission. Within the Department of Defense, for example, hazy lines of responsibility drawn between the services and among the Operations and Maintenance (O&M), Military Construction (MC), and Procurement Programs accounts leaves in question what resources should be used for any given stage of an operation. However, most inflexibility in account structure comes from the infighting over interpretation of what accounts should be used, as discussed in the "Coherence" section of this chapter.

[23] FAA of 1961, §660(b)(6) provides a waiver for limited programs to reconstitute civilian police forces in post-conflict countries. This exception is seldom relied upon, however, and USAID has tended to interpret it narrowly. The exception has also fallen victim to politically charged decisionmaking processes. For a further discussion of §660, see, in this volume, chapter 6 by Flournoy and Pan, "Dealing with Demons: Enhancing Justice and Reconciliation."

[24] There was so much contention over the interpretation of the International Disaster account statute that in the 2001 Foreign Ops appropriation a separate "Transition Initiatives" line item drawing on IDA's statute was created. In FY 2001, the TI account was appropriated a small $50 million, compared to the less risky programs to be funded with $165 million under the IDA. FAA 1961, as amended, §491 & 492(a). U.S. House of Representatives, "House Report 106-997-Making Appropriations for Foreign Operations, Export Financing, and Related Programs for the Fiscal Year Ending September 30, 2001, and for Other Purposes," October 24, 2000.

[25] Notwithstanding authorities essentially override other prohibitions in law about providing assistance. According to USAID, for example, there are a number of "notwithstanding" authorities in the Foreign Assistance Act and appropriations acts that "permit the furnishing of assistance notwithstanding

prohibitions on furnishing assistance." See section 23.3.5.6 on "Notwithstanding" Authorities on the "USAID Policies and Procedures Website," www.usaid.gov/policy/ads/600.

Another tool often thought to gain flexibility is the use of transfer authorities. The broadest transfer authority is the "Economy Act," 31 U.S.C. 1535, which allows the transfer of monies for services or goods between any U.S. government agencies. This act is generally used because one agency has a standing capacity in a particular area lacking in the agency to which funds were appropriated. The Department of State and USAID more commonly use FAA §632(a) and §632(b), which are specific transfer authorities for FAA funds. Transfer authorities, however, are not that helpful in gaining real flexibility because monies transferred are to be used for the purposes stated in their appropriation.

[26] FAA 1961, as amended, §614(a)(1): "The President may authorize the furnishing of assistance under this Act without regard to any provision of this Act, the Arms Export Control Act, any law relating to receipts and credits accruing to the United States, and any Act authorizing or appropriating funds for use under this Act, in furtherance of any of the purposes of this Act, when the President determines…that to do so is important to the security interests of the United States."

[27] "Report together with Additional Views [To accompany H.R. 5410] (see note 9), pp. 36, 38. The report is highly critical of USAID procurement systems, even directing that priority be given to hiring engineers to help draft contracts.

[28] The Bush administration proposed the creation of an "Emergency Fund for Complex Foreign Crises" account to meet some of these needs in its fiscal year 2004 budget, but it struggled to persuade Congress to include this provision in the fiscal year 2004 budget. Stricken from draft legislation multiple times, in October 2002 the president included a line item for this account (at a level of $100 million) in his supplemental appropriation request for ongoing operations in Iraq and Afghanistan.

[29] The key points making the Emergency Refugee and Migration Assistance Fund successful are that its use is authorized by the president, it has notwithstanding authority, it is to be maintained at a consistent funding level, and monies remain available until expended. 22 U.S.C. 2601(c) states: "Whenever the President determines it to be important to the national interest he is authorized to furnish on such terms and conditions as he may determine assistance under this chapter for the purpose of meeting unexpected urgent refugee and migration needs….There is authorized to be appropriated to the President from time to time such amounts as may be necessary for the fund to carry out the purposes of this section, except that no amount of funds may be appropriated which, when added to amounts previously appropriated but not yet obli-

gated, would cause such amounts to exceed $100,000,000. Amounts appropriated hereunder shall remain available until expended."

[30] Directors of reconstruction would be appointed by the president for a specific crisis and would not be a standing position. For details of the proposal, see, in this volume, chapter 4 by Orr, "Governing When Chaos Rules: Enhancing Governance and Participation."

[31] The MSDA monies can be thought of in two parts. The first is a "surge capacity" that covers immediate although not all emergency humanitarian, unanticipated costs that cannot be taken from existing, already-disbursed accounts and before supplemental appropriations are available. A notional estimate of need in this area is between $150 million and $200 million annually. The second batch of monies are those to cover U.S. contributions to necessary tasks of post-conflict reconstruction that are not fully authorized in existing accounts; the largest of these tasks include reintegration of ex-combatants (and disarmament, demobilization, and reintegration, or DDR, more generally), funding of recurrent civil administration expenditures, and policing. A preliminary estimate of U.S. contributions (at 25 percent of total cost) for these three areas is $17 million, $70 million, and $135 million, respectively, per year. These figures assume 1-2 contingencies per year and are drawn from a baseline established in recent post-conflict operations, data taken from the United Nations Development Program, Department of State, Department of Defense, GTZ, Dyn-corp, and the government of East Timor. For all of these tasks, every country presents its own unique needs; however, the U.S. government must have immediately deployable resources to respond until a more thorough assessment of a given country is available. For more information, see Office of the Secretary of Defense, "Critical Factors in Demobilization, Demilitarization and Reintegration," February 2002; Kees Kingma. "Demobilisation and Reintegration of Ex-combatants in Post-war Transition Countries," Deutsche Gesellschaft für Technische Zusammenarbe. Eschborn, 2001); United Nations Development Program, "Immediate and Transitional Assistance Programme for Afghan People 2002," January 2002; Ministry of Planning and Finance, East Timor Public Administration, "The Democratic Republic of East Timor Combined Sources Budget 2002-2003," June 2002). For a good review of aid to post-conflict states, see Shepard Forman and Stewart Patrick, eds., *Good Intentions: Pledges of Aid for Postconflict Recovery* (Boulder, Colo.: Lynne Rienner, 2000).

[32] According to the president's fiscal year 2004 budget request, spending for the "050" account will total $390.4 billion while the "150" account is allocated $25.6 billion. Using these estimates, the United States will spend 15.2 times more on defense than on international affairs. See *Historical Tables, Budget of the United States Government, Fiscal Year 2004*, www.whitehouse.gov/omb/budget/fy2004/pdf/hist.pdf.

[33] FAA §492(a) in the Foreign Operations, Export Financing, and Related Programs Appropriations Act, 2001 (§101(a) of P.L. 106-429).

[34] This figure does not include the $70 million supplemental appropriation TI received in the fiscal year 2003 emergency wartime supplemental request for Iraq.

[35] A new Conflict Mitigation and Prevention office at USAID has been set up and is being developed, currently with a budget of $50 million. Once the new office's mandate and operations are clearly established, appropriations to both it and the TI account should be adjusted accordingly.

[36] FAA§491 and §492(a). The language "reconstruction" was added in the Foreign Operations, Export Financing, and Related Programs Appropriations Act, 2001 (§101(a) of P.L. 106-429), which also divided the account into two line items: "International Disaster Assistance" and "Transition Initiatives." This chapter refers to the two accounts as distinct even though they draw upon the same section of the FAA.

[37] It is reported that USAID requested from the administration a $150 million supplemental appropriation; however, only $40 million was submitted to Congress. See Elizabeth Turpen and Victoria K. Holt, "Following the Money: The Bush Administration FY03 Budget Request and Current Funding for Selected Defense, State, and Energy Department Programs" (Washington, D.C.: Henry L. Stimson Center, April 2002). Given this underfunding and the possibility of future large-scale reconstruction needs (in the Democratic Republic of the Congo, the Middle East, etc.), the recommended increase is a low estimate and additional supplemental appropriations will need to be sought.

[38] See FY 2004 International Affairs (Function 150) Budget Request, U.S. Department of State, at www.state.gov/m/rm/rls/iab/2004/.

[39] 22 U.S.C. 2601(c).

[40] For a fuller discussion of demining in a wider security context, see, in this volume, chapter 3 by Feil, "Laying the Foundation: Enhancing Security Capabilities."

[41] Another chapter in this volume calls for the expansion of TDA funds to post-conflict countries. See chapter 5 by Mendelson Forman, "Restoring Hope: Enhancing Social and Economic Well-being."

[42] 50 U.S.C. 1431 states: "The President may authorize any department or agency of the Government which exercises functions in connection with the national defense...to enter into contracts or into amendments or modifications of contracts heretofore or hereafter made and to make advance payments thereon, without regard to other provisions of law relating to the making, performance, amendment, or modification of contracts, whenever he deems that such action would facilitate the national defense." The statute further puts mon-

etary caps on use of this authority and maintains certain contracting regulations. Executive Order 10789 of November 14, 1958 ("Authorizing Agencies of the Government to Exercise Certain Contracting Authority in Connection with National Defense Functions and Prescribing Regulations Governing the Exercise of Such Authority"), as amended, authorizes the following departments and agencies to use this authority in the national defense: Defense, Treasury, Interior, Agriculture, Commerce, Transportation, General Services Administration, NASA, Tennessee Valley Authority, Government Printing Office, and the Federal Emergency Management Agency (FEMA). In October 2001, President Bush authorized the Department of Health and Human Services to use this contracting authority. In March 2003, FEMA authority was replaced by the Department of Homeland Security.

PART FOUR

POST-CONFLICT RECONSTRUCTION
CASE STUDIES

First Generation:
Post–World War II Occupation—Japan

Second Generation:
Post–Cold War "Humanitarian
Intervention"—Kosovo, East Timor, Sierra Leone

Third Generation:
Post–September 11 Interventions—Afghanistan, Iraq

CHAPTER ELEVEN

JAPAN

OCCUPATION AS MEANS TO A "CITADEL OF DEMOCRACY IN THE EAST"

Robert C. Orr

Following World War II the United States occupied the defeated Axis powers and some of the countries previously controlled by them, including Japan, Germany, Austria, and Italy. Driven by the imperative to "win the peace," the United States sought to refashion these countries along democratic lines as a way of preventing the revival of the militarism and fascism that had led to the war and, increasingly, to neutralize the perceived threat to U.S. interests posed by resurgent communism in the aftermath of the war.

While the four immediate postwar cases were handled very differently, the United States did pursue a common general approach insofar as there was a U.S. commitment to democratization, a relatively consistent postwar set of assumptions about political development, a set of policies designed to put into practice these assumptions, and military occupation troops with substantial civilian guidance and support as the main actors to implement them.[1]

Of all the occupations, that of Japan stands out as perhaps the most interesting and important of the postwar reconstruction efforts undertaken by the United States. First, the occupation of Japan was in fact a "pure" American project. Whereas the occupation of Germany was a four-power operation in which the United States often had to accommodate differing goals and approaches of its allies, the occupation of Japan was a fully unified, U.S.-controlled operation. Although forces from the British Commonwealth were stationed in Japan, they were essentially limited to tactical garrison duty rather than actively participating in the policymaking and governance of Japan.[2] The United States was determined to keep Soviet (and to a lesser extent other allies') influence out of

Japan, and it completely marginalized the multicountry bodies designed to oversee and provide advice on occupation matters. General Douglas MacArthur, the Supreme Commander for Allied Powers in Japan (SCAP), in particular was responsible for holding the Far Eastern Commission (comprising all 11 nations at war against Japan) and the Allied Council (comprising the United States, Britain, the USSR, and China) at arm's length, turning them, in his own words, into "little more than a debating society."[3] The structure of the occupation ensured that this would be the case. All forces were placed under the command of the U.S.-designated Supreme Commander, and it was U.S. policy that in cases of differences of opinion, "the policies of the United States will govern."[4]

If the occupation of Japan was the most American of the post-World War II occupations, it was also the most ambitious, given the relatively greater challenges and more limited resources. While the Allies could build on the institutions and draw on the personnel of the Weimar Republic in the German case, Japan had never fully experienced democracy in the same way that Germany had for 15 years under the Weimar constitution. Indeed, Japan had so little experience with democracy, and such a profound recent authoritarian experience, that Washington's initial post-surrender policy for Japan was circumspect about what the United States could accomplish, seeking only to "bring about the eventual establishment of a peaceful and responsible government" that would "conform *as closely as may be* to principles of democratic self-government."[5] Despite this cautious beginning, the occupation of Japan proved to be quite successful in putting Japan on a stable, sustainable, democratic path.

THE U.S. OCCUPATION OF JAPAN: GOALS AND ASSUMPTIONS

According to the "bible" of the occupation, the Basic Initial Post-Surrender Directive (JCS 1380/15), the ultimate objective of the occupation was to "foster conditions which will give the greatest possible assurance that Japan will not again become a menace to the peace and security of the world."[6] This was to be achieved not only through disarmament and demilitarization, but also through "strengthening of democratic tendencies and processes in governmental, economic, and social institutions; and the support of liberal political tendencies in Japan." Two years after the Japanese surrender, General MacArthur spoke of making Japan "a new and impregnable citadel of democracy in the East" that would "provide its people with the blessings of a truly free way of life and thereby prove a factor for stability in a world torn by the uncertain ties of confusion and fear."[7]

If democracy was assumed to be the path to the ultimate goals of peace and stability in the world, the question arose as to how the United States could bring about democracy. In this area, U.S. policymakers made a large assumption—that democracy is a universal desire of all people and that its realization therefore, depended largely on removing artificial barriers to its functioning. As spelled out in the Potsdam Declaration, allied efforts were to focus on "removing obstacles to the revival and strengthening of democratic tendencies among the Japanese people."[8]

The general methodology of the occupation derived from this assumption. In the words of MacArthur: "I knew that the whole occupation would fail if we did not proceed from this one basic assumption—the reform had to come from the Japanese."[9] The United States and MacArthur himself, however, generated a great deal of the agenda and intervened repeatedly on such issues as the constitution, purges, labor difficulties, local government, and the decentralization of the police when it was deemed necessary. The occupation forces did take great pains, however, to work through Japanese institutions and minimize the appearance of control, rather than administering the country directly as in Germany.[10] Consistent with MacArthur's exhortation to avoid interference with Japanese acts in search of an excessive degree of perfection, U.S. occupation forces let stand many Japanese government decisions considered suboptimal so as not to undermine the Japanese sense of ownership of the changes.

Growing out of this concern, the United States sought to temper its desire to remake Japan in its own image. MacArthur freely acknowledged that the pattern of the occupation lay "deeply rooted in the lessons and experiences of American history," but he understood that the Japanese system could not follow the U.S. system too closely, opting in specific cases such as the constitution and the Diet to follow the British model more closely.[11]

One final assumption by the drafters and implementers of the U.S. occupation of Japan was that to create democracy in an inhospitable climate, a total approach would be necessary. The project had to have military, social, economic, educational, cultural, and even religious foundations as well as a political one. This was most evident in the setup of an occupation apparatus that included a division to address each of these different sets of issues.

THE OCCUPATION IN PRACTICE

JCS 1380/15 laid out a very specific set of actions that occupation forces should undertake. These included political and administrative reorganization; demilitarization; arrest and internment of Japanese war criminals; control of proscribed political activity; reform of education and preservation of arts and archives; economic disarmament; restructuring and democratization of economic institutions, including deconcentration of trusts and strengthening of labor; civilian supply and relief; and oversight of the financial system.

MacArthur sought in particular to emphasize reforms that would "bring Japan abreast of modern progressive thought and action" through the following formula:

> First, destroy the military power. Punish war criminals. Build the structure of representative government. Modernize the constitution. Hold free elections. Enfranchise the women. Release the political prisoners. Liberate the farmers. Establish a free labor movement. Encourage a free economy. Abolish police oppression. Develop a free and responsible press. Liberalize education. Decentralize the political power. Separate church from state.[12]

The total cost of the occupation for the first five years was approximately $500 million per year, with over 50 percent of this going to food.[13] Although these amounts were criticized by many, in fact this was a relatively modest sum compared to the more than 100 billion taxpayer dollars spent in the Pacific Theater for the war.[14]

The occupation had two distinct stages. The first was the ambitious, reformist, democratizing stage from 1945 to 1948. The second was the phase from 1948 to 1952 that many have called the "reverse course." This chapter will focus principally on the active constructive phase of the occupation from 1945 to 1948. The "reverse course" phase will be addressed only insofar as it had an impact on the reforms of the earlier period.

Purges of Despotic Elites

The first major element of the United States' democracy promotion efforts was that of destroying the old system. From the Potsdam Declaration to the Initial Post Surrender Policy and the Basic Directive, the United States made it clear that "those who have deceived and misled the people of Japan," especially the "active exponents of militarism and militant nationalism," would need to be removed from positions of authority.[15] On January 4, 1946, MacArthur issued SCAPIN 550, providing the basis for a "purge" removing and excluding "undesirable personnel" from public office.

The initial focus was on militarism and ultranationalism, with the principal targets the "triple oligarchy" of the military, economic, and bureaucratic elites in the Japanese war machine.[16] Concretely, this meant war criminals, career military and naval officers, leaders of ultranationalistic organizations, leaders of the Imperial Rule Assistance Association, officers of companies involved in economic colonialism, governors of occupied territories, and a catchall encompassing "additional militarists and ultranationalists" vaguely defined.[17] The purge was also extended to include the media, local officials (before the first local elections), and the highly ambiguous category of "those who oppose the goals of the military occupation."[18]

In practice, this meant that between January 1946 and May 1948, 2,308,863 people were screened, with 210,287 people either removed or excluded from public life.[19] Although this was a significant number of people, the scope of the purge in Japan was much more limited than that taking place in Germany. It was also undertaken as an administrative procedure dictated by membership in certain groups, not as a judicial one as in Germany, which was perceived as proceeding far too slowly.[20] This administrative purge was very different in scope, process, and results from the war crimes process in which action was pursued against 28 suspected war criminals (27 of them top military officers), 25 of whom were brought to trial and all of whom were found guilty in court proceedings.[21]

The purge hit the military the hardest, with 79.6 percent of those purged coming from their ranks, followed by a significant 16.5 percent coming from among political elites.[22] A mere 0.9 percent of those purged came from business elites and an equivalent 0.9 percent drawn from the bureaucracy, a result of needing the latter to help run the occupation and the former to help rebuild Japan so as to be able to terminate the occupation as soon as possible. A similarly tiny number of 1,200, or 0.6 percent, was drawn from the media and entertainment industries.[23]

The basic motivation for the purge was to open space for democrats and large-scale democratic engineering. These goals become particularly clear when one considers the timing of the purges and the targets. SCAPIN 550 was issued three months before the first general election under the occupation and included 80 percent of the Diet and 50 percent of Prime Minister Shidehara's cabinet.[24] With the political housecleaning accomplished under the purge, room was created for a new political regime.

In 1950, due to changes in the international scene and the increasing militancy of the left in Japan, the purge was turned against communists. By January 1950, the Soviet-organized Cominform had induced the Japanese Communist Party to abandon its "peaceful revolution" strategy in favor of a more militant "people's liberation war" hard-line anti-American approach.[25] On June 6, 1950, MacArthur removed from public life all 24 members of the Central Committee of the party, including 7 members of the Diet. This was followed by the suspension of the Communist newspaper *Akahata* and arrest of these new purgees immediately after outbreak of the Korean War.[26] Between 1950 and 1952, the Japanese government, with the backing of occupation forces, accompanied these new purges with a de-purging of many of the original targets. The purge had come full circle.

Establishing a New Constitutional and Political Order

If the purges were seen as a crucial step in destroying the old order in Japan, the writing and implementation of a new constitution were seen as the key to creating a new order. Only 32 days after the surrender, on October 4, 1945, the Supreme Commander for Allied Powers issued a "Bill of Rights Directive" that instructed the Japanese government to release all political prisoners and to "remove all restrictions on political, civil, and religious liberties on the grounds of race, nationality, creed, or political opinion."[27] He initially left the task of revising the constitution, however, to a Japanese commission appointed by Prime Minister Shidehara. When in early 1946 an initial draft was leaked that made few significant changes in the 1889 Meiji constitution, however, MacArthur set his Government Section to work on a new draft constitution. After only ten days, between February 4 and 13, 1946, 27 members of the Government Section—military officers, lawyers, teachers, civil servants, and secretaries (without a single constitutional lawyer)—turned out a draft constitution that would ultimately be accepted and, with only minor revisions, enter into force on May 3, 1947.[28]

The new Japanese constitution differed markedly from the old Imperial constitution in many respects. First, it established a representative democracy in which power and sovereignty were vested in the people and the emperor became a constitutional monarch on the British model. Second, the constitution for the first time guaranteed fundamental human rights to the Japanese people, specifically enumerating 31 civil and human rights. Third, the constitution banned the sovereign right of war and the maintenance of military forces. Fourth, the new constitution established three independent branches of government. Although the legislative branch was designated "first among equals" and SCAP worked closely to build the Diet, the judicial and legal system was freed from the executive for the first time.[29] In addition, the executive branch was thoroughly decentralized, with various functions being handled at the local level for the first time ever, including elections, collection of taxes, control over police, and choosing of school boards.[30]

According to MacArthur, the new constitutional order was to make possible a reshaping of the national and individual character of the Japanese people.[31] It would appear to have been quite successful in doing so. MacArthur himself identified the new constitution as "probably the single most important accomplishment of the occupation."[32]

Because the new constitutional system depended on democratically elected and democratically inclined leaders, the United States gave a great deal of attention to creating a new political system in which elections would play a central role. Occupation forces not only contributed to the process of drafting a new set of election laws and helped to establish a new set of electoral institutions; they also undertook an extensive election-monitoring role in a number of elections during the occupation.[33] On April 10, 1946, Japan held its first completely free election. Women's suffrage having been extended under the occupation, over 13 million women voted for the first time, and the percentage of eligible voters who voted surpassed 75 percent.

In addition to the effort to establish new electoral mechanisms, SCAP also sought to democratize the parties and the party system in Japan. Indeed, one of the four major objectives of the political reorientation program of the occupation was "to develop a political party system in which democratically controlled parties can be held responsible by the nation for the conduct of the government."[34] Sometimes, SCAP held up legislation proposed by the Japanese because it did not put enough emphasis on democratizing internal party structures, including the use of secret ballots, nominating procedures, and party conventions, as well as ensuring accountability of party finances.[35] Yet even though great attention was given to these issues, participants in the efforts were generally disappointed in their personal effectiveness at rooting out old antidemocratic tendencies within the parties.[36]

While national elections and reform of the party system were important, the changes at the local level were no less important. As part of the
decentralization effort, the occupation promoted prefectural and local
elections as well as national ones. These were deemed important not only
in their own right, but also because participation at the local level was
thought to encourage people to take an active interest in the selection of
officials, and hence to strengthen democratic tendencies at the national
level as well.[37] Trying to ensure that new local structures created under
the Local Autonomy Law could actually start with as clean a slate as possible, MacArthur ordered that no local incumbent could run in the
first-ever local elections in April 1947.[38] Although some may have
slipped through the net, this approach ensured that local government
got an infusion of new blood just as the national government and the
parties had.

Economic Democratization

Speaking before the Senate in September 1945, Secretary of State Dean
Acheson noted that the occupation would seek to change the "present
economic and social system in Japan which makes for a will to war."[39]
Reform efforts thus focused not only on dismantling the capabilities of
the Japanese war machine, but also on the economic structures that
were assumed to contribute to Japan's aggressive behavior. The economic democratization program designed to underpin political democratization consisted of three major components: "deconcentration" of the
centers of excessive economic power; enhancing the strength and role of
labor; and promoting the wider distribution of income and ownership
(of both land and industry). These economic democratization efforts
were accompanied by a concern for revitalizing the economic capacity
of Japan after the war, a concern that grew in importance in the later
stages of the occupation.

Following the war, the U.S. occupation immediately set about dismantling "excessive concentrations" of economic power. It was estimated that over 60 percent of the total economic life of Japan before the war
was concentrated in the hands of only eight families, with over 70 percent of Japan's entire export trade in the hands of the Mitsui and Mit-
subishi families.[40] In the first months of the occupation, even before the
economic purge (which ultimately removed or barred a mere 668 people),[41] the United States embarked on a program to dismantle the
zaibatsu, or large family holding companies and industrial combines.

Conceived with U.S. antitrust efforts to wrest power from large combines in the 1930s in mind, the *zaibatsu* deconcentration program was pre-figured in the Basic Directive for Post-Surrender Military Government (JCS 1380/15) and approved by the State-War-Navy Coordinating Committee in 1946 to promote a democracy-enabling "wide distribution of income and of ownership of the means of production and trade."[42]

In addition to the *zaibatsu* family groups, occupation sought to break up other powerful holding companies as well. Eighty-three holding companies, including those of the four major *zaibatsu* were dissolved (with 32 of those completely liquidated). Minor holding companies were either dissolved or allowed to continue to exist by divesting some of their assets.[43] In 1948, pressure grew to "reverse course." George Kennan—who argued that "the ideological concepts on which these anti-*zaibatsu* measures rested bore so close a resemblance to Soviet views about the evils of 'capitalist monopolies' that the measures could only have been eminently agreeable to anyone interested in the future communization of Japan"—prevailed, and in 1948 the occupation moved from seeking the breakup of 325 combines representing 75 percent of Japanese industry to announcing the "completion" of the dissolution program with orders for the breakup of only 9 combines.[44]

"Deconcentration" programs were not the only method used by the United States to distribute wealth and economic influence more equitably. Changes in the tax system were also designed to influence the distribution of resources as well as enhance efficiency and promote economic revitalization. U.S. tax experts were brought in and produced a four-volume study that set out a comprehensive tax plan, ultimately adopted in large part, designed to rationalize the system, expand local governments' powers to tax, and encourage greater equity.[45] SCAP helped the government to strengthen tax enforcement, especially for large evaders, and to institute a capital-levy tax in 1946 that taxed personal capital assets at steeply rising rates from 25 percent to 90 percent on assets over 100,000 yen.[46]

The occupation also sought to promote a distribution of power in the economic arena conducive to democracy by encouraging the development of labor unions. In October 1945, only a week after giving a directive establishing civil liberties and ordering the immediate abrogation of all restrictive legislation barring labor organization and collective bargaining, MacArthur instructed the prime minister to "encourage labor unionization" in Japan.[47] The result was a dramatic increase in union membership from a pre-war peak of 400,000 to over 4 million by the end of 1946, and over 7 million members of 25,000 unions by 1951.[48] This growth was facilitated by a host of new legislation guaranteeing the right to organize and bargain collectively (for the first time in Japanese history), an active education program and overtly pro-labor stance of SCAP's Labor Division, the establishment of a labor ministry and other related administrative agencies, and the reigning in of police intimidation.[49]

As the United States became increasingly concerned with growing Communist strength and potential manipulation of the labor movement, the occupation shifted to a harder line on labor questions. In addition to outlawing a planned general strike in February 1947, SCAP also sponsored a 1948 law denying government workers the right to bargain collectively and strike. This was consistent with the occupation's focus on labor largely as a political question. According to Theodore Cohen, the chief of the Labor Division, the mission of the Labor Section was to build up Japanese labor, "giving it the stake in a peaceful society it had never had and ensuring its participation in Japanese public life to protect that stake."[50] While "reverse course" policies may have eroded some of the gains in this area, there is little doubt that the occupation's labor programs on the whole achieved part of their principal goal— making labor a player, if a constrained one, in Japan's democratic system.

Breaking up the Feudal Social and Economic System

Despite its industrial development, Japan in 1945 was "more nearly a feudal society" than a twentieth-century civilization in the eyes of its occupiers.[51] To attack the roots of the feudal social and economic structures, the occupation undertook agrarian reform in rural areas as well as various programs societywide designed to change attitudes and enhance social mobility. These efforts included significant changes in the areas of the status of women, education, the civil service, culture, and religion.

Agrarian reform. The heart of the "anti-feudal" effort was an agrarian reform program. Prior to the war, over half the Japanese people—more than 35 million in 7 million households—toiled on 5,698,000 farms.[52] Seventy percent of the Japanese farmers rented all or part of the land they cultivated, and population pressure on limited land resources perpetuated a feudalistic land tenure system requiring payment of exorbitant rents in kind often amounting to 50 to 70 percent of gross farm production.[53] Despite the fact that the agrarian reform was not mentioned in the Initial Post-Surrender Directive, MacArthur aggressively pursued this issue from the early days of the occupation. In October 1946, the Diet passed land reform legislation that sought to arrange for the transfer of land to the farmers who worked it and that would improve the farm tenancy practices for those who continued on as tenants.[54]

Between 1947 and 1950, the government bought and distributed 5 million acres, over one-third of Japan's cultivated land, to 33,000 cooperatives with 8.2 million members. Because the resale prices did not allow for inflation, this essentially amounted to expropriation, with each acre selling for the equivalent of a black-market carton of cigarettes.[55] Between August 1947 and February 1950, the percentage of owner-operated land jumped from 54 percent to 90 percent.[56] In addition to the transfer of land, the occupation-sponsored programs also helped solidify the position of the new owners and those remaining tenants by providing credit, expanding agricultural extension, and reducing the undue tax and debt burdens afflicting farmers. Similarly, the occupation also arranged for complete reformation of the feudalistic fisheries rights system and for the organization of 4,000 democratic cooperatives.[57]

Virtually all analysts of the Japanese agrarian reform agree that the program was a huge success. MacArthur himself considered this a key part of the program not only because it helped to destroy the feudal system that had supported the militarists and ultranationalists, but also because it was seen as crucial to erecting a bulwark against communism and to creating a path to modernization in Japan.[58]

Raising the status of women. A second, less well-known aspect of the anti-feudalism drive of the occupation was the conscious effort to raise the status of women. This effort is best understood as part of a larger project to reform the "antidemocratic family system" that was seen as a root cause of the militarism that had led to the war. Under the occupation, women were granted legal equality and guarantees, some of which went beyond what was accepted at the time in the United States.[59] The most visible and dramatic change was the enfranchisement of women, with 13 million women voting for the first time in 1946, electing 38 women to the Diet.[60] Soon after, 23 women were elected to prefectural assemblies, 74 to city councils, and 707 to town assemblies. By 1948, a tradition had been established that every national cabinet must include a woman vice-minister. Within five years, 14,000 women were serving as social workers in villages and more than 2,000 as policewomen, an unprecedented development in Asia. One and one-half million women joined unions. Laws concerning marriage, divorce, and adultery were revised. Contract marriages and concubinage were forbidden. High schools became coeducational, and 26 women's universities were founded. Women were incorporated into the media as experts, making weekly appearances on radio programs sponsored by the occupation's Civil Information and Education section.[61] Perhaps most importantly for the survival of these various reforms, one of the five bureaus created within the new Labor Ministry was a Women's and Minors' Bureau, which effectively kept the momentum for improving women's status even after the end of the occupation.[62]

Educational reform. Similar dramatic changes were pursued in the field of education. To break down the old system, 120,000 of 500,000 teachers were purged under the occupation.[63] Militaristic textbooks were discarded, and by 1950 over 250,000 new ones were being produced annually.[64] Education was decentralized, and for the first time people were given the right to choose their own school boards at the local and prefectural levels. Nine years of education became free and compulsory as opposed to the previous standard of six years, and conditions for teachers improved as unionization of teachers was promoted.[65] In the field of higher education, new universities were promoted, with 48 universities in 1945 growing to 220 by 1952. Perhaps most important, after the visit of the U.S. education mission in 1946, a new education law was drafted that declared the right to equal opportunity of education without discrimination regardless of race, creed, sex, social status, or family origin.[66] Although this standard was by no means immediately realized, it created an opening for many in the educational system that had not existed before.[67]

Civil service reform. To enhance social mobility, the occupation also addressed the civil service. Civil service reform had not been included in the Basic Post-Surrender Directive, but the issue gained notoriety as other dominant issues like constitutional revision and elections were taken care of. The stated goal of civil service reform was to "not only enhance the governmental efficiency but [also] break up the ruling cliques of pre-surrender Japan—the tightly knit, exclusive and self-perpetuating bureaucracy which exercised the powers of government over the people in the feudal concept of dynastic rule by divine right."[68] In 1947 and 1948, laws were passed fundamentally reorienting the civil service system, with appointments based on competitive examinations, dismissals based only on poor performance, and promotions based on merit rather than simply seniority.[69] One of the principal goals was to enhance social mobility through creating an American-like civil service based on a merit system. In the end, however, the Civil Service Mission, and later the newly created Civil Service Section, ended up focusing almost solely on the question of strikes and collective bargaining as well as technical issues affecting the efficiency of the civil service.[70] As a result, while efficiency may have been enhanced and some level of systematization introduced, the deeper issue of breaking up a system based on "old school ties" was not profoundly affected.

Culture. While many of the efforts to democratize Japan's culture were undertaken through the educational system, a host of other efforts tried to change "feudal mentality" by selling democracy to the Japanese people directly through the propaganda organs of the occupation forces.[71] Among these efforts was the creation and distribution of two-and-a-half million copies of *A Primer for Democracy* and the launching of an accompanying program over the broadcast media.[72] Perhaps the most imaginative efforts to create a new democratic culture were the attempts by the Civil Information and Education Division throughout Japan to sponsor square dancing and billiards to replace the Japanese staples of *geisha* dances and *kendo* sword fighting.[73]

Religion. Another way in which the occupation sought to break the grip of feudalism in Japan was through breaking the link "between church and state." While the vocabulary was pure Americana, the issue was a real one. State Shintoism as it existed at the time was as much a nationalistic dogma as a religion and, as such, needed to be addressed if the militaristic, ultranationalistic mindset was to be changed.[74] The Supreme Commander for Allied Powers took this issue head on, abolishing state Shinto by directive on December 15, 1945. This set in motion a complex process that involved, on the one hand, eliminating state funding to religious organizations and, on the other hand, transferring land titles from the state to religious organizations in order to effect a clear separation of church and state. The process also included removing Shinto doctrine from textbooks and Shinto symbols from public buildings, as well as national Shinto holidays.[75]

While establishing freedom of religion was a general goal for democratizing Japan, MacArthur had a more specific, personal goal—that of promoting "Christian morals." When asked how he wanted to be remembered, the general once responded that he would like to be seen as "one whose sacred duty it became...to carry to the land of our vanquished foe the solace, hope and faith of Christian morals."[76] To visiting clergy he often stated, "The more missionaries we can bring out here, and the more troops we can send home, the better." Indeed, in response to these requests, 1,900 missionaries poured into Japan in the first four years to "help fill the spiritual vacuum" with Christianity as well as democracy, and the Pocket Testament League at MacArthur's request distributed 10 million bibles in Japanese.[77] In a very short space of time, over 2 million Japanese had become Christian.[78]

OVERALL EVALUATION

Given the deplorable state of Japan at the time of its surrender in 1945 and the much-improved condition in which the United States left the country in 1952, the occupation must be considered a success. Perhaps its most significant accomplishment was the establishment of an entirely new constitutional order, one that has remained fully intact since the occupation and has presided over positive developments in a number of spheres of Japanese life. In the course of seven years the Japanese people were converted from "subjects to citizens," governed by a newly democratic constitutional order in which executive, legislative, and judicial powers were effectively separated and the Parliament made the chief organ of state power. Japanese citizens—especially women, who made up the majority of the population—were granted a host of civil and political rights they had never enjoyed. One unique and ultimately successful aspect of the new constitutional order was the stringent limitation placed on the military under Article 9 of the constitution. Though successive Japanese governments have had to resist U.S. pressure to rearm, they have done so relatively successfully, enabling an unprecedented amount of resources to go toward facilitating the Japanese economic "miracle."

In the economic arena, the results of the occupation, like the policies themselves, were mixed. Economic democratization—composed principally of deconcentration efforts, enhancing distribution, and empowering labor—was an intensely ambitious agenda that yielded some positive results as well as some failures between 1945 and 1948. Labor development and some distributional efforts advanced, while deconcentration efforts stalled. Parallel efforts in the area of economic revitalization were even more successful, especially after the 1948 "reverse course" that made this the principal focus of occupation efforts from that point forward. In a very short time, the United States helped Japan regain its economic footing, successfully re-oriented trade flows so as to eliminate the motivation for imperial expansion, and left in place a re-built economic infrastructure that would form the launching pad for the Japanese "miracle."[79]

According to one Japanese expert, "the deconcentration by the occu-pation was the most important factor in making the Japanese industrial structure competitive."[80] Numerous other analysts of the Japanese economy, including some directly affected by the deconcentration poli-cies, agreed and pointed in particular to the importance of the separa-tion of the ownership of capital and the management of capital in bringing about Japan's prosperity.[81] In the area of finance, reorganiza-tion and expansion of the number of banks was pursued instead of de-concentration, also resulting in increased competition and efficiency.[82] Thus, economic democratization efforts, even though they may have largely come to a halt in 1948, made some fundamental changes that were critical to the economic growth for which Japan is well known.

Similarly, while many of the purges enacted by the occupation in the early years were reversed near the end, they nonetheless had an impor-tant impact on Japan's political, social, and economic development. The purges created space for a new generation of leaders, giving the young democracy some breathing room at a critical early stage. By the time the old leaders were cleared to re-enter it, the system had fundamentally changed. At the same time, the reverse course policies of cracking down on labor and shifting the purge to go after the left did have serious long-term negative consequences. By allowing the conservatives to crack down on their political opponents, strengthening the position of busi-ness and weakening that of labor, the United States facilitated the shift from a competitive, alternating party system to a less democratic system dominated by one party for more than 40 years.

One area in which the success of the occupation is not at all in ques-tion is agrarian reform. This program not only freed millions of Japanese tenant farmers from feudal servitude as intended; it also increased rural productivity, lessening the immediate burden on the United States and strengthening the rural base for Japan's dynamic industrial develop-ment. Indeed, agrarian reforms, combined with labor reforms, helped to create an internal consumer mass market for the first time in Japanese history.[83] Agrarian reform thus not only helped to directly democratize Japan by freeing a large part of the population from a feudalistic system and incorporating them as citizens in the new democratic system; it also helped to spur the economic growth that helped to consolidate all the political and social gains in the postwar period.

SOURCES OF SUCCESS

Given the notable success of the U.S. occupation of Japan, it is important to explore the roots of this success. One of the first reasons for success was that the occupiers had an important foundation on which to build. Despite the physical devastation in Japan, they were not starting from scratch. In the economic sphere there was a significant, if heavily damaged, industrial base, an extensive commercial infrastructure, and a reservoir of managerial and technical expertise. In the political realm, Japan had experienced a proto-democratic period in the 1920s and 1930s, exposing people to new ways of thinking and creating an all-important cadre of democrats from which the occupation forces could draw for leadership after the war. In addition, Japan had important governmental structures in place that could be utilized to further the ambitious goals of the occupation. As one distinguished analyst has noted, "We will probably never have an intact government with such bureaucratic perfection as the Japanese presented us with in the summer of 1945."[84]

If the occupation forces had a human, institutional, and material foundation on which to build, they also had a country psychologically and spiritually ready to be remade. The trauma of war and defeat left the Japanese looking for a new path. As MacArthur characterized the situation, "Never in history had a nation and its people been more completely crushed than were the Japanese at the end of the war.... Their entire faith in the Japanese way of life, cherished as invincible for many centuries, perished in the agony of their total defeat."[85]

A third source of success lay in the fact that fundamental U.S. interests were at stake in "winning the peace." As such, nothing that was needed was denied. The Supreme Commander of Allied Powers was provided with all the people, resources, and autonomy that were necessary to accomplish the mission. By the narrowest estimates, the United States poured over 2 billion dollars into Japan during the occupation, and the General Headquarters bureaucracy of the Supreme Commander grew to 3,500 people, not counting all the field personnel and special missions that he could and did draw on.[86] And though Washington did press certain changes on MacArthur, he was generally allowed to pursue his democracy promotion agenda without undue interference.

Another key to success was the choice to observe the principle of subsidiarity in the implementation of the occupation to the extent possible. By leaving as much as possible to the occupied people themselves, the Japanese took ownership of many of the reforms, allowing them to persist after the occupation was over. At the same time, the Supreme Commander did intervene quite regularly, but he did so as unobtrusively as possible. The ultimate example of this was his handling of the new draft of the constitution, letting the Japanese debate it and take credit for it when in fact his own staff members were the sole authors and only minimal changes were allowed.

Another major source of success was the all-encompassing scope of the project. Political, social, economic, cultural, religious, and military dimensions were addressed, as well as the relationships between them. The occupation forces obtained and maintained information on everything from economic production statistics throughout the land, to thorough investigations of Japanese nutritional requirements and dietary habits, as well as religious practices.[87] A broad basket of goods was pursued throughout, enabling the overall mission to survive and prosper even when specific elements failed.

Good leadership and decisions were crucial to the success of the occupation. MacArthur understood very early on that democratization would be impossible if the punitive project envisioned by some in Washington was pursued. He adroitly steered U.S. efforts away from punishing Japan's emperor and pressing reparations toward constructive efforts to build a new society. In particular, some of the biggest successes—from a new constitution and its novel renunciation of the sovereign right to war (lifting from the Japanese the burden of armament), to land reform and the liberation of women—were those things pushed by the Supreme Commander himself.

A final important source of the occupation's success lay in its long duration. Though most of the "democratizing" policies of the occupation took place between 1945 and 1948, the fact that the occupation continued until 1952 is important. Seven and a half years was a very long time—enough for Japan to absorb a great deal of American attitudes and culture. These not only had a direct impact on Japanese democracy;

they also helped cement a positive relationship with the United States. This relationship, and its importance to the Japanese, helped to keep Japan on the democratic path long after the occupation was over.

CONCLUSIONS: IMPLICATIONS FOR SUBSEQUENT EFFORTS

Many lessons could be drawn from any effort as significant and complex as the U.S. occupation of Japan. Because this effort was both successful and novel—being the first major political development effort of a new era in American foreign policy—it was especially formative in creating a postwar mindset about what was possible and desirable in terms of democracy and development in a wide range of countries. One transmission mechanism was through the many personnel of the occupation who became foreign aid workers and consultants all over the world.

There were a multitude of problems with extrapolating from the experience in Japan to the very different challenges facing the United States in subsequent decades. Few countries coming out of war had what Japan did: a great reservoir of managerial and technical expertise; an industrial base and extensive commercial infrastructure; an uncommonly strong institutional base; a high set of expectations based on seeking to regain what had been lost; a coherent cultural, ethnic, and historical identity; and a polity with a well-integrated, well-established identity.[88] Nor would the United States again have the virtually absolute control that it exercised in Japan, the same level of resources for such projects, or the luxury of concentrating so intensively on a single country. Despite this, the record of transforming Japan in seven short years helped to solidify a particularly American attitude that societies coming out of war could and should be rebuilt by the United States.

Notes

[1] On Germany, see: John D. Montgomery, *Forced to Be Free: The Artificial Revolution in Germany and Japan* (Chicago: University of Chicago Press, 1957; Robert Wolfe, ed., *Americans as Proconsuls: United States Military Government in Germany and Japan, 1944–1952* (Carbondale, Ill.: Southern Illinois University Press, 1984); Peter H. Merkl, "Allied Strategies of Effecting Political Change and Their Reception in Occupied Germany," *Public Policy* 17 (1968): 1–26; Carl J. Friedrich, "The Legacies of the Occupation of Germany," *Public Policy* 17 (1968): 59–103; and Ekkehart Krippendorff, ed., *The Role of the United States in the Reconstruction of Italy and West Germany, 1943–1949* (Berlin: John F. Kennedy Institut Fur Nordamerikastudien Freie Universitat Berlin,

1981). On Italy, see: John Lamberton Harper, *America and the Reconstruction of Italy, 1945–1948* (Cambridge: Cambridge University Press, 1986); James Edward Miller, *The United States and Italy, 1940–1950: The Politics and Diplomacy of Stabilization* (Chapel Hill: University of North Carolina Press, 1986); and David W. Ellwood, *Italy 1943–1945* (New York: Holmes and Meyer, 1985). On Austria, see: U.S. General Staff, *General Marshall's Report: The Winning of the War in Europe and the Pacific*, Biennial Report of the U.S. Army Chief of Staff to the Secretary of War, July 1, 1943 to June 30, 1945 (Washington, D.C.: GPO, 1945), p. 94; Oliver Rathkolb, "National Security Decision Making of the Eisenhower Administration and the Austrian Question 1953–1955–1960" (paper presented at the Conference on Patterns of U.S. Occupation Policies, Hoover Institution and Stanford University, May 1986); and, Milton Colvin, "Principal Issues in the U.S. Occupation of Austria, 1945–1948," in *U.S. Occupation in Europe after World War II,* ed. Hans A. Schmitt (Lawrence, Kans.: Regents Press of Kansas, 1978).

[2] For an account of the role of the Commonwealth forces, see Peter Bates, *Japan and the British Commonwealth Occupation Force, 1946–1952* (London: Brassey's, 1993).

[3] Douglas MacArthur, *Reminiscences* (New York: McGraw-Hill, 1964), p. 293.

[4] State-War-Navy Coordinating Committee directive (SWNCC 150/3), August 30, 1945. As cited by Marlene J. Mayo, "American Wartime Planning for Occupied Japan: The Role of Experts," in Wolfe, *Americans as Proconsuls*, p. 467.

[5] State-War-Navy Coordinating Committee, *United States Initial Post-Surrender Policy for Japan* (SWNCC 150/4), approved by the President of the United States September 6, 1945. Emphasis added. In Supreme Commander for the Allied Powers, *Political Reorientation of Japan* [hereafter *PRJ*] (Washington, D.C.: GPO, 1949), p. 423.

[6] JCS 1380/15, in *PRJ*, p. 429. Key members of the Occupation forces have confirmed that the main ideology and practical implementation matters of the Occupation came from Washington in the form of the Basic Initial Post-Surrender Directive (JCS 1380/15), not through the Initial Post-Surrender Policy (SWNCC 150/4). Although the latter was the public face of the policy for the Japanese, the former was what was used paragraph by paragraph on a daily basis to determine how the Occupation should proceed. See Theodore Cohen, *Remaking Japan: The American Occupation as New Deal,* ed. Herbert Passin (New York: Free Press, 1987), p. 13.

[7] Douglas MacArthur, *A Soldier Speaks: Public Papers and Speeches of General of the Army Douglas MacArthur* (New York: Praeger, 1965), p. 198.

[8] *Potsdam Declaration*, Proclamation by the Heads of Government of the United States, the United Kingdom, and China, July 26, 1945. In *PRJ*, p. 413.

[9] MacArthur, *Reminiscences*, p. 294.

[10] Direct intervention was logically most prominent in the beginning of the occupation. Over 1,000 directives by the Supreme Commander for Allied Powers (SCAP) were issued in the first ten months of the occupation and mass participation did not really get going until two years into the occupation. See Ralph Braibanti, "The MacArthur Shogunate in Allied Guise," in Wolfe, *Americans as Proconsuls*, p. 84. For examples, see *Catalogue of Administrative Directives to the Japanese Government*, vol. 1 (Tokyo: General Headquarters SCAP, 1947). U.S. control over developments did not end, however. Rather, the instruments used were simply less obvious after SCAP shifted to governing the Japanese by advice and pressure tactics rather than by directive. See Richard B. Finn, *Winners in Peace: MacArthur, Yoshida, and Postwar Japan* (Berkeley: University of California Press, 1992), p. 88.

[11] Letter from MacArthur to Charles M. Englisby, February 14, 1948. Included as an appendix to *PRJ*, p. 785.

[12] MacArthur, *Reminiscences*, pp. 282–283.

[13] John Gunther, *The Riddle of MacArthur: Japan, Korea, and the Far East* (New York: Harper Collins, 1951), p. 146.

[14] Eleanor M. Hadley, *Antitrust in Japan* (Princeton: Princeton University Press, 1970), pp. 134, 138.

[15] See Proclamation of the Three Powers: The United States, Great Britain, and China, July 26, 1945. www.ibiblio.org/pha/policy/1945/450802.a.html. See also, State-War-Navy Coordinating Committee, "U.S. Initial Post-Surrender Policy for Japan" (SwNCC 150/4/A), September 21, 1945. www.ndl.go.jp/constitution/shiryo/01/022 2/022 2tx.html

[16] *PRJ*, p. xxiv.

[17] Hans H. Baerwald, "The Purge in Occupied Japan," in Wolfe, *Americans as Proconsuls*, p.189.

[18] On the evolution of the purge through various stages, including the refocusing on new targets as the occupation entered its later stages, see the accounts of principal participant Hans J. Baerwald, *The Purge of Japanese Leaders Under the Occupation* (Berkeley: University of California Press, 1959), and ibid., pp. 188–197.

[19] Montgomery, *Forced to Be Free*, p. 26; and Finn, *Winners in Peace*, p. 85.

[20] See Eli E. Nobleman, "United States Military Courts in Germany," in Wolfe, *Americans as Proconsuls*, pp. 181–187; and Meirion and Susie Harries, *Sheathing the Sword: The Demilitarization of Japan* (London: Hamish Hamilton, 1987), p. 46.

[21] Finn, *Winners in Peace*, pp. 75–82.

[22] For a breakdown of these, as well as the following statistics, see Tetsuya Kataoka, *The Price of a Constitution: The Origin of Japan's Postwar Politics* (New York: Crane Russak, 1991), p. 67.

[23] Baerwald in Wolfe, *Americans as Proconsuls,* p. 196.

[24] Finn, *Winners in Peace,* p. 86.

[25] Steve (Sei Young) Rhee, "SCAP Purge of Left-wing Elements during the Korean War," in William F. Nimmo, ed., *The Occupation of Japan* (Norfolk, Va.: General Douglas MacArthur Foundation, 1991), p. 88.

[26] Gunther, *The Riddle of MacArthur,* p. 163.

[27] Ibid., p. 125.

[28] For primary documentation, see *Framing the Constitution of Japan: Primary Sources in English, 1944–1949* (Bethesda, Md.: Congressional Information Service, 1989). For a full treatment of the overall constitutional process, see Robert E. Ward, "Presurrender Planning: Treatment of the Emperor and Constitutional Changes," Theodore H. McNelly, "'Induced Revolution': The Policy and Process of Constitutional Reform in Occupied Japan," and Tanaka Hideo, "The Conflict between Two Legal Traditions in Making the Constitution of Japan," in *Democratizing Japan: The Allied Occupation,* ed. Robert E. Ward and Sakamoto Yoshikazu (Honolulu: University of Hawaii Press, 1987); and Finn, *Winners in Peace,* pp. 89–104.

[29] *PRJ,* pp. 133–134. On SCAP's efforts to rebuild the Diet, see Hans H. Baerwald, "Early SCAP Policy and the Rehabilitation of the Diet," in Ward and Sakamoto, *Democratizing Japan,* pp. 133–156.

[30] Gunther, *The Riddle of MacArthur,* p. 126; *PRJ,* pp. 298–299.

[31] MacArthur, *A Soldier Speaks,* p. 167.

[32] MacArthur, *Reminiscences,* p. 302.

[33] On some of the laws and institutions, see *PRJ,* p. 361. See also Justin Williams Sr., *Japan's Political Revolution Under MacArthur: A Participant's Account* (Tokyo: Tokyo University Press, 1979).

[34] Edwin M. Martin, *The Allied Occupation of Japan* (Stanford, Calif.: Stanford University Press, 1948), p. 64.

[35] *PRJ,* p. 358.

[36] See *PRJ,* p. 362; and, Martin, *The Allied Occupation of Japan,* p. 72.

[37] Martin, *The Allied Occupation of Japan,* p. 70.

[38] On the Local Autonomy Law, see Amakawa Akira, "The Making of the Postwar Local Government System," in Ward and Sakamoto, *Democratizing Japan,* pp. 253–283. On MacArthur's prohibition, see Gunther, *The Riddle of MacArthur,* p. 153.

[39] As cited in Justin Williams, "American Democratization Policy for Occupied Japan: Correcting the Revisionist Version," *Pacific Historical Review* 57, no. 2 (May 1988): 185.

[40] Gunther, *The Riddle of MacArthur*, p. 154.

[41] *PRJ*, p. 54.

[42] JCS 1380/15 in *PRJ*, p. 435. This language was the same in SWNCC 150/4 (*PRJ*, p. 425) and was used consistently by MacArthur. See, for example, Gunther, *The Riddle of MacArthur*, p. 155.

[43] Michiko Ariga in *The Occupation of Japan: Economic Policy and Reform*, pp. 230–231; Gunther, *The Riddle of MacArthur*, p. 154.

[44] George Kennan, *Memoirs* (Boston: Little Brown, 1967), p. 409; and Howard Schonberger, "A Rejoinder," *Pacific Historical Review* 56, no. 2 (May 1988): 214.

[45] Carl Shoup et al., *U.S. Tax Mission to Japan: Report on Japanese Taxation* (Tokyo: General Headquarters SCAP, 1949).

[46] On enforcement and early successes in prosecuting evasion cases, see Supreme Commander for the Allied Powers, *Mission and Accomplishments of the Occupation in the Economic and Scientific Fields* (Tokyo: General Headquarters SCAP, 1949), p. 6.

On the capital-levy tax, see Wolfe, *Americans as Proconsuls*, p. 143.

In 1946, 100,000 yen was equal to between $16,700 and $25,000.

[47] *Mission and Accomplishments of the Occupation in the Economic and Scientific Fields*, p. 23.

[48] MacArthur, *Reminiscences*, p. 308; Cohen, *Remaking Japan*, p. 197; and Gunther, *The Riddle of MacArthur*, p. 143.

[49] See *PRJ* p. 134; Cohen, *Remaking Japan*, pp. 187–276; Supreme Commander for Allied Powers, *Mission and Accomplishments of the Occupation in the Economic and Scientific Fields*, pp. 22–26; Lawrence H. Redford ed., *The Occupation of Japan: Economic Policy and Reform*, Proceedings of a Symposium Sponsored by the MacArthur Memorial, April 13-15, 1978, (Norfolk, Virginia: The MacArthur Memorial, 1980), pp. 162–201; and Supreme Commander for the Allied Powers, *Final Report of the Advisory Committee on Labor* (Tokyo: General Headquarters SCAP, 1946).

[50] See interview with Theodore Cohen in Redford, ed., *The Occupation of Japan: Economic Policy and Reform*, pp. 162–163.

[51] MacArthur, *Reminiscences*, p. 283.

[52] William Manchester, *American Caesar: Douglas MacArthur, 1880–1964* (Boston: Little, Brown and Company, 1978), p. 462.

[53] Supreme Commander for the Allied Powers, *Mission and Accomplishments of the Occupation in the Natural Resources Field* (Tokyo: General Headquarters SCAP, 1949), p. 9

[54] Ibid.

[55] Manchester, *American Caesar,* p. 508.

[56] Supreme Commander for Allied Powers (SCAP), *Mission and Accomplishments of the Supreme Commander for the Allied Powers in the Economic, Scientific, and Natural Resource Fields* (Tokyo: General Headquarters SCAP, 1952), p. 64.

[57] Supreme Commander for Allied Powers (SCAP), *Selected Data on the Occupation of Japan* (Tokyo: General Headquarters SCAP, 1950), p. 43.

[58] Ibid.; MacArthur, *Reminiscences,* pp. 313–314.

[59] See Susan J. Pharr, "The Politics of Women's Rights," in Ward and Sakamoto, *Democratizing Japan,* p. 222.

[60] For these and the following statistics, see Gunther, *The Riddle of MacArthur,* pp. 130–133.

[61] On changes in the status of women during the occupation, see Gunther, *The Riddle of MacArthur,* p. 132, MacArthur, *Reminiscences,* p. 305, and Manchester, *American Caesar,* p. 504. On the women in the media, see Marlene J. Mayo, "Civil Censorship and Media Control in Early Occupied Japan: From Minimum to Stringent Surveillance," in Wolfe, *Americans as Proconsuls,* p. 317.

[62] Pharr in Sakamoto and Ward, *Democratizing Japan,* pp. 234–245.

[63] Eleanor M. Hadley, "From Deconcentration to Reverse Course in Japan, in Wolfe, *Americans as Proconsuls,* p. 153.

[64] Gunther, *The Riddle of MacArthur,* p. 147.

[65] Ibid.; Toshio Nishi, *Unconditional Democracy: Education and Politics in Occupied Japan, 1945–1952* (Stanford: Hoover Institution Press, 1982), pp. 196–197.

[66] Nishi, *Unconditional Democracy,* p. 198.

[67] For a complete discussion of the educational reforms by one who held an important position in the Education Division of the Civil Information and Education Section, see Mark Orr, "Education Reform Policy in Occupied Japan" (doctoral dissertation, University of North Carolina, 1954–1955).

[68] *PRJ,* p. 246.

[69] SCAP, *Selected Data,* p. 20.

[70] Gunther, *The Riddle of MacArthur,* p. 126; Cohen, *Remaking Japan,* pp. 378–400.

[71] See Mayo, "Civil Censorship and Media Control in Early Occupied Japan," in Wolfe, *Americans as Proconsuls,* pp. 263–320.

[72] Ibid., p. 316.

[73] Cohen, *Remaking Japan*, p. 9.

[74] For the most complete account of the treatment of religion under the Occupation, see William Woodard, *The Allied Occupation of Japan, 1945–1952, and Japanese Religions* (Leyden, The Netherlands: Brill, 1972).

[75] From an official occupation document as cited in Gunther, *The Riddle of MacArthur*, pp. 141–142.

[76] Manchester, *American Caesar*, p. 466.

[77] MacArthur, *Reminiscences*, p. 311; and SCAP, *Select Data*, pp. 26–27.

[78] Manchester, *American Caesar*, p. 474.

[79] Industrial resurgence reached an amazing index of 145 (1932–1926=100) by the end of the Occupation. See Supreme Commander for Allied Powers, *Mission and Accomplishments of the SCAP in the Economic, Science and Natural Resource Fields*, p. 1.

[80] Michiko Ariga in Redford, *The Occupation of Japan: Economic Policy and Reform*, p. 231.

[81] See Gengo Suzuki in *The Occupation of Japan: Economic Policy and Reform*, pp. 245–247; Robert S. Ozaki, Eleanor Hadley, and Professor Uekesa in the same volume, pp. 233–245; and Eleanor M. Hadley, "Discussion," in Wolfe, *Americans as Proconsuls*, p. 175.

[82] See Tristan Beplat in Redford, *The Occupation of Japan: Economic Policy and Reform*, pp. 236–240.

[83] Cohen, *Remaking Japan*, p. 375; and Professor Uekusa as cited in Redford, *The Occupation of Japan: Economic Policy and Reform*, p. 232.

[84] John D. Montgomery, "Artificial Revolution Revisited: From Success to Excess," in Wolfe, *Americans as Proconsuls*, p. 445.

[85] MacArthur, *Reminiscences*, p. 281.

[86] Kennan, *Memoirs*, pp. 382–383.

[87] See, for example, U.S. Naval Medical Research Institute, *Far Eastern Nutritional Relief (Japanese Culture)* (Washington, D.C.: Office of the Chief of Naval Operations, 1944).

[88] Braibanti, "The MacArthur Shogunate in Allied Guise," in Wolfe, *Americans as Proconsuls*, pp. 81, 83, and 91.

CHAPTER TWELVE

KOSOVO

LEARNING TO LEVERAGE "LIBERATOR" STATUS

Bathsheba N. Crocker

The United States has been Kosovo's preferred patron since leading the calls for air strikes against Yugoslavia in March 1999. Although the ensuing military campaign to drive Serbian president Slobodan Milosevic's forces from Kosovo was a NATO effort, the United States was the biggest player militarily. It bore the brunt of the burden for the war in terms of commitment of troops, equipment, technical expertise, and money. It also played a crucial role in concluding the negotiations between the Serbs and NATO to end the war and in defining the postwar military and civilian efforts.

As a result, Kosovar Albanians see the United States as their great liberator.[1] A main thoroughfare in downtown Pristina was renamed Bill Clinton Boulevard after the war. And in practical terms, the political capital the United States amassed during the quick and decisive military campaign largely shielded it from criticisms and complaints lobbed at the postwar international presence.

During the post-conflict phase, the United States translated its preferred patron status into actual outcomes on the ground in very particular ways. Sometimes the results were positive—such as the encouragement of donor support and assistance to the Kosovo Police Service (KPS). Sometimes, however, they were counterproductive—for example, the United States' wartime ties to the Kosovo Liberation Army (KLA) undermined early efforts to establish law and order, as did its failure to hold the Kosovo Protection Corps (KPC) accountable for criminal and insurgency activities, and its hesitation to address the issue of Kosovo's final status. The overriding lesson of Kosovo for future post-conflict missions is that better management of the opportunities and obligations that accompany "preferred" status must be a priority for the United States.

BACKGROUND

On June 9, 1999, after a 78-day bombing campaign, NATO and the Serbian armed forces signed a Military Technical Agreement calling for the immediate and complete withdrawal of all Serb forces from Kosovo and the establishment of an international peacekeeping force.

On June 10, 1999, the United Nations Security Council passed Resolution 1244, calling, among other things, for the establishment of a United Nations Mission in Kosovo (UNMIK) to function as the civil administration; the appointment of a Special Representative of the Secretary General (SRSG) who would function as the transitional administrator of Kosovo; NATO control over the peacekeeping force; the establishment of an international civilian police force; and the demobilization of the Kosovo Liberation Army (KLA), an opposition group that had assisted NATO's campaign.[2] Notably, Resolution 1244 left open any determination of Kosovo's "final status"—whether it would become independent or remain part of Serbia—mandating only that autonomy would gradually be transferred to newly established Kosovo government institutions, but recognizing the territorial sovereignty of the Federal Republic of Yugoslavia (FRY).[3]

The NATO-led Kosovo Force (KFOR) entered Kosovo on June 12, 1999, and Yugoslav withdrawal was completed by June 20, as scheduled. UNMIK began its deployment simultaneously, although it was severely understaffed during the first several months of its existence due to resource and personnel constraints. At its height, KFOR had 49,400 troops,[4] and the civilian presence was about 11,000 strong, including UNMIK administrators and international civilian police (CIVPOL).[5]

THE INTERNATIONAL COMMUNITY'S EARLY RECORD

Despite the high-level focus of the United States and other major countries, the international community's record in the early years of the Kosovo mission was mixed.

Security

KFOR failed early on to address some critical security problems—revenge killings, ethnic violence, and nascent organized criminal activity. This created a dangerous security vacuum that, over time, has undermined UNMIK's leverage and longer-term efforts to establish the rule of law and reconciliation among Kosovo's ethnicities. In part, NATO underestimated the level of revenge violence that would occur; but policy-makers in Washington and other major capitals also failed to properly mandate KFOR for law enforcement needs. Politically and ethnically motivated violence declined over time, but many years into the mission, KFOR and CIVPOL officers still guarded Serb patrimonial sites to protect them against destruction by ethnic Albanians. Serbs and other ethnic minorities, to the extent they had returned to Kosovo at all, continued to live as virtual prisoners in well-guarded enclaves with effectively no freedom of movement. Ordinary criminal activity markedly declined, but Kosovo became a haven for organized crime, from prostitution and human trafficking to drugs and weapons smuggling and money laundering.[6]

Governance and Participation

UNMIK's slow deployment into Kosovo resulted in a political vacuum that enabled competing power structures to take hold, in particular enabling KLA officials to assert civilian authority in most of Kosovo's municipalities. This forced UNMIK and other international actors to treat former KLA officials as legitimate governing partners from the start.

Once UNMIK assumed control, however, it enacted a series of measures designed to foster coordination with Kosovar authorities, such as setting up joint administrative structures and Kosovo advisory groups. Gradually, UNMIK transferred considerable authority to Kosovo's self-government institutions. It was slower to transfer authority over key functions, including the judiciary, the police, legislation, the economy, and the budget, leading to criticisms that it was effectively a colonial administration. Moreover, the SRSG retained virtually unlimited authority to override decisions of Kosovo's governing institutions, to validate or overturn laws passed by Kosovo's nascent National Assembly, and to promulgate laws without input or debate from the assembly. During its early years, UNMIK quite simply failed to pass certain laws that were critical to the establishment of the rule of law in Kosovo, including the criminal and criminal procedure codes, which sat with UN lawyers in Pristina and New York for years after being drafted.

In just four years, the international community oversaw three rounds of the most free and fair elections in Kosovo's history, although voter turnout declined in each successive election.[7] Nonetheless, the development of transition strategies to turn authority over to Kosovo institutions was ad hoc, as was training and mentoring of Kosovar civil servants and government officials, often a direct reflection of which donor happened to be in charge of any particular agency or function.[8] Thus, the level of preparedness among Kosovar ministries for self-government varied, perpetuating the perceived—and in some cases actual—need for UNMIK to retain overall control.[9] Four years into its mission, UNMIK had yet even to formulate a workable plan for transferring authority to the justice ministry.

Justice and Reconciliation

UNMIK did not adequately prioritize the need to establish the rule of law and focus on the judiciary in the immediate post-conflict phase.[10] Initial confusion in deciding on an appropriate body of interim law, severe delay in CIVPOL deployment, and the late decision to bring in international judges and prosecutors to supplement the nascent Kosovar judiciary all contributed to lasting problems in instilling the rule of law in Kosovo.

During UNMIK's first months on the ground, Kosovo's judiciary was not equipped to handle cases related to post-conflict revenge and ethnic violence, and judges routinely released suspects KFOR had arrested. UNMIK and KFOR, however, seemed unwilling or unable to handle cases involving war crimes or revenge violence, fostering doubts about the international community's commitment to address the issue systemically.

Several years after NATO's intervention, the justice system was still unprepared to handle war crimes cases against Serbs and Albanians and sensitive cases involving former KLA officers. War crimes in Kosovo remained largely unpunished, as did postwar crimes against Kosovo's minority populations.[11] Until these cases are addressed, efforts to foster reconciliation among Albanians and Serbs will founder. The need to address war crimes and other sensitive cases means that there is a continuing need for international judges and prosecutors in Kosovo. Yet, UNMIK lagged in establishing training and mentoring programs for local judicial capacity, needed to ensure the sustainability of any transition strategy.

Some of the early problems in establishing the rule of law stemmed from what has been called UNMIK's "scandalous lack of resources,"[12] including the lengthy delay in staffing the CIVPOL presence. At the same time, however, UNMIK's efforts to create an indigenous police force—the Kosovo Police Service—are widely regarded as a success story. By June 2003, around 5,500 KPS officers had graduated from the Kosovo Police Service School and were policing the streets of Kosovo, carrying out sensitive arrests, and in some areas operating on their own authority.[13] As of late 2002, minorities made up 15 percent of the KPS, and women accounted for 16 percent of the force—making the KPS one of the most multiethnic and gender-balanced police forces in all of Europe.[14]

Economic and Social Well-being

During the first years of the Kosovo mission, there was progress in rebuilding much of Kosovo's damaged infrastructure, but the economy remained very weak: estimates of unemployment ranged as high as 60 percent;[15] Kosovo was still heavily dependent on international funding and had seen little foreign investment; about 50 percent of Kosovars lived under the poverty line;[16] there had been little progress on privatizing Kosovo's state-owned enterprises; and most of the territory still experienced rolling power blackouts on a daily basis. Donor support for Kosovo was consistently high, close to the World Bank and European Community's joint projected needs assessment for Kosovo.[17] But initial delay in funding UNMIK's budget and severe donor coordination problems undermined UNMIK's performance and overall reconstruction efforts.[18]

There is very real concern about massive economic destabilization when the "internationals" pull out. Major discrepancies in salaries received by Kosovo's civil servants, judges, lawyers, and police officers versus those received by Kosovars employed as UNMIK drivers, security officers, and translators leave Kosovo's police forces and judges vulnerable to bribery and create little incentive for Kosovars to remain in Kosovo once UNMIK leaves. There was little initial focus on longer-term development needs, including the creation of long-term business opportunities. The apparent lack of a comprehensive employment generation plan is particularly worrisome given Kosovo's demographics: about 50 percent of Kosovars are under the age of 20, by far the youngest population in Europe.[19]

Resolution 1244 charged UNMIK to foster "the safe and unimpeded return of all refugees and displaced persons to their homes in Kosovo," but refugees were slow to return. As of early 2004, close to 10,000 of an estimated 230,000–280,000 displaced Kosovar minorities had returned to Kosovo.[20] Security and the consequent lack of freedom of movement have been the biggest constraints to returns.[21] The severe and lasting restrictions on minorities' freedom of movement have limited their access to basic government services, including health care, education, and social services. Over the long term, Kosovo's dim economic prospects, assuring better access to basic services, and acceptance by Kosovar Albanians will be the more difficult hurdles with respect to the returns process.[22]

ASSESSING THE UNITED STATES IN ITS ROLE AS PREFERRED PATRON

Burden Sharing

Because it shouldered most of the military burden, the United States has felt from the start that the European Union and its member states should have primary responsibility for Kosovo's reconstruction. Nonetheless, throughout the post-conflict reconstruction phase, the United States continued to wield significant power and authority—in KFOR, with respect to civilian administration, and financially. The United States announced that it would participate in a Kosovo peacekeeping force even before the start of air strikes, and indeed, the United States assumed control of one of Kosovo's five multinational brigades (MNBs) and has consistently supplied between 11 and 15 percent of KFOR's troops.[23] The commander of KFOR has never been an American, but the United States has still determined security policy.

The United States has maintained a robust diplomatic and political presence throughout the Kosovo post-conflict mission, establishing a U.S. Office in Pristina that functions as the diplomatic presence and a large U.S. Agency for International Development (USAID) mission. Moreover, the first three principal deputy SRSGs in Kosovo were Americans.

During the early reconstruction years, the United States was the second largest single donor, pledging 15 percent of overall funds, or a total of $350 million from July 1999 to November 2002.[24] The European Community was the largest single donor during that time, at 40 percent.[25] Donors initially failed to meet UNMIK's baseline budget requirements, which led to severe problems of underfunding and delays in staffing the mission. U.S. pressure—in the form of public statements by high-level U.S. officials and congressional action—helped persuade European donors to fulfill their pledges and ensure UNMIK could become operational.[26] At certain times, USAID has financed over half of the EU's "pillar" in UNMIK, to compensate for slow EU funding mechanisms.[27]

Political Will

Where the United States has taken a particular interest in certain reconstruction activities, a combination of high-level attention and significant financial and personnel contributions has led to some real successes. For example, the United States has contributed substantially in the area of policing; U.S. police officers consistently made up about 12 percent of the overall CIVPOL force in the early years of the mission.[28] It has been the largest financial contributor to the Kosovo Police Service and, as such, had leverage to encourage its goals, such as multi-ethnicity and the inclusion of women.[29] The United States also used its leverage to maintain pressure on UNMIK to keep on track with the transfer of authority from CIVPOL to KPS, considered a highlight of UNMIK's overall record on transitioning authority to Kosovar institutions.[30]

In other cases, however, political expediency led the United States to make choices that have hindered or hamstrung progress. Three examples stand out.

KFOR's Early Ambivalence toward Albanian Violence

During its first few months on the ground, KFOR failed to minimize the rampage of revenge and ethnic violence by Kosovar Albanians. Although the UN's plans in the summer of 1999 had called for the rapid deployment of 3,000 international police officers, it was three months before the first 1,400 CIVPOL officers were in Kosovo. Even one year later—in June 2000—CIVPOL was only at 77 percent of its authorized total of 4,718.[31] This lengthy delay, together with the abrupt and complete withdrawal of all Serb armed forces and police officers, meant that KFOR was the only game in town for months.

Still, it was several months before KFOR started to tackle the law enforcement vacuum systematically, and the interim period saw major violence and a wholesale exodus of Serbs and other minorities from Kosovo—representing "a profound failure of the international community to uphold the principles that had been hailed as the driving force behind the war effort."[32]

The complete security vacuum in Kosovo and the lack of any meaningful support on the civilian side meant that KFOR had to take on myriad tasks simultaneously without proper mandates, training, or equipment—everything from monitoring the withdrawal of Serb troops, to overseeing the disarmament of KLA fighters, establishing law and order, repairing local infrastructure, protecting Serbs and other minorities, resolving housing disputes, and administering towns.[33]

KFOR troops never received coordinated guidance from Washington and other NATO capitals as to how to handle violence by Albanians—the protection of whom was the impetus for the bombing campaign and who had been NATO allies during that campaign. KFOR troops sometimes stood by and watched as Albanians, including KLA members, looted and drove Serbs from their homes, because they had orders "to let them plunder."[34] The failure to stop ethnic violence in the first months after the war signaled that Albanian violence was somehow acceptable, causing lasting problems with respect to establishing the rule of law and respect for human rights and efforts to foster reconciliation among Albanians and Kosovo's minority populations. It also led to a long-term need for KFOR and CIVPOL officers to provide round-the-clock protection for minorities.[35]

The dual chain of command between the military and civilian presence—necessary to secure U.S. participation in KFOR—created its own difficulties. It took several years for KFOR and UNMIK to develop a workable system for intelligence sharing in order that CIVPOL could successfully prosecute sensitive criminal cases for which only KFOR had the necessary intelligence. There are numerous reports suggesting that serious crimes have gone unsolved in large part because KFOR had crucial intelligence that it would not share with UNMIK and CIVPOL.[36] After NATO requested that Italy's *carabinieri* track organized crime in Kosovo, U.S. army forces and *carabinieri* working in the same town would not even share intelligence with each other or discuss what each side was doing.[37] KFOR and UNMIK eventually developed a Central Intelligence Unit that enabled KFOR to share military intelligence with UNMIK police.[38]

There are also allegations that concern for the safety of KFOR soldiers led KFOR and UN officials to block or oppose some trials against former KLA officials.[39] This has undermined the establishment of an independent judiciary in Kosovo. It was only in the spring of 2002, when it publicized investigations into sensitive cases involving former KLA members, that UNMIK began to shed its reputation of failing to pursue an impartial and effective system of justice.[40]

KFOR and the KLA: A Marriage of Convenience?

NATO—and the United States in particular—had developed close ties with the KLA before and during the 1999 bombing campaign that made it difficult for U.S. policymakers to confront the KLA at the first signs of its direct involvement in violence against Kosovo's minorities. UNMIK's leverage over the KLA was limited by KFOR's reluctance to tackle the issue. Because of its position as political sponsor of the KLA, it is arguable that only the United States could have succeeded in pressuring the KLA leadership to take steps to end revenge activities. U.S. officials, however, waited months before beginning to deliver high-profile warnings to KLA leaders.[41]

Despite Resolution 1244's mandate to demilitarize the KLA, KFOR never developed a comprehensive plan for doing so.[42] Instead, certain early decisions by KFOR—and the United States—have enabled the KLA to survive in various forms.[43] It is widely acknowledged (although not recorded in writing) that in order to secure the KLA leadership's agreement on demobilization, KFOR and UNMIK accepted KLA demands that 50 percent of the original classes of KPS officers would be made up of former KLA members. Although UNMIK stopped honoring this quota in June 2001, senior CIVPOL officers have said that law and order in Kosovo will suffer because of the continuing presence of active KPS officers who are loyal to former KLA leaders rather than to the KPS.[44] This will be particularly problematic with UNMIK's transfer of authority to the KPS because KPS officers will be required to handle sensitive cases involving allegations against former KLA members.

Similarly, the Kosovo Protection Corps was established in 1999 as a compromise between KFOR's need to demilitarize the KLA and the KLA leadership's determination that Kosovo be allowed to maintain some kind of standing force.[45] The KPC was established as a civil emergency force that would provide disaster response service, deliver humanitarian assistance, clear mines, and assist with reconstruction.[46] The KPC was meant to be nonmilitary, but it was allowed to preserve the KLA command structure, wear military-like uniforms and badges similar to those of the KLA, and carry weapons. From the first, KPC members have been completely open about their intent that the KPC is the nucleus of a future national army of an independent Kosovo.[47]

The United States helped conceive and design the KPC, including determining its command structure, perhaps out of deference to the KLA's role during the war.[48] It is clear that KFOR and UNMIK agreed to create the KPC as a means of absorbing a large core of the former KLA fighters, in part to address the lack of an overall strategy for their demilitarization. KPC members have allegedly been directly involved in militant Albanian insurgency activities in southern Serbia and Macedonia as well as in organized and other criminal activities. By 2003, several senior KPC officers had been arrested for serious crimes, including murder, but the KPC largely operated with near impunity during UNMIK's early years. KFOR,

UNMIK, and the United States did not take seriously the need to oversee KPC activities and hold KPC officers accountable; they instead sought to downplay reports of the KPC's links to crime and other illicit activity.[49] This only added to the general feeling that former KLA members operate outside Kosovo's nascent system of justice.

Despite these problems, neither KFOR nor UNMIK developed a long-term plan as to how to handle the KPC. Although it was originally envisioned that the KPC might take over some duties from KFOR, the KPC's demonstrated links to undesirable activities made this problematic in practice. Further, the open questions related to final status effectively chilled any incentive on the part of the KPC and other former KLA members to fully disarm.

Final Status

The third U.S. policy choice that has hampered Kosovo's reconstruction was the deliberate decision of the U.S. government to "keep its head in the sand" with respect to final status.[50] The continued refusal by the international community to set a course for determining whether Kosovo will remain part of Serbia, become independent, or be a semiautonomous part of a loose federation with Serbia and Montenegro has created an inherently unstable situation for Kosovo, Serbia, and the region. As a group of prominent policy experts has written, it "fuels misplaced hopes for some in Serbia that all or part of Kosovo will again come under the authority of Belgrade, postpones stability in Southeast Europe, and most disturbingly, contributes to increased tensions, political and economic stagnation, and an unhealthy culture of dependence among Kosovo's ambitious, youthful, and growing population."[51]

The United States and other major bilateral players consistently refused to be pinned down as to when final status discussions should begin; as late as four years into the mission, high-level U.S. officials reiterated that such discussions are some way off.[52] In July 2002, SRSG Michael Steiner announced a policy of "standards before status," laying out a series of benchmarks that Kosovo's institutions must meet before discussions on final status can take place.[53] The UN Security Council endorsed the benchmarks process, as did the U.S. government, which noted its continuing support for the graduated approach to questions of self-government, autonomy, and future political status.

Although Resolution 1244 intentionally left open the question of final status, by its own terms, the resolution took a position on the question by calling for the establishment and transfer of autonomy to self-governing institutions. As a result, UNMIK's early actions created both the expectation of independence on the part of Kosovars and a sort of de facto independence—even though the international community continued to recognize formally that Kosovo is still a part of Serbia.

In fact, since the end of the conflict, the United States and most European and regional countries except Albania have expressed strong opposition to independence. More than one commentator has described this policy as incoherent. Worse, it has affected the reconstruction efforts across the board, from killing incentives for Kosovars to disarm, to chilling foreign investment, to ensuring the single-minded pursuit by Kosovo's political parties of independence rather than domestic issues, to lengthy delays in the promulgation of important and necessary legislation. UNMIK was effectively paralyzed by indecision over how to accomplish certain goals—such as privatization—without prejudging final status issues. UNMIK's lengthy hand-wringing over Kosovo's criminal codes reportedly stemmed from similar concerns.

Regardless of what Kosovo's final status should be, it is apparent that continued ambiguity over final status has undermined Kosovo's progression. Moreover, because under the terms of Resolution 1244 UNMIK's exit hinges on a final status determination, the decision not to address the question ensures that the international community will not leave Kosovo anytime soon.[54] The United Nations has recognized an inherent tension among Kosovars' aspirations for independence, respecting Serbia's territorial integrity, and UNMIK's mandate as described in Resolution 1244: "There seems no alternative, in these circumstances, to a continuing UNMIK presence, and a strict implementation of resolution 1244 (1999), until such time as an agreement on final status can be reached."[55]

CONCLUSION

Several years into the Kosovo mission, it remained clear that continued U.S. involvement will be indispensable. As one journalist wrote, "The fact is that everyone in the Balkans, even the bad guys, look to America as the broker, as the one to exert pressure, to deliver what's promised."[56]

Yet the case of Kosovo demonstrates that when the United States has dominant influence by virtue of an overwhelming military victory, a large political role, or a major financial commitment, it has an obligation not to duck tough issues or kick them down the road, as has been the case with the initial security vacuum, Albanian violence, establishing the rule of law, and the final status issue in Kosovo. If the "preferred patron" does not lead, who will?

Kosovo also illustrates how alliances and policies formed of wartime necessities or political expediency can cloud later policy decisions or undermine important reconstruction goals. Better coordination between wartime and post-conflict goals could help avoid the types of problems seen in Kosovo. It is understandable that the United States wanted to co-opt former KLA members into legitimate security organizations. But this should have been accompanied by a commitment to exercise oversight over its wartime allies, rather than delaying decisions when problems became evident.

The United States has used its influence in Kosovo wisely on some issues. But the ad hoc nature of its involvement has contributed to the mixed record of the international community in Kosovo. It remains to be seen whether the United States will seek to translate its dominant status into an active, sustained, and well-planned drive toward peace and reconstruction.

Notes

The author would like to thank Stephan Anagnost of the Organization for Security and Cooperation in Europe (OSCE) for his invaluable assistance in arranging the author's visit to Kosovo in November 2002. The author would also like to thank Milan Vaishnav and Neil Fletcher for their excellent research assistance.

[1] While many Kosovars considered the United States their "liberator," I will use that term only when referring to Kosovar views. I will use the term "preferred patron" when referring to the relationship through the eyes of Americans or third parties to avoid a normative bias when describing the relationship.

[2] United Nations Security Council Resolution 1244, June 10, 1999, at http://ods-dds-ny.un.org/doc/UNDOC/GEN/N99/172/89/PDF/N9917289.pdf?OpenElement.

[3] The Federal Republic of Yugoslavia at that time included Serbia and Montenegro, which have since split into a loose union of two republics that was officially renamed Serbia and Montenegro on February 4, 2003.

[4] *Report of the Security Council Mission to Kosovo and Belgrade, Federal Republic of Yugoslavia*, S/2002/1376, December 19, 2002, at www.un.org/Docs/sc/missionreports.html. In July 2002, NATO agreed to a force ramp-down that would take it to 32,000 troops by the end of 2002 and 29,000 troops by the end of June 2003. See Steven J. Woehrel and Julie Kim, *Kosovo and U.S. Policy*, Congressional Research Service Report for Congress, updated January 3, 2003, p. 10, at www.usembassy.it/pdf/other/RL31053.pdf. KFOR's overall numbers were actually 25,000 as of May 2003. Janet Bogue, Deputy Assistant Secretary of State for South Central Europe, "U.S. Policy Toward Kosovo," testimony, House International Relations Committee, May 21, 2003, at www.state.gov/p/eur/rls/rm/2003/20900pf.htm.

[5] Yaroslav Trofimov, "UN's Long Stay and Power in Kosovo Stir Resentment," *Wall Street Journal*, January 3, 2003.

[6] Woehrel and Kim, *Kosovo and U.S. Policy*. As one UN spokesperson noted, "This isn't really a society with an organized crime problem. In many ways, this is a society based on organized crime." See Sylvia Poggioli, "UN Nation-building Mission in Kosovo Moving Slowly," on *Morning Edition*, National Public Radio, May 19, 2003 (quoting Barry Fletcher, spokesperson for UN CIVPOL in Kosovo).

[7] In the October 26, 2002, municipal elections, overall voter turnout was 54 percent, down from 79 percent in the first round of municipal elections. Fisnik Abrashi, *Kosovo Moderates Win Local Elections*, Associated Press, November 3, 2002.

[8] One report has noted that Kosovo departments that were supported by the U.S. Agency for International Development (USAID) have proved better able to assume responsibility transferred from internationals, reflecting U.S. policy to focus on mentoring and training locals from the start, than those departments supported by the United Nations, for example. *A Review of Peace Operations: A Case for Change: Kosovo*, Conflict Security and Development Group report, London, March 10, 2003, p. 54 [hereinafter *CSDG Report*].

[9] In January 2003, Michael Steiner, the Special Representative for the Secretary-General (SRSG) at that time, said: "To think that they [the Kosovars] are already ready to take over the whole administration is an illusion." Trofimov, *UN's Long Stay*.

[10] See, for example, William G. O'Neill, *Kosovo: An Unfinished Peace*, International Peace Academy Occasional Paper, 2002; Simon Chesterman, *Justice Under International Administration: Kosovo, East Timor and Afghanistan*, International Peace Academy report, September 2002.

[11] *Finding the Balance: The Scales of Justice in Kosovo*, International Crisis Group Balkans Report No. 134, September 12, 2002, pp. 16–17.

[12] *A Fragile Peace: Laying the Foundations for Justice in Kosovo*, Lawyers' Committee for Human Rights Report, October 1999.

[13] Hedi Annabi, Assistant Secretary-General for Peacekeeping Operations, Security Council briefing, June 10, 2003, at www.un.org/News/Press/docs/2003/sc7785.p2.doc.htm.

[14] *Pillar 1: Police and Justice*, UNMIK presentation paper, November 2002, p. 9, at www.unmikonline.org/justice/documents/PillarI_Presentation_Paper.pdf. See also *A Kosovo Roadmap (II): Internal Benchmarks*, International Crisis Group Balkans Report No. 125, March 1, 2002, p. 14.

[15] The unemployment rate for Kosovo's minorities was 85 percent as of the end of 2002. *Return to Uncertainty: Kosovo's Internally Displaced and the Return Process*, International Crisis Group Balkans Report No. 139, December 13, 2002, p. 22.

[16] *Kosovo, Federal Republic of Yugoslavia Transitional Support Strategy*, World Bank document, July 2, 2002, p. 4, at www.seerecon.org/Kosovo/KosovoDonor-Programs/WBTSS-Kosovo.pdf.

[17] In the first year and a half of the mission, donors pledged around 90 percent of the projected medium-term reconstruction needs for Kosovo. Ibid., p. 2.

[18] A Council on Foreign Relations high-level independent task force described the coordination of international donors in the Balkans as ranging from close to nonexistent, noting that different stakeholders often work at cross-purposes, lack any coherent or consistent strategy, and resemble a "morass of uncoordinated agencies." *Balkans 2010: Report of an Independent Task Force*, Council on Foreign Relations, 2002, p. 31.

[19] European Commission—Humanitarian Aid Office (ECHO), *ECHO in Kosovo: 1998–2001*, ECHO report, Pristina, November 2001, p. 27.

[20] UN High Commissioner for Refugees, "Minority Returns to Kosovo," January 31, 2004, available at www.db.idpproject.org/sites/idpsurvey.nsf/wviewcountries/94C34C4084558E231C1256C7C003A50B6.

[21] Author interview with Peggy Hicks, Director, UNMIK Office of Returns and Communities, Pristina, November 12, 2002.

[22] Ibid.

[23] In March 2000, KFOR had 38,000 troops, 5,600 of whom were American (around 15 percent). Steve Bowman, *Kosovo: U.S. and Allied Military Operations*, July 24, 2000 at www.globalsecurity.org/military/library/report/crs/IB10027_000724.pdf. In November 2002, U.S. troops also made up 15 percent of KFOR. *Bush Reports to Congress on U.S. Forces in Kosovo*, November 15, 2002, at www.usembassy.it/file2002_11/alia/a2111506.htm. By May 2003, the

United States had about 2,700 troops in Kosovo, out of a total of 25,000 KFOR troops (around 11 percent). Andrew Higgins, "Chief Supporters for U.S. in Kabul: France, Germany," *Wall Street Journal,* June 17, 2003.

[24] *U.S. Statement at Kosovo Donors Meeting,* November 5, 2002, at http://belgrade.usembassy.gov/current/021112b.html.

[25] *Kosovo Transitional Support Strategy* (note 15), Annex 2, p. 2.

[26] See Curt Tarnoff, *Kosovo: Reconstruction and Development Assistance,* Congressional Research Service, Report for Congress, updated January 16, 2001, pp. 8–11.

[27] *CSDG Report* (note 7), p. 53 and n.160. UNMIK oversees four pillars that collectively carry out its mandate: Pillar I, Police and Justice (UN leadership); Pillar II, Civil Administration (UN leadership); Pillar III, Democratization and Institution Building (OSCE leadership); and Pillar IV, Reconstruction and Humanitarian Development (EU leadership). The Police and Justice pillar replaced the Humanitarian Aid pillar, which was phased out in mid-2000.

[28] For example, in September 2002, there were 4,468 CIVPOL officers in Kosovo, 535 of whom were from the United States. *UNMIK Police Personnel,* UNMIK information, at www.unmikonline.org/civpol/factsfigs.htm.

[29] Author interview with Henry Wilkins, Chief Law Enforcement Officer, U.S. Office, Pristina, November 8, 2002.

[30] See Stephan M. Minikes, U.S. Ambassador to the OSCE, *Statement on Kosovo,* Vienna, Austria, July 11, 2002.

[31] See Independent International Commission on Kosovo, *Kosovo Report,* 2000, p. 110.

[32] Ibid., p. 105.

[33] For an in-depth look at the various roles U.S. KFOR troops have played, see Dana Priest, *The Mission: Waging War and Keeping Peace with America's Military* (New York: W. W. Norton, 2003), pp. 247–384.

[34] Chesterman, *Justice Under International Administration,* p. 4. As Priest writes, "The former Albanian rebels, whom NATO had worked with during the war, became the new enemies. But troops were not authorized to kill or capture this enemy, or to even arrest him. There were no jails big enough to hold them all. There was no criminal justice system to convict them." Priest, *The Mission,* p. 291.

[35] As late as June 2003, Serbs were being brutally murdered in Kosovo, demonstrating ongoing difficulties in efforts to foster reconciliation between Albanians and Serbs. "Serb Family's Murder is Heinous Crime Against Multi-Ethnic Society," UNMIK News Release, June 4, 2003, at www.unmikonline.org/news.htm#0606.

[36] *Finding the Balance*, p. 12; R. Jeffrey Smith, "Rule of Law is Elusive in Kosovo: U.N., NATO Criticized for Inaction on Violence," *Washington Post*, July 29, 2001, p. A1.

[37] Priest, *The Mission*, pp. 325–26.

[38] *Finding the Balance*, p. 12; author interview with Wilkins. UNMIK was also required to change a FRY-era law that prohibited courts from considering as evidence any information that had been collected covertly.

[39] Charles Karphammer, a Swedish jurist who worked as a prosecutor and judge in Kosovo, claims that during his 18 months in Kosovo, the judiciary was not allowed to function independently because UN and KFOR officials intervened in cases against former KLA members. O'Neill, *Kosovo: An Unfinished Peace*, p. 91.

[40] See *CSDG Report*, pp. 60–63 and 69.

[41] Tyler Marshall, "U.S. in Kosovo for the Long Haul," *Los Angeles Times*, June 10, 2000.

[42] The KLA turned over 10,000 weapons to KFOR in the summer of 1999 in observance of a demilitarization agreement signed on June 21, 1999, but this did not come close to a full disarmament of the KLA. KFOR has admitted that it did not prioritize such disarmament during UNMIK's first year, and KFOR continues to find huge weapons caches throughout Kosovo. Bonn International Center for Conversion (BICC), *Wag the Dog: The Mobilization and Demobilization of the Kosovo Liberation Army*, BICC Brief, no. 20, 2001, pp. 19–21, at www.bicc.de.

[43] The International Crisis Group (ICG) argues that KFOR never set out to fully demilitarize the KLA but rather had a policy of "tolerant confrontation" that allowed former KLA members to survive in various forms, engaging in politically and ethnically motivated violence as well as organized and other criminal activity. According to ICG, the KLA remains a powerful and active element in "every aspect of Kosovo Albanian life." International Crisis Group (ICG), *What Happened to the KLA?* ICG Balkans Report, no. 88, March 3, 2000, pp. 1, 20.

[44] Author interview with Tom Hacker, Deputy UNMIK Police Commissioner, Pristina, November 15, 2002.

[45] ICG, *What Happened to the KLA?* p. 1.

[46] *On the Establishment of the Kosovo Corps*, UNMIK Regulation No. 1999/8, September 20, 1999, at www.unmikonline.org/regulations/1999/reg08-99.htm.

[47] The KPC commander, Agim Ceku—one of the most senior KLA officers—has stated that "[w]e see the KPC as a bridge towards the future, from the KLA as a wartime organization towards a regular, modern army of Kosovo." BICC, *Wag the Dog*, p. 22.

[48] *CSDG Report*, p. 34.

[49] O'Neill, *Kosovo: An Unfinished Peace*, pp. 120–22. The Council on Foreign Relations-sponsored independent task force has called the KPC's lack of accountability "unacceptable." *Balkans 2010*, p. 60.

[50] Author interview with senior official at the U.S. Office, Pristina, November 13, 2002.

[51] Janusz Bugajski, R. Bruce Hitchner, and Paul Williams, *Achieving a Final Status Settlement for Kosovo* (Washington, D.C.: CSIS, April 2003), p. 2.

[52] Bogue, *U.S. Policy Toward Kosovo.*

[53] The benchmarks cover the areas of functioning democratic institutions, rule of law, freedom of movement, returns and reintegration, economy, property rights, dialogue with Belgrade, and the Kosovo Protection Corps. A chart describing the benchmarks can be found at www.unmikonline.org/pub/focus-kos/apr02/benchmarks_eng.pdf.

[54] See International Crisis Group (ICG), *A Kosovo Roadmap (I): Addressing Final Status*, ICG Balkans Report, no. 124, March 1, 2002, pp. ii, 2. In this regard, it should be noted that senior UN and U.S. officials have expressed a desire for the European Union to take over from UNMIK once it leaves, and for the international role to morph into a more traditional development and monitoring role at that point. Author interview with Minna Jarvenpaa, senior policy adviser to SRSG Steiner, Pristina, November 8, 2002.

[55] *No Exit Without Strategy: Security Council Decision-making and the Closure or Transition of United Nations Peacekeeping Operations,* UN Document S/2001/394 (April 21, 2001), paragraph 41, at http://ods-dds-ny.un.org/doc/UNDOC/GEN/N01/343/62/PDF/N0134362.pdf?OpenElement.

[56] Marshall, "U.S. in Kosovo for the Long Haul."

CHAPTER THIRTEEN

EAST TIMOR

THE UNITED STATES AS JUNIOR PARTNER

Robert C. Orr

On May 20, 2002, the Democratic Republic of East Timor celebrated its independence—officially becoming the first new country of the twenty-first century and, indeed, the new millennium. On the reviewing stand UN Secretary General Kofi Annan, former U.S. president Bill Clinton, Australian prime minister John Howard, Indonesian president Megawati Sukarnoputri, and Portuguese president Jorge Sampaio watched solemnly. While it was East Timor and its people's day, the unusual guest list of top-level international players in the tiny country underscored the fact that it also represented a major success for the international community.

East Timor was an unlikely success story. After more than 400 years as a tiny, poor, remote colony of Portugal, East Timor was on the verge of independence when in 1975 Indonesia invaded and declared the territory its twenty-seventh province. For the next 24 years, East Timor was subject to an ongoing guerrilla war, brutal suppression by the Indonesians, and a horrendous standard of living—with over 200,000 East Timorese, almost a third of the population, dying in the years following the annexation from disease and famine.[1] As troubling as Timorese history was in its own right, it was compounded by the problematic role of the international community as well. Since 1975, when Indonesia invaded, East Timor was synonymous with international capitulation in the face of naked aggression, weakness of international law, and the failure of countries and international organizations to live up to their ideals.

For two and a half long decades, East Timor struggled under the yoke of external domination, constantly at war as a clandestine independence movement carried on an armed struggle against Indonesian occupiers. Long a backwater caught in an eddy of global power politics that swirled around regional power Indonesia, East Timor's strategic context changed markedly in the late 1990s as a post-Cold War international environment opened the doors to increasing external pressure on Indonesia to end its illegitimate occupation.

In 1999, East Timor had its first real chance to turn its troubled history around. A change of government in Indonesia and increasing pressure from the international community related to East Timor caused the government in Jakarta to allow an internationally monitored referendum on independence to go forward. When the East Timorese voted overwhelmingly for independence, however, all hell broke loose. Indonesian-backed militias went on a rampage throughout the territory.[2] The ensuing period of organized mayhem left over a thousand dead, the entire population terrorized, and the territory a smoldering ruin.[3]

How East Timor moved from one of the worst places on earth in 1999 to a hope-inspiring success in three short years is a compelling story. It is the story of a resilient people, strong internal leadership, neighboring countries moved by increasingly enlightened self-interest, an international organization that finally lived up to its exacting mandate, and a distant superpower that began to learn how to catalyze success in a new way.[4]

Many in positions of authority in the United States recognized the peace operation and subsequent post-conflict reconstruction effort in East Timor as a notable success story. Even though U.S. participation in the intervention took place during the Clinton administration, President George W. Bush's secretary of state, Colin Powell, held up the operation as representative of a "model" that is "very, very deserving of our support."[5] Senators from across the political spectrum argued, "We got it about right," and identified East Timor as "a promising recipe for U.S. engagement in the world today."[6] While the success in East Timor was real, it received a great deal of extra attention from U.S. policymakers because it provided a model for intervention that did not require the United States to take the lead and bear the accompanying costs. In this "new" model the world's dominant superpower could be actively involved and work with a range of other partners, but unlike in other circumstances, in this case the United States would be a junior partner.

BUILDING A NEW EAST TIMOR: THE INTERNATIONAL ROLE

Following the rampage of militias and Indonesian soldiers, East Timor lay in ruins. On September 15, 1999, Australia led a 31-country intervention force (INTERFET) authorized by UN Security Council Resolution 1264 to restore order. The intervention force drove out violent pro-Indonesian militias, established a stable border with the neighboring province of West Timor, and restored general law and order throughout the territory. Over 100,000 East Timorese, however, were driven or fled into West Timor. The general conditions for East Timorese refugees in West Timor were deplorable, and the camps in which many lived also served as bases from which attempts were made to destabilize East Timor. The United Nations, recognizing the problem, made concerted efforts to repatriate the refugees and reintegrate the redeemable pro-integrationist forces. It eventually succeeded in closing the camps and returning over 50,000 to East Timor. Concurrent with these efforts, the international community attempted to facilitate the demobilization and reintegration of ex-combatants, mostly through the International Office on Migration (IOM). Some of the ex-combatants were given jobs in the newly created East Timorese Defense Force.

Internal law and order posed as many challenges as managing the border with neighboring Indonesia. Few if any police remained who were trusted by the population and capable of maintaining a semblance of order. During the transition to independence, international troops and civilian police provided what little protections they could. Slowly, as international efforts to train a new police force of 3,300 officers moved forward, new police officers began to appear on the streets. At the same time, however, the country-to-be lacked a court system, judges, legal codes, penal institutions, and many other elements of a functioning legal system.

One of the most pressing needs in post-conflict East Timor was for a government. Having never governed itself in over 500 years, and having lost virtually all Indonesian and pro-Indonesian government administrators at the time of the international intervention, East Timor desperately needed help to run its affairs. The United Nations set up the Transitional Administration in East Timor (UNTAET) to run most governmental and administrative affairs in the period to lead up to independence. This apparatus, while not considered terribly efficient by either the local population or many of the internationals present in the territory, managed to field administrators for all parts of the territory and to run basic government functions. To the great credit of UN transitional administrator Sergio Vieira de Mello, the UN not only delivered the needed administrative goods; it managed to incorporate a range of

Timorese into the operations in such a way that they would be ready to take over the governing functions at independence.

East Timor's social and economic situation posed a severe problem in the aftermath of the militias' rampage. Never a wealthy place to begin with, and suffering from extremely high infant mortality and illiteracy rates, East Timor had 75 percent of its physical infrastructure destroyed by retreating militias and Indonesian soldiers.[7] Social institutions were gutted by the killings and forced displacement of large numbers of Timorese, as well as by the withdrawal of the Indonesian and pro-Indonesian civil servants who held virtually all senior positions in schools, clinics, and government offices. The shortage of local Timorese with education and management expertise posed one of the largest impediments to building the new country. East Timor also faced huge funding gaps due to the withdrawal of over $100 million in annual Indonesian subsidies. The withdrawal of this infusion of external cash, however poorly spent previously, could not help but have a serious impact on the economy.

Against this bleak economic backdrop, East Timor's only apparent bright spot was the prospect of significant oil and natural gas revenues from the Timor Gap. Even prior to independence, a Timorese and international team representing Timorese interests negotiated an agreement with Australia, securing a deal thought at the time to be worth approximately $3.6 billion over 20 years. Although significant, these revenues were not guaranteed, and East Timor faced an estimated fiscal gap of approximately $200 million before these revenues would kick in approximately four years later. The international community rallied to the challenge, pouring relatively significant development monies into the tiny territory for rebuilding infrastructure and starting to develop a new economy, based at least in part on agriculture and tourism—high priorities for the Timorese leadership.[8]

Another fundamental problem facing both East Timor and the international community following the intervention was coming to terms with crimes committed during Indonesian rule, including accountability for the 1999 mass killings. Primary responsibility for doing so rested in the hands of the Indonesian legal system, although the UN Security Council passed a resolution that provided for an international justice process should the Indonesian courts fail. The absence of any extensive legal system in East Timor made reconciliation efforts even more crucial. Timorese leaders, both political and religious, sponsored a series of reconciliation meetings with pro-integrationist Timorese in the two-year run-up to independence.

THE UNITED STATES' CONTRIBUTION: LEARNING TO BE AN EFFECTIVE JUNIOR PARTNER

At the time of the intervention, the United States had modest but notable interests at stake in East Timor. A failure could have adversely affected stability in neighboring Indonesia, where over 40 percent of the world's shipping passes on a daily basis. Timor was also important to the United States because it was important to Australia, an ally that had fought with the United States in every war of the twentieth and twenty-first centuries. The United States also had an interest in seeing the United Nations succeed in its role as midwife of a new nation state. If the UN were to fail at this type of mission, more would be left to the United States in similar situations in the future. Furthermore, the United States had and has a stake in re-enforcing the principles of international law, many of which had been violated by Indonesia's invasion in 1975 and in atrocities committed from that time until Indonesia was dislodged in 1999.

Because of its interests and values at stake in East Timor, the United States adopted a supporting or "junior partner" role—one that was somewhat unnatural for the world's sole superpower. The U.S. contribution to the overall effort was important in helping secure a successful outcome, but one cannot ignore the fact that the United States' steps down the path of "junior partnerdom" were tentative and less than robust. East Timor will not be the last case where the United States finds its interests served by ensuring that an intervention led by a friend or ally succeeds. Evaluating the significant but limited role the United States has played in East Timor provides insight into how the United States can improve its leverage and impact in missions where it chooses to be a junior partner.

Military Support

Four types of U.S. military engagement are important elements of the success achieved in East Timor and should be considered for similar operations in the future. First, the United States made significant contributions of logistics, intelligence, and other support. Some form of dedicated support arrangement is often necessary when friends and allies maintain significant forces on the ground. The United States accomplished this through the U.S. Support Group East Timor (USGET), a task force set up expressly to fill critical needs during both the Australian-led and UN-led phases of the operation.

Second, the United States showed the flag on the arms of American military personnel who went ashore to perform civil affairs functions. These visits bolstered friends on the ground and even more importantly sent strong signals to the local population. The abilities and discipline of U.S. troops were lost on no one. As Sergio Vieira de Mello, the UN administrator of East Timor at the time, noted, "people talk about the Marines for weeks" after they build a school or health post, interacting with the local population.[9] Perhaps equally important, the presence of uniformed U.S. military in various parts of the territory over time sent the signal to the militias and Indonesian elements that might be tempted to destabilize the situation that they could make an enemy of the most powerful nation on earth if they attacked the rebuilding project under way.

Third, a retired U.S. general was recruited to work with the Timorese military leadership to establish the East Timor Defense Force, helping with everything from the design of a concept of operations for the new force to writing training, human resources, and logistics plans. This type of support is easy, very valuable, and should be considered in other circumstances as well.

Fourth, three Americans soldiers were assigned to serve as UN military observers and realized huge returns on a minimal investment. The American chief of operations' high visibility and extreme competence running a network of multinational observers throughout the country not only enhanced U.S. prestige; it significantly enhanced the chances for the mission's success.[10] As much as many Americans would like it to be otherwise, however, U.S. commitment is measured not just by the quality, but also by the quantity of "boots on the ground." Providing only three soldiers to a force of more than 8,000 was interpreted by many as verging on a vote of "no confidence" in the mission. In the future, the United States should consider modest double-digit to triple-digit contributions to selected UN forces as a way of drastically improving mission capabilities and overall confidence in the enterprise.

Political and Diplomatic Support

When the United States plays the role of junior partner, political and diplomatic support is crucial. In the case of East Timor, the United States not only led the charge in the UN Security Council and pressured

Indonesia through various channels to accept a multinational force; it also helped Australia assemble and field the multinational coalition.

This initial investment, however, was not matched on the ground. Even as East Timor was moving quickly toward independence, U.S. diplomatic and political presence in East Timor was minimal. No U.S. flag flew in East Timor, and the United States was represented by a mid-level officer who worked for the U.S. ambassador in Indonesia. This arrangement rankled many Timorese, thereby diminishing U.S. influence at a crucial time. It also ensured that U.S. interests in Timor continued to be filtered through the all-powerful lens of Indonesian interests. While inadequate funding for the State Department led to many embassy closures worldwide over the last decade, in those instances where the United States deems its interests sufficiently at stake to engage military and political assets, it must also be prepared to follow through with a commensurate diplomatic presence on the ground.

Transitional Economic and Social Support

Given its baseline economic and social conditions, East Timor needed just about anything that the United States and other countries could give. The United States made a distinctive contribution to the economic and social needs of East Timor, according both to Timorese and to other donors, through assistance provided by USAID's Office of Transition Initiatives (OTI). This flexible, fast assistance—for everything from temporary employment programs to work with political groups and the media sector—filled a gap that other donors could not. Based on this case and others, policymakers in Washington should explore options for enhancing this, and other, flexible civilian rapid response capabilities.

Equally important, the United States helped to establish a basis for a potentially sustainable economy over the long term. In an act little known to most outside East Timor, an American ambassador seconded to the UN Transitional Authority in East Timor negotiated East Timor's rights to the Timor Gap oil and gas, leading to the Timor Sea Treaty.[11] Given the distinct asymmetry of the negotiations between Australia and the struggling territory, employing a hard-nosed American ambassador to conduct the negotiations on behalf of East Timor proved to be a wise strategy. This type of creative use of U.S. diplomatic personnel should be considered in the future.

The United States could also play a bigger role in promoting private-sector involvement in post-conflict reconstruction efforts. Even in East

Timor, with the prospect of developing a reasonably robust economy, there has been little interest from the private sector in long-term investments. Instead, lacking any mechanism to ensure against risk in post-conflict countries, the U.S. government has stood by while business contracts go to buccaneer capitalists who do little to enhance the long-term prospects of the country. The U.S. government needs to find a way to enable quality American businesses to reduce the heightened risk of an early entry into a market like East Timor. Currently, all of the mechanisms in the Overseas Private Investment Corporation (OPIC) and the Export-Import Bank (Ex-Im Bank) are designed for "normal" countries, not for a post-conflict environment and the special risks that involves. Broadening the authorities in those two institutions would be good for U.S. economic interests as well as for the target country's stability and for U.S. foreign policy interests.

Support for Justice and Reconciliation

The United States used minimal leverage with the Indonesian government to advance the cause of justice and reconciliation in East Timor. Sustained U.S. involvement along with other international actors could have helped ensure that Indonesia's domestic tribunals deliver results. Unfortunately, minimal efforts were minimally effective in persuading the Indonesian government to hold high-level Timorese militia leaders (such as Euricco Guterres) and Indonesian military leaders accountable. Almost two years after independence, East Timor's political progress and basic stability remained compromised by a lack of reconciliation throughout the territory. As noted in a common local phrase— "reconciliation after justice"—the country will not be able to achieve basic reconciliation and stability until some reasonable level of justice has been achieved, especially for the high-level militia and military leaders most responsible for ordering and implementing the mass atrocities and destruction in East Timor. The United States could have done more through direct aid and working with other international partners to fund reconciliation efforts between East and West Timor and to accelerate police reform and training.

Support for Democracy and Governance

Various U.S. entities took the lead in supporting the development of a democratic system in East Timor. USAID's Office of Transition Initiatives was instrumental in supporting civic education to prepare

Timorese for their independence. Similarly, the International Republican Institute did good work on developing political parties. While many international actors can support democracy and governance activities, the United States has a comparative advantage due to its own history and superior experience in this field.

Accountability is necessary not only in politics and economics, but in the foreign assistance business as well. One of the biggest problems in a complex operation like East Timor is the lack of sufficient planning and coordination among the countless bilateral, nongovernmental, and international organization actors on the ground. This inevitably leads to overlap, inefficiencies, and possible corruption. All such operations need some sort of watchdog, governmental or nongovernmental, to keep local officials and the international community honest. In the case of East Timor, a joint local/international NGO called Lao Hammutuk served this function by publishing a regular newsletter monitoring the activities of the international community and pointing out failures of common sense. Although the United States did not provide funding to Lao Hammutuk, it should seek opportunities to support watchdogs, both inside and outside government, to reduce corruption and put pressure on donors to respond to local needs.

REMAINING CHALLENGES

Independence does not a success make, at least not a complete one. East Timor has come a long way since the dark days of 1999. And yet it has a long way to go to become a viable country.

Security

A year and a half after East Timor's independence, the United Nations remains in charge of security in the country—both the incipient army and the police. By September 2003, the international force had dropped from highs of over 10,000 to 3,500 international peacekeepers and 300 civilian advisers in the various government ministries.[12] Turnover of the security functions to Timorese control is anticipated around 2004–2005. Yet major threats remain. Externally, 30,000–50,000 East Timorese remained in West Timor as of the end of 2003, many of them militias or sympathizers who fled there when the international intervention took place. In 2003, militia attacks across the West Timor border resumed, leaving nine dead.[13] Trouble in the form of raids, stealing, and pure provocation can be expected to continue. How East Timor's security forces and their outside partners handle these challenges will deeply shape East Timor's crucial relationship with its dominant neighbor, Indonesia. The United States can play a very important role in this regard. U.S. relations with the Indonesian military, which had been suspended due to the role of Indonesian troops in the violence in East Timor in 1999, were newly upgraded in 2003. The U.S. military can and should use the increased leverage that comes with regular contact and training of the Indonesian military to ensure that Indonesian troops do their part to rein in disgruntled elements living in West Timor and that they guarantee safety and security for all in the border area.

Internally, frustrations from disappointed expectations of great improvements following independence and an overzealous reaction to a political demonstration by the new police force resulted in riots in the capital of Dili in December 2002, leaving at least two protesters dead and many injured. While it is hoped that such occurrences can be avoided in the future, a certain level of internal tension can be expected. How the local police forces react to both crime and political demonstrations will be crucial, as it has proved to be, both positively and negatively, in the past. The United States should continue to support UN efforts to train the new police force and hold it accountable to international standards.

Justice

In 1999, the United Nations set up the Serious Crimes Unit (SCU) to collect information on Timorese and Indonesians who committed atrocities. By mid-2003, the SCU had issued 169 arrest warrants for alleged perpetrators at large in Indonesia, including former Indonesian defense chief General Wiranto.[14] Unfortunately, the Indonesian government has not handed any of the culprits over for trial and has consistently sought to undermine the authority of the United Nations on this matter. If the United States and other partner governments are interested in securing a stable future for East Timor, they cannot afford to look the other way on the question of accountability for Indonesian and Indonesian-backed Timorese culprits. Without U.S. and other international pressure on the government in Jakarta to produce the suspects for real trials, nothing will happen. If this occurs, a sore will continue to fester in East Timor's relations with Indonesia, a situation that could lead to disasters for both countries.

Governance

East Timorese have never had the opportunity to run their own affairs. After nearly 500 years of Portuguese rule, 3 years of Japanese occupation during World War II, 24 years of Indonesian occupation, and 3 years of UN tutelage, learning the ways of self-government will take some time. In particular, realizing the democratic ideals of Timorese nationalists may be made more difficult by the dangers of a possible single-party state. As might be expected, the party of the resistance movement— FREITILIN (the Revolutionary Front for an Independent East Timor)— is dominant in the political affairs of the new country. It received 58 percent of the vote in the foundational elections in August 2001. In 2003, Prime Minister Mari Alkatiri noted that FREITILIN could be in power for 50 years.[15] This does not bode well for democracy or for stability over the long run. FREITILIN will have to learn how to be open to a loyal opposition, and the opposition elements will have to learn how to organize themselves and participate in constructive debate and governance. If not, animist cults such as Colimau 2000 and Sacred Family may prosper outside legitimate political boundaries, endangering the political system itself. U.S. programs for political development of all parties and institutions are desperately needed.

Economic and Social Well-being

East Timor was born poor. At independence it was ranked as one of the ten poorest countries on earth, with an annual per capita gross domestic product of $478.[16] Two out of five people live on less than 55 cents a day, deemed the bare minimum for food, clothes, and housing, while three-fourths of the population are without electricity and half are without safe drinking water.[17] The Timor Sea Treaty, signed with Australia in April 2003, gives East Timor a potentially viable future.[18] Turning oil and natural gas revenues into a sustainable, balanced economy, however, is an imposing challenge. Lacking an established institutional environment that could help ensure that oil and gas wealth is not squandered, East Timor will have to build strong governance structures to avoid the corruption that has plagued other countries in similar circumstances. It has only one shot at creating a sustainable economy—in the coming years that it will be receiving large inflows of money from the Timor Sea Treaty.

Even if that is handled well, East Timor faces a very difficult two years until those revenues come on line in 2006. In the meantime, the reduced infusion of foreign capital resulting from the winding down of UNTAET caused economic growth to slow dramatically, from 15 percent in 2000 and 18 percent in 2001, to 3 percent in 2002.[19] As if to highlight the fragile, dependent state of the Timorese economy, the World Food Program warned in 2003 that 110,000 people could face starvation by the end of the year unless they received emergency aid.[20] The United States must live up to its best traditions by supporting the World Food Program's humanitarian appeals, even as it supports the World Bank's efforts to provide infrastructure and ensure a fiscally responsible macroeconomic plan. Likewise, the United States can and should support the development of new sectors such as tourism and niche agricultural exports through USAID and the multilateral development banks.

A NEW FORM OF LEADERSHIP

The United States is used to being the dominant player in just about any crisis in just about any part of the world. When it leads, the United States strives, and expects, to succeed. When it chooses to play a supporting role, it should strive to be no less effective. In East Timor, the United States took an important step and made significant, if limited, contributions in a number of key areas. At the same time, if U.S. experience in East Timor is to become a new "promising recipe for U.S. engagement," U.S. policymakers will have to hone their approach. Deferring to others to take the lead will continue to be an appropriate response in some cases, but only if an intervention succeeds on the ground will it truly be a "model." The United States therefore needs to continue to develop the policy tools that will maximize U.S. leverage to lead to decisive and positive outcomes. Being a "junior partner" has to become less about doing less, and more about doing more focused tasks better. If the United States further develops this form of leadership from below when others are willing and able to take the lead, "junior partner" will become a real badge of honor.

Notes

[1] Sylvia Pfeifer, "The Citizens of East Timor Danced in the Streets," *The Business,* May 26, 2002, p. 16.

[2] Of those East Timorese voting, 344,580, or 78.5 percent, rejected a proposal for "autonomy" within Indonesia, opting instead for independence. Report of Secretary General Kofi Annan to the UN Security Council, September 3, 1999.

[3] The estimates of people killed in the violence range from 1,000 to 1,300. For a summary of the incidents, patterns of destruction, and responsibility, see United Nations International Commission of Inquiry on East Timor, "Question of East Timor," A/54/726, S/2000/59, January 31, 2000.

[4] Until this period, all the key international protagonists had very poor records on the question of East Timor. On the problematic histories of the UN, Australia, and the United States, see: William Maley, "The UN and East Timor," Mathew Jardine, "East Timor, the United Nations, and the International Community: Force Feeding Human Rights into the Institutionalized Jaws of Failure," and Jose Ramos Horta, "From Kissinger to Albright: the US and East Timor," all in *Pacifica Review* 12, no. 1 (February 2000).

[5] Secretary of State Colin Powell, speaking before the Commerce, Justice, State and the Judiciary Subcommittee of the Senate Appropriations Committee, May 3, 2001. The Federal News Service, May 3, 2001. According to Powell, the "model" consists of four essential elements: (1) The United States not provide troops if other troops are available; (2) the United States provide political and diplomatic support; (3) the United States provide funding; and (4) there is a clear endpoint to the operation.

[6] Senator Kay Bailey Hutchison (R-Tex.) on the floor of the U.S. Senate, April 12, 2000. Senator Russell Feingold (D-Wisc.) on the floor of the U.S. Senate, May 28, 2000.

[7] Report of the Joint Assessment Mission, World Bank, August 12, 1999, p. 1. This damage affected housing, schools, clinics, government buildings, and even many churches.

[8] Interview with Mari Alkitiri, the then shadow minister of finance, later to become the first elected prime minister of independent East Timor. Dili, May 23, 2001.

[9] Remarks at USGET change of command ceremony, Dili, March 14, 2001.

[10] The chief of operations, Lt. Col. Michael Bailey, was one of the best-known internationals in East Timor because of his nationality, his position at the hub of a territory-wide network of observers, and his willingness to engage the local population.

[11] The ambassador, Peter Galbraith, had served previously as U.S. ambassador in Croatia.

[12] Interview with the president of East Timor, Xanana Gusmao, by Slobodan Lekic, Associated Press, September 24, 2003.

[13] Jill Jolliffe, "East Timor Endures Freedom's Growing Pains," *Montreal Gazette*, May 22, 2003.

[14] Jill Jolliffe, "A Year to Remember," *The Age* (Melbourne), May 20, 2003.

[15] As quoted in "Freedom's disappointments," *The Economist*, March 22, 2003, U.S. edition.

[16] United Nations Development Assistance Framework 2003–2005, p. 6, www .unagencies.east-timor.org/06_ccaundaf/dcm/1%20-%20undaf%20.PDF. The IMF estimated GDP per capita at $427 in 2002, www.imf.org/external/pubs/ft/ scr/2003/cr03228.pdf.

[17] World Bank statistics, as cited in Alan Sipress, "Independence Breeds Frustration in East Timor," *Chicago Tribune*, October 10, 2003.

[18] Estimates of the potential income stream for East Timor vary wildly, from $5 billion over 17 years, to $25 billion over 20 years, to $33 billion over 30 years.

[19] According to World Bank representative Elizabeth Huybens, cited in Jill Jolliffe, "A Year to Remember," *The Age* (Melbourne), May 20, 2003.

[20] World Food Program, as quoted in Alan Sipress, "East Timor Learns How to Go it Alone; Lesson 1: Nation-Building Takes Time," *Washington Post*, October 12, 2003, p. A26.

CHAPTER FOURTEEN

SIERRA LEONE

MAKING MULTILATERALISM WORK

Milan Vaishnav and Bathsheba N. Crocker

In May 2000, 500 United Nations peacekeepers were captured by rebel forces in Sierra Leone and held hostage for over three weeks. The peacekeepers had been sent to Sierra Leone to try to ensure a fragile peace between the government and the rebel army. But lightly armed and not mandated to use combat force, they were easily overwhelmed by the infamously brutal, if disorganized, young rebel fighters. The peacekeepers were eventually released, unharmed, thanks in large part to the intervention of elite British forces, but the episode suggested little hope for lasting peace in war-ravaged Sierra Leone.

The decade-long war against the government of Sierra Leone was launched by a rebel force known as the Revolutionary United Front (RUF)—with the support of future Liberian president Charles Taylor—in 1991. The rebels instilled a culture of fear among the citizenry with their brutal brand of terror, which included systematic mutilation, raping, and pillaging. Sierra Leone seemed well on its way toward becoming a classic failed state.

Yet in just a few years from the war's end in May 2000, Sierra Leone went from one of the world's basket cases to a state working its way down the long road to recovery. International intervention and support played a key role in this turnaround.

The post-conflict reconstruction efforts in Sierra Leone have been largely unheralded. But the relative success of those efforts warrants closer study. Four key factors have helped jumpstart Sierra Leone's journey to recovery. First, the international community used a winning formula in applying a "UN-plus model," with the United Kingdom taking the lead role as part of a broader United Nations' effort.[1] Second, the UN proved its flexibility, with the United Nations Security Council adjusting the mandate and size of the peacekeeping force in Sierra Leone in response to early missteps; the result was a robust, well-equipped, and clearly mandated UN mission. Third, early focus on security and the rule of law helped spur economic growth and provided a reasonably stable environment for the new government to operate. Fourth, the United States played a catalytic role as a "junior partner,"[2] decisively changing outcomes when it weighed in with political, economic, and even military assistance.

The United States has provided strategic, targeted assistance at crucial junctures in the international intervention in Sierra Leone, helping to consolidate what United Nations Secretary General Kofi Annan calls "steady and remarkable progress."[3] In particular, the United States' provision of key financial, political, and diplomatic support for the United Nations and British efforts in Sierra Leone—including backing a robust and effective UN peacekeeping mission; facilitating justice and reconciliation; efforts to stem the illegal trade in "conflict diamonds"; and assistance in support of anticorruption and good governance programs—have been integral to the initial successes in post-conflict Sierra Leone.

BACKGROUND

The U.S. role in Sierra Leone has not always been positive. In May 1999, after almost ten years of civil war, the United States helped broker the Lomé Peace Accord between the government of Sierra Leone and the RUF rebels. According to Lomé's terms, RUF leader Foday Sankoh was named Sierra Leone's vice president and placed in charge of the country's natural resources, including its lucrative diamond mines. The RUF was also granted amnesty for its horrific crimes.[4] To oversee implementation of the accord, the UN Security Council passed Resolution 1270 (October 22, 1999), authorizing the United Nations Mission in Sierra Leone (UNAMSIL), which called for the deployment of international peacekeepers and civilian police and the establishment of a limited UN civilian mission.[5]

Resolution 1270 authorized only 6,000 lightly armed troops, and UNAMSIL's mandate was too limited to effectively combat continuing RUF activity. In February 2000, in response to growing calls for a more robust international presence, the Security Council used its chapter VII authority to strengthen UNAMSIL's mandate and increase its troop level to 11,000.[6] This early decision to change UNAMSIL's mandate is in contrast to other situations—such as in Afghanistan and the Congo—in which a collective lack of member states' political will delayed or obstructed changes to the makeup, mandate, or size of peacekeeping forces in response to needs on the ground. Although the Security Council had initially failed to create a mission that could be effective in Sierra Leone, its willingness to change the original mandate—known as the shift from UNAMSIL I to UNAMSIL II—has been widely praised.[7]

Still, it was not until the UNAMSIL peacekeepers were taken hostage in May 2000 and Freetown was surrounded by RUF militiamen that the international community finally marshaled the effort that was needed to end Sierra Leone's conflict. Later that month, approximately 800 elite British military troops arrived in Sierra Leone to rescue UK citizens and UN hostages, secure Freetown's airport, and take back the capital. This marked a critical shift in Britain's involvement in the post-conflict effort. With Britain, Sierra Leone's former colonial overseer, firmly in the lead, UNAMSIL was able to wrest control of the country back from the RUF in a matter of weeks, including by facilitating the arrest of Sankoh on May 17, 2000.

In the two years following the British troops' arrival in Freetown, the country held relatively free and fair nationwide elections; a UN-backed tribunal began trying the war criminals responsible for the country's decade-long nightmare; international peacekeepers helped to quell violent crime; and Sierra Leone's economy began showing signs of life.[8]

Until May 2000, the United States, the United Nations, and the United Kingdom had all continued to insist that Lomé form the basis of any future peace accord in Sierra Leone, despite the overwhelming evidence that it was flawed.[9] Once the British took the lead, however, the United States and the United Nations revisited their positions on Lomé. The United States eventually drafted a Security Council resolution calling for the establishment of a tribunal to try Foday Sankoh and his RUF cronies for war crimes, which was passed in August 2000.[10] This signaled the formal end of Lomé and its amnesty provisions, and the tipping point for peace in Sierra Leone.

ASSESSING THE RECONSTRUCTION EFFORTS

Britain's leadership has been crucial to bringing Sierra Leone back from the brink. As a key UN Security Council member, Britain has been able to garner and maintain high-level support for the UN mission from other major states—in particular the United States. Moreover, the UK's prime role has provided symbolic value to those efforts, demonstrating Western commitment to Sierra Leone's recovery.

Although it is too early to declare a post-conflict success story, the international community's efforts in Sierra Leone resulted in significant, early progress in the four key areas of post-conflict reconstruction: security, justice and reconciliation, governance and participation, and social and economic well-being. It was particularly important that the United Nations, the United Kingdom, and the United States made establishing security, justice, and the rule of law immediate priorities.

Security

The British deployment of 800 soldiers armed with a combat mandate in May 2000 served as an important boost for UNAMSIL, signaling to the RUF that the UN peacekeepers were not to be interfered with. The UK's heightened engagement paved the way for a series of Security Council decisions that eventually increased UNAMSIL's force size to 17,500, making it the largest peacekeeping mission in UN history. [11]

UNAMSIL was able to bring order to the streets of Freetown and throughout the country, take control of the diamond mines, and help stem illicit border activities. Traveling outside of Freetown—once described as a "life-or-death lottery"—became routine, and international nongovernmental organizations and humanitarian aid workers were operating freely in most parts of the country by the summer of 2003. [12] After a decade of bloody civil war, Sierra Leone found itself enjoying relative peace and stability.

Conflicts in neighboring Liberia and Cote d'Ivoire continued to threaten Sierra Leone's fragile peace in the early post-conflict years. RUF loyalists regrouped in Liberia, where they were protected and replenished by former Liberian president Charles Taylor, who was responsible for many—if not all—of West Africa's conflicts in recent years. [13] Security along the Liberia-Sierra Leone border remained tenuous even as late as April 2003 due to spillover from Liberia's civil war.

At the same time, the security situation had improved enough by May 2002 that Sierra Leone held its first elections in six years. UNAMSIL troops helped protect election sites and provided highly technical logistics support at thousands of polling stations nationwide.

Stabilizing the security situation was also a necessary precondition to Sierra Leonean refugees returning home. By June 2003, the United Nations High Commissioner for Refugees (UNHCR) had repatriated over 200,000 Sierra Leonean refugees out of an estimated 300,000 who had fled during the civil war. The remaining 100,000 continued to live in refugee camps in neighboring countries.[14]

British efforts have also been essential to train and equip a reconstituted Sierra Leonean army. Through its International Military Assistance and Training Team (IMATT), the United Kingdom has helped retrain and restructure the Republic of Sierra Leone Armed Forces (RSLAF) and also build capacity in the Ministry of Defense by training key senior officials.[15] In just three years, the RSLAF has made significant progress toward transforming itself into a legitimate, capable military force that respects the rule of law and civilian oversight.

In a country in which thousands of armed combatants had easy access to an ample supply of weapons, one of the highest priority tasks was disarming, demobilizing, and reintegrating the various warring parties. This task was handled by the National Committee for Disarmament, Demobilization, and Reintegration (NCDDR), coordinated by the government and run by UNAMSIL. Between October 1998 and January 2002—when the disarmament of ex-combatants was declared successfully completed—over 72,000 combatants laid down their arms.

Although the United Nations began the gradual drawdown of UNAMSIL troops in November 2002, more than 13,000 UNAMSIL troops were still stationed throughout the country as of June 2003. The UN has laid out a series of critical benchmarks that must be met before UNAMSIL is significantly reduced in numbers.[16] Despite considerable progress in the country, many of those benchmarks were a long way from being fulfilled even three years into the mission, suggesting that UNAMSIL troops could remain in large numbers for some time.

Justice and Reconciliation

The international players in Sierra Leone gave early attention to the area of justice and reconciliation. After the breakdown of the Lomé accord, the UN Security Council—with strong U.S. backing—decided to create a tribunal to prosecute and try Sierra Leone's war criminals. In August 2000, it passed Resolution 1315, which called for the establishment of a Special Court for Sierra Leone, charged with trying those who "bear the greatest responsibility" for crimes against humanity and other serious violations of international humanitarian law.[17] The court was established pursuant to a treaty between the United Nations and the government of Sierra Leone signed in January 2002. Staffed with international and Sierra Leonean judges, the tribunal operates under both international and local laws, drawing on local forms of justice.

The court differs from the international courts established to try war criminals from the Yugoslavia and Rwanda conflicts in several ways. First, the Special Court issued its first ten indictments in just over a year, making it far more efficient than the aforementioned tribunals. Of those indicted, seven were in the court's custody as of June 2003, including notorious former RUF leader Foday Sankoh. Second, the majority of the Special Court's professional staff (approximately 60 percent) are native Sierra Leoneans, unlike the Rwanda and Yugoslavia tribunals that are managed primarily by international officials. Finally, the Special Court sits in the heart of Freetown—in the actual country where the atrocities took place. This fact adds a certain amount of credibility and visibility to the court's work, which is lacking in the Rwanda and Yugoslavia instances.

The Special Court did face problems early on. Donors were slow to respond to the United Nations' calls for funds. Neighboring countries also proved uncooperative. The Special Court consistently battled with Liberian authorities over their obstruction of the court's work; in early June 2003, the Ghanaian government refused to arrest Liberian president Taylor while he was in Ghana, despite the court having issued an indictment against him;[18] and in October 2003, Taylor was ensconced in Nigeria with no signs that the government of Nigeria intended to hand him over to the court. Nonetheless, the court has been widely hailed as a promising new model for post-conflict criminal tribunals.

A truth and reconciliation commission (TRC), mandated by the Lomé accord to create an unbiased, historical record of the conflict and promote nationwide healing and reconciliation, was formally established on February 22, 2000. The TRC was plagued early on by donor fatigue, mismanagement, and rocky relations with the United Nations. Donors viewed the TRC's $6.6 million budget as too costly and were discouraged by allegations of biased hiring practices and lack of transparency.[19] Eventually, the TRC began to make headway: it held its first public hearings in April 2003 and announced that it had collected over 6,000 written statements documenting rights abuses committed over the past ten years.[20]

UNAMSIL also focused early on establishing the rule of law. The British in particular have made substantial contributions to reconstituting Sierra Leone's justice system through their Department for International Development (DFID). Sierra Leone's judicial infrastructure before the conflict was barely developed, and what did exist was destroyed in the years of fighting. Three years into the reconstruction efforts, Sierra Leone's judicial infrastructure was still skeletal, and the national judiciary did not reach much beyond Freetown.[21] At the same time, there had been a series of small but steady improvements—such as setting up magistrate courts throughout the country.[22] In late 2002, the Commonwealth Human Rights Initiative was able to report that Sierra Leone had seen "a steady build up of hopeful events which portend well for rule of law and from which judicial functioning will benefit."[23]

UNAMSIL and United Kingdom efforts to reconstitute the Sierra Leone Police (SLP) have been a key component of instilling a culture of the rule of law. Crime rates throughout the country have been surprisingly low since the end of the conflict, and the predicted vigilantism and retributive violence did not come to fruition. The SLP, long maligned for corruption and oppressive and unprofessional behavior, was further decimated by years of fighting. By the end of the conflict, only 6,600 civilian police officers remained in the entire country (down from a previous high of over 9,300).[24] By late 2003, 6,500 SLP officers had been either retrained or newly hired and trained and were deployed throughout Sierra Leone. [25] But the police force still lacked even basic physical infrastructure, necessitating ongoing assistance from UNAMSIL troops and UN and UK civilian police advisers and trainers.

Governance and Participation

With international assistance, Sierra Leone has made progress since the end of the war in instilling good governance and transparency. Efforts to strengthen the central government and improve governance structures and capacity throughout the country, however, have proved slower going.

Less than two years after international intervention, UNAMSIL oversaw relatively free and fair elections, in which Ahmed Tejan Kabbah was reelected as Sierra Leone's president. This marked the first free, fair, and truly nonviolent set of elections in the country's history. Several years into the postwar mission, however, many government officials outside Freetown still lacked the basic necessities to perform their jobs, complicating efforts to restore and consolidate the government's power at the local, district, and provincial levels.[26] This will be essential if the government of Sierra Leone is to be truly effective.[27]

Widespread corruption has plagued successive Sierra Leonean governments. In fact, Sierra Leone's rebels claimed that they launched the war to end decades of government-driven exploitation of Sierra Leone's diamonds. The rebels, in turn, funded their war efforts through illicit sale of those diamonds, eventually focusing international attention on what came to be known as the conflict or "blood" diamonds issue.

With assistance from the World Bank, the European Commission, the United Kingdom, and the UN Development Program, the government established a "Good Governance Program," which includes efforts to decentralize power and create a more transparent, accountable government.[28] In February 2002, the government of Sierra Leone, with the help of Britain's DFID, set up an Anti-Corruption Commission composed of government and British officials, which is mandated to expose instances of government corruption. The commission's early efforts received mixed reviews, largely because it lacks any enforcement mechanisms.[29]

International efforts also focused on curbing the trade in conflict diamonds, including by developing the so-called Kimberley process, which was codified in November 2002.[30] At the same time, the Security Council focused on the problem in Sierra Leone itself, passing Resolution 1306 on July 5, 2000, which banned the sale of diamonds from Sierra Leone unless they had been certified by the government of Sierra Leone according to a process approved by the Security Council.[31] The government instituted its certification regime in September 2000. By June 2003, the Security Council was able to determine that the government's efforts to control and manage the country's diamond industry and its full adherence to the Kimberley process warranted the lifting of the ban.[32]

Social and Economic Well-Being

After the early focus on security and justice issues, Sierra Leone began to emerge from the post-conflict emergency phase, slowly making the difficult transition to longer-term development. Efforts to build a sustainable economy in Sierra Leone started nearly from scratch. Despite the country's wealth of natural resources, most notably diamonds and rutile,[33] the United Nations' annual Human Development Index rated Sierra Leone the world's worst place to live in 2002, ranking it dead last out of 173 countries—reflecting the country's low rates of life expectancy, literacy, and per capita GDP.[34]

In 1999, during the heart of the civil war, the economy of Sierra Leone contracted by 8.1 percent. By 2001, the economy began improving with a growth rate of around 3.8 percent, and by 2002, it was experiencing economic growth upwards of 6 percent. Inflation, once as high as 35 percent, was brought to less than one percent, and in July 2002, the United States and other "Paris Club" countries forgave Sierra Leone's sovereign debt obligations. In all, over 90 percent of the country's massive debt burden has been forgiven.[35]

Within just a few years of the end of Sierra Leone's civil war, diamond exports had risen "meteorically."[36] The conflict's end meant that revenue collected from diamond sales—previously used by the RUF to finance the war—could be used to provide jobs and tax revenues for a central government lacking adequate resources.[37] It is estimated that with enough investment, diamond export sales could more than triple by 2006, to over $180 million. The government has also announced the discovery of significant offshore oil and gas deposits that could provide a much-needed economic boost. Exploratory drilling, which is projected to commence in 2005, could generate substantial government revenue not to mention much-needed foreign direct investment.[38]

Sierra Leone still has a long way to go to economic recovery, including the difficult task of reintegrating the country's former combatants into society and providing them some economic livelihood. More than 72,000 combatants in Sierra Leone's civil war have been successfully disarmed and demobilized, but the process of reintegrating these ex-combatants has proved much more challenging. Most of the funds provided to the World Bank trust fund for disarmament, demobilization, and reintegration have been spent on the first two steps of the process, leaving little money for reintegration. This has left thousands of disarmed and demobilized soldiers with no gainful employment, creating a dangerous pool of young, disenfranchised ex-combatants.

THE ROLE OF THE UNITED STATES

With the United Kingdom having taken the leading role, the United States has opted for the part of best supporting actor. Relative to Kosovo, Afghanistan, and Iraq, for instance, U.S. financial and military assistance to Sierra Leone has not been significant. Nevertheless, the United States has contributed in key strategic ways to critical aspects of the reconstruction.

Support for UNAMSIL and Other Security Efforts

The United States was instrumental in securing the passage of UN Resolution 1270, which established UNAMSIL. Once UNAMSIL was up and running, U.S. officials helped, publicly and privately, to establish a UN peacekeeping force that was properly sized, trained, equipped, and mandated to keep the peace in Sierra Leone.

Throughout the process, the United States supported the enhancement of UNAMSIL's mandate to ensure consistency with mission objectives. In spite of a strengthened mandate after February 2000, significant complications arose due to inadequate troop numbers and a confused command structure. Spearheaded by then-U.S. Ambassador to the United Nations Richard C. Holbrooke, the United States took an active leadership role to rectify the situation. Holbrooke relentlessly fought "to straighten [UNAMSIL] out, which means cleaning up the existing command, cleaning up the missions and tasks, and giving it the resources to achieve its mission and tasks."[39] Holbrooke was aided by allies on Capitol Hill, who comprised a unique coalition of strange bedfellows. This coalition, which consisted of human rights proponents, Africa followers, anti-peacekeeping advocates, and those seeking curbs on conflict diamonds, worked together to push reform of UNAMSIL.

As a result, in October 2000, UN Secretary General Annan replaced the force commander and the deputy force commander and established two new senior-level positions responsible for streamlining operations and linking the UN's military and humanitarian efforts.[40] After these structural issues were addressed, the United States worked to ensure that UNAMSIL had sufficient troops to keep the peace by actively supporting the increase of the force size to 17,500 troops.

The United States also provided key diplomatic support to the United Kingdom when it deployed forces to Sierra Leone in the spring of 2000, and it has been one of the primary financial contributors to UNAMSIL, covering approximately 25 percent of its operating costs with over $600 million in funds provided to the UN mission in 2000–2003.[41]

The United States has made three other important contributions to security needs in Sierra Leone. First, since the inception of the UK-led efforts to revamp Sierra Leone's armed forces, the United States has provided training, equipment, and helicopter support to the RSLAF through the IMATT program.[42] The United States also has provided IMATT with three military officers to assist in its ongoing efforts; although small in number, this U.S. contingent has great symbolic effect within Sierra Leone.

Second, in August 2000, President Clinton announced the creation of "Operation Focus Relief," a U.S. initiative to train and equip seven West

African peacekeeping battalions set to deploy to Sierra Leone as part of UNAMSIL. Under international pressure to help reverse the souring security situation in Sierra Leone and with President Clinton unwilling to commit U.S. soldiers, the United States decided to help fill the security gap in Sierra Leone by spending around $90 million over two years to train and equip hundreds of troops from Nigeria, Ghana, and Senegal with rifles, mortars, M-60 machine guns, antitank weapons, and transport vehicles.[43]

Third, the United States issued an important waiver that allowed Pakistani troops to participate in UNAMSIL after the government of India pulled its troops out in February 2001. The United Nations warned that without an infusion to make up for the loss of the Indian contingent—which had been in command of UNAMSIL to that point—UNAMSIL would lack real combat readiness.[44] But the Pakistanis demanded as a precondition of their participation that the United States provide them with military spare parts, the sale of which was prohibited under U.S. law because of Pakistan's nuclear status.

To help stave off a crisis for UNAMSIL and Sierra Leone, on August 9, 2001, President Bush waived the ban on supplying military equipment and spare parts for the purpose of equipping Pakistani peacekeepers deployed in Sierra Leone.[45] This move shocked many in Washington and around the world and risked raising congressional—not to mention the government of India's—ire. But the Pakistani forces provided a much-needed lift to UNAMSIL; they were well-trained, well-equipped, and well-coordinated, augmented by attack helicopters and substantial artillery.[46] The U.S. decision to facilitate Pakistan's participation was seen as an important symbolic gesture of U.S. support for the UN peacekeepers in Sierra Leone.

Support for Justice and Reconciliation

When discussions began about setting up a war crimes tribunal for Sierra Leone, the United States and other UN Security Council member states were very reluctant to finance yet another costly, bureaucratic international war crimes tribunal along the model of the International Criminal Tribunals for Yugoslavia and Rwanda (ICTY and ICTR, respectively).[47] At the same time, the United States was determined to demonstrate moral leadership on the transitional justice issue, in part to restore credibility it had lost due to brokering and supporting the Lomé accord.[48] Thus Ambassador Holbrooke insisted that the United States draft Resolution 1315, calling for the establishment of a hybrid war crimes tribunal for Sierra Leone. He was also instrumental in drumming up support for the key resolution and facing down the prospect that creation of the court might lead to renewed fighting in Sierra Leone. "Let the United Nations do the right thing, and let the evil people face up to the consequences of their actions," challenged Holbrooke at a press conference immediately following the passage of 1315. "[D]o you think the international community should be immobilized by fear of a handful of machete-wielding thugs who are trying to upgrade their weaponry to machine guns and...surface-to-air missiles? I don't think so."[49]

The rhetoric of the United States was meaningful, however, only because it was backed up by concrete support for the court. The United States pressed for the appointment of David M. Crane, an American appointed by Annan to the post of chief prosecutor of the court in April 2002. The first chief investigator for the Court was also an American. In addition, the United States has been the largest financial contributor to the court, providing nearly 40 percent of its overall budget.[50] About one quarter of the prosecutor's staff is American; and several U.S. agencies—including the Defense, Justice, and State Departments—have provided crucial support for the court's work, including helping to gather intelligence, conduct investigations, and round up war criminals.

Two actions by the U.S. Congress in 2003 also supported the court in important ways. First, Congress authorized the expansion of the State Department Rewards for Justice program to cover crimes committed in Sierra Leone and prosecuted by the Special Court.[51] The Rewards for Justice program authorizes the secretary of state to provide rewards for information leading to the arrest or conviction of an individual responsible for committing serious crimes, including violations of international humanitarian law.

Second, Congress authorized the president to provide $30 million in goods and services for international war crimes tribunals (including the Sierra Leone court) should he determine that "doing so will contribute to a just resolution of charges regarding genocide or other violations of international humanitarian law."[52] In addition to the political support implicit in it, this authorization also provided the president with the authority to provide extra assistance for the court should circumstances so warrant.

Although neither of these additional authorities has yet been exercised by the executive branch (and there is some skepticism that they ever will be), the U.S. Congress acted in crucial ways to bolster the support the United States is able to provide the court, should circumstances warrant additional resources.

Support to Curb the Illicit Trade in Conflict Diamonds

In May 2000, Africa's diamond-producing states convened a meeting in Kimberley, South Africa to initiate a process aimed at stemming trade in conflict diamonds (the "Kimberley Process"). For various reasons, the United States—the world's largest diamond importer—was slow to fully endorse Kimberley's extensive certification scheme, which hampered early efforts to get the process off the ground.[53] At the same time, though, at the United Nations, Ambassador Holbrooke strongly advocated for the adoption of Resolution 1306—banning the export of uncertified diamonds from Sierra Leone—helping to ensure its passage.

Despite its initial reluctance to sign on to Kimberley, the United States eventually became an ardent supporter, even pushing for an early start-up date of January 1, 2003, for the certification regime during the November 2002 meeting in Interlaken, Switzerland at which 47 nations signed onto the regime. The United States delayed its own implementation slightly, due to the need to secure implementing legislation; but on April 25, 2003, President Bush signed into law the Clean Diamonds Act, which mandates that shipments of rough diamonds into and out of the United States must be accompanied by a certification that they are from a legitimate source. U.S. officials claim that the United States has worked "intensively" through the Kimberley Process to combat the flow of conflict diamonds.[54]

In addition, since the passage of Resolution 1306, the United States has provided substantial financial and technical assistance to Sierra Leone's diamond industry. The United States led efforts to establish Sierra Leone's Commission on the Management of Strategic Resources. The commission's central mission is to integrate key figures in Sierra Leonean civil society and traditional leadership structures into the government's efforts to regulate and manage the diamond industry. The commission is intended to "provide oversight at the local level and expose efforts to circumvent or undermine the system of controls the government of Sierra Leone is putting in place" regarding the diamond sector.[55] In addition to helping launch the commission, the United States dedicated $1 million and provided technical assistance to help develop the commission's capacities.

Recognizing the importance of good governance and anticorruption programs, the work of the U.S. Agency for International Development (USAID) in Sierra Leone has focused on helping to improve the internal management and control of Sierra Leone's diamonds. USAID was instrumental in helping the government of Sierra Leone establish a "certification of origin" regime, as called for under the Kimberley Process. USAID's "Diamond Management Program" has been effective in bringing Sierra Leone's diamonds under the control of the central government and helping the government and local communities monitor the mining sector. Finally, USAID organized and funded, along with the UK's DFID, the Kono Peace Diamond Alliance that aims to enhance management capacity and ensure that the benefits of the country's diamond wealth begin to flow to the people of Sierra Leone in a transparent manner.[56]

This key assistance by the United States helped build Sierra Leone's local capacity to manage its diamond industry such that the UN Security Council was able to lift its ban on exports of Sierra Leone's diamonds after only two years.

CONCLUSION

Sierra Leone has achieved tremendous progress in only a few short years. To be sure, the path to recovery is littered with potential pitfalls. Regional instability still threatens the country's fragile peace. Conflicts in Liberia, Guinea, and Cote d'Ivoire have tremendous spillover potential. And while the country's great mineral wealth is finally being marshaled for the good of the citizenry, corruption persists.

Ensuring control, transparency, and accountability of the diamond mines will be a top priority for Sierra Leone and the international community. Maintaining donor support will be crucial to making sure that the peace in Sierra Leone sticks. Internationals are still relied upon to assist in the provision of basic services, and UNAMSIL's presence continues to be essential as the domestic security apparatus gets back on its feet.

Yet Sierra Leone is a good case study of how the United States— though providing modest tangible assistance—has effectively used its influential position to further the interests of peace. In an era of limited resources and seemingly unlimited problems—more than a few of which are in Africa—Sierra Leone offers a model of how the United States can leverage strong partners and wise policy choices to maximize the impact of its investment. Called upon to play a role similar to that of Britain's Sierra Leone role in Liberia, the United States has thus far declined, leaving the security role to the Nigerians. Sierra Leone's "UN-plus" model could nonetheless serve as a model for future peacekeeping in Africa.

The U.S. role in Sierra Leone also illustrates how critical personalities can be to the success or failure of reconstruction efforts. Ambassador Holbrooke—a dogged and persistent player in Sierra Leone's recovery while he was in office—was a key instrument of the United States' effectiveness in Sierra Leone. Along with the key role played by the United Kingdom, Ambassador Holbrooke's determination not to let Sierra Leone slide back into chaos helped maintain the focus and attention of the United Nations and the U.S. government (both the executive and legislative branches) on that country, without which Sierra Leone would not have been set on such a promising road after surviving its gruesome and devastating civil war.

Notes

[1] The "UN-plus model" has been described as follows: "The international response works best when a single nation is willing to take a substantial lead role with the United Nations assuming responsibilities suited to its strengths. . . . In Sierra Leone, for instance, the United Kingdom served as 'guardian angel' and came through with the critical elements of robust military and political intervention." Stanley Foundation, *Laying a Durable Foundation for Post-Conflict Societies* (final report, Stanley Foundation "37th United Nations of the Next Decade" conference, June 15–20, 2002), June 2002, p. 20, http://reports.stanleyfoundation.org/UNND02.pdf.

[2] The concept of the United States as a "junior partner" in post-conflict reconstruction operations was developed in Robert C. Orr, "Making East Timor Work: The United States as Junior Partner," *National Security Studies Quarterly* 7, no 3 (Summer 2001): 133–140.

[3] Fifteenth Report of the Secretary General on the United Nations Mission in Sierra Leone, S/2002/987, September 5, 2002, http://daccess-ods.un.org/TMP/3324873.html.

[4] Lomé Peace Accord, at www.sierra-leone.org/lomeaccord.html. When he signed the Lomé peace agreement on behalf of the United Nations, the Special Representative of the UN Secretary General (SRSG) added a disclaimer that the United Nations did not recognize the amnesty as applying to international crimes of genocide, crimes against humanity, war crimes, or other serious violations of international humanitarian law.

[5] United Nations Security Council Resolution 1270, S/RES/1270, October 22, 1999.

[6] United Nations Security Council Resolution 1289, S/RES/1289, February 7, 2000.

[7] Prior to UNAMSIL I, the Security Council authorized the creation of a UN Observer Mission in Sierra Leone (UNOMSIL) in June 1998. UNOMSIL was charged with monitoring and advising efforts to disarm combatants and restructure the country's armed forces. As military observers, the mission was unarmed and could merely stand by and watch as RUF forces launched an offensive in December 1998 in which they successfully recaptured Freetown. In October 1999, UNAMSIL was created, and the Security Council disbanded UNOMSIL.

[8] For an analysis of the progress in Sierra Leone in these areas, see International Crisis Group (ICG), *Sierra Leone: The State of Security and Governance*, Africa Report No. 67, September 2, 2003, www.crisisweb.org/home/index .cfm?id=1492&l=1.

[9] Susan Rice, then assistant secretary of state for African affairs, would later admit that "[t]he Lomé Agreement, like many others before it, was a calculated risk that didn't play out as the people of Sierra Leone, the international community, or the United States would have hoped." Testimony to U.S. Senate Foreign Relations Committee, Subcommittee on African Affairs, October 11, 2000, http://usinfo.state.gov/regional/af/security/a0101102.htm.

[10] United Nations Security Council Resolution 1315, S/RES/1315, August 14, 2000.

[11] United Nations Security Council Resolution 1346, S/RES/1346, March 30, 2001.

[12] "After the Horror, a New Beginning," *The Economist*, May 16, 2002.

[13] On June 4, 2003, the chief prosecutor for the Special Court for Sierra Leone, David M. Crane, announced the indictment of Charles Taylor for "'bearing the greatest responsibility' for war crimes, crimes against humanity, and serious violations of international humanitarian law within the territory of Sierra Leone since 30 November 1996." Statement of David M. Crane, Chief Prosecutor, Special Court for Sierra Leone, June 4, 2003, on file with author. At the time of publication, Taylor had stepped down from the presidency and was granted exile in Nigeria. He had not been arrested or turned over to the Sierra Leonean Special Court.

[14] UN Office for the Coordination of Humanitarian Affairs (OCHA), *Sierra Leone: Humanitarian Situation Report, Mar-Apr 2003*, April 30, 2003, www .reliefweb.int/w/rwb.nsf/ByCountry/Sierra+Leone?OpenDocument &StartKey=Sierra+Leone&Expandview; OCHA, *Inter-Agency Appeal for Relief & Recovery for Sierra Leone 2003: Mid-Year Review*, May 2003, wwww.reliefweb.int/

w/rwb.nsf/6686f45896f15dbc852567ae00530132/f52cab8d463050b6c1256d 390062cc18?OpenDocument.

[15] Mark Malan, "Security and Military Reform," in Mark Malan, Sarah Meek, Thokozani Thusi, Jeremy Ginifer, and Patrick Coker, *Sierra Leone: Building the Road to Recovery*, monograph no. 80 (Pretoria, South Africa: Institute for Security Studies, 2003), p. 97.

[16] See note 3.

[17] Ibid.

[18] Statement of David M. Crane, Chief Prosecutor, Special Court for Sierra Leone, June 5, 2003, on file with author; Douglas Farah, "Tribunal Indicts Liberia's Leader; Taylor Charged with War Crimes during Long Conflict in Sierra Leone," *Washington Post*, June 5, 2003.

[19] International Crisis Group (ICG), "Sierra Leone's Truth and Reconciliation Commission: A Fresh Start?" *Africa Briefing*, December 20, 2002, www.crisisweb .org//library/documents/report_archive/A400858_20122002.pdf.

[20] "Sierra Leone: Public Hearings Start at Truth Commission," Integrated Regional Information Networks (IRIN), United Nations Office for the Coordination of Humanitarian Affairs, April 16, 2003.

[21] Mark Malan, "The Challenge of Justice and Reconciliation," in Malan et al., *Sierra Leone: Building the Road to Recovery*, pp. 140–141.

[22] National Recovery Strategy, p. 22.

[23] *In Pursuit of Justice: A Report on the Judiciary in Sierra Leone*, Commonwealth Human Rights Initiative report, 2002, www.humanrightsinitiative.org/ publications/sierra_leone/Sierra%20Leone%20Report.pdf.

[24] Sarah Meek, "Policing Sierra Leone," in Malan et al., *Sierra Leone: Building the Road to Recovery*, p. 105. It is estimated that more than 900 Sierra Leone police officers were killed by RUF members during the 1990s.

[25] National Recovery Strategy, p. 21.

[26] Ibid., pp. 19–20.

[27] Like Afghan president Hamid Karzai, dubbed the "mayor of Kabul," President Kabbah has often been mocked as the "mayor of Freetown" because of his perceived lack of authority outside the capitol.

[28] *Transitional Support Strategy for the Republic of Sierra Leone*, World Bank document, March 3, 2002, p. 6; *Sierra Leone: Post-Conflict Development Agenda: Strategies for Growth and Poverty Reduction*, Government of Sierra Leone document, November 13–14, 2002, p. 14.

[29] Michael Peel, "Sierra Leone to Lead in Fighting Corruption," *Financial Times*, May 21, 2002; John Prendergast, testimony, U.S. House International Relations Committee, Africa Subcommittee, May 16, 2002.

[30] The Kimberley process, named after the South Africa city where representatives of the diamond industry and importing nations first met to discuss the challenge of stemming the trade in "conflict diamonds," is a global initiative backed by the UN aimed at severing the link between legitimate trade in diamonds and the illicit trade of diamonds from conflict zones. What originally began as a consultative process culminated in the adoption of the Kimberley Process Certification Scheme (KPCS) at a meeting in Interlaken, Switzerland, in November 2002, which aims to ensure that conflict diamonds are not traded on the legal market. For an in-depth treatment of the process, see www.kimberleyprocess.com.

[31] United Nations Security Council Resolution 1306, S/RES/1306, July 5, 2000.

[32] "U.N. Ending Ban on Diamonds," Associated Press, June 6, 2003.

[33] Rutile is a titanium ore used as paint pigment and welding rod coatings. Sierra Leone has the largest deposit of natural, high-quality rutile in the world.

[34] *Human Development Report 2002: Deepening Democracy in a Fragmented World* (New York: United Nations Development Programme, 2002), p. 152.

[35] Sierra Leone Country Report, Economist Intelligence Unit, March 2003; Fiscal Year 2004 Congressional Budget Justification for Foreign Operations, U.S. Department of State, www.state.gov/m/rm/rls/cbj/2004/. A large part of the debt has been forgiven as part of the World Bank's Heavily Indebted Poor Countries (HIPC) initiative.

[36] In 2001, diamond exports generated $26 million in revenue; in 2002, revenues increased to $37 million; during the first three months of 2003 alone, export revenues were $23.8 million. U.S. Agency for International Development, "Peace Diamonds from Sierra Leone," www.usaid.gov/gn/sierraleone/news/030203_peacediamonds/; Rod MacJohnson, "'Blood Diamonds' Initiative a Mixed Success in War-scarred Sierra Leone," Agence France Presse, May 18, 2003.

[37] "After the Horror, a New Beginning," *The Economist*, May 16, 2002; "Britain's Short Asks Sierra Leone to Clean Up Diamond Trade," Agence France Presse, March 1, 2002.

[38] Sierra Leone Country Profile, Economist Intelligence Unit, 2002.

[39] Remarks by Ambassador Richard C. Holbrooke, U.S. Permanent Representative to the United Nations, on the Situation in Sierra Leone, at the UN Security Council Stakeout, July 27, 2000, www.un.int/usa/00_100.htm.

[40] In late 2000, Annan replaced almost the entire senior leadership of UN-AMSIL and created new positions and relationships in hopes of rectifying the mission's confused command structure. Specifically, Annan provided that the Special Representative of the Secretary General would have two deputies, one responsible for governance and stabilization, the other for operations and

management. The DSRSG for governance and stabilization would also serve as director of the UN Development Group, serving as a bridge between UN military and humanitarian operations. This new arrangement allowed for greater flexibility on the part of the UN and straightened out previously confused chains of command. For an in-depth analysis of UNAMSIL and its restructuring, see Clifford Bernath and Sayre Nyce, *UNAMSIL: A Peacekeeping Success Lessons Learned*, Refugees International report, October 2002, www.refugeesinternational.org/files/reports/RIUNAMSIL.pdf.

[41] See International Affairs (Function 150) Budget Requests for Fiscal Years 2002–2004, www.state.gov/m/rm/c6112.htm.

[42] Statements by U.S. Delegation to Sierra Leone Consultative Group, November 13–14, 2002, www.sierra-leone.org/usgovernment112002.html.

[43] Andrew Maykuth, "Nigeria Army Balks at U.S. Training," *Philadelphia Inquirer*, November 15, 2000; Danna Harman, "Sierra Leone: The Path from Pariah to Peace," *Christian Science Monitor*, September 18, 2002.

[44] Mark Doyle, "Indian Troops Quit Sierra Leone," BBC News, February 14, 2001, http://news.bbc.co.uk/l/hi/world/africa/1170237.stm; David Buchan, Carola Hoyos, and William Wallis, "UN Struggles to Replace Indian Peacekeepers in Sierra Leone," *Financial Times*, September 22, 2000.

[45] "Waiver of Sanctions for the Export of Select U.S. Munitions List U.S.-Origin Helicopter and Armored Personnel Carrier Spare Parts and Ammunition from the United States to Pakistan," Presidential Determination No. 2001-23, August 9, 2001, www.fas.org/terrorism/at/docs/2001/PakWaiverAug01.pdf.

[46] International Crisis Group, *Sierra Leone: Managing Uncertainty*, Africa Report No. 35, October 24, 2001, p. 7.

[47] U.S. Ambassador to the UN Richard Holbrooke repeatedly stated that the United States would not support the creation of "a third war crimes tribunal like ones we have in Rwanda and the former Yugoslavia, because those are expensive and time-consuming." William M. Reilly, "US Tables Sierra Leone Tribunal Resolution," United Press International, July 27, 2000.

[48] Michelle Sieff, *A Special Court for Sierra Leone*, Crimes of War Project Magazine, May 2001, www.crimesofwar.org/tribun-mag/sierra_print.html.

[49] Richard C. Holbrooke, transcript, UN press stakeout following the Security Council session on Sierra Leone, August 14, 2000, www.un.int/usa/00_111.htm.

[50] The court has a three-year mandate and a budget of approximately $15 million a year. The United States provided $5 million for the court's first year; U.S. budgetary plans called for the United States to provide $10 million for the court's second year and $5 million for its third year. See *Joint Resolution Making Consolidated Appropriations for the Fiscal Year Ending September 30, 2003,*

and for Other Purposes, Public Law 108-7, February 20, 2003; and International Affairs (Function 150) Budget Requests for Fiscal Years 2002–2004.

[51] Ibid.; see also *Foreign Relations Authorization Act, Fiscal Year 2003,* Public Law 107-228 (HR 1646).

[52] *Joint Resolution Making Consolidated Appropriations for FY2003.*

[53] Holly Burkhalter, "Blood on the Diamonds," *Washington Post,* November 6, 2001, p. A23.

[54] Charles W. Corey, "Kimberley Process 'Good News' for Africa, Says Kansteiner," Washington File, International Information Programs, April 23, 2003, http://usinfo.state.gov/regional/af/security/a3041601.htm.

[55] Statement by Howard Jeter, deputy assistant secretary of state for African affairs, *Exploratory Hearing on Sierra Leone Diamonds,* UN Security Council, August 1, 2000, www.un.int/usa/00_105.htm.

[56] "Peace Diamonds" from Sierra Leone," USAID, April 25, 2003, www.usaid.gov/gn/sierraleone/sl_democracy/news/030203_peacediamonds/index.htm.

CHAPTER FIFTEEN

AFGHANISTAN

THE CHIMERA OF THE "LIGHT FOOTPRINT"

Milan Vaishnav

Shortly after the September 11, 2001, attacks, the United States—and the world—turned its attention to remote and desolate Afghanistan. As the primary base of operations for Osama bin Laden and the Al Qaeda terrorist network, Afghanistan served as a recruiting ground for Islamic terrorists, an important training hub for members of the Al Qaeda network, and a launching pad for worldwide terrorist operations. The ruling Taliban regime had granted Al Qaeda safe haven in Afghanistan and was regarded by the Bush administration as a co-conspirator in the 9/11 attacks.

Thus, it came as no surprise when less than a month after the attacks, Afghanistan became the first target in the United States' global "war on terrorism." After months of air strikes and grueling battles with Al Qaeda and Taliban holdouts, the coalition succeeded in unseating the Taliban, and subsequently, Afghanistan became the site for the twenty-first century's first major post-conflict reconstruction.

After ousting the Taliban from power and weakening Al Qaeda's operations in Afghanistan, the United States was expected to play a central role in the country's reconstruction. President George W. Bush pledged to the Afghan people that the United States would undertake a Marshall Plan-like effort to rebuild the war-torn country, which had been wrecked by decades of civil war, foreign invaders, and external meddling. Afghanistan was a vast country with scarce resources, a fractionalized populace, and nonexistent infrastructure. Many Afghans who had suffered under the brutal Taliban regime hoped that the Americans would be their liberators and the guarantors of a future that would be more prosperous, peaceful, and promising than the country's troubled past.

A close examination of the American record in post–9/11 Afghanistan suggests, however, that the U.S. role in the post-conflict rebuilding of that country has fallen far short of those expectations. Relying on a "light footprint" approach that placed the onus of the reconstruction burden on Afghans themselves, the Bush administration sought to distinguish its efforts from the costly forays into "nation building" undertaken during the 1990s.[1] Such exercises, the administration argued, overextended the U.S. military and entangled the United States in expensive and lengthy commitments overseas. Unfortunately, in practice this light-footprint approach has amounted to "nation-building lite,"[2] or "nation building on the cheap."

While the United States has helped achieve progress in several areas—throwing out a repressive Taliban regime, for starters—significant challenges remained a full two years into the enterprise. Most importantly, the United States' failure to secure the country colored all other aspects of the reconstruction. Hostilities rose throughout 2003, leaving the overarching security situation significantly worse than a year before. As a result, the pace of reconstruction lagged behind, causing many to worry that Afghanistan was in severe danger of receding back into the dark days that it had briefly left behind.

Second, the United States' reliance on the Northern Alliance and Afghanistan's warlords during the combat phase helped entrench the warlords and consolidate their power throughout the country. Because of rampant insecurity and a limited number of U.S. troops on the ground, the U.S. military had no choice but to work with and to rely on regional warlords during the post-combat phase to provide day-to-day security and to assist in the fight against rebel elements. The American partnership with the warlords undercut the authority of the central government and strained relations between the center and the periphery.

Finally, preoccupation with the deteriorating security situation occurred to the detriment of other elements of U.S. strategy, namely social and economic reconstruction. The United States spent roughly 11 times more money on its efforts to defeat Taliban and Al Qaeda remnants than it did on civilian reconstruction (including humanitarian assistance).[3] America's inadequate dedication of resources to the reconstruction — in the form of financial and human resources—served as an uninspiring model for international donors, who were troubled by the unstable environment for rebuilding.

With its staying power in question and its reputation in the region and the world on the line, one might have expected the United States to place a higher priority on the reconstruction, providing it with the resources and assistance necessary to make the transition. Yet, two years into the effort, there was still far too great a likelihood that Afghanistan could descend back into the ranks of the world's failed states.

STATUS OF THE RECONSTRUCTION: A MIXED RECORD

Despite the initial attention that the United States, the United Nations, and the international community focused on Afghanistan, reconstruction proceeded over the first two years at a modest pace. Immediately following the overthrow of the Taliban, the international community repeatedly pledged to stay the course in Afghanistan. Likening the effort to rebuild Afghanistan to the multiyear Marshall Plan after World War II, President Bush said, "By helping to build an Afghanistan that is free from this evil and is a better place in which to live, we are working in the best traditions of George Marshall."[4] British prime minister Tony Blair made a similar promise: "To the Afghan people we make this commitment. The conflict will not be the end. We will not walk away, as the outside world has done so many times before."[5]

The reality, however, has fallen far short of the inflated rhetoric. Although the reconstruction is still in its nascent stages, critics have assailed the lack of progress made in Afghanistan since the overthrow of the Taliban in the fall of 2001. One reporter who spent a considerable time traveling throughout the country wrote that the rebuilding of Afghanistan "has so far been a sputtering, disappointing enterprise, short of results, short of strategy, short...of money."[6]

A report issued in 2003 by a panel of South Asia experts reached a similar conclusion, albeit in a much more measured tone: "The failure to stem deteriorating security conditions and to spur economic reconstruction [in Afghanistan] could lead to a reversion to warlord-dominated anarchy and mark a major defeat for the U.S. war on terrorism."[7]

There are three interrelated areas where the United States has come up short: enhancing security throughout the country; bolstering the standing of the central government while reducing the power wielded by regional warlords; and increasing the level of resources for reconstructing Afghanistan, especially those channeled through the central government. The United States, in conjunction with the international community, must devise a coherent approach that addresses these three deficits if reconstruction in Afghanistan is to have a chance of ultimately succeeding.

FIGHTING THE WAR, PLANTING THE SEEDS OF RECONSTRUCTION

As most Americans were still reeling from the September 11 attacks, military planners inside the Pentagon were hard at work on the blueprints for Operation Enduring Freedom (OEF). To address the president's reluctance about placing a large number of American "boots on the ground" in Afghanistan, U.S. military plans called instead for a massive aerial bombardment. On October 7, U.S.-led coalition aircraft began bombing Taliban and Al Qaeda targets, from military bases to command and control stations to suspected terrorist training camps.

But the Taliban resistance was steadfast. By mid-October, it became conventional wisdom within the U.S. government that linking the U.S. military and intelligence operatives with proxy forces on the ground could assure swift victory. Because the Bush administration was loath to commit large numbers of U.S. ground troops, this quickly became the option of choice.

To amass those proxy forces, the United States turned to the Northern Alliance, a multiethnic group of mujahideen fighters who had been engaged in an internecine war against the Taliban since the mid-1990s, and who had successfully carved out an enclave within northern Afghanistan as a base of operations. OEF paired highly skilled, well-trained U.S. Special Forces and CIA personnel with the Northern Alliance. By coupling a limited number of U.S. personnel, massive amounts of airpower, and the Northern Alliance troops, the war began to shift in favor of the United States. In a matter of weeks, the Northern Alliance captured the capital of Kabul and shortly thereafter the southern Taliban stronghold of Kandahar.

Because the attacks on Afghanistan began less than a month after September 11, there was insufficient time to prepare a full-scale plan for the war, much less the reconstruction. As a result, the framework for the reconstruction grew out of the war plans. Utilizing Northern Alliance ground troops meant the United States did not have to put a substantial number of its troops in harm's way. It also meant, however, that the United States would be forced to cut less than optimal deals with the Northern Alliance leaders and Afghan military commanders when it came to time to crafting a political framework for the future of Afghanistan. The

Northern Alliance had captured the Afghan capital of Kabul well before the international community had devised a framework for a future Afghan national government. That meant that any negotiations would have to take into account the distribution of power as it existed in Afghanistan immediately following the war.

ESTABLISHING SECURITY

Endemic security problems plagued the Afghan reconstruction from the start. As has been demonstrated in numerous prior reconstruction efforts, the inability to provide security renders it impossible to achieve progress in all other aspects of reconstruction. Security is the precondition and the very foundation on which reconstruction must build.

In Afghanistan, this lesson was learned once again—the hard way. Two years into the post-conflict phase, remnants of the Taliban regime aimed to undermine the transitional government of Hamid Karzai and continued to threaten the peace in Afghanistan. This insecurity further strengthened the hand of the warlords, which slowed efforts to disarm illegitimate militias and empower the national armed forces and police. The resulting public security vacuum paved the way for an overall sense of lawlessness and disturbing levels of banditry, which beleaguered regime officials, international aid workers, and the Afghans who cooperated with them.

While America's overwhelming military might, expressed in the form of Operation Enduring Freedom, forced the Taliban from power and degraded Al Qaeda's capacities in Afghanistan, OEF did not eliminate either group. Although many of their safe havens were systematically destroyed, these rebels merely scattered across porous borders or regrouped in smaller units in hard-to-reach parts of the country. Much of the country remained vulnerable to attack by Taliban remnants and their sympathizers. In particular, southern Afghanistan and those areas that share a border with neighboring Pakistan consistently came under attack by Taliban guerillas who used the rugged, mountainous border region as a base of operations.

Insecurity throughout Afghanistan created an environment in which warlordism was allowed to thrive. On the one hand, the United States cooperated with the warlords and their militias—whom they relied on to provide security in parts of the country. On the other hand, the United States assisted the Afghan central government to develop its own military capacity. Many regional warlords refused to disarm and demobilize their soldiers, setting up a showdown with a central government that was desperately trying to develop its own army. By playing to both sides, the United States made it very difficult for a legitimate, capable, and truly national Afghan army to emerge.[8]

Finally, many of the attacks that contributed to the slow pace of reconstruction were attributed to bandits, ordinary criminals, and "narco-criminals," all of whom prospered in the security vacuum. Because Afghanistan lacked forces capable of effectively enforcing the rule of law, those that sought to profit off of insecurity did quite well. Roving bandits of disenchanted Afghans, pro-Taliban militiamen, and greedy spoilers thrived on this lack of security. According to statistical figures, Afghanistan's share of global opium production shot up from 12 percent in 2001 to 76 percent in 2002.[9] This increase in narcotics production and trafficking helped ingrain the drug trade and allowed organized crime to gain a foothold.

FLAWS IN U.S. STRATEGY

The roots of the inability to secure the majority of the country can be traced to three facets of U.S. strategy.

First, in the initial period, the U.S.-led military coalition focused almost exclusively on "anti-terrorist" operations against remnants of Al Qaeda and Taliban holdouts, rather than on securing the country through broader peace enforcement and peacekeeping operations. This resulted in a serious security gap for areas outside of Kabul. By October 2003, there were approximately 12,000 coalition troops (the U.S. contingent is roughly 8,500) charged with preventing Taliban elements from regrouping and with combating rebel incursions, primarily in southern Afghanistan. By using the bulk of its military to perform combat missions, the United States chose not to utilize its military to perform peacekeeping duties. This narrow mandate precluded large numbers of U.S. soldiers from taking part in noncombat-related activities. The coalition, under U.S. command, essentially absolved itself from the responsibility of providing everyday security for ordinary Afghans. "Even from the narrow angle of the war against terrorism, you have got to do a little bit more than trying to damp down threats from Al Qaeda," quipped Lakhdar Brahimi, referring to the U.S. military's unwillingness to expand the scope of its mission.[10]

As a result of this intransigence, the United States de facto ceded the provision of day-to-day security to the warlords—and in Kabul, to the multinational International Security Assistance Force (ISAF). What began as a matter of convenience quickly turned into one of necessity. Although regional militias proved unfit (or unwilling) to protect the citizenry against the regular attacks of pro-Taliban forces, remnants of the old regime, and criminal elements, the question that stared U.S. decisionmakers in the face was: If not the militias, then who? According to Lt. Gen. John R. Vines, commander of U.S. forces in Afghanistan in 2003, "Militias are part of the existing reality. Some are legitimate, and some are predators...but the challenge is, if you disestablish a militia, who provides security? The vacuum can be filled by anarchy."[11] Intense rivalry among the warlords was rampant, deepening existing fault lines within the country. This infighting frequently manifested itself as violent conflict between the militias of skirmishing warlords, which contributed to the fragility of the security environment.

In Kabul, security was handled by ISAF, a United Nations-mandated operation established in December 2001 to assist the Afghan transitional government in maintaining security in Kabul.[12] Hampered by a limited mandate, ISAF was unable to operate outside of the immediate outskirts of the capital. Thus, while it succeeded in stabilizing Kabul, it had no impact on security throughout the rest of the country, which was largely insecure.

Many people, including President Karzai and Lakhdar Brahimi, the UN Secretary General's Special Representative (SRSG) for Afghanistan, repeatedly called for expanding ISAF's reach beyond Kabul. But the U.S. administration balked. During the early months of the reconstruction, the United States argued against expanding ISAF beyond the confines of Kabul, choosing instead to focus its efforts on rebuilding indigenous Afghan military and policing capacity.[13] The United States explained its reluctance to expand ISAF in the initial reconstruction years by arguing that efforts to build an Afghan national army were a higher priority. Still, although rebuilding Afghan military capacity was essential to a stable Afghanistan in the long run, the American position did not address the short-term and medium-term stability and security needs. By ignoring pressing security concerns, the United States encouraged the creation of a dangerous, multiyear security gap.[14]

In August 2003, the North Atlantic Treaty Organization (NATO) assumed permanent command of ISAF, whose troops at the time numbered close to 5,500. NATO was successful in convincing the United States to actively support an expansion of the mandate, resulting in UNSCR 1510, which lifted the "Kabul-only" restrictions on ISAF's operations.[15] As a first step in this expansion, Germany agreed to send approximately 450 peacekeepers to the (largely peaceful) city of Kunduz in northern Afghanistan.

The United States' initial opposition to ISAF expansion eventually evolved into indifference and later lukewarm support. Yet its initial inflexibility on this question severely damaged the prospects for a speedy reconstruction. In the intervening 18 months between the creation of ISAF and the expansion of its area of operation, much damage had been done. U.S. reluctance to support an expansion of ISAF allowed spoilers to disrupt reconstruction in areas outside Kabul, which over time degraded popular support of the Karzai government, not to mention the initial goodwill toward the American presence.

Succumbing to pressure to alleviate chronic insecurity and speed up the pace of reconstruction, in 2003 the United States stood up deployable reconstruction units in several cities across Afghanistan. These units, called Provincial Reconstruction Teams (PRTs), consisted of between 50 and 100 U.S. soldiers and were complemented by development, diplomatic, and economic civilian specialists from the U.S. government. In essence, PRTs functioned as mini-reconstruction agencies designed to win the hearts and minds of the Afghan populace. The United States established three PRTs in the relatively safe cities of Gardez, Bamiyan, and Kunduz. The United Kingdom later established a fourth PRT in Mazar-e-Sharif. New Zealand has since taken over the U.S. PRT in Bamiyan, and the United States expressed interest in establishing additional PRTs in Jalalabad, Kandahar, Herat, Bagram, and Ghazni.[16]

A brainchild of the U.S. Department of Defense, PRTs were created to bolster reconstruction efforts, extend the influence of the central government beyond Kabul, and monitor and assess the local and regional developments. In addition, PRTs were intended to increase the feeling of security in places outside of the capital. While PRTs did possess the capability to enhance security for Afghan citizens, they were not explicitly mandated to provide security. Instead, PRTs functioned as "small-scale reconstruction agencies, but with overheads off the charts."[17]

PRTs were not a perfect substitute for peacekeeping troops. Several critics have assailed the concept of PRTs as "trying to achieve security in Afghanistan on the cheap,"[18] and many humanitarian organizations also criticized the PRTs for blurring the distinction between military and civilian missions. However, PRTs did have a great deal of success in

undertaking small reconstruction projects that markedly improved relations between local Afghans and U.S. officials. As far as enhancing security, PRTs had a net positive impact on security, but they also were
intentionally established in relatively safe areas where security was better than average.

STRENGTHENING GOVERNANCE

The U.S. military strategy in Afghanistan also had lasting political ramifications that made it difficult to establish effective governing institutions. A distinguishing feature of the strategy behind Operation
Enduring Freedom was "the degree to which military expediency determined strategic choices."[19] Relying on warlords like Mohammed Fahim,
Ismail Khan, and Abdul Rashid Dostum to topple the Taliban made
sense from a military perspective, but led to a political black hole. The
United States did not have a long-term political vision for Afghanistan
that dealt with the warlords in any realistic fashion. Many within the
U.S. government believed that it would be able to rein in the warlords
over time, but during the first two years of the reconstruction, that
proved impossible.

Continued insecurity throughout the country meant that the U.S.
military could not sever its ties with the warlords. Rather, during the first
two years of the reconstruction, the United States directly contributed
to the continued empowerment of the warlords. Lacking boots on the
ground to perform the required security duties, the U.S. government
found itself in the untenable position of supporting a central government whose stated aim was to reduce the power of the warlords, while
providing financial and other material resources to the warlords themselves.

This contradictory policy severely weakened the authority of the
central government. As a result, Karzai's transitional government experienced significant difficulty consolidating its power and spreading its
influence from Kabul to the far reaches of the country. Karzai constantly
battled with the warlords—many of whom resided within his government—for authority, money, and legitimacy.

The origins of this tension between the center and the warlord-dominated periphery can be found in the Bonn agreement of 2001. Under
the auspices of the United Nations, representatives of the Northern Alliance and Afghan expatriate groups convened in Bonn, Germany, in No-

vember 2001 to decide the future political structure of Afghanistan. After nine days of tense negotiations in which the United States played a central role, an agreement was reached to form an interim government that represented each of the four major ethnic groups within Afghanistan: Tajiks, Uzbeks, Hazara, and Pashtuns. This compromise, though an uneasy one, was crucial to preserving the long-term interests of the Afghan nation-state.[20] In an effort to promote national conciliation, leaders of each of these factions—many of whom had less than glowing reputations—were brought into the new government. In essence, Bonn codified the standing of the warlords and legislated the unworkable relationship between the warlords vis-à-vis the central government.

As stipulated in the terms of the agreement, the interim government, headed by Pashtun Hamid Karzai, was in power for six months before giving way to a transitional administration. The structure of the transitional administration was decided upon by a *loya jirga* (grand council) of Afghan representatives, which convened in June 2002 with assistance from the United Nations as well as the United States and its allies. With behind-the-scenes U.S. support, the charismatic Karzai was elected by the quasi-democratic *loya jirga* to head the Afghan transitional government. This government was charged with overseeing a constitutional *loya jirga* in 2003, which would ratify a new constitution and pave the way for national elections in 2004.

Following the agreement established at Bonn, the United Nations Security Council passed Resolution 1401, which created the UN Assistance Mission in Afghanistan (UNAMA). UNAMA was granted a limited, narrowly defined mandate in Afghanistan, compared to the much larger UN missions in Kosovo (UNMIK) and East Timor (UNTA-ET). In Afghanistan, the UN's primary task was to assist in the implementation of the Bonn agreement. This meant, among other things, supervising Afghanistan's political process, overseeing the drafting of a new constitution, organizing for future elections, and assisting in the creation of an effective civil administration.[21]

The UN's efforts to implement the Bonn agreement and to adhere to its timeline proceeded with a great deal of difficulty. For starters, the constitutional process was fraught with controversy. The lack of security made it nearly impossible for systematic public consultation. Growing insecurity in provincial centers (especially in the south) reduced opportunities for public debate, and as a result there was little public legitimacy accorded to the process or the final document.[22] In September

2003, Karzai delayed the convening of the constitutional *loya jirga* until mid-December in order to provide more time for consultation and public education.[23]

As the final step in the constitutional process, national elections are to be held in June 2004. The document that emerges from the constitutional *loya jirga* will provide the framework for these elections. The timing of the elections themselves, however, was also subject to debate as many observers voiced concerns that poor security and a lack of funding and strategic planning might warrant a delay. As of August 2003, the widely held view was that the security environment on the ground was not conducive for free and fair nationwide elections. In his report to the Security Council, UN Secretary General Kofi Annan also warned of delays in the electoral timetable, citing that as of July 2003 "too many areas are inaccessible for lack of security.... Without the appropriate security environment, communities in some areas of the country are bound to be disenfranchised."[24] In addition, UNAMA struggled to receive adequate financing to implement important facets of the electoral process, such as conducting voter registration programs and educating Afghans about the electoral process. While a nationwide census was slated to begin in 2004, delays in implementation imperiled the chances that the data could be used effectively for a nationwide voter registration exercise.

Having played a crucial role in defeating the Taliban, the position of most of the warlords was deeply embedded in society. As a result, the U.S.-brokered Bonn agreement had little choice but to legitimize the standing of many of these warlords. Most of them were independent operators who only nominally pledged their allegiance to the central government. Each warlord had his own bureaucracy, security, and loyal following. Thus, "while the country [had] an interim government...it [was] much less than the sum of its parts—and those parts [were] largely controlled by warlords."[25]

The Karzai government pledged to remove those warlords who did not comply with the authority of the central government, but it had few means at its disposal to implement such a policy. Struggling to extend the reach of the central government beyond Kabul, President Karzai was often ridiculed as the "mayor of Kabul" and the "vice president of public relations."[26] Unable to effectively govern most of the country, Karzai had to rely on demonstrating to the Afghan people the tangible change that the central government had effected. With growing insecurity, inadequate funding, and a slow pace of reconstruction, this was extremely difficult.

PROVIDING ADEQUATE FUNDING FOR RECONSTRUCTION

Since the fall of the Taliban, social and economic reconstruction in Afghanistan has suffered tremendously from the lack of security. In fiscal year 2003, the United States spent roughly $1 billion on reconstruction and humanitarian assistance for Afghanistan—less than 10 percent of what it spent on ongoing military operations in the country. The security gap made donors hesitant to invest money in such an unstable environment for fear that their money would be wasted. For reasons mentioned previously, the security gap also had the unintended consequence of strengthening the hand of the warlords vis-à-vis the central government. As a result, much of what was spent in Afghanistan did not go through the central government, which found itself in a difficult fiscal position. Donors refused to channel money through the central government due to what was commonly referred to as a lack of "absorptive capacity," and the central government countered this with allegations that donors refused to "invest adequately in building that capacity or to allow the government to learn how to manage its resources."[27]

Nonetheless, in 2002 the Afghan central government produced a National Development Framework that articulated its vision for the reconstruction of Afghanistan. The comprehensive document laid out priorities in four sectors: humanitarian and human and social capital; physical reconstruction and natural resources; private-sector development; and governance and security. Within each of these four pillars, it devised broad strategies for specific program areas ranging from refugee return to urban management to a national police force.[28] In 2003, the Karzai government issued a detailed national budget whose individual line items corresponded closely with the National Development Framework. This budget was widely praised by the international donor community for its clear articulation of national priorities and its realistic financial allocations.

Yet, despite the fact that a strategy was in place for potential funding, the international community was reluctant to provide the resources necessary to address the central government's needs. Unfortunately, this fact tracked with the overall record of foreign assistance to Afghanistan dating back to early 2002. In January 2002, international donors met in Tokyo to discuss financing the reconstruction in Afghanistan. At this conference, donors pledged $5.2 billion for the reconstruction over the course of five years.[29] Though initially hailed as a success, the pledges made at Tokyo represented much less that what many experts considered adequate for reconstructing a country that lacked significant infrastructure. A joint needs assessment conducted by the Asian Development Bank, the United Nations Development Program, and the World Bank estimated that $10.2 billion would be needed over five years for reconstruction purposes.[30] The Afghan government conducted a needs assessment of its own, which anticipated international donors would have to contribute $15 billion over five years to cover the costs of reconstruction.[31]

On a per capita basis, actual aid spent in other post-conflict countries far exceeded what was pledged for Afghanistan. According to one study, "[I]f Afghanistan were to receive the average of aid spending levels per capita from four other recent post-conflict settings [Rwanda, Bosnia, Kosovo, and East Timor], it would receive…more than $30 billion over five years."[32] As of May 2003, $2.1 billion had been disbursed—$1.6 billion of which was committed for reconstruction projects. The total expenditure on reconstruction projects completed by May 2003 totaled only $192 million, a small fraction of what had been disbursed.[33]

Furthermore, according to an analysis conducted by the Afghan Assistance Coordination Authority, only 16 percent of the money that was disbursed since the Tokyo donors' conference actually passed through the central government.[34] By bypassing the central government, donors helped to undercut the embryonic authority of the Karzai government, already under attack by the operations of the semiautonomous warlords.[35] Regional warlords regularly hijacked customs revenue for themselves, diverting a major source of funds away from the central government. The central government's inability to control the flow of customs revenue was repeatedly identified as a central economic weakness of the Kabul government, yet the international community refused to devise means to deal with the problem. Ismail Khan, governor of Herat and commander of four provinces in western Afghanistan, allegedly took in $100 million in customs revenue in 2002—more than the entire central government took in that year nationally.[36] As a result of this influx of revenue, Khan was able to reconstruct a good deal of Herat, but simultaneously deprived the Karzai government of a significant source of income.

The nexus between security and social and economic reconstruction was so acute that even when the Afghan government and the United States (and the international community) did agree on what reconstruction priorities to fund, implementation was extremely difficult. For instance, the rebuilding of the 300-mile highway connecting Kabul and Kandahar was one of the Afghan government's most heralded reconstruction projects—as well as a cornerstone of U.S. reconstruction efforts. Funded in large part by the U.S. Agency for International Development (USAID), this key road became the symbol of national reconstruction efforts, signifying not only physical unification but also the practical facilitation of the domestic transfer of goods and services.[37] But gangs, many of whom are suspected to be working in cooperation with Taliban militants, continued to stage regular attacks on those who are rebuilding the road as well as those who seek to protect it. Progress on the highway occurred at a "painfully slow" rate; and in the Afghan psychology, the inability to construct this thoroughfare was a constant reminder of the country's decrepit infrastructure. [38]

Unfortunately, the struggle to rebuild this key transport link was indicative of many of the country's reconstruction projects that foundered due to a lack of security. Aid workers were forced to restrict their areas of operation and many of them became targets of resurgent violence. Humanitarian NGOs such as the United States-based Mercy Corps, which had a large presence in Afghanistan, ceased operations in 2003 in some provinces that were deemed too dangerous. "Certainly the humanitarian community feels badly about this. We have no hesitation to work in the entire southwestern provinces," explained Mercy Corps's coordinator for southern Afghanistan, "but at the end of the day security for our staff is very important."[39]

In July 2003, the Bush administration re-launched its Afghanistan reconstruction policy. To fend off accusations of underfunding Afghan reconstruction and neglecting Afghanistan in favor of Iraq, the United States stated its intention to devote an additional $1 billion per year to revitalize the reconstruction. This would bring the total amount of U.S. assistance to nearly $1.8 billion in fiscal year 2004. According to the Bush administration, the new monies were designed to bolster civilian programs to reconstruct decrepit infrastructure, rebuild schools, and pave key roads. The shift in policy (dubbed "Accelerate Success") was advertised as more than just additional dollars in the pipeline. The United States also announced its plans to increase the number of civilian officials posted in the U.S. Embassy and to pair up key civilian technical experts with the various Afghan ministries.[40] However, many questioned whether these new monies would be channeled through the central government, or if they would bypass Kabul altogether.

Despite these policy pronouncements, U.S. policy hardly amounted to a "Marshall Plan"-like effort, as had been suggested by senior Bush administration officials in the fall of 2001. As leader of the coalition and the wealthiest donor country, the United States did not place enough emphasis on civilian reconstruction during the early stages of the post-conflict phase. Moreover, the money that was spent did not pass through the central government, placing U.S. assistance policy at odds with U.S. political objectives of strengthening government institutions and ensuring the continued legitimacy of Hamid Karzai.

CONCLUSION

In March 2003, Afghanistan's finance minister Ashraf Ghani briefed an annual gathering of donor nations in Brussels. Looking five years into the future, he described three potential outcomes for Afghanistan: "The first possibility was a Western-friendly democracy with a strong central government and enough new infrastructure to establish a thriving private sector. The second was yet another floundering third-world country that borrows money it cannot repay and lifts virtually no one out of poverty. The third was a narco-mafia state where opium producers and warlords create enough mayhem to thrust the nation into the whirlwind of anarchy."[41]

Based on its current trajectory, the first of Ghani's scenarios is doubtful; the second is likely; and the third is conceivable. Afghanistan does not appear to be on the verge of state collapse—especially while the world's superpower maintains a watchful eye. However, the United States will not be able to indefinitely provide Afghanistan with the military or economic assistance it currently requires. If Afghanistan and donor nations such as the United States do not take concrete steps to consolidate the power of the central government, minimize the stature of the warlords, and make significant headway on social and economic reconstruction in the near term, Afghanistan could turn into the drug-riddled, feudal state Ghani describes.

The inter-connectedness of security, governance, and social and economic reconstruction was amply demonstrated in the Afghan case. The failure to provide adequate security has hampered efforts to achieve political development. Political development has also been stymied by slow movement on the economic front—greater economic progress could have helped to shore up the central government. A stronger central government in Kabul, in turn, could take more ownership of providing security throughout Afghanistan.

Initial decisions by the United States to build on its "light footprint" combat model have ended up forcing the United States into a devil's pact with the warlords and militia leaders whose survival depends on continuing insecurity. This insecurity has been the root of all other problems in reconstruction efforts in Afghanistan. Although the light footprint worked in the combat phase, it has complicated reconstruction efforts. In order to protect against Afghanistan falling victim to one of the two pessimistic outcomes described by Ghani, the United States (in conjunction with the international community) must move beyond this approach.

Compounded by a lack of adequate funding for reconstruction, the United States' effort in Afghanistan has been one of contradictions. A light footprint approach may be workable in Afghanistan, but it will depend on sustained commitment and generous resources that are designed for maximum impact.

Notes

General note: The author would like to thank Joel T. Meyer, Carl A. Robichaud, and Courtney Rusin for their help in performing research for this chapter. Bathsheba Crocker provided important feedback on earlier versions of this chapter.

[1] This "light footprint" approach was also adopted by the United Nations and the larger international community as a whole, whose presence in Afghanistan has been significantly smaller than it was in earlier post-conflict operations in Kosovo or East Timor. The United Nations, cautious about appearing too heavy-handed with regard to the political aspects of rebuilding, has been careful to play a supporting role in a deliberate attempt to ensure that Afghans—not international bureaucrats—control Afghanistan's destiny.

[2] Michael Ignatieff, "Nation-Building Lite," New York Times Magazine, July 28, 2002.

[3] In 2003, the United States spent roughly $11 billion on military goals that in and of themselves do not directly achieve reconstruction goals, compared to roughly $1 billion on civilian reconstruction in Afghanistan.

[4] Remarks by President George W. Bush to the George C. Marshall ROTC Award Seminar on National Security, Virginia Military Institute, April 17, 2002, www.whitehouse.gov/news/releases/2002/04/20020417-1.html.

[5] Remarks by Prime Minister Tony Blair to the 2001 Labour Party Conference, October 2, 2001, http://politics.guardian.co.uk/speeches/story/0,11126, 590775,00.html.

[6] Barry Bearak, "Unreconstructed," *New York Times Magazine*, June 1, 2003.

[7] Frank G. Wisner II, Nicholas Platt, and Marshall Bouton, *Afghanistan: Are We Losing the Peace?* Chairmen's Report, Independent Task Force Cosponsored by the Council on Foreign Relations and the Asia Society, June 2003.

[8] *Good Intentions Will Not Pave the Road to Peace*, Policy Brief, CARE International and Center on International Cooperation, New York University, September 2003, www.cic.nyu.edu/pdf/goodintentions.pdf.

[9] Ibid.

[10] Victoria Burnett and Edward Luce, "Rebuilding after the Taliban Is Still a Huge Undertaking," *Financial Times*, July 17, 2003.

[11] Pamela Constable, "Key Security Initiatives Founder in Afghanistan," *Washington Post*, September 19, 2003.

[12] United Nations Security Council Resolution 1386 (2001), S/RES/1386, December 20, 2001.

[13] This policy has perhaps best been articulated by U.S. Secretary of Defense Donald Rumsfeld as follows, "[W]hy put all the time and effort and money into [expanding ISAF]? Why not put it into helping [the Afghans] develop a national army, so that they can look out for themselves over time?" See Rachel Bronson, "When Soldiers Become Cops," *Foreign Affairs* 81, no. 6, (November/December 2002): 122–132.

[14] For a more in-depth analysis, see Anja Manuel and P. W. Singer, "A New Model Afghan Army," *Foreign Affairs* 81, no. 4 (July/August 2002): 44–59.

[15] United Nations Security Council Resolution 1510, S/RES/1510, October 13, 2003.

[16] See U.S. Department of Defense "Afghanistan Update: September 23, 2003," www.defendamerica.mil/afghanistan/update/oct2003/au101603.html.

[17] Larry Thompson and Michelle Brown, "Security on the Cheap: PRTs in Afghanistan," Refugees International, July 7, 2003, www.refugeesinternational .org/cgi-bin/ri/bulletin?bc=00613.

[18] Ibid.

[19] Carl Conetta, *Strange Victory: A Critical Appraisal of Operation Enduring Freedom*, Project on Defense Alternatives, Commonwealth Institute, PDA Research Monograph 6, January 30, 2002, p. 29, www.comw.org/pda/ 0201strangevic.pdf.

[20] James Dobbins et al., *America's Role in Nation-Building: From Germany to Iraq* (Santa Monica, Calif.: RAND, 2003), p. 132.

[21] United Nations Security Council Resolution 1401, S/RES/1401, March 28, 2002.

[22] International Crisis Group, *Afghanistan's Flawed Constitutional Process*, Asia Report No. 56, June 12, 2003. According to Special Representative of the Secretary General Lakhdar Brahimi, "The Constitutional Commission [did] its best to mitigate the lack of security...in the Constitution making process....It had to avoid more vulnerable district level meetings. They held public consultations in provincial capitals only, and through smaller, focused groups that could more easily be protected from intimidation." See briefing by Lakhdar Brahimi, SRSG for Afghanistan to the UN Security Council, August 13, 2003, www.unama-afg.org/docs/sc/Briefings/SRSG%20Briefing%20to%20the%20Security%20Council%2013%20Aug%202003.htm.

[23] "Afghanistan: Karzai Postpones Constitutional Loya Jirga," Radio Free Europe/Radio Liberty, September 7, 2003, www.rferl.org/nca/features/200309/07092003164238.asp.

[24] *The Situation in Afghanistan and its Implications for International Peace and Security*, Report of the United Nations Secretary-General, July 23, 2003, Report A/57/850–S/2003/754, available at www.un.org/Docs/sc/sgrep03.html.

[25] Bearak, "Unreconstructed," p. 41.

[26] Ignatieff, "Nation-Building Lite."

[27] *Good Intentions Will Not Pave the Road to Peace* (see note 8).

[28] National Development Framework, Version 2, April 2002, www.afghanistangov.org/resources/itsa/ig-april/NDF_Revised_Draft.pdf.

[29] Of the $5.2 billion, $3.8 billion would come in the form of grants and $1.4 billion as loans.

[30] For more information, see Asian Development Bank, United Nations Development Program, and World Bank, *Afghanistan: Preliminary Needs Assessment for Recovery and Reconstruction*, January 2002, www.reliefweb.int/library/documents/2002/undp-afg-15jan.pdf.

[31] Barnett Rubin, Humayun Hamidzada, and Abby Stoddard, *Through the Fog of Rebuilding: Evaluating the Reconstruction of Afghanistan*, Policy Brief, Center on International Cooperation, New York University, May 2003, www.cic.nyu.edu/pdf/EvaluatingAfghReconst.pdf.

[32] It is estimated that between 2002 and 2006 Afghanistan will receive the equivalent of $42 of aid per person. This is significantly lower than the per-person amount of aid to Rwanda ($193), Bosnia ($326), Kosovo ($288), and East Timor ($195). For more information, see *Rebuilding Afghanistan: A Little Less Talk, A Lot More Action*, CARE International in Afghanistan Policy Brief, October 2002, www.careusa.org/newsroom/specialreports/afghanistan/09302002_policybrief.pdf.

[33] Rubin, Hamidzada, and Stoddard, *Through the Fog of Rebuilding.*

[34] *Analysis of Aid Flows to Afghanistan,* Afghan Assistance Coordination Authority, April 2003, www.af/resources/aaca/cU-GoA-AidAnalysis.pdf.

[35] "The easy talk about helping Afghanistan stand on its own two feet does not square with the hard interest that each Western government has in financing not the Afghans, but its own national relief organizations....The unpleasant underside of nation-building is that the internationals' first priority is building their own capacity....The last priority is financing the Afghan government," writes Michael Ignatieff. See Ignatieff, "Nation-Building Lite."

[36] Wisner, Platt, and Bouton, *Afghanistan: Are We Losing the Peace?* pp. 2, 16. Barry Bearak comments, "It is as if the governor of New York also declared himself the emir of New Jersey and Connecticut, keeping federal taxes from the region for his own purposes." See Bearak, "Unreconstructed," p. 3.

[37] Pamela Constable, "Attacks Slowing Key Afghan Road," *Washington Post,* September 6, 2003; and Carlotta Gall, "Potholes and Promises Line an Afghan Highway," *New York Times,* August 31, 2003.

[38] Constable, "Attacks Slowing Key Afghan Road."

[39] According to government and UN documents, approximately 16 of Afghanistan's 32 provinces are deemed high-risk for aid workers and 3 are classified as medium-risk (as of September 2003). See *Good Intentions Will Not Pave the Road to Peace* (note 8); "Afghanistan: Special Report on the Insecurity in the South," IRIN News (United Nations Integrated Regional Information Network), UN Office for the Coordination of Humanitarian Affairs, August 14, 2003.

[40] Victoria Burnett, "Washington to Relaunch Afghan Reconstruction," *Financial Times,* July 28, 2003; April Witt, "Afghan Says Aid Will Help Rebuild Peace," *Washington Post,* July 28, 2003.

[41] Bearak, "Unreconstructed."

CHAPTER SIXTEEN

IRAQ

GOING IT ALONE, GONE WRONG

Bathsheba N. Crocker

Reconstructing Iraq after the 2003 war to oust Saddam Hussein is the largest and most strategically significant post-conflict challenge the United States has undertaken since World War II. If Iraq becomes a stable, prosperous democracy, it could exert a powerful and positive influence on the region and the Muslim world more generally. But if Iraq descends into chaos, the consequences will be disastrous, not only for the Iraqi people, but for Middle East stability, U.S. relations with the Arab and Muslim world, and U.S. authority in the international community as a whole.

The war in Iraq was characterized by U.S. determination, might, and technologically superior war-fighting capabilities. Relations with key allies and the role of the United Nations were subordinated to America's resolve, and Saddam Hussein's regime was toppled in a mere three weeks. Yet, as the first year of the U.S. occupation of Iraq confirmed, the United States failed to prepare for or implement the peace as it had the war.

The United States chose to use a different model for postwar reconstruction in Iraq than those used throughout the 1990s. The reconstruction was led by the United States—with only a skeletal coalition—in contrast to the United Nations or a robust multinational coalition. It was also led by a U.S. government institution—the Department of Defense—with relatively untested capacities in planning for and carrying out post-conflict reconstruction.

Five aspects distinguish the Iraq reconstruction model. First is its sheer enormity—in terms of scale and commitment. By the time the United States went to war to topple the country's ruler, Iraq's 24 million people and its infrastructure and service delivery mechanisms had suffered decades of severe degradation and underinvestment, in addition to three wars and over 10 years of crippling international sanctions. Both before and after the 2003 war, the United States made enormous promises about what regime change would bring for the Iraqi people and about the United States' commitment to set Iraq on a more promising course for the future. As the months after the war made clear, those promises would require a larger commitment of U.S. troops than at any time since the Vietnam War and the expenditure of U.S. funds on par with the Marshall Plan for Germany after World War II.

Second, during both the war and the reconstruction, the United States acted virtually unilaterally. Attempts to garner an international consensus on going to war failed, and U.S. relations with key allies suffered as a result of differences over the decision to go to war. There was no United Nations Security Council resolution authorizing the use of force in Iraq, and the United States fought the war largely on its own—although Britain provided considerable troops, and some other countries provided troops or other support for the war effort. In part because of the diplomatic breakdown before the war, and in part because of differences over how the United States was conducting the reconstruction efforts, U.S. efforts to build an international consensus for the reconstruction of Iraq also foundered.

During the first year of the reconstruction, the United States was unsuccessful in getting major commitments of troops or funds from other countries. Although the United States was able to garner Security Council support for three resolutions seeming to confirm the U.S. postwar actions, the resulting resolutions had little if any effect on the ground in Iraq. The Security Council passed a fourth resolution in June 2004 that endorsed Iraq's interim government that took power from the United States on June 30, 2004, and authorized the continued presence of the U.S.-commanded multinational force in Iraq. Unlike the earlier resolutions, the June 2004 resolution provided some real hope of setting Iraq on the right track for the first time since the fall of Saddam.

Third, the Iraq effort was an almost pure military operation through key phases of the reconstruction. Admittedly, in other situations—Kosovo, for example—military forces have had to undertake some "nation-building" activities until the civilian operations were up and running, giving rise to concerns in the United States about "mission creep." But in Iraq, all such concerns were quickly abandoned, as soldiers were called on to do everything from fighting insurgents and keeping law and order to setting up political councils and handing out salaries. Even the U.S. civilian operation—the Coalition Provisional Authority (CPA)—was run by the Department of Defense (DOD), rather than the Department of State, which typically oversees the civilian side of U.S. post-conflict operations.

DOD oversight did produce some early successes; for example, DOD was able to field a civilian administration office in Iraq relatively quickly. But that speed was completely overshadowed by the lack of preparation, which led to several fundamental early mistakes, such as the CPA's decision to disband the Iraqi army and a draconian de-Ba'athification order that was premised on Germany without any attention to local facts. DOD does not have the necessary background or core competencies to run a post-conflict operation on its own, and it rebuffed calls for greater collaboration with other U.S. government agencies.

Fourth, the Department of Defense decided to use large, private U.S. contractors to provide most key services in the postwar phase—such as restoring electricity, building schools and hospitals, revamping Iraq's economy, training Iraqi security forces, and organizing community-level political activities—rather than the usual assortment of U.S. and foreign government agencies, international organizations, nongovernmental organizations (NGOs), and smaller private contractors. Companies with untested capacities in post-conflict reconstruction were entrusted with handling major parts of the reconstruction. Moreover, the United States largely kept the bidding process limited to U.S. companies, shutting companies from other countries out of the potentially lucrative business prospects in Iraq and further alienating close friends and allies—not to mention fueling mistrust of U.S. motives in Iraq.[1]

Finally, like Afghanistan, the Iraq war and its aftermath were billed by the U.S. government as being central to the war on terrorism. In building its case for war, the United States had argued that Saddam was linked to and provided support to terrorist groups, including Al Qaeda. After deposing Saddam, the United States argued that a successful reconstruction in Iraq was a key part of its overall anti-terrorism efforts. At the same time, Iraq post-Saddam became a magnet for foreign terrorists, who crossed Iraq's porous borders to join ranks with Iraqi resistance fighters, creating a growing problem for the United States in implementing reconstruction activities.

The postwar Iraq model provides an interesting case study, both of the virtues and shortfalls of the model itself, and also of the relative capacities of the U.S. government to carry out post-conflict reconstruction. With respect to crosscutting issues—strategic planning and interagency coordination—and substantive areas—security, governance, economic and social well-being, and justice and reconciliation—the record of the United States in Iraq during the first year was poor.

Despite wildly optimistic prewar predictions that the reconstruction efforts would be quick and relatively easy, U.S. government officials soon acknowledged that rebuilding Iraq would be a long-term and exceedingly challenging and costly endeavor. Fairly early on in the effort, it became clear that the U.S. model for reconstructing Iraq was flawed, and that the reconstruction would have gone more smoothly were the U.S. government better prepared and set up to address post-conflict reconstruction.

THE PERILS OF POOR PLANNING AND INADEQUATE COORDINATION

U.S. post-conflict reconstruction efforts consistently suffer from inadequate planning, and Iraq was no exception. The strategic plan for the military aspects of the 2003 war in Iraq has been lauded as brilliant. But neither the U.S. military nor U.S. civilian agencies have a corresponding capacity to plan for postwar reconstruction.[2] Compounding this problem is the lack of an effective coordinating mechanism among those U.S. government agencies involved in reconstruction activities.[3]

Indeed, in some ways the root of the troubled response in Iraq can be traced to the abdication of the interagency process and the role of the National Security Council (NSC) before the war and during the early reconstruction months. The lead-up to the war in Iraq saw a breakdown in relations not only between the United States and many of its allies but also among U.S. government agencies. Major cleavages developed between the Defense Department and the State Department in particular. Those departments clashed over fundamental issues related to the war itself; and their clashes spilled over to planning for the reconstruction, with different agencies carrying out separate planning exercises—often based on conflicting underlying assumptions—and disagreeing on key issues, such as whether to establish a provisional government made up of exiled Iraqis.

Rather than working to resolve the differences among agencies and integrate the various actors, the NSC opted to let the Defense Department take over the planning and implementation of the reconstruction. Although the State Department and the U.S. Agency for International Development (USAID) are the U.S. government civilian agencies with the most post-conflict reconstruction experience, an office was established at the Defense Department to oversee and coordinate U.S. reconstruction, humanitarian, and civil administration efforts in Iraq.

That office—the Office of Reconstruction and Humanitarian Assistance (ORHA)—was not created until late January 2003, just two months before the war itself began. The State Department's early planning efforts, which included a series of "Future of Iraq" working groups with Iraqi exiles that began in late summer 2002, were largely shelved.[4] Instead, ORHA quickly recruited hundreds of U.S. government employees, former diplomats, and military officers and began planning anew for the expected humanitarian and reconstruction needs.

Despite the presence of personnel from other agencies, though, ORHA—which later became the CPA—was decidedly a Defense Department operation. Personnel problems on the ground in Iraq during the reconstruction—in particular the dearth of U.S. civilians with relevant experience and language skills—reflected this. Thus the early coordination breakdown hampered the implementation as well as the planning of reconstruction. As one expert noted, "cooperation inside the government broke down."[5]

Lack of adequate planning frustrated ORHA's efforts to hit the ground running. U.S. policymakers appear to have seriously underestimated the enormity and complexity of the undertaking, and ORHA's plans were based on a series of faulty assumptions. First, ORHA prepared for a massive humanitarian emergency that never materialized in postwar Iraq. Second, U.S. planners assumed that coalition military forces would be warmly welcomed throughout Iraq as liberators. Instead, those forces encountered resistance from the beginning, which only grew as the months wore on. This assumption, in turn, led to the third—a serious underestimation of the postwar security challenges, which meant that the United States did not prepare in advance a post-conflict security (or "constabulary") force that could handle those challenges. Nor were U.S. combat forces deployed in adequate numbers or adequately prepared or mandated to handle those challenges. Fourth, the United States had assumed that Iraq's military and police forces would remain intact and could be used immediately for post-conflict law enforcement, security, and rebuilding needs. Instead, those forces melted almost immediately back into their communities or went into hiding. Finally, ORHA planners overestimated the ease with which basic services—particularly Iraq's electricity grid—and oil production could be restarted, largely because of a lack of knowledge about how degraded Iraq's key infrastructure had become.

A review of lessons learned from previous post-conflict experiences could have informed certain planning assumptions or decisions, in particular on the security front.[6] But it also appears that the failure to plan as needed resulted from two fundamental, ideological beliefs on the part of some senior U.S. officials: that the U.S. military should not be engaged in "nation-building" activities at all; and that the United States could do the job better and faster alone than with the United Nations and a broad coalition of allies.

Planning for the reconstruction in Iraq should have started much earlier—after all, the military planning for the war effort began over a year before the start of hostilities. Once ORHA was established, its planning processes should have built on the early State Department efforts, and should have allowed for better coordination among relevant U.S. government agencies and nongovernmental organizations that were also preparing for the postwar. In belated recognition of this, the president attempted a modest reorganization of U.S. government roles and responsibilities in early October 2003, theoretically bringing the oversight and coordination roles back to the NSC, although the Defense Department remained the lead implementing agency.[7]

SECURITY: THE MISSING LYNCHPIN

The Problems

Coalition military forces seemed completely unprepared for and unwilling to fill the security vacuum that took hold immediately after the war. Whether as a release after decades of oppression or as the earliest indications of planned and organized resistance to U.S. efforts, Iraqis went on a massive looting spree in the first weeks after Baghdad fell. Across the country, government buildings, schools, hospitals, museums, and key infrastructure sites were completely ravaged; looters stole everything from computers and ancient artifacts to copper electrical wires and ceiling tiles.

As the months passed, what had appeared at first to be the ad hoc work of criminals and petty thieves morphed into much more serious and long-term security problems, which completely overwhelmed other reconstruction tasks. Crime continued on a large scale. Theft, rape, and car jackings were common occurrences in Baghdad and other Iraqi cities, and Iraqis felt unsafe venturing outside of their homes after dark. Some complained that they had felt safer under Saddam. Women suffered in particular, with many afraid to go out of their homes at all without a male escort.

The CPA's efforts to provide basic services and restart oil production were continuously undercut by what gradually appeared to be an organized sabotage campaign. Iraq's power lines and electricity grids were consistently targeted by small bombs and people stealing copper wire and other equipment. Oil pipelines and fields were similarly attacked, slowing efforts to increase oil production and move oil for export—key to funding the reconstruction efforts.

The sabotage campaign was linked to larger and more worrisome Iraqi resistance activities. Indeed, as early as July 2003, U.S. military officials had begun characterizing the resistance efforts as guerilla warfare. Coalition troops (particularly U.S. troops) continued to be attacked and killed on a regular basis throughout the first year of the occupation.

There were several devastating, major bomb attacks against international civilian targets, beginning in August 2003, including at the Jordanian Embassy on August 11 (killing 17 people); at the UN headquarters in Baghdad on August 19 (killing 22 people, including Sergio Vieira de Mello, the Special Representative of the Secretary-General); at the Imam Ali mosque in Najaf on August 29 (killing 126 people, including a prominent Shi'a cleric, Ayatollah Mohammad Baqir al-Hakim); and at the Baghdad headquarters of the International Committee for the Red Cross on October 27 (killing 12 people). By spring 2004, Iraqi insurgents were targeting international civilians more regularly with an upsurge in kidnappings and murders, including several particularly gruesome assassinations.

At the same time, the insurgency began to target Iraqis who were seen to be collaborating with the CPA. Police officers were killed in cities around Iraq, and police stations across the country were bombed. In September 2003, a member of Iraq's Governing Council was shot and killed, allegedly by Ba'ath Party loyalists. A second Governing Council member was killed in May 2004.

Iraqi resistance efforts were largely confined to Baghdad and the so-called Sunni triangle—the area to the north and west of Baghdad where the population is considered most loyal to Saddam and the former re-gime. But there were also occasional attacks in southern Iraq, where the UK forces were in command; in Najaf and Karbala, the Shi'a heartland of Iraq; and in Mosul and other northern cities, where the Kurds are in the majority. Moreover, although the resistance efforts were at first at-tributed to former Ba'athists and regime loyalists—as well as to foreign fighters coming across Iraq's porous borders—ordinary Iraqis began to grow more openly hostile to the U.S. presence, and there were increasing signs of Shi'a opposition to the occupation. By spring 2004, a so-called second front of the insurgency had opened up, pitting U.S. forces against an Iraqi militia, known as the Mahdi Army, under the leadership of Moktada al-Sadr, a radical Shi'ite cleric.

Complicating the post-war security picture even further was the presence of foreign terrorists in Iraq, including some with ties to Al Qae-da, who were believed to be acting in concert with indigenous Iraqi resis-tance forces to undermine reconstruction efforts.

The dire security situation undermined all other aspects of the re-construction during the first year of the occupation. Governance, jus-tice, and economic activities all were slowed and in some cases halted due to the security environment. More than 800 U.S. troops were killed during the first year of the occupation, and it is estimated that more than 10,000 Iraqis died violent deaths (due to the war, political violence, and crime) during that time.[8]

The U.S. Response

Because the United States had not prioritized the advance preparation and swift deployment of security forces dedicated to post-conflict con-stabulary duties, U.S. and British combat forces were the only ones avail-able to maintain civil security in the immediate aftermath of the war.[9] But in the first days and weeks after the war, U.S. military commanders and Defense Department officials announced that the U.S. military "does not do policing" and that it was up to the Iraqis to bring themselves under control.[10] Coalition forces eventually began to take responsibility for po-licing and other security needs, but U.S. combat forces are not trained for and do not tend to be best placed to address post-conflict security tasks. In the absence of a standing constabulary capacity in the U.S. mil-itary, the United States should have turned to other countries that have constabulary capacity (such as Italy and France), or should have trained and mandated a core of U.S. troops in such duties before the war began.[11]

Many military experts and others also argued that there were simply not enough coalition forces on the ground after the war to handle the myriad security issues. By June 2004, there were 166,500 coalition forces in Iraq, 140,000 of which were U.S. These numbers had remained more or less constant during the first year of the occupation. U.S. officials had planned several drawdowns in U.S. troop numbers throughout the year, but as violence in Iraq increased during the spring of 2004, U.S. officials announced that troop numbers were likely to increase even more. [12]

Having gone to war without the support of the UN Security Council or most of its close allies—and having resisted several early attempts by other countries to give the United Nations some meaningful authority over the reconstruction efforts in Iraq—the United States faced an up-hill battle to persuade other countries to contribute peacekeeping troops to Iraq. A year into the occupation, non-U.S. coalition troops to-taled only 26,500, and 11,000 of those were British.[13] Moreover, Spain pulled out its troop contingent in April 2004, and other coalition members threatened to do so as well. President Bush himself expressed skepticism in early summer 2004 that any major troop contributions would be forthcoming. It seemed inevitable that the United States would bear the brunt of the military responsibilities in Iraq for the foreseeable future.

As the security situation in Iraq deteriorated in the early postwar months, U.S. officials began placing high expectations on reconstituted and retrained Iraqi security forces, including police, civil defense forces, soldiers, facilities protection guards, and border guards. But Iraqi securi-ty forces will be neither a panacea nor an exit strategy. Expectations of how quickly Iraqi security forces could realistically handle security re-sponsibilities on their own seemed overinflated—particularly in light of the rapid speed with which the coalition began training those forces in order to get them out on patrol sooner.[14] Indeed, those forces proved to be wholly inadequate to deal with the heightened violence in Iraq in spring 2004, with many abandoning their posts and other joining forces with the insurgents. As in all post-conflict settings, new Iraqi security forces will need significant international oversight and rapid response capacity for at least two to five years before they can reasonably be ex-pected to handle security tasks on their own.[15]

The United States was right to focus on Iraqis taking responsibility for security, as a key to long-term management of those problems and to decreasing anti-Americanism. But it was unreasonable to expect that training those forces would obviate the need for effective international forces—military and police—to remain in Iraq to address serious security issues like insurgency and terrorist activities. It was six months into the postwar period, however, before the United States began to rethink its own concept of operations in Iraq with a view to reconfiguring its forces more effectively to address all the security problems.[16]

A major problem for the United States on the security front was that it lacked good intelligence about the nature and membership of the resistance forces. U.S. military officials continuously cited the need for better intelligence—as opposed to the need for greater force numbers—as the key reason behind continuing security problems in Iraq. Indeed, the scandal of abuses at Abu Ghraib prison, which broke in the spring of 2004, was allegedly related to attempts by U.S. military intelligence operations to glean better information about resistance activities.

The intelligence problems were linked in part to the nature of the U.S. presence in Iraq—both the CPA and U.S. forces were largely cut off from Iraqis, remaining ensconced in heavily fortified areas. (This was less true of the forces stationed outside Baghdad and the Sunni triangle, which tended to engage more directly with the local populations.) In addition, few in the CPA or the U.S. military spoke Arabic, adding to difficulties in effectively communicating with Iraqis and highlighting a more endemic lack of qualified Arabic speakers within the U.S. government.

Disarmament, Demobilization, and Reintegration (DDR)

DDR typically is an "orphan" issue within the U.S. government, not having a logical home in any particular U.S. government agency, with the result that programs are neither coordinated nor cohesive.[17] In Iraq, the U.S. government seemed to have no plan at all for DDR—particularly reintegration—even well into the reconstruction effort.

The CPA had mistakenly assumed that the "self-demobilization" of the Iraqi army during and after the conflict meant that it had demobilized in actual fact, leading CPA officials to believe there was no need to tackle the DDR issue. In fact, Ambassador Bremer's decision to formally disband the 400,000 or so former members of Iraq's military forces in June 2003 has been criticized as one of the signal policy mistakes the CPA made. After mass protests and considerable international criticism, the CPA partially reversed itself, deciding at least to pay stipends to former soldiers and to incorporate some of them into the newly formed security services.

The decision to put several hundred thousand angry, young, and armed people out of work—in the face of already severe unemployment—was a poor one, particularly in the absence of any coherent plan for alternative employment, education, training, or reintegration of rank and file soldiers. There was some evidence that laid-off former officers and soldiers were part of the anti-U.S. insurgency in Iraq, and in some cases even directed those attacks.[18] Nonetheless, the CPA continued to put off the need to launch a major initiative to reintegrate former soldiers—and militia members—into civilian society to minimize the opportunity for them to pose security threats in the future.

In fact, the presence of numerous private militias throughout Iraq—such as the Bad'r Brigade and al-Sadr's Mahdi Army in south-central Iraq and the Kurdish Peshmerga in northern Iraq—was another serious security concern. Despite official CPA pronouncements outlawing such militias and demanding that they disarm, efforts to implement these orders were lackluster. Although Afghanistan by this time had well demonstrated the dangers of allowing extra-legal military forces to take root, the United States proceeded to make the same mistake in Iraq. The serious fighting between U.S. forces and the Mahdi Army throughout the spring of 2004 was only one illustration of the longer-term problems that will be caused by the failure to systematically address Iraq's many militias.

GOVERNANCE: WHO'S IN CHARGE?

The question of who should govern Iraq after Saddam was much debated, perhaps especially within the U.S. government itself. Before the war, some experts had cautioned against a U.S. occupation; others had called for the creation of a provisional government made up of exiled Iraqis; and still others had advocated a UN-led civilian administration in Iraq similar to that in Kosovo and East Timor. But the United States bucked all advice and opted for a U.S.-led occupation, akin to that in Germany and Japan after World War II, directed first by ORHA and then by the CPA.

Confusion reigned in the early days of the occupation. Within the span of barely over a month, the CPA's governance plans shifted multiple times, which resulted in a widespread belief—in Iraq and elsewhere—that the United States had no plans for postwar Iraq.

Eventually, on July 13, 2003, the Iraqi Governing Council was formed. A body of 25 Iraqis, chosen by the CPA, the council consisted of Iraqis from all of Iraq's major ethnicities and religions and included three women.[19] Nonetheless, from its inception, the council suffered from a lack of legitimacy among Iraqis, within the region, and in the international community more broadly.

Because the United States handpicked the members, many viewed the council with skepticism and as a mere extension of the CPA. The Iraqi Governing Council was also seen to lack clear and robust enough authorities. The CPA retained ultimate veto authority over all council decisions, and the lines of authority between the CPA and the council were never clearly articulated by the United States.

Iraqis and U.S. allies alike also argued that the United States failed to articulate the political transformation process for Iraq—the process toward self-rule. In fact, the CPA shifted course in terms of that process multiple times, finally settling on a political transition plan on November 15, 2003. The "November 15 Agreement" called, inter alia, for the Iraqi Governing Council to draft an interim constitution by the end of February 2004 and for an elaborate, tiered caucus system that would choose an interim government to take over from the CPA by June 30, 2004. Although the Governing Council did pass an interim constitution—known as the Transitional Administrative Law (TAL)—in early March 2004, the other pieces of the November 15 agreement were largely scrapped. The only other piece that stuck firmly was the plan to transfer sovereignty to an Iraqi interim government on June 30, a date that ultimately took on near-mythic importance during the Iraqi occupation. The United States ran into stiff resistance to the rest of the plan almost immediately, in particular from Grand Ayatollah Ali al-Sistani, the most prominent Shi'ite cleric in Iraq, who insisted that only an elected government would have the legitimacy to run Iraq and take actions such as drafting a constitution. By April 2004, the United States was essentially forced to turn to the United Nations to devise a political transition plan. Having failed, despite myriad attempts, to come up with a workable solution, the U.S. government had to acknowledge that it lacked the credibility and objectivity to oversee the formation of an interim government in Iraq.

On June 1, 2004, the UN's Iraq envoy, Lakhdar Brahimi, and senior U.S. officials announced the selection of an Iraqi interim government that was to manage the Iraqi government and oversee the lead-up to elections, scheduled under the TAL to be held no later than the end of January 2005. The United States planned to end its occupation, close down the CPA, and hand over the keys of power to the interim government less than one month later, on June 30, 2004. The crucial question going forward would be whether the Iraqi interim government would be accepted as legitimate by the Iraqi people, and whether it would be able to oversee free and fair elections a mere six months after assuming office, especially given the security problems throughout the country.

In the end, the U.S.-driven political process in the first year of the reconstruction saw few successes. The coalition military forces and the CPA made considerable progress in the early postwar months in setting up municipal and provincial political councils throughout Iraq. Yet, the councils largely foundered because their roles vis-à-vis the central government were never clearly defined, and they were not given the resources that could have allowed them to begin responding to citizens' demands. The CPA also made some progress in political party development and encouraging town hall-style meetings throughout Iraq.

Moreover, to bolster its progress in this area, the CPA itself would have needed to decentralize, but the United States was slow to place CPA civilian personnel out in Iraq's provinces, cities, and towns. This may have been due in part to legitimate security concerns. But it meant that coalition military forces—rather than civilians with more relevant expertise—were carrying out political, social, and economic transformation tasks throughout the life of the occupation. Those forces did exceptional work in helping to establish local governance throughout Iraq, but even they began to express concern that they were far past their "comfort zones" in terms of knowledge and experience and needed the help of practiced civilians.[20]

Questions of governance, constitution drafting, and elections were critical to long-term stability in Iraq and to the U.S. goal of democratization, and because most other countries and international institutions were hesitant to wholeheartedly participate in Iraq's reconstruction efforts until a legitimate governing body was in place. Yet, despite the importance, the U.S. efforts in the governance realm seemed bumbling, driven more by political considerations in the United States than by the necessity of establishing a political process that Iraqis would feel a stake in. Indeed, the vast majority of Iraqis did not participate in defining the political transition process or in choosing the Governing Council and the interim government. Rather than opening up the political process to involve Iraqis, the United States allied itself from early on with a group of exiled Iraqis who had little if any credibility or legitimacy inside Iraq. This alliance hampered U.S. credibility in executing tasks on the governance front and did not give the Iraqi people the sense that participation in the political process was the most viable means of their survival.

This led not only to increasing anti-Americanism throughout the first year after Saddam fell but also to a growing number of Iraqis sympathizing with the insurgents' cause and to the resistance against the U.S. presence, as well as to radical groups such as that led by al-Sadr.

Indeed, one particular concern about the U.S.–driven process in Iraq early on was its marginalization of Iraq's Sunni population. Pushed from power once Saddam fell, the Sunnis of Iraq were understandably threatened by any notion of true democracy—as elections would likely result in a government that reflected the Shi'as' numerical strength. Early CPA actions seemed to equate Ba'athists with Sunnis; the CPA's sweeping "de-Ba'athification" order and decision to disband the army only compounded for Sunnis the feeling that they were being shut out of the political process. The use of the term "Sunni triangle" to refer to that area in Iraq where former regime loyalists were most aggressively resisting coalition efforts seemed to conflate all Sunnis with those Ba'athists and former regime loyalists who were actively fighting against the coalition. As one expert noted, it was "no coincidence that the worst violence [was] in Sunni regions."[21]

In addition, because the United States was reluctant until the spring of 2004 to consider a real role for the United Nations in overseeing the political transformation process, it did not have the assistance of a body with considerable, valuable, and relevant experience in overseeing those processes in post-conflict countries. When the Bush administration eventually did turn to the United Nations, it initially declared that Ambassador Brahimi would have a free rein in choosing the members of the Iraqi interim government that took power on June 30. In fact, however, Ambassador Bremer and the Iraqi Governing Council played a large role in the selection process. Moreover, because the United Nations was involved at such a late date, Brahimi's ability to fundamentally change the nature of Iraq's governing body and political process was limited. His hands were largely tied— by previous U.S. policy decisions, by the continuing involvement of Bremer and the White House in determining the political process, and by a last-minute power play by an Iraqi Governing Council that seemed reluctant to give up power.

Indeed, the U.S. efforts on the governance front were stymied in large part because the CPA, Ambassador Bremer, and officials in Washington exercised far too tight control over political matters in Iraq, rather than turning earlier to the United Nations (which would have imbued those matters with the stamp of international legitimacy) and to Iraqis themselves. Not only did the CPA fail to decentralize itself; it also focused too intently on political issues on the national plane rather than on local-level, decentralized efforts that would plant the seeds of democracy in Iraq. By the time the Iraqi interim government was appointed in June 2004, it would be hamstrung from the beginning by a perceived lack of legitimacy in the way it was selected, the serious continuing security problems it inherited from the U.S.-led CPA, the short timetable until elections were to be held, and the lack of focus on building democracy from the grassroots level up during the first year of the reconstruction.

ECONOMIC AND SOCIAL WELL-BEING: LIGHTS AND JOBS

Restarting Basic Services

Aside from security, no issue captivated the minds and frustrated the Iraqis more than the lack of electricity in the early months of the reconstruction. As with so many issues, U.S. planning for restarting Iraq's power system after the war fell far short. The United States seriously underestimated the level of degradation of Iraq's electricity infrastructure due to decades of severe underinvestment and war damage. The United States' early plans called for spending a relatively small amount of money on electricity needs, believing the problem would be easily tackled. Looting and sabotage of the power infrastructure by Iraqis after the war only compounded the prewar damage.

It was a full six months into the postwar period before the CPA announced that electricity production throughout Iraq was back to prewar levels, and even then, power delivery continued to be spotty. The United States had to revise its early cost estimates from $230 million for emergency repairs to over $5 billion for restoring Iraq's power supply. The World Bank, in fact, estimated that up to $12 billion would be needed over time to rehabilitate this sector. The power supply gradually improved—helped in part by the use of gas-supplied generators—but the problems in restarting power also impacted water supply and oil production, as all were linked to electricity in Iraq.

By late summer 2003, Iraqis' frustration about the power situation was palpable, and patience for the U.S. efforts dwindling. Their anger highlighted the importance of planning for and immediately addressing basic needs—power, water, sanitation—in post-conflict situations, in order to allow the population to feel some semblance of normalcy, or even improvement, in their lives.

Under the U.S. model for Iraq, major U.S. private contractors were given responsibility for electricity and most other services. But such contractors did not necessarily have the relevant post-conflict experience—including political and cultural sensitivities—of government agencies, international organizations, or NGOs in implementing reconstruction activities. Moreover, using private contractors proved significantly more expensive than turning to Iraqis themselves to tackle reconstruction needs.

Although there is clearly a vital role to be played by the private sector in post-conflict reconstruction settings, the U.S. officials' belief that private contractors could replace the role of government agencies, international organizations, and NGOs across the board was misplaced. So too was their belief that handing the jobs to the private sector would cut through the usual bureaucratic hold-ups and significantly speed up the process.

As Iraq's electricity troubles amply demonstrated, private contractors may be no more able to get things done quickly than the "usual cast of characters." Indeed, in those few instances when Iraqis were given responsibility for addressing problems, the process was much more efficient—and cheaper—than using U.S. contracting mechanisms.[22] Even more important, Iraqi ownership over the reconstruction process will be key to its ultimate success.

Iraq also became a showcase for the controversies surrounding the use of private military contractors to carry out a wide range of tasks, from military logistics to outright security operations (including military interrogation work). Due to the murky legal framework and accountability mechanisms regarding the use of these contractors, this issue began to gain higher visibility on Capitol Hill and among scholars and policymakers during the Iraq occupation.

For future efforts, instead of a model that relies completely on the capacities of the private sector, the United States should develop a model for providing services in post-conflict environments that draws on the relative capabilities of the private and public sectors, recognizing the complementary benefits of using both and of incorporating local talent from the outset.

Rebuilding Iraq's Economy

In addition to decades of underinvestment in its infrastructure, Iraq's economy had also suffered from decades of heavily controlled, state-run economic policies. Simply rebuilding even a functioning economy out of those failed economic structures would have been a daunting task.

But the United States entered Iraq after the war with a dramatic plan to remake Iraq into a liberal market economy, including privatizing its state-owned enterprises and opening up the country to foreign investment.

Prewar unemployment levels were high; postwar estimates ranged as high as 60 percent. Yet the CPA only added to those levels by dismissing 400,000 former Iraqi soldiers, and by keeping another 400,000 to 750,000 employees of state-owned enterprises out of work, as most such enterprises remained closed many months after the end of the war. Still, at the CPA's direction , the Iraqi Governing Council decided to implement a series of sweeping economic reforms, including allowing for the direct foreign ownership of Iraq's assets (except oil and other natural resources).[23] (Although the Governing Council's reforms also would have allowed for immediate privatization of Iraq's state-owned enterprises, the CPA eventually had to back away from that idea, deciding that privatization decisions should be left to a sovereign Iraqi government.) In a country traditionally resistant to outside ownership of Iraqi property and enterprises, moreover, it was worrisome that a group of unelected officials—to some, an illegitimate body—would initiate such massive reforms and brought into question their longer-term viability.

The CPA instituted major reforms in other areas of the economy as well. It oversaw the successful introduction of a new Iraqi currency to replace the old "Saddam dinar." An Iraqi central bank was established, and private banks began carrying out some transactions. Yet Iraq continued to lack a functioning regulatory framework for the financial sector, and economic activity was stifled due to security concerns and political instability. Moreover, some international legal experts argued that certain activities of the CPA in the economic sector went beyond the bounds of its authority as an occupying power. Indeed, the continuing validity of laws issued under the CPA's tenure after the June 30, 2004, handover date was an open question.

JUSTICE AND RECONCILIATION

Iraq's Justice System: Slowly Returning to Life

A functioning justice system is a critical underpinning of democracy. But the area of justice is traditionally given short shrift in post-conflict environments, and here too Iraq has been no exception. Based on lessons learned from other post-conflict settings, experts had advocated the

creation of a "justice package"—to include lawyers, judges, police officers, and prison officials—that could be deployed to Iraq immediately to
begin the critical task of reopening courts, hearing cases, and sentencing
criminals.[24] But, as in most other areas, the United States was slow to
bring in civilian experts, relying for too long on coalition military forces
to restart Iraq's justice system.

Those forces faced a daunting task, as all of Iraq's prisons and most of
its courthouses were badly looted in the war's immediate aftermath;
records were missing, prisoners had been let out of jail by Saddam, and
Iraqi police vanished. Although the military performed as admirably
here as in other areas, it lacked the resources and expertise to perform all
the necessary tasks, which ranged from repairing buildings and paying
salaries to modernizing courts and training judges and lawyers. Still, the
CPA and coalition forces had some modest early success.

Iraqi courts reopened and began to hear cases, although the process
was slow, leaving many suspected Iraqi criminals to languish in detention
awaiting appearance before a judge and Iraqis unsure of how their legal
system worked. Early recruiting of international legal experts could have
helped speed the justice process. A related problem was that even after
Iraqi courts had been set up, coalition military officers counteracted decisions by Iraqi judges and police officers—for example, releasing prisoners before their cases had been heard in court. In other cases, prisoners
were kept in jail for extended periods without appearing before a judge.
Such actions could undermine longer-term efforts to gain the trust of
Iraqis in their own justice system, which will be vital to efforts to build
democracy in Iraq. Iraqis must begin to see the justice system as working
transparently and fairly rather than on the seemingly arbitrary basis of
the decision of a coalition military officer. On that note, the severe abuse
of Iraqi prisoners being held at Abu Ghraib prison outside Baghdad,
which came to light in the spring of 2004, further undermined U.S. credibility and heightened anti-Americanism. Although that issue is not covered in depth in this chapter, it was one more example of the problems
posed by asking U.S. soldiers to take on virtually every task in post-Saddam Iraq. Trained and reputable corrections officers presumably could
have been hired to oversee Iraq's prisons.

In early December 2003, Iraq's Governing Council—with the approval of the CPA—announced the creation of the Iraqi Special Tribunal for
Crimes against Humanity to try former regime members for war crimes
and other crimes against humanity. International jurists, human rights

groups, the United Nations, and many U.S. allies expressed immediate concern over the plans for the court to include Iraqi judges only, use Iraqi criminal laws, and authorize imposition of the death penalty. Indeed, in a letter to Ambassador Bremer, the UN's acting High Commissioner for Human Rights expressed concerns that the court's statute was incompatible with international humanitarian law. The Special Tribunal was not expected to start hearing cases until the summer of 2004—after governing authority was turned over to an Iraqi provisional government. But the fact that it (1) was set up under U.S. auspices during the time of occupation, (2) did not have international or UN backing, and (3) was not expected to include international lawyers except as advisers also led to real concerns that it will be seen as meting out victor's justice or be used as a tool of vengeance, rather than as a legitimate arbiter of past crimes.

The trial of Saddam, who was captured by U.S. forces on December 13, 2003, will pose an especially dramatic challenge to Iraq's recovering justice system, particularly the Special Tribunal. The crimes with which Saddam might be tried have been described by an international law expert as "absolutely staggering."[25] Trying such cases would be an delicate, time-consuming, and difficult task even for well-established courts with full international backing and the involvement of international jurists, as evidenced, for example, by the trial of former Yugoslav president Slobodan Milosevic by the UN's International Criminal Tribunal in The Hague. Iraqi support for the idea of trying Saddam inside Iraq "appeared almost universal."[26] The Bush administration too seemed to favor the idea of trying Saddam in Iraq, perhaps at the newly created Special Tribunal, although it made clear that Iraqis should determine how and where to try Saddam and other regime members. But again, legal and human rights experts expressed real concerns over whether a trial of Saddam by the barely functioning Iraqi justice system would be perceived as fair. Indeed, like most other courts in Iraq, space, staff, resources, judges, and security were the most immediate issues the Special Tribunal faced after it was established. The idea that it would soon be ready to try Saddam, and that it could do so in a fair, transparent manner that would gain acceptance among the international community and in Iraq, seemed optimistic.

Iraqi and International Police

Recruitment and deployment of CIVPOL has been painfully slow in all recent post-conflict endeavors—in Kosovo, for example, it took six months before CIVPOL were in place in sufficient numbers. Notwithstanding these examples, the United States did not take early steps to recruit international or U.S. police for the Iraq effort, and six months into the reconstruction, coalition military forces were still in charge of training and overseeing the newly trained, reconstituted Iraqi police force. Although a U.S. contractor was awarded a police training contract early on in the reconstruction, it was not until October 2003 that plans began to move forward on hiring up to 1,000 U.S. police trainers and setting up an Iraqi police training camp in Jordan. In their absence, stretched coalition forces had to retain responsibility for training and overseeing Iraqi police officers.

The United States placed enormous expectations on the Iraqi police as one key to stabilizing the security situation in Iraq. But training efforts were insufficient. During the heightened violence in Iraq in 2004 it became clear that Iraq's newly trained officers would not be fully capable of maintaining law and order in Iraq for some time to come.[27]

GOING IT ALONE, A RISKY VENTURE

President Bush and his senior officials made lofty promises to the Iraqi people about what a post-Saddam Iraq might look like—a democratic, multiethnic, free, and open society that would no longer be a threat to its neighbors and that would maintain its territorial integrity—and what democracy in Iraq would mean for the Middle East region. Administration officials often argued that the transformation of Iraq into a stable democracy could produce a democratizing domino effect throughout the Middle East. President Bush stated that "[t]he establishment of a free Iraq at the heart of the Middle East will be a watershed event in the global democratic revolution."[28]

Although a stable, democratic Iraq—and Middle East—is clearly central to the United States' strategic interests, the administration's grand goals for postwar Iraq were not matched by U.S. actions on the ground. Yet, despite its flawed and inadequate planning and preparation for the postwar phase—as well as its serious difficulties in the first year of the occupation—the United States remained steadfast in its go-it-alone approach to Iraq and in sticking to its model for the reconstruction. Caution was warranted about this unilateral model, however. Previous unilateral attempts by the United States to build democracies in conflict-torn places have rarely succeeded, and have tended instead to lead to military dictatorships and corrupt autocracies. Cuba and Nicaragua in the early 1900s and Cambodia and Vietnam in the early 1970s are a few examples.[29]

It was almost a year into the reconstruction effort before the United States began to turn to the United Nations for help on the political front in Iraq, garnering the passage of UN Security Council Resolution 1546 on June 8, 2004. By that point, the problems, particularly on the security and governance fronts, were significant, and the options for improvement limited. Having suffered severe setbacks across every issue discussed in this chapter, the United States found itself almost desperate for help it had previously shunned and clearly desperate for troop reinforcements that were unlikely to materialize. The United States' early record in Iraq was telling in terms of the effectiveness of the U.S. reconstruction model for Iraq. And that record was troubling. Moreover, the Iraq case clearly points to the need for a systemic overhaul of the way the U.S. government engages in post-conflict reconstruction, as discussed elsewhere in this volume.

Whether the United States will engage in another enormous, unilateral reconstruction effort in the future is open to question. But given the significance of the post-conflict challenge in Iraq, it will be crucial that the United States stick to its promises to remain in Iraq—with the necessary troops, resources, and personnel—for as long as necessary. Otherwise, it risks leaving an unstable, nonviable state with little chance of becoming the lasting democracy the United States would like to see. At the same time, it was clear as a longer-term lesson that earlier internationalization of the effort—and in particular greater Iraqi buy-in and responsibility—were two key missing ingredients of the U.S.-led occupation in Iraq.

Notes

[1] An October 30, 2003, report by the watchdog organization Center for Public Integrity highlights some of the early concerns over lack of transparency and perceived political favoritism in awarding contracts. *Winning Contractors: U.S. Contractors Reap the Windfalls of Post-War Reconstruction* (Washington, D.C.: Center for Public Integrity, October 30, 2003), www.publicintegrity.org/wow/default.aspx.

[2] Center for Strategic and International Studies and Association of the U.S. Army, *Play to Win: Final Report of the Bi-partisan Commission on Post-Conflict Reconstruction* (Washington, D.C.: CSIS, January 2003), p. 10, www.csis.org/isp/pcr/playtowin.pdf.

[3] Ibid., pp. 11–12.

[4] See, for example, David Rieff, "Blueprint for a Mess: How the Bush Administration's Prewar Planners Bungled Postwar Iraq," *New York Times Magazine*, November 2, 2003, p. 28.

[5] John Hamre, testimony, House Committee on Armed Services, October 8, 2003, www.csis.org/hill/ts031008hamre.pdf.

[6] See, for example, Frederick Barton and Bathsheba Crocker, *A Wiser Peace: An Action Strategy for a Post-Conflict Iraq* (Washington, D.C.: Center for Strategic and International Studies, January 2003), pp. 12, 14–15, www.csis.org/isp/wiserpeace.pdf.

[7] Experts in this field have proposed a much more central role for interagency planning and coordination. See *Play to Win*, pp. 10–12; and, in this volume, chapter 7 by Flournoy, "Interagency Strategy and Planning for Post-Conflict Reconstruction."

[8] Daniel Cooney and Omar Sinan, "Morgue Records Show 5,500 Iraqis Killed," Associated Press, May 24, 2004.

[9] For a discussion of the need to institutionalize constabulary capacity within the United States or the international community, see, for example, chapter 3 by Feil, "Laying the Foundation: Enhancing Security Capabilities."

[10] For example, during a Central Command briefing on April 11, 2003, Brigadier General Vincent Brooks, the deputy director of operations for Operation Iraqi Freedom, stated, "At no point do we see [the U.S. military] really becoming a police force. What we see is taking [military] actions necessary to create conditions of stability." CENTCOM Operation Iraqi Freedom Briefing, April 11, 2003, www.centcom.mil/CENTCOMNews/transcripts/20030411.htm.

[11] Barton and Crocker, *A Wiser Peace*, p. 14.

[12] U.S. force numbers were expected to increase slightly to 145,000 during the summer of 2004. Tom Squitieri and Dave Moniz, "U.S. Force in Iraq to Grow as Marine Deployment Pushed Up," *USA Today*, June 8, 2004.

[13] The number of British troops was also expected to rise by a few thousand during the summer of 2004. See "Non-U.S. Forces in Iraq—20 May 2004" at www.globalsecurity.org/military/ops/iraq_orbat_coalition.htm.

[14] The rapid growth in numbers of Iraqi security forces out on patrol by November 2003 "was accomplished by allowing Iraqi policemen and building guards to start work with little or no formal training in democratic standards and relevant job skills." Bradley Graham and Rajiv Chandrasekaran, "Iraqi Security Crews Getting Less Training," *Washington Post*, November 7, 2003, p. A1.

[15] The author's interviews with coalition military commanders in charge of training and equipping new Iraqi security forces in Baghdad, Basra, Najaf, and Karbala, Iraq, June 27–July 6, 2003, confirmed this point.

[16] During a press conference in early November 2003, Secretary of Defense Donald Rumsfeld noted that the United States would begin shifting to "forces that are appropriate to deal with the evolving threats in Iraq today, including more mobile infantry units." Secretary Rumsfeld, Department of Defense News Briefing, Washington D.C., November 6, 2003, www.defenselink.mil/transcripts/2003/tr20031106-secdef0862.html. A group of post-conflict reconstruction experts that traveled to Iraq in June-July 2003 to assess reconstruction efforts had recommended such a re-look several months earlier; see *Iraq's Post-Conflict Reconstruction: A Field Review and Recommendations* (Washington, D.C.: CSIS, July 17, 2003), www.csis.org/isp/pcr/IraqTrip.pdf.

[17] See, for example, *Play to Win*, pp. 12–13.

[18] Mark Fineman, Warren Vieth, and Robin Wright, "In an Iraq without an Army, Perils Abound," *Los Angeles Times*, August 24, 2003.

[19] One of those three women—Akila Hashimi—was shot and killed in late September 2003.

[20] Author's interviews, Basra, Najaf, and Karbala, Iraq, June 27–July 7, 2003.

[21] Jessica Mathews, "Iraqis Can Do More," *Washington Post*, September 29, 2003.

[22] Ariana Eunjung Cha, "Success Traced in Cement: Iraqis Rebuild Factory at a Fraction of Estimate," *Washington Post*, November 10, 2003, p. A1.

[23] Coalition Provisional Authority Order Number 39 on Foreign Investment, www.cpa-iraq.org/regulations/20030921_CPAORD39.pdf.

[24] See Barton and Crocker, *A Wiser Peace*, pp. 21–22; United States Institute of Peace, *Establishing the Rule of Law in Iraq*, special report 104 (Washington, D.C.: USIP, April 2003), www.usip.org/pubs/specialreports/sr104.pdf. For a detailed discussion of this issue, see, in this volume, chapter 6 by Flournoy and Pan, "Dealing with Demons: Enhancing Justice and Reconciliation."

[25] Steve Wick, "New Tribunal Might Be Option for Saddam," December 14, 2003 (quoting Diane Orentlicher), www.newsday.com.

[26] Susan Sachs, "The Prosecution of a Dictator: A Decade's Digging Is Already Done," *New York Times*, December 16, 2003.

[27] See, for example, Jim Krane, "U.S. General: Iraq Police Training a Flop," Associated Press Online, June 9, 2004.

[28] Remarks by President Bush at the twentieth anniversary of the National Endowment for Democracy, Washington D.C., November 6, 2003, www.whitehouse.gov/news/releases/2003/11/20031106-2.html.

[29] Minxin Pei and Sara Kasper, *Lessons from the Past: The American Record on Nation Building*, policy brief (Washington, D.C.: Carnegie Endowment for International Peace, May 24, 2003), www.ceip.org/files/pdf/Policybrief24.pdf.

PART FIVE

CONCLUSION

CHAPTER SEVENTEEN

AN AMERICAN STRATEGY FOR POST-CONFLICT RECONSTRUCTION

Robert C. Orr

Creating additional American capacities to rebuild countries after conflict is necessary, but not sufficient for protecting U.S. interests in an age of global terrorist networks, weapons of mass destruction, and highly interdependent economies. To use post-conflict reconstruction capacity effectively, the United States will need to adopt a strategy for when, where, how, and with whom it will use this capacity.

A U.S. strategy is particularly needed at this moment in history. The United States has unprecedented power, but simultaneously faces new, unpredictable, and unprecedented threats. It is already deeply engaged in major post-conflict reconstruction projects in Iraq and Afghanistan at the start of the twenty-first century. The outcomes of these cases will not only determine how safe the United States will be in the future and how it will be viewed around the world; they will also help to determine what next generation post-conflict reconstruction will look like in the coming years. Will the United States learn the lessons of over 50 years of post-conflict reconstruction efforts, or will it continue to struggle, as is currently the case in Iraq and Afghanistan?

The complex challenges facing the United States now and in the future require not simply capacity, but also a strategy. The lessons of reconstruction efforts from the post-World War II era, the post–Cold War period, and the post–9/11 period help point the way. Following are ten building blocks that, if taken to heart and implemented, would lay a solid foundation for a U.S. strategy that answers the questions of when, where, and how to use the enhanced U.S. post-conflict reconstruction capabilities described in this book.

One: Define national interest and triage cases accordingly.

The question of where and when to engage in post-conflict reconstruction will never be an easy one. The need around the world for internally stronger and more stable states will always outstrip the United States' ability to enhance the strength of states. Not all states will be equally important to the United States. The United States will need to gauge its involvement according to a clearly articulated, generally agreed-on concept of its own interests. Nonetheless, even though the process of articulating and agreeing on national interests will be ongoing and played out in both the policy and political arenas, there are a few key identifiable issues today that should help the triaging process.

The first major criterion that will not go away is ensuring that countries with weapons of mass destruction are not allowed to implode or explode in such a way that either the weapons themselves or the people and systems used to create them are exported. Nuclear countries like North Korea and Pakistan are obvious candidates for special concern along these lines.

A second category of countries of concern would be those that have been and are being used by terrorists as bases for international operations. These range from Afghanistan and Pakistan in Central and South Asia, to Somalia and Yemen in the Horn of Africa, to Indonesia and the Philippines in Southeast Asia. While terrorist operations can move from country to country, of greatest concern are those in which a major region or the entire territory of a country has proved a place of choice for global terrorist organizations to train, recruit, and operate.

A third category of states or territories that might merit special U.S. attention for rebuilding efforts are those that affect the prospects of achieving top U.S. foreign policy objectives, such as Middle East peace. An obvious contender for such attention would be the Occupied Territories, especially if a peace deal were reached that depended on outside support to anchor a positive outcome.

A fourth category of states that might need special rebuilding attention are those whose collapse could flood U.S. shores with refugees. This happened previously in Haiti and could easily happen again there, as in neighboring Cuba.

A fifth category of countries whose rebuilding might be of particular interest to the United States are those that supply the world with significant amounts of the energy needed to keep the world's economy running. Because of the relatively diversified nature of the world oil market, oil alone will seldom justify or require an intervention, but it could tip the balance if other concerns also come into play. Countries of concern on this list range from Iraq in the Middle East to Venezuela in the Americas, and a range of countries in Africa that could include Angola and the Sudan.

None of these categories of interests or individual cases automatically impels the United States to rebuild a failed or weak state. What this list of interests and countries does imply, however, is that the United States does not have an option to ignore the potential need for reconstruction capabilities. Recent history, trends in a number of countries, and U.S. interests in many of them would suggest that the United States would likely need to become involved in some form of rebuilding in one or more of these countries in the coming three to five years. A structured ongoing process of matching up a defined set of U.S. national interests with potentially weak and failing states is clearly required. Such an exercise would give U.S. planners a sense of the range of potential challenges that the United States could be expected to face in coming years.

Two: Be prepared to assist allies and provide priority international public goods.

Direct threats to U.S. interests will define most of the universe of cases where the United States needs to deploy its military and, correspondingly, its rebuilding capabilities. It is very likely, however, that there will also be a need to deploy rebuilding capacity when international allies or partners' interests are at stake. Essentially, this boils down to acknowledging American primacy and the responsibilities that it entails. As the paramount global power in the twenty-first century, the United States does not have the luxury of ignoring "other people's problems." Yet the United States needs to be careful to avoid becoming, or being seen as, a global crusader. At the same time, when specific situations become bad enough in someone else's "backyard," it will need to be prepared to consider requests for help. Clearly, the United States should have a different threshold for becoming involved in such cases and will provide a different investment in these less-directly self-interested "global public goods" cases. The easiest cases will be those where a close U.S. ally asks for support and is prepared to make a major investment itself, as in the cases of East Timor and Sierra Leone examined in this volume.

The harder cases, but ones that a global hegemon cannot ignore, are those where there may not be a single "lead nation," but where there may be a chance of success and where U.S. involvement might leverage enough contributions to make a difference. If American power and wealth are used only to benefit narrow American interests over time, the United States will lose vital cooperation in building a secure and prosperous international environment for all. If, on the other hand, the United States makes strategic investments of its capacity that show that American leadership benefits more than just American citizens, more countries and people will be prepared to work with the United States rather than banding together to resist American primacy. U.S. investments to support international rebuilding efforts in the Congo and Liberia in 2003, while extremely modest, are a step down this path. By proving to countries in the region and beyond that the United States is willing to use some of its capacity to help "non-strategic" countries, the United States can help secure its status as a benign hegemon, whose power benefits the many, not just the few.

Three: Balance "high-end" and "low-end" capabilities.

To tailor U.S. reconstruction support to its national interests and to international needs in a discrete manner, the United States needs to develop a better balance of "high-end" and "low-end" capabilities. In some instances, high-tech, complex, expensive, macro-level instruments are called for, while in others simple, low-tech, inexpensive, people-focused instruments may be more likely to produce the desired result. In the security realm, this means redesigning a part of U.S. forces to be able to better perform "low-end" stabilization functions, and leading international efforts to build integrated international forces that can fill the "constabulary" gap.[1] In the political, economic, social, and justice realms, this means building up "high-end" civilian capacity (such as supporting constituting processes, creating legal and regulatory frameworks for macroeconomic development, and deploying integrated justice packages) as well as "low-end" civilian capacity (such as setting up local councils and doing quick impact projects), and being able to deploy it in an integrated fashion much more quickly.[2] In short, the United States needs a range of capabilities that matches its range of interests.

The cases of Iraq and Afghanistan reinforce the need for low-end security capabilities and high-end civilian capabilities in today's world. The cases of Japan and Iraq demonstrate that occupation adds a whole range of additional demands on the capacity of the occupier, just as Kosovo and East Timor demonstrate the range of additional capabilities needed by the United Nations and the international community in order to run transitional administrations effectively. Facilitating local governing functions and taking them over are two totally different challenges, especially if the latter is done without the consent of the local population.

Yet, the issue is not just about creating more capacities for these different types of cases. It is also about designing a coherent group of U.S. capacities to assist others as a "junior partner." This involves following another country's lead in a distinctly subordinate role with more focused and targeted assistance. The United States effectively served as a junior partner in both East Timor and Sierra Leone, following the lead of Australia in the first instance and the United Kingdom in the second. The package that the United States had to offer each was helpful, but could have been tailored much more to what the circumstances and the lead nations required.

Creating still more effective junior partner capacities, and ensuring that they are able to easily link into and support other international actors, would give the United States a level of flexibility that it does not currently enjoy. Becoming more effective at helping allies and the United Nations succeed is perhaps the best way to ensure that the United States can protect its interests, maintain its alliances, and continue to play an international leadership role without exhausting itself through nonstop interventions. If the United States does not improve its range of capabilities, it will continue to be stuck in an "all or nothing" position of either using overwhelming military force to perform nonmilitary tasks or doing nothing at all.

Four: Ensure basic agreement on goals and objectives for each reconstruction.

Once the United States has built a broader range of capabilities, balanced them so as to maximize success, and decided where and when it is in its interests to intervene to help rebuild a country, it faces a major decision about setting the bar for what it hopes to achieve in any given case. Balancing American values and interests is always a challenge. On the one hand, U.S. democratic, human rights, and humanitarian values motivate U.S. leaders to try to rebuild countries in such a way that their citizens might enjoy some of the rights and privileges that Americans enjoy. On the other hand, in many cases American interests may not dictate the kind of investment necessary to fulfill such grand designs. In any event, the United States needs to be clear on what it aspires to accomplish in each case.

To secure agreement on objectives, a vigorous interagency process must serve as the foundation to ensure that various agency perspectives are fully aired. This must include a full discussion between the military and other U.S. government agencies in order to ensure a sustainable strategy. Obviously, such a process must avoid the kind of mission-endangering split between agencies as occurred during the Bush administration between the Defense and State Departments in the run-up to the mission in Iraq. Securing intra-administration buy-in, however important, is not sufficient. Simultaneously, the administration must actively consult Congress and international partners to guarantee that there is a sustainable strategy both domestically and internationally.

This internal and external consultation and planning process must create a clear, concise formulation of what the intervention is trying to achieve. If the planning, consultation, and buy-in process is robust, it will help to insulate decisionmakers from pressures to tack sharply when the situation on the ground gets difficult, as often happens. Somalia is a textbook case of insufficient agreement on the ultimate objectives. The Clinton administration began to formulate new objectives for the mission, but the military and some in Congress perceived the new objectives as "mission creep." When American soldiers were killed, the resulting pressure caused the Clinton administration to abandon the mission. Goals can evolve with the situation on the ground, but only if that evolution is sustainable in the target country, domestically in the United States, and internationally. This is a very high bar for changing fundamental mission goals. Tactical changes are of course necessary in many cases; and should be dictated by the senior civilian and military leaders on the ground.

Another danger to be avoided is leaving a dramatic gap between rhetorical goals and actual goals pursued on the ground. Following up on inflated rhetoric with modest action leaves expectations in the target country unfulfilled, potentially endangering the mission itself. In the case of Afghanistan, for example, President Bush's high-octane rhetoric about a "Marshall Plan" for the country created high expectations in Afghanistan and among potential partner nations. This was followed by anemic support, leaving the Karzai government not only weakened, but demoralized as well. The government's repeated public calls for the United States and its partners to live up to their commitments did little to solidify its standing either domestically or internationally. Indeed, two years after the intervention the combination of overblown rhetoric and weak support had achieved the opposite of the desired result—a weakened central government, entrenched warlords, emboldened remnants of the Taliban and Al Qaeda, a disempowered and demoralized Afghan population, cynical neighboring countries, and a weakly committed international community.

A third danger to be avoided is fostering negative perceptions of U.S. intentions. The United States, as the dominant global power, must be extremely careful about how its intentions are perceived. The case of Iraq demonstrates how difficult it can be to manage local and international expectations. Despite President Bush's desire to cast the intervention in Iraq as one designed to "build a democracy" and to establish "a free Iraq at the heart of the Middle East" as a "watershed event in the global democratic revolution," the Bush administration's decision to pursue a war of choice (as opposed to one forced upon the United States) without broader international support or legitimating actions such as a UN resolution led people around the world to express grave doubts about U.S. intentions.[3] Many governments voted with their feet by not supporting the U.S.-led intervention, and the vast majority of people around the world not only questioned the United States' intentions and its broader role in the world—many actually felt that the United States had become a "threat to peace in the world."[4] In essence, one intervention poorly handled rekindled a debate about U.S. imperialism that had been largely dormant for almost a century.

One final caution: Goals for the country in question must be realistic, especially in cases where a lower level of economic and political development may dictate a more modest set of goals. Post-conflict reconstruction can succeed in even the most humble of countries as long as outside interveners set the bar appropriately and shape their efforts depending on the base conditions of the country in question. As the case studies of Sierra Leone, East Timor, and Afghanistan all indicate, even a country at or near the bottom of the development ladder can be assisted. At the same time, a weaker institutional environment means the external intervention must be adjusted accordingly to focus more on basic capacity building than on a full-service reconstruction effort.

Five: Build and maintain bipartisan consensus.

One of the keys to success will be to maintain a consistent U.S. approach to post-conflict reconstruction over time. Consistency of purpose, as was marshaled and maintained during the Cold War, is essential if the United States is to steadily improve its capabilities and enhance its ability to use them effectively. Dramatic zigs and zags in policy approach undermine U.S. credibility internationally and squander valuable capacity built up. George W. Bush's politicizing of the "nation-building" issue during the 2000 campaign was regrettable, but it was even worse when he and his administration proceeded in the first two years of his presidency to discard and disinvest in all the capacity and knowledge built up during the 1990s. There can be little doubt that the ad hoc, inconsistent efforts in Afghanistan and Iraq were weaker as a result. Had the Bush administration used some version of its predecessor's Presidential Decision Directive (PDD)-56 framework, for example, these interventions would have been much better planned and been able to draw on the strengths of the various agencies that had built up some experience and level of cooperation previously. Instead, by trying to improvise a system for interagency cooperation in the midst of crisis, the quality of the U.S. planning and response suffered greatly.

A lasting bipartisan consensus on how to build U.S. post-conflict reconstruction capacity and how to use it is essential. This set of issues is neither Democratic nor Republican, and politicians and policymakers should not allow it to be treated as such. Just as during the Cold War—when the concepts of "rollback," "missile gap," and "détente" could find their way into political campaigns, but "containment" and arming the United States to combat Soviet expansionism were not called into question— there has to be agreement on core principles and capacities even as there is leeway for some disagreement about the specifics of how and when to apply them. This will necessarily involve ongoing negotiations and consultations between key players in both parties not only about what capacity should be built, and where it should be housed, but also about the uses to which it should be put. Only if there is some basic level of agreement, publicly ratified, can the United States ensure consistency on this crucial subject from one administration to the next.

Ensuring stable handoffs from one administration to the next is only half the battle, however. The other key to continuity is ensuring that the executive branch and the legislative branch come to some agreement about what capacities to build and how to use them. Congress, in this area as in other foreign policy questions, cannot be expected to simply follow the president's lead. It is therefore imperative that the ground rules for building and sustaining reconstruction capacity are agreed on before a crisis comes to a head. In particular, mechanisms for funding and reasonable oversight need to be well established in advance. This applies not only to the "big" cases when the United States deploys its military on top-priority national security grounds, but also to those cases where the United States could benefit from deploying civilians and "low-end" capacity to help on missions led by allies and international organizations. The disastrous record of congressional-executive branch relations over funding UN peacekeeping in the 1990s provides a cautionary tale about what must be avoided.

Six: Design flexible instruments and use an adaptive strategy.

As is clear from a reading of the cases in this volume, every post-conflict reconstruction situation is distinct. As such, there can be no "one-size-fits-all" approach to successful reconstruction efforts. The broad diversity of countries where reconstruction might be required necessitates flexible reconstruction instruments and an adaptive strategy. As was learned throughout the 1990s, and indeed relearned the hard way in the first cases of the twenty-first century, the United States is much better prepared to prevent and deal with humanitarian emergencies than to address the security and political vacuums that often cause them. This is due in large part to the fact that humanitarian missions have broad bipartisan support in both the executive and legislative branches, significant flexible funding, pre-agreed mechanisms for fielding human and material assets expeditiously, on-call lists of well-trained people, and broad and deep links with comparable capacity in other governments and international organizations. As described in many of the chapters in this volume, what is now required is a set of mechanisms in the areas of security, political processes, economic well-being, and justice that would allow comparable flexibility.

Having flexible instruments is useless, however, if policymakers simply try to fight the last war or reconstruct the last reconstruction. Lessons from previous interventions must be learned and broadly disseminated if people and institutions are to move up the learning curve. Indeed, experience from the 1990s suggests that lessons learned from difficulties in Somalia, Haiti, Bosnia, and Rwanda helped to improve the quality of the interventions in the second half of that decade. Kosovo, East Timor, and Sierra Leone, for example, all applied important lessons about the fundamental importance of security, designing an effective international division of labor, and dealing with justice issues in a new manner. While none of those latter cases was exactly alike, they all benefited from application of previous lessons learned and an adaptive strategy process that allowed the U.S. government to learn its lessons and tailor its approach to each case.

Seven: Focus on speed.

One lesson that cannot be overlearned is that speed matters. Slow reconstruction responses and initial missteps are very hard to undo. This is especially important in cases where the United States is involved in the conflict, since its dominant war-fighting ability means that its wars are becoming increasingly short, allowing for less preparation for reconstruction. In Iraq, for example, being unprepared to deploy constabulary assets to secure major sites necessary for reconstruction (from hospitals to government ministries) led to widespread destruction and a devastating loss of momentum and moral authority that would have accrued to the victorious forces if they had been able to maintain the economic and social infrastructure intact. As it was, crucial infrastructure was devastated and the reconstruction in Iraq was set back significantly, forcing the United States to dig itself out of a deep hole from the start of the operation.

In Afghanistan, a quick and successful humanitarian response saved hundreds of thousands of lives and set up conditions for a major repatriation of refugees and the return of many internally displaced persons to their points of origin. At the same time, the failure to quickly fund and follow through on the priorities outlined at the Tokyo donors' conference led to a weakening of the central government that will extend the need for international involvement for years and decrease that intervention's likelihood of success. Likewise in Sierra Leone, a slow U.S. and international response led to near disaster in 1999, rescued only by timely British intervention.

Just as early missteps matter, so does early positive investment. A few well-placed early resources are more effective than a lot of resources thrown at the problem down the road. An effective campaign of quick-impact projects and community-centered development in East Timor, for example, created the momentum needed to move the political and security situation forward toward an early independence and stable new nationhood.

Eight: Ensure sustainability of interventions.

As all of the case studies in this volume show, success, to the extent it is achieved, is won only over the course of many years. While initial goals of stabilization may be achieved in a year or two in some cases, lasting stability and a sustainable successful trajectory are generally only achieved over a course of three to seven years. The United States and the international community, however, seldom display the staying power to maximize the effect of their interventions. No matter how important a reconstruction effort appears at any given time, attention virtually always shifts to other, newer crises and challenges.

As such, it is imperative for the United States, if it is to succeed, to follow through on its commitments and design a system for ensuring that other international actors do so as well. The only way to do this is to lock in up front not only the commitments but also the finances and human resources needed to do the job. To ensure sustainability, the United States must work with its international partners to create real disincentives for grandstanding, backsliding, and cheating on commitments. This will require major changes in the ad hoc system currently used to put together donors' conferences. On the U.S. side, it will require working with Congress to design longer-term flexible funding and multiyear commitments, accompanied by appropriate oversight.

Another key to ensuring sustainability over time is to improve the United States' and the international community's ability to measure progress. Staying power depends on political will, which in turn depends upon understanding and support for the intervention over time on the part of politicians and citizens back home. Knowing what constitutes success in any given case and how one might measure progress toward top goals gives politicians and policymakers the tools they need to sustain support at home. Additional work on metrics for defining success in a broad range of cases is in order. With stronger tools in this area, those who commit the country to a given reconstruction effort will have a better chance of maintaining the support they need to succeed.

Nine: Pursue multilateralism first, not as a last resort.

The United States needs partners for reconstruction. The scope of activities, the cost in human and material terms, and the complex politics of reconstruction efforts all highlight the need for broad international involvement. The United States, for all its resources, needs three things that the international community can offer: additional capacity, legitimacy, and burden sharing.

There is already a great deal of reconstruction capacity spread around the international community. Bosnia and Kosovo highlight increasing capacity in Europe to take the lead on political management and administrative challenges across a wide range of substantive areas (though it needs further developing as well). Bosnia, Kosovo, and Afghanistan highlight NATO's increasing capacity to perform stabilization functions and its willingness to use this capacity outside the borders of its member countries. East Timor and Kosovo highlight the unique capacity of the United Nations to run transitional administrations. Sierra Leone and East Timor highlight the capacity of bilateral partners in the United Kingdom and Australia. In short, in case after case history has proved the importance of creating capability centers outside the United States and then lashing up U.S. capabilities with those of other international actors. In this process, it is crucial that the United States focus on ensuring that international capacities grow in parallel to U.S. capacities. The United States cannot afford to do in post-conflict reconstruction what it has done on the military side—build capacity so far beyond everyone else's that we cannot even integrate others' forces even when we want to do so. In this regard, the United States needs to learn from its NATO experience, and build capacities across a range of potential partners, as well as design a workable system for how to use them together.

As the predominant global power, the United States needs to be greatly concerned about the perceived legitimacy of its actions when intervention is contemplated. Multilateral responses are the best option for securing broad-based legitimacy. Even when multilateral solutions are not adopted, the United States pays a huge price if it has not at least made a good faith effort to secure multilateral agreement up front. Coalition building after the fact is an option, but it is a poor second to formal multilateral acceptance and participation. Iraq clearly highlights this problem most acutely. Little effort was made to seek a multilateral solution initially, leading to strong, broad, and lasting resistance to American plans. In contrast to the Bush administration's approach on Iraq, the Clinton administration, facing a similar situation with respect to Kosovo, went ahead with an intervention not endorsed by the UN Security Council, but took many steps to multilateralize and legitimize the intervention all along the way. This ultimately produced a more effective, more widely accepted intervention.

Afghanistan, in contrast to both Iraq and Kosovo, was a broadly accepted intervention. The United States, however, decided in favor of a faster military response with a narrower coalition and resisted a broadly mandated multilateral stabilization force in the early stages of the effort.

Despite changing its tack on multilateral engagement later on, the United States was never able to recover the international momentum it had at its disposal in the early days. As a result, the United States has borne a disproportionate share of the financial and military burdens in Afghanistan. But multilateralizing post-conflict reconstruction is not just a question of coalition building. It involves having international structures available for integrating different actors' capacities. In this regard, the United States needs to provide more consistent support for institutional development in multilateral venues like the United Nations, the World Bank, NATO, and other regional organizations.

When the United States decides that it must go it alone, without formal authorization by the UN Security Council, it needs to come up with an alternative legitimization strategy. Sheer expenditure of effort in this regard helps to generate good will. When the United States follows its own path, it needs to clearly enunciate its interests and the principles at stake that have led it to part ways with other international actors. In all cases, knowing what to expect from the United States—a basic level of predictability—is important to potential future partners in multilateral efforts.

The third reason for pursuing multilateral solutions aggressively is the need for burden sharing. Post-conflict reconstruction is generally very complex, demanding, and expensive. A range of actors brings an appropriately broad set of capabilities and needed variety of strengths to the table. Sometimes other countries can do things the United States cannot, either for historical, political, geographic, or capacity-based reasons. Bilateral donors, international organizations, development banks, and military alliances all have different mandates, different tools, different political profiles, and different resources. This diversity gives strength if harnessed properly. Thus, even as the United States builds up its own capacity, it needs to simultaneously build up complementary international capacity. This should be accompanied by agreements and understandings about which actors will use what capacities under what circumstances. An international division of labor creates more effective missions.

Ten: Prioritize and master handoffs.

A final building block toward a successful U.S. strategy for post-conflict reconstruction is recognition of the importance of handoffs. Transitions from one stage of a reconstruction effort to another, and from one set of actors to another, are almost always messy. This does not have to be so. The key is to design into the process clearly understood criteria and mechanisms for effective handoffs. There are three sets of handoffs that are particularly important: from military to civilian actors; from U.S. actors to international actors; and from international (including U.S.) actors to local actors.

The sharp dichotomy between U.S. funding for the military and for civilian agencies leads to suboptimal uses of the military in many instances. U.S. military forces, in every case considered in this volume, have wanted to hand off key civilian functions to civilians long before civilian agencies or entities were ready to perform them. Not only does civilian capacity need to be improved; it needs to be better integrated into the operation before reaching the "post-conflict" phase. In this regard, planning and pre-intervention "dress rehearsals" are essential. In the field, experiments like the integrated Provincial Reconstruction Teams (PRTs) in Afghanistan are worthy of further study and development.

The second set of handoffs that needs to be improved is that from U.S. actors to other international actors. The United States, feeling unduly burdened in some cases, often drops major functions quite abruptly into the lap of the UN or other international bodies. The United States, when it takes the lead as it did in Somalia, Haiti, Kosovo, Afghanistan, and Iraq, needs to involve international players in the planning from the start. If these other players know what is coming, they can prepare for it much more effectively. Deciding that "we have paid for this long enough" and handing the operation over to the UN or other international institutions, as is done all too often, is just not effective.

The last set of handoffs, and the most important ones, are those from all the international actors, including the United States, to the population of the country in question. The local population must participate in, and indeed own, the reconstruction process from the start. Attaching locals to shadow all the major international actors from an early stage is a strategy that has proved effective. The handoff to the local population also requires more priority attention to, and mechanisms for, creating transitional governance structures among the local population if legitimate ones do not already exist. Afghanistan is a case of constituting processes done well and relatively quickly, at least at the national level, while the national-level process in Iraq has left a great deal to be desired. If security is the key to creating an environment for all other post-conflict reconstruction activities, governance structures are key to ensuring that all the activity that is undertaken will be adopted by the local population and made sustainable.

WINNING PEACE: LAUNCHING VIRTUOUS CYCLES

Creating and applying a conscious American strategy for rebuilding states after conflict is a pressing need for both the United States and the world. Putting the post-conflict reconstruction capacity outlined in this volume to good effect will pay huge dividends, in terms of both national and international security. "Post-conflict reconstruction," far from being simply a matter of cleaning up old messes, is really about preventing future ones. A shockingly high recidivism rate—almost half of "post-conflict" societies return to conflict within five years—is a major threat to regional stability in various parts of the globe where the United States has significant interests at stake.[5] Increasing the success rate for peaceful and stable outcomes advances America's interests not only in the specific places where peace and stability are achieved, but also in far-off countries that see the world's most powerful country using its power and wealth to help others.

Successful post-conflict reconstruction launches virtuous cycles. Countries that the United States has helped to achieve a stable and enduring peace over the years have become important partners in building peace in other parts of the globe. Japan, one of the United States' most important success stories, now helps to anchor stability in an important region and provides significant amounts of funding for enhancing peace prospects around the world. Soldiers from El Salvador, themselves all too familiar with the costs of war to their own society, now work to build peace in Iraq. Sierra Leone, once the heart of instability in West Africa, is now a source of hope in a troubled region. Even the Federal Republic of Yugoslavia, only recently at war on multiple fronts and a world pariah, has offered up Serbian soldiers to advance peace in Afghanistan.

Starting virtuous cycles of peace and stability is in America's interests. It is also profoundly consistent with American values. Achieving stable peace not only advances humanitarian ideals; it also creates an environment in which freedom, democracy, and prosperity have a chance to flourish. To the extent that the United States helps to create these conditions, it launches yet other virtuous cycles that improve the lot of people around the world. If the United States is to be a successful world leader, it will have to prove that it can become as adept at winning peace in the twenty-first century as it became at winning war in the twentieth century.

Notes

[1] See, in this volume, chapter 3, "Laying the Foundation: Enhancing Security Capabilities" by Feil. The long-simmering debate over the question of reconfiguring U.S. forces to be better able to perform the stabilizing mission gained more prominence with the evident inability of U.S. forces to achieve this mission in Iraq with anywhere near the success with which they accomplished the war-fighting mission. Secretary of Defense Donald Rumsfeld's director of force transformation, Adm. Arthur K. Cebrowski, circulated a paper to this effect among senior defense officials in November 2003. See Bryan Bender, "Pentagon Seeing New Keys to Victory," *Boston Globe*, November 15, 2003, p. A10.

[2] See, in this volume, Orr, Mendelson Forman, and Flournoy and Pan on the challenges in the governance, socioeconomic, and justice sectors, chapters 4, 5, and 6 respectively. See also chapter 8, by Mendelson Forman and Pan, on civilian rapid response.

[3] George W. Bush, "Remarks by the President at the 20th Anniversary of the National Endowment for Democracy," November 6, 2003, text available at www.whitehouse.gov/news/releases/2003/11.

[4] See "Views of a Changing World 2003: War with Iraq Further Divides Global Publics," Pew Research Center for the People and the Press, June 2003, which documents a precipitous drop in positive attitudes toward the United States worldwide, but especially among Muslim populations. In a survey commissioned by the European Commission and conducted October 8–16, 2003, 53 percent of Europeans thought that the United States posed a "threat to peace in the world," ranking it after Israel alone and tied with Iran and North Korea. See EOS Gallup Europe, "Iraq and Peace in the World," Flash Eurobarometer 151, European Commission, November 2003, available at www.eosgallupeurope .com/webreports/ReportFL151aIraqandPeaceintheWorld.

[5] According to a World Bank study, countries emerging from civil war face a 44 percent risk of returning to conflict within five years. See Paul Collier et al., *Breaking the Conflict Trap: Civil War and Development Policy*, World Bank Research Report (Washington, D.C.: World Bank, 2003), p. 83.

APPENDIX 1

JOINT CSIS/AUSA
POST-CONFLICT RECONSTRUCTION TASK FRAMEWORK

Countries emerge from conflict under differing and unique conditions. Therefore, the priority, precedence, timing, appropriateness, and execution of tasks will vary from case to case. The Post-Conflict Reconstruction Task Framework presents the range of tasks often encountered when rebuilding a country in the wake of violent conflict. It is designed to help indigenous and international practitioners conceptualize, organize, and prioritize policy responses. By laying out the universe of options, the framework is intended to help identify shortfalls and gaps in reconstruction processes and capabilities. It is also geared to assist planning and coordination efforts. The framework is not a political-military plan; nor is it a checklist of mandatory activities for all cases or a strategy for success. Rather, it provides a starting point for considering *what* needs to be done in most cases. It does not suggest *how* it should be done or *who* should do it.

The framework places tasks between the cessation of *violent conflict* and the return to *normalization*. For the purposes of this framework, normalization is reached when (1) extraordinary outside intervention is no longer needed; (2) the processes of governance and economic activity largely function on a self-determined and self-sustaining basis; and (3) internal and external relations are conducted according to generally accepted norms of behavior.

The framework is organized into three conceptual phrases, defined as *initial response, transformation*, and *fostering sustainability*. These phases occur over a time span that varies according to local conditions and by each individual task. As such, this framework should be read horizontally, as transitions are task-specific. Comparing different tasks vertically is misleading because not all of the tasks that appear in a given phase will occur at the same time.

Security

Violent Conflict ──────────────────────────────▶ *Normalization*

	Initial response	Transformation	Fostering sustainability
	Goal: Establish a safe and secure environment	**Goal: Develop legitimate and stable security institutions**	**Goal: Consolidate indigenous capacity**
Control of belligerents			
Cease-fire	Enforce cease-fire; supervise disengagement and withdrawal of belligerent forces (including foreign); identify and neutralize potential spoilers; establish and maintain secure conditions for relief workers; negotiate terms for exchange of prisoners of war (POWs)	Supervise truces and cease-fires; separate civilian population from soldiers and militias; establish and control buffers, including demilitarized zones; monitor exchange of POWs	Transfer monitor requirements to indigenous security institutions
Enforcement of peace agreement	Provide security for peace monitors and observers; provide security for negotiations among belligerents; develop confidence-building measures with and among belligerents; employ information operations and other needed operational measures; conduct counterinsurgency operations	Investigate complaints and alleged breaches of agreements; provide military support to civil authorities; support and enforce political, military, and economic terms of peace plan; support confidence-building measures among belligerents; support and enforce territorial adjustments directed in peace plan	Transfer enforcement requirements to indigenous authorities; support and sustain confidence-building measures
Disarmament	Establish and enforce weapons control regimes, including collection and destruction; identify international arms merchants and their activities; identify indigenous arms control capacity; provide reassurances and incentives for disarmed faction	Disarm belligerents; reduce availability of unauthorized weapons; collaborate with neighboring countries on weapons flows, including apprehension of illegal arms dealers; cooperate with legal authorities to prosecute arms dealers	Secure, store, and dispose of weapons; develop indigenous arms control capacity

(continued)

Demobilization	Establish demobilization camps; ensure adequate health, food provisions, and security for belligerents	Identify, gather, and disband structural elements of belligerent groups; monitor and verify demobilization; ensure safety of quartered personnel and families	Decommission camps
Reintegration	Design reintegration strategy, including assessment of absorptive capacity of economic and social sectors	Provide job training, health screening, education, and employment assistance for demobilized forces; provide stipends and material support for demobilized forces	Reintegrate ex-combatants into society; provide follow-up services for reintegration
Territorial security			
Border and boundary control	Establish border/boundary monitoring mechanism; prevent arms smuggling; interdict contraband (i.e., drugs and natural resources); prevent trafficking of persons; regulate immigration and emigration	Develop indigenous capacity to control border/boundary; develop capacity to interdict contraband and arms smuggling; develop capacity to manage immigration and emigration	Begin transfer of border/boundary control functions to indigenous actors
Movement	Establish and disseminate rules relevant to movement; ensure freedom of movement for security forces and humanitarian assistance; establish freedom of movement for civilian population and international observers/monitors; dismantle roadblocks and establish checkpoints; regulate air and overland movement	Disseminate and enforce rules pertaining to movement	Provide full freedom of movement; transfer responsibility to indigenous actors
Points of entry	Establish control over major points of entry (e.g., airports, airspace, overland and maritime navigation)	Protect air and shipping operations; regulate movement of commercial air and naval operations; enforce controls with the assistance of indigenous authorities	Ensure air and naval freedom of movement; establish indigenous port and airport authority

(continued)

Protection of the populace

Noncombatants	Protect vulnerable elements of population (refugees, internally displaced persons [IDPs], women, children); ensure humanitarian aid and security force access to endangered populations and refugee camps; designate protection zones	Establish and maintain order in refugee camps and population centers; disarm and remove belligerents from camps and population centers; provide interim security programs for at-risk populations
Public order	Provide public order, including international police or constabulary operations	Enforce public order; maintain positive relations between international military and police forces and indigenous population; prevent reprisals; design and implement civic education programs for law and order and public security	Transfer public security responsibilities to indigenous police force
Clearance of unexploded ordnance (UXO)	Conduct emergency de-mining and UXO removal; conduct mapping and survey exercises of mined areas; mark mine fields; identify and coordinate emergency requirements; establish priorities and conduct de-mining operations	Initiate large-scale de-mining and UXO removal operations; promote mine awareness; train and equip indigenous de-mining elements	Transfer de-mining and UXO removal operations to indigenous actors

Protection of key individuals, infrastructure, and institutions

Private institutions and individuals	Protect political and religious leaders, judges; protect and secure places of religious worship and cultural sites; protect private property and factories	Create indigenous capacity to protect private institutions and individuals	
Critical infrastructure	Protect and secure critical infrastructure (e.g., airports, roads, bridges, hospitals, telecommunications, banks, electricity plants, dams, water reservoirs, pipelines)	Create indigenous capacity to protect critical infrastructure	

(continued)

Military infrastructure	Identify, secure, and protect stockpiles of nuclear and chemical materials; secure military equipment and means of communication	Create indigenous capacity to protect military infrastructure	Identify modernization needs and means to achieve them
Public institutions	Protect and secure strategically important institutions (e.g., government buildings, courthouses)	Create indigenous capacity to protect public institutions	

Reconstitution of indigenous security institutions

National armed forces	Identify roles, missions, and structure of indigenous national security institutions; vet individuals for past abuses	Assist in and monitor the rebuilding and reorganization of official national security institutions; promote civilian control of military; professionalize and enhance the capabilities of indigenous military forces; support use-of-force policies based on rule of law; establish transparent entry, promotion, and retirement systems	Provide conventional military assistance programs; establish military-to-military programs with the host country's forces
Nonmilitary security forces	Plan for the reorganization and transformation of police force and/or paramilitary; develop recruitment practices that promote more representative security forces; vet individuals for past abuses; develop training programs for police forces	Professionalize and provide assistance to indigenous nonmilitary security forces; establish transparent entry, promotion, and retirement systems; create a nonmilitary intelligence capacity	Establish community requirements for indigenous public safety

Regional security

Regional security arrangements	Negotiate or modify regional security arrangements with all interested parties	Establish mechanisms for implementing regional security arrangements	Monitor compliance with and reinforce arrangements

Governance and Participation

ViolentConflict ———————————————————————▶ *Normalization*

	Initial response	Transformation	Fostering sustainability
	Goal: Determine governance structure and establish foundation for citizen participation	**Goal: Promote legitimate political institutions and participatory processes**	**Goal: Consolidate political institutions and participatory processes**

Governance

National constituting processes

National dialogue	Establish process at national, regional, and/or local levels to represent views of citizenry	Commence dialogue at national level to define national identity (citizenship criteria, languages, etc.)	Implement conclusions of national dialogue and support constitutional process
Constitution	Establish constitutional commission and determine method of adoption; provide legal advisers	Draft or reform constitution; ensure fair, inclusive process for drafting or reform of constitution; launch public information campaign to promulgate new/revised constitution	Adopt constitution; create outlet for popular discussion of new constitution

Transitional governance

International transitional administration	Consult with indigenous and international actors to establish interim government; restore transitional political authority	Design structure of future governance system; establish interim civil administration; include indigenous actors in decisionmaking process	Phase out and transfer authority through elections or other means
National transitional administration	Establish rules and timetable for interim national government	Determine power-sharing arrangements and recruit individuals to serve in and advise the national transitional government; determine process of choosing permanent national government	Phase out transitional government in favor of permanent national government through previously decided means

(continued)

Executive authority

Public sector	Identify unmet institutional needs for structuring major government functions	Establish ministries and independent agencies, including specifying organization and lines of authority	Provide ongoing technical support for institutional development of the public sector
Civil service	Determine structure and affordable size of civil service to meet ongoing and future needs	Select and train indigenous civil servants; establish transparent entry, promotion, and retirement systems	Implement civil service reforms; appoint and empower civil servants at national and regional levels
Revenue generation	Identify sources and design a workable, efficient system that is able to generate revenue for government services	Implement plans for revenue generation, banking, customs, taxation, and financial services; create capacities to manage budget and personnel issues	
Recruitment and training	Identify key individuals in executive authority to receive training; educate executive leaders and staff about principles of responsible governance; encourage diaspora with leadership skills to return to country	Provide management and technical assistance training to selected civil servants; develop ethical standards and code of conduct	
Infrastructure		Improve physical infrastructure of executive branch (i.e., buildings, libraries, information systems, and office equipment)	Establish line items in budget to sustain physical infrastructure of executive branch

Legislative strengthening

Mandate	Establish role and mandate of legislative branch in national and indigenous decisionmaking processes	Develop guidelines concerning passage of laws and regulations through legislature; increase legislative influence on national policy and budgets	Determine mechanisms to resolve disputes between various branches of government; ensure enforcement of laws passed by legislature

(continued)

Citizen access	Identify obstacles and potential means to facilitate citizen access	Facilitate avenues for advocacy and interest group activities; enable communication between legislators and their constituents	Guarantee public's right to attend meetings, hearings, and examine records; establish means to provide indigenous constituent services
Technical assistance	Identify infrastructure and training needs	Provide legislators and staff with training and support; develop ethical standards and code of conduct; improve physical infrastructure (i.e., buildings, libraries, information systems, and office equipment)	Conduct parliamentary exchanges to strengthen democratic principles and encourage legislative independence
Local governance			
Legal basis	Establish legal foundation for indigenous governing structures; determine method of indigenous representation and participation	Implement new structures for indigenous control that ensure compatibility with national laws and community traditions	Allow for indigenous decisionmaking and budgetary control
Decentralization	Conduct review of political organizational structure; determine scale and form of decentralization	Conduct decentralization in administrative, financial, and political areas; ensure civilian authority	Establish liaison process between national and local governing institutions
Institution building	Identify indigenous capacity and needs for institutional development	Provide technical and financial assistance to indigenous governmental structures	Monitor indigenous governance performance
Traditional representation	Identify traditional community structures	Utilize traditional structures to help govern and ensure participation	Reconcile traditional structures with formal government structures

(continued)

Transparency and anticorruption

Anticorruption	Develop laws promoting anticorruption, accountability, and transparency within government and private sector; create mechanisms to curtail corruption, including special prosecutors, witness and judge protection; design and implement anticorruption campaign, including education	Enforce anticorruption laws, including removal of corrupt officials; dismantle organized crime networks; empower legal and civil society mechanisms to monitor governmental behavior; foster transparent governing practices in public and private sectors	Prosecute violators and enforce standards; seek international cooperation to combat corruption
Watchdogs	Encourage formation of watchdog organizations in public and private sectors to monitor international and national institutions	Establish legislative protections for indigenous watchdog groups; ensure adequate resources and standing for oversight mechanisms	Promote indigenous transparency monitoring presence in public and private sectors

Participation

Elections

Planning and execution	Set timetable and goals for elections; determine mode of representation; conduct census; establish independent national electoral commission; establish and verify voter registry	Develop appropriate procedures and rules for election, including security of candidates and ballot box; promulgate rules of election; ensure secure and fair election campaign	Provide logistical support for elections (ballot boxes, voting stations, etc.); assist in planning and execution of election; promote sustainable election methods and mechanisms
Monitoring	Secure agreements for international and domestic monitoring presence	Recruit and organize indigenous and international election monitoring teams	Deploy monitoring team
Citizen outreach	Advertise election timetable and encourage citizen participation	Disseminate information about electoral process; undertake voter education campaign	Make election results widely available to avoid fraud and misperception

(continued)

Political parties

Task		
Formation	Define political party system; ensure clear legal status, protections, and regulations of political parties	Encourage creation of multiple competitive parties in multi-tiered system through transparent and legal funding mechanisms; register political parties in accordance with election laws	Support political activities by backing democracy promotion objectives; link parties to legitimate international counterparts
Training	Identify potential political party leaders	Sponsor workshops to develop political parties (i.e., advertisement, issue analysis, media relations, fundraising, voter mobilization, campaign strategy)	Facilitate democracy, management, and negotiation skills education for party leaders; encourage women candidates in leadership roles

Civil society

Task		
Development	Promote participation in society through establishment of unions, professional associations, religious groups, and civic associations	Provide funding, technical assistance, and training to civil society groups	Develop indigenous capacity to advise, fund, and train new indigenous groups
Enabling environment	Review existing regulations on nongovernmental organizations (NGOs) and civil society actors; conduct survey of existing NGOs	Draft or alter statutes establishing rights and restrictions of NGOs (including taxation status, etc.)	Create and strengthen an umbrella organization of NGOs to represent civil society views to the government; encourage intergroup partnerships and community-building functions at the town and village levels

Media

Task		
Public information	Establish international news media outlet; utilize media as public information tool to provide factual information and control rumors	Widely disseminate news; lobby for fair free speech and free press rules and regulations; provide regular updates on the peace process and other critical developments	Foster indigenous media presence and promote establishment of open broadcast networks; continue to use media as facilitator of dialogue and information

(continued)

Training	Recruit and train media personnel; encourage media professionals to return	Establish journalism schools	Turn over media programming to indigenous actors; provide incentives for the creation of new, independent newspapers and TV/radio stations
Professionalism/ethics	Develop media code of conduct	Educate reporters and media executives about best practices and role of media; establish indigenous journalist association	Foster continued journalistic independence

Social and Economic Well-Being

Voilent Conflict ——————————————————→ *Normalization*

	Initial response	Transformation	Fostering sustainability
	Goal: Provide for emergency humanitarian needs	**Goal: Establish foundation for development**	**Goal: Institutionalize long-term development program**

Social Well-Being

Refugees and internally displaced persons (IDPs)

	Initial response	Transformation	Fostering sustainability
Prevention of displacement	Provide emergency food, water, shelter, and medicine in situ; prevent flow of refugees	Ensure reliable and adequate supply of assistance to population centers	Develop and provide economic opportunities and services to support permanent populations
Management of refugees	Negotiate agreements to establish IDP camps; build camps to provide adequate services; establish registration and identification system; establish public information campaign to manage refugee flows	Obtain services from and provide support to host countries; provide assistance to refugee camps and surrounding communities; provide reintegration services and develop repatriation plans; continue information campaign	Close camps; repatriate refugees; monitor conditions for refugees after their return
Management of IDPs	Negotiate agreements to establish IDP camps; provide services to IDPs and surrounding communities; establish public information campaign to manage IDPs; establish registration and identification system	Continue provision of assistance to IDPs and surrounding communities; develop relocation plans	Relocate IDPs to permanent locations; monitor conditions for IDPs after their return

Food security

	Initial response	Transformation	Fostering sustainability
Emergency distribution	Secure emergency food aid distribution channels; deliver emergency food to most vulnerable populations; protect food distribution network; supply adequate storage facilities to prevent food contamination	Collaborate with international and local relief actors to implement distribution programs; prevent and punish theft and misappropriation of food resources; reassess distribution programs	Phase out emergency relief distributions; transition to traditional food aid programs

(continued)

Market mechanisms	Identify and try to procure locally to support existing markets	Channel food aid to promote indigenous market activities; establish transportation and distribution networks for markets	
Agricultural development	Reestablish domestic food production and seed supply; supply tools and seeds to farmers in affected regions; reopen markets and ensure ability to secure needed imports to sell food to prevent food accompanying price explosions	Rehabilitate agricultural system; restore rural irrigation systems; create agricultural credit plan to provide low-interest loans to farmers; develop land reform plan and extension service for farmers.	Implement land reform measures; promote diversification of agriculture
Public health			
Water and waste management	Ensure proper sanitization, purification, and distribution of drinking water; provide interim sanitation and waste disposal services	Evaluate water sources to protect against contamination and ensure that plans are environmentally sustainable; support indigenous waste management capacity; develop geographic plan of action for waste management	Build indigenous capacity to deliver clean drinking water; expand regular waste management activities to rural areas
Medical capacity	Stockpile and distribute emergency medical supplies and drugs; set up or reopen accessible clinics to deal with emergency health problems (disease, infection, wounds); recruit doctors, nurses, and staff	Ensure sufficient stockpile of medical supplies and drugs; review status of medical resources; establish ambulance service; provide sufficient external medical support while integrating indigenous expertise; train health care providers	Modernize medical equipment and solidify public health sector; expand hospitals to provide specialized care for greater numbers; build capacity for local administration of clinics; transfer administration of clinics to indigenous actors
Prevention of epidemics	Prevent epidemics through immediate vaccinations	Establish vaccination and screening programs to deal with potential epidemics (especially in refugee camps) through local clinics	Institutionalize country-wide vaccination programs to prevent infectious diseases

(continued)

Health education	Educate population about crisis-induced health risks	Develop community-based programs geared to identify, prevent, and reduce health risks	Implement long-term health care education programs, including family planning and HIV/AIDS education
Shelter			
Construction	Provide emergency shelter for immediate needs; develop housing development strategy to address refugees/IDPs as well as reintegration of ex-combatants	Repair existing housing stock using local labor and supplies, if available; establish standards for housing construction and development; clear devastated housing and assess damage	Construct affordable housing by stimulating competition in the construction market
Adjudication of property disputes	Develop roster of contested property; establish criteria and mechanisms for property dispute resolution	Conduct investigations and hearings; create commission to adjudicate disputes	Administer remuneration and compensation system
Educational system			
Human resources	Identify and recruit teachers and administrators; register school-aged population; create equal opportunity education policy	Train teachers and administrators and provide incentives to educate kids, but especially girls	Strengthen continued education for teachers and administrators
Infrastructure	Evaluate need for new schools; build and repair schools and universities; help develop educational materials with local input.	Open schools and universities	Maintain and enlarge new or restored schools and universities
Curriculum	Develop curriculum that respects diversity	Distribute curriculum and supporting teaching materials	
Literacy campaign	Survey literacy levels and linguistic groups; develop literacy campaign	Conduct literacy campaign and focus on girls and women, and men ages 15–25	Institutionalize opportunities for adult education to sustain efforts of literacy campaign

(continued)

Social safety net

Pension system	Evaluate existing pension systems for government and parastatal employees	Design or reconfigure pension system based on agreed criteria and ability of new government to support	Secure funding stream and institutionalize pension system
Social security	Evaluate existing social security system	Design or reconfigure social security system based on agreed criteria and ability of new government to support	Secure funding stream and institutionalize system

Economic Well-Being

Economic strategy and assistance

Strategy	Assess macroeconomic situation for budget and create transparency in all sectors	Work with country officials to create short-, medium-, and long-term growth strategies	Implement and institutionalize strategic planning capability
International financial assistance	Define indigenous representation at donor conferences; develop mechanism for donor and in-country coordination; recruit donors	Hold donor conferences to mobilize resources; negotiate agreement between indigenous authorities and donors concerning terms of aid conditionality	Secure grants and loans; monitor status of contributions and implementation; work with specialists on managing commercial and public debt
Absorption	Identify capacity of key institutions and individuals	Enhance government ability to absorb and administer donor funds; enhance NGO ability to absorb and administer funds	Develop funding capacity for long-term institution building

Physical infrastructure

Power	Restore power (electricity and fuels) to critical institutions	Expand power to private and public consumers in densely populated areas; design and implement system for administering energy resources	Integrate power demands and generation capabilities with overall economic strategy

(continued)

Transportation	Ensure access to airports, roads, rail lines, and ports for humanitarian and crucial economic functions; regularize urban transportation	Reconstruct major arteries and bridges; upgrade capacity for more intensive commercial usage	Develop and diversify transportation networks
Telecommunication and information technology (IT)	Restore critical telecommunications and IT capacities	Design and implement telecommunication and IT networks, beginning with major population centers	Expand telecommunications and IT capability to rural regions
Employment generation			
Public works	Design initiatives to provide immediate employment as part of a larger sectoral strategy for soliciting projects ideas from local communities	Implement public works projects	Rationalize public works projects with long-term development program
Microenterprise	Create microenterprise mechanisms with appropriate credit mechanisms; solicit proposals at local level	Identify funding sources and implement priority projects	
Markets			
Market reconstitution	Create basis for legal markets through reform of contract law	Supplant black market activities with legal alternatives; facilitate transformation of informal markets	Expand reach of national markets
Legal and regulatory reform			
Property rights	Draft laws and codes to establish or strengthen property rights	Adopt laws and codes	Ensure equitable implementation of laws and codes
Business	Design laws and regulations to provide incentives for economic growth and development	Implement laws and regulations, including provisions to protect intellectual property rights	Promote business growth through regulatory streamlining and tax incentives
Labor	Design flexible laws and regulations to protect labor rights, including workplace safety, minimum wage, child labor, and union rights provisions	Implement and enforce labor laws and regulations	Promote management-labor dispute mechanisms

(continued)

International trade

Enabling environment	Evaluate tariffs, tax structures, and barriers to trade	Reduce tariffs, taxes, and barriers to trade	Foster economic integration through local, regional, and global organizations
Trade facilitation	Set trade priorities and explore new trade opportunities; initiate dialogue between country economic team and international actors responsible for granting preferential trading status	Provide technical assistance to firms and trade groups to develop nontraditional export capacities; take steps to qualify for preferential market access under General System of Preferences (GSP) and regional trade arrangements	Increase export diversification to enhance economic stability; seek accession into regional or global trade organizations

Investment

Private	Establish business environment conducive to economic growth	Assist businesses with start-up grants and loans; encourage investment by international actors, including diaspora communities; provide all investors with legal protections and incentives	Offer risk protection to facilitate sustained investment
Public	Consider top public investment needs	Invest in critical projects neglected by the private sector (i.e., large-scale investment in education, health care)	Continue to use government resources to promote public needs; consider private-public investment partnerships
Subsidies	Evaluate subsidized sectors, industries, and firms	Rationalize subsidies with regard to cost to government and impact on employment levels	
Natural resources and environment	Secure and account for valuable natural resources; safeguard/eliminate most dangerous health hazards; draft and adopt specific environmental standards for industry and agriculture	Promote development of natural resources to attract potential investors; establish environmental protection and regulatory mechanisms	Rationalize national resource policies with long-term economic development strategies; enforce environmental protection provisions; contain or reverse environmental damage

(continued)

Banking and finance

Central banking authority	Gain agreement on recognized interim currencies; create independent central banking authority	Introduce national currency and develop monetary policy if it doesn't exist, and stabilize the currency.	Enforce banking regulations through legislative changes and implementation of existing laws; monitor banking transactions; enforce violations of banking regulations
Banking regulations and oversight	Develop transparent regulatory system to govern financial transactions by banks as well as private and public entities	Recruit and train regulators; emphasize transparency in banking system to prevent corruption and enhance economic stability	
Capital markets			Create conditions conducive to formation of capital markets

Justice and Reconciliation

Violent Conflict —————————————————————————————→ *Normalization*			
Initial response	**Transformation**	**Fostering sustainability**
Goal: Develop mechanisms for addressing past and ongoing grievances	**Goal: Build legal system and process for reconciliation**	**Goal: Functioning legal system based on international norms**
Justice			
Transitional justice	Deploy transitional justice package, including international police, police monitors, judges, prosecutors, defense attorneys, corrections capacity, court administrators, codes, and procedures	Dispense justice in central or sensitive jurisdictions	Transfer responsibilities to permanent justice institutions
Law Enforcement			
International police	Establish international civilian police authority; disseminate rules, purpose, and objectives of the international force	Conduct co-patrols with indigenous police; provide police monitors	Phase out international police and reduce monitoring presence; retain minimal international oversight of policing
Indigenous police	Vet and reconfigure existing police forces; recruit law enforcement and administrative personnel; establish police academies; train, educate, and equip/resource existing indigenous police in international policing standards; deploy police monitors	Develop investigative capability and institutionalize procedures for national police; secure funding to maintain police academies and administrative support to law enforcement; establish transparent entry, promotion, and retirement systems for national police	Provide ongoing technical support and training; encourage relationships with relevant national and international law enforcement associations

(continued)

Accountability/oversight		Establish Office of Inspector General to investigate police corruption and abuse; establish ombudsman's office to address citizens' complaints and criticisms of law enforcement	Institutionalize offices of inspector general and ombudsman by securing line-item budgetary funding
Judicial system			
Reorganization	Review existing court system	Pass laws and statutes to foster judicial independence; review role of prosecutor and promote role of defense lawyer	Institutionalize new structures and responsibilities
Training/recruitment	Inventory indigenous legal professionals; select individuals for judicial positions; establish professional code of conduct for judicial system	Vet and train judges, prosecutors, defense attorneys, and court personnel; ensure diversity of selection of court personnel; establish law schools and recruit professors to educate next generation of legal professionals	Provide additional training for judicial specializations; develop pay structure for legal professionals to counteract "brain drain"
Infrastructure	Inventory courts, law schools, legal libraries, and bar associations	Rehabilitate or construct necessary facilities	
Citizen access	Establish liaison mechanism between civilians and transitional authorities (or international forces) on legal matters	Educate indigenous population on accessing the judicial system	Extend legal representation to underprivileged community through a public defender system and legal services organizations; institute formal alternative dispute resolution mechanisms (e.g., arbitration and mediation)
Laws			
Code and statutory reform	Review existing laws	Promulgate revised legal code and statutes (civil and criminal) consistent with protection of basic human rights	Implement legal code through legislation

(continued)

Participation	Create and strengthen legal aid and NGO groups; channel citizen input into law-drafting process	Initiate public dialogue with all sectors of civil society on legal reform	Provide oversight and monitoring of code implementation
Human rights			
Capacity building	Assess capacity of indigenous human rights groups	Establish government mechanisms to protect human rights; support citizen advocacy organizations	Create mechanisms for organizing human rights NGOs; design processes for government/NGO interaction on human rights
Monitoring	Establish international monitoring presence; develop indigenous human rights monitoring capacity	Conduct joint human rights monitoring missions with indigenous monitors	Create sustainable indigenous human rights monitoring mechanism
Security force reform	Vet security forces for human rights abuses	Purge violators and train reconstituted forces in humanitarian law and practices; revise military code and doctrine to comply with laws of war and domestic criminal law	Institutionalize human rights education into training programs; ensure legal system prosecutes violators
Corrections			
Incarceration and parole	Determine status of prisoners held (political prisoners and war prisoners)	Evaluate release on case-by-case basis; reconfigure probations and parole system	Transfer penal authority to indigenous authorities; monitor compliance with internationally accepted corrections standards
Infrastructure	Refurbish prison facilities at key sites; provide emergency lock-up facilities	Rebuild correctional institutions, including administrative and rehabilitative capacities	Ensure continued funding of correctional facilities
Training		Vet existing and recruit new corrections officers; train officers according to internationally accepted standards	Establish indigenous sustainable corrections training programs

(continued)

International courts and tribunals

Establishment of courts and tribunals	Establish jurisdiction and mandate of international courts and tribunals; ensure compatibility of international court with national and international legal mechanisms	Recruit court staff; identify secure facilities; provide logistical and technical support to international courts and tribunals; develop intelligence-sharing agreements; second expert personnel (prosecutors, forensics)	Bring cases to trial
Investigation and arrest	Document and preserve evidence of mass atrocities; coordinate efforts with UN and NGO investigations	Assist in investigation, arrest, and transfer of suspected war criminals to international courts	Assist efforts of indigenous forces to arrest and transfer human rights violators and war criminals
Citizen outreach	Publicize progress and work; publish indictments and statements	Broadcast court proceedings; support media access	Translate and disseminate court records and decisions

Reconciliation

Truth commissions

Organization	Solicit voluntary contributions from international donors; hire indigenous and international staff to set up commission; create indigenous dialogue on structure and mandate of commission; involve diverse groups in establishment of court, including teachers, unions, ex-combatants, women's groups, and police	Determine mandate, mission, size, duration, and enforcement powers; train international and indigenous staff; provide infrastructure and technical assistance; ensure indigenous involvement and ownership in the process; ensure compatibility and coordination of commission with national and international mechanisms	Support commission's work and final recommendations; deploy investigators; hold hearings; collect testimony; prepare reports and recommendation; provide restitution, reparations, and compensation
Citizen education	Identify misperceptions stemming from miscommunication; establish broad public information programs to promote efforts for reconciliation	Dispel myths through educational curricula; support programs that publicize and raise awareness of truth and reconciliation activities	Evaluate reconciliation mechanisms; widely disseminate proceedings and documents produced by commission
Reparations	Determine appropriate means and levels of reparations	Identify classes of eligibility	Implement reparation measures

(continued)

Community rebuilding

Confidence building	Provide neutral meeting places for discussions and activities; identify and use third-party advisers and mediators to build trust and cooperation; enhance participation through public outreach	Provide reconciliation training and resources; bring adversaries together where possible; incorporate a wide range of stakeholders; establish mutually beneficial resource-sharing arrangements; organize recreational and educational activities	Foster informal, indigenous mechanisms for dispute resolution; provide resources for community projects; publicize successful confidence-building programs
Religion and traditional practices	Identify religious institutions and leaders on local and national levels; provide interim meeting locations for religious groups to congregate; design community programs to support reconciliation based on religious and traditional practices	Ensure participation of diverse religious elements; rebuild places of worship and sacred sites; implement traditional reconciliation mechanisms, such as purification rituals and reburial ceremonies	Create and implement faith-based initiatives to rebuild communities
Women	Assess traditional role of women in society and their potential to contribute to reconciliation process	Support initiatives devised by women's groups	Ensure women's rights and influence

Individual healing and empowerment

Closure	Provide localized counseling to victims and perpetrators of the conflict; establish missing persons initiatives; solicit funds and technical experts for identifying bodies and running missing persons programs	Implement counseling programs focusing on victim's redress and post-violence trauma; create citizen's councils to establish memorials, scholarship funds, performances, and other commemoration activities	Routinize memory through public activity and historical records (e.g., museums, archives, and oral histories)
Individual empowerment	Identify individual needs	Develop activities promoting sense of self-worth through employment, education, and recreational opportunities; provide counseling and training to enhance contributions to society	Ensure sufficient employment opportunities and avenues to participate in civil society

JOINT CSIS/AUSA
POST-CONFLICT RECONSTRUCTION PROJECT

Joint CSIS/AUSA Project Commissioners

J. Brian Atwood
Former Administrator, USAID
Dean, Hubert H. Humphrey School
of Public Policy

Peter Bell
President and CEO, CARE USA

Doug Bereuter
United States House of Representatives

Paul Brest
President, The William and Flora
Hewlett Foundation

Susan Collins
United States Senate

Chester Crocker
Former Assistant Secretary of State
for African Affairs
Schlesinger Chair, Georgetown
University

John Edwards
United States Senate

Sam Farr
United States House of Representatives

George Folsom
Former Deputy Assistant Secretary
of the Treasury
Deputy Director, Iraq Management
and Reconstruction Office

John J. Hamre
Former Deputy Secretary of Defense
President and CEO, CSIS

Richard Holbrooke
Former U.S. Ambassador to the
United Nations
Vice Chairman, Perseus LLC

George Joulwan (USA, Ret.)
Former SACEUR and CINC,
EUCOM

Geoffrey Kemp
Former Special Assistant to the President for National Security Affairs
Director of Strategic Programs,
Nixon Center

Jeane Kirkpatrick
Former U.S. Ambassador to the UN
Director of Foreign and Defense
Policy Studies, AEI

Nancy Lindborg
Executive Vice President,
Mercy Corps

T. Joseph Lopez (USN, Ret.)
Former CINC, Southern Forces
Europe
Senior Vice President, Halliburton
KBR

(project commissioners, continued)

C. Payne Lucas
Former President, Africare

Jan Piercy
Former World Bank U.S. Executive
Director

Jack Reed
United States Senate

Pat Roberts
United States Senate

Walter B. Slocombe
Former Undersecretary of Defense
for Policy
Member, Caplin & Drysdale

Gordon R. Sullivan (USA, Ret.)
Former Chief of Staff, U.S. Army
President, AUSA

Julia Taft
Former President and CEO, InterAction
Assistant Administrator, UN Development
Program

Larry D. Welch (USAF, Ret.)
Former Chief of Staff, U.S. Air Force
President and CEO, Institute for
Defense Analyses

Charles Wilhelm (USMC, Ret.)
Former CINC, SOUTHCOM
Member of the Board, MIC
Industries

Timothy E. Wirth
President, United Nations
Foundation

Frank Wolf
United States House of Representatives

Joint CSIS/AUSA Project Cochairs

John J. Hamre
President and CEO, CSIS

Gen. Gordon R. Sullivan, (USA, Ret.)
President, Assocation of the United
States Army

Joint CSIS/AUSA Project Codirectors

Phase One

Scott Feil
Operational Evaluation Division,
Institute for Defense Analyses

Johanna Mendelson Forman
Senior Program Officer,
Peace, Security, and Human Rights,
United Nations Foundation

Michèle Flournoy
Senior Adviser, International
Security Program, CSIS

Robert Orr
Executive Director, Belfer Center for
Science and International Affairs,
John F. Kennedy School of Government, Harvard University

(project codirectors, continued)

Phase Two

Frederick D. Barton
Senior Adviser and Codirector,
Post-Conflict Reconstruction Project,
CSIS

Bathsheba N. Crocker
Fellow and Codirector, Post-Conflict
Reconstruction Project, CSIS

Joint CSIS/AUSA Project Staff

Sasha Kishinchand
Research Director

Michael Pan
Project Coordinator

Elizabeth Latham
Research Associate

David Fuhr
Research Assistant

Milan Vaishnav
Research Assistant

Daniel Werbel-Sanborn
Research Assistant

Alex Daskalakis
Events Coordinator

Sami Fournier
Information Systems

INDEX

Page numbers followed by the letter n *refer to notes on those pages.*

Abizaid, John, 22–23
Abu Ghraib prison (Iraq), 272, 280
Accountability: of host country, 30–31; interagency planning and, 108–9; of international actors, 30–31; of police, 324
Acheson, Dean, 176
ACOTA. *See* African Contingency Operations Training Assistance Program
Afghanistan, 244–59; background on, 39, 244; Bonn Agreement (2001) for, 20, 252–53, 254; central government in, weaknesses of, 132, 240n.27, 252, 256; constituting processes in, 130, 253–54, 302; ethnic groups within, 253; funding inadequacy and delays, 30, 35n.20, 255–58, 261n.32, 298; future of, scenarios for, 258–59; governance and participation in, 252–54; humanitarian response in, 298; indigenous participation in reconstruction of, 28, 255–56; interagency planning for, lack of, 107; international police in, 250–51; long-term political vision for, lack of, 252; *loya jirga* in, 130, 253; multilateral engagement in, U.S. failure to secure, 7, 300–301; National Development Framework for, 255; opium

production in, 249; Provincial Reconstruction Teams (PRTs) in, 251–52, 302; security problems in, 44–45, 245, 248–52, 253, 255, 257, 259; status of reconstruction, 246–47; as terrorist-sponsored state, 39; trade relations with U.S., restoration of, 88n.20; U.S.-led intervention in, 247, 248, 252; U.S. policy inconsistencies and problems in, viii, 7, 296; U.S. promises to, 244, 246, 294–95; U.S. role in post-conflict reconstruction of, 245–46, 257–58; U.S. strategy in, flaws in, 249–52; U.S. troops in, x, 15; warlords in, 248–50, 252, 254; women's rights in, 28
Africa: information and intelligence problems in, 53; UN-plus model for peacekeeping in, 224, 238, 238n.1; weak states in, 8. *See also specific countries*
African Contingency Operations Training Assistance Program (ACOTA), 51
African Crisis Response Initiative, 153
African Growth and Opportunity Act (AGOA), 82
Agrarian reform, in Japan, 178–79, 183–84

sion of labor in, 113; and funding
of post-conflict reconstruction,
141; importance of, 105; and international liaison, 114–15; for Iraq,
failure in, 45–46, 107–8, 266–68;
leadership of, 109; process of, 105–
6; recent efforts in, 106–8; rehearsals and training for, 112; resistance
to, 107, 114; responsiveness of,
109–10; secure intranet for, 114;
shared frame of reference in, 110–
11; skepticism about, 105; stum-
bling blocks for, 108; template/
generic plan in, 111, 113; training
for, 112, 127, 129, 133–34
Interests: of key actors, taking into
account, 21; U.S. national, 3, 214,
290–91
INTERFET. *See* Intervention Force in
East Timor
Intergovernmental organizations
(IGOs): coordination with U.S.
government agencies, 46; and information and intelligence, 53
Internally displaced persons (IDPs):
management of, 316. *See also* Refugees
International actors, 19–33; accountability of, 30–31; burden sharing by,
301; chaotic response of, 19; codes of
conduct for, 31; conditionalities used
by, 69; coordination among, 21–22,
206n.18; field representatives of,
empowering, 24–25; funding by, 28–
30; and governance and participation issues, 58, 61–70; holistic
approach of, 22–23; host country
counterparts for, creating or developing, 20, 59; negative influences of,
minimizing, 27–28; security tasks of,
23–24, 41, 54; sequencing of activities of, 26–27; strategy development
by, 21–22; timing of involvement of,
31–32. *See also specific countries and
multinational organizations*

International Commission for Missing
Persons, 102n.9
International Criminal Court, U.S.
legislative restrictions on, 102n.8
International Criminal Investigative
Training Assistance Program (ICI-
TAP), 97, 118, 131–32
International Criminal Tribunal for
Yugoslavia (ICTY), 102n.9
International Crisis Group (ICG),
208n.43
International Disaster Assistance fund,
144, 145, 152–53
International Military Education and
Training Program (IMET), 56n.18
International Office on Migration
(IOM), 212
International organizations (IOs):
coordination with U.S. government
agencies, 46; and information and
intelligence, 53
International Republican Institute, 65,
218
International Security Assistance Force
(ISAF), in Afghanistan, 250–51
International Trade Administration
(ITA), 119
Internews, 96
Intervention Force in East Timor
(INTERFET), 212
Investment, encouraging in post-
conflict environment, 79–81, 216–
17, 321
IOM. *See* International Office on Migration
IOs. *See* International organizations
Iraq, 263–83; casualties of war and
occupation in, 270; civilian response
mechanism in, 118; coalition forces
in, 271; Coalition Provisional Authority (CPA) in, 46, 265, 267; disarmament, demobilization, and
reintegration (DDR) in, 272–73;
doubts about U.S. intentions in, 295;
electricity infrastructure in, 277;

ABOUT THE AUTHORS

Bathsheba N. Crocker is a fellow and codirector of the Post-Conflict Reconstruction Project at the Center for Strategic and International Studies (CSIS), as well as an adjunct professor at the Johns Hopkins School of Advanced International Studies and at George Washington University's Elliott School of International Affairs. During 2002–2003, she was an International Affairs Fellow at the Council on Foreign Relations. Prior to that, she served as an attorney in the Legal Adviser's Office at the U.S. Department of State, as deputy U.S. special representative for the Southeast Europe Initiative, and as executive assistant to the deputy national security adviser at the White House.

Scott Feil is a research staff member of the Institute for Defense Analyses in Alexandria, Virginia. Colonel Feil's 27–year career in the United States Army culminated in the command of an armored brigade and service as chief of the Strategy Division of the Directorate for Strategic Plans and Policy of the Joint Staff. After his retirement, he was executive director of the Association of the United States Army's Program on the Role of American Military Power and codirector of the joint CSIS/AUSA Post-Conflict Reconstruction Project.

Michèle Flournoy is senior adviser in the International Security Program at the Center for Strategic and International Studies (CSIS), where she works on a broad range of defense policy and international security issues. She was a codirector of the joint CSIS/AUSA Post-Conflict Reconstruction Project. Previously, she was a Distinguished Research Professor at the Institute for National Strategic Studies at the National Defense University. In government, she served as principal deputy assistant secretary of defense for strategy and threat reduction and as deputy assistant secretary of defense for strategy.

Johanna Mendelson Forman is senior program officer for Peace, Security, and Human Rights at the United Nations Foundation in Washington, D.C. An expert on post-conflict reconstruction and political development, she was a cofounder of USAID's Office of Transition Initiatives and a social scientist at the World Bank's first Post-Conflict Unit. Previously she served as a senior adviser at the Association of the United States Army and a codirector of the joint CSIS/AUSA Post-Conflict Reconstruction Project. An historian and attorney, she has written extensively on civil-military relations in Latin America and on post-conflict and security sector reform. She holds academic appointments at Georgetown University and the American University in Washington, D.C.

Robert C. Orr is the executive director of the Belfer Center for Science and International Affairs at Harvard University's John F. Kennedy School of Government. Prior to this appointment, he served as director of the Council on Foreign Relations in Washington, D.C., and as senior fellow and codirector of the joint CSIS/AUSA Post-Conflict Reconstruction Project at the Center for Strategic and International Studies. He has served in government as deputy to the U.S. ambassador to the United Nations and as director for Global and Multilateral Affairs at the National Security Council in the White House.

Michael Pan is a senior policy analyst for national security and international policy at the Center for American Progress in Washington, D.C. Previously he served as the political adviser to the chief prosecutor for the Special Court for Sierra Leone. Prior to joining the tribunal in Freetown, he was an associate and coordinator of the joint CSIS/AUSA Post-Conflict Reconstruction Project at the Center for Strategic and International Studies. Prior to that, he served as the special assistant for the ambassador-at-large for War Crimes Issues at the Department of State.

Milan Vaishnav is a researcher for the Commission on Weak States and U.S. National Security at the Center for Global Development in Washington, D.C. He also serves as special assistant to the center's president. Previously, he served as program coordinator in the Washington, D.C., office of the Council on Foreign Relations. He served as research assistant on the joint CSIS/AUSA Post-Conflict Reconstruction Project at the Center for Strategic and International Studies.